POLICY EVALUATION
Making Optimum Decisions

POLICY EVALUATION
Making Optimum Decisions

Stuart S. Nagel

University of Illinois

PRAEGER

PRAEGER SPECIAL STUDIES • PRAEGER SCIENTIFIC

Library of Congress Cataloging in Publication Data

Nagel, Stuart S., 1934–
  Policy evaluation.

  Bibliography: p.
  Includes index.
  1. Policy sciences—Methodology—Case studies.
I. Title.
H61.N275   361.6′1   81-12123
ISBN 0-03-059646-7   AACR2
ISBN 0-03-059644-0 (pbk.)

Published in 1982 by Praeger Publishers
CBS Educational and Professional Publishing
A Division of CBS, Inc.
521 Fifth Avenue, New York, New York 10175 U.S.A.

© 1982 by Praeger Publishers

23456789   145   987654321

Printed in the United States of America

Dedicated to the idea of
"Why not the best?"

List of Tables, Figures, and Appendix Tables

Appendix Tables

Introduction

This book is about policy evaluation or policy optimizing. Its purpose is to bring together for a student and professional audience a set of principles and applications to apply the optimizing methods of operations research, management science, and related disciplines to public policy problems. The book can be used in the newly developing courses on policy evaluation and policy analysis that are being offered in political science, other social sciences, and interdisciplinary programs. It can also stimulate relevant ideas on the part of government practitioners whose training may not have included these new methodological developments. Sophisticated, concerned citizens are also becoming increasingly interested in the logic of decision sciences as applied to public and private sector problems.

As the title indicates this book represents a combination of the basic orientations that are in the process of being combined to form the policy evaluation field. One orientation is policy studies or policy analysis, which is associated with political science and economics. The other orientation is evaluation research or program evaluation, which is associated with psychology and sociology. Policy studies differs from evaluation research in that it emphasizes a relatively greater concern for (1) evaluating policies before, rather than after, they are adopted; (2) taking goals as givens and seeking to maximize or achieve them, rather than taking policies or programs as givens and seeking to determine their effects; and (3) a concern for problems that relate to economic regulation, civil liberties, and foreign policy, more than health, education, and welfare. Policy evaluation, as reflected in this book, attempts to combine all of these concerns.

Policy-optimizing models involve three separate concepts. By the word "policy" we mean governmental decisions designed to deal with social problems on which governmental action is considered desirable. By "optimizing" we mean an attempt to arrive at a governmental decision that represents the best choice among discrete alternatives in light of various constraints and conditions, or the best level or mix along a continuum of alternative possibilities. By "models" we mean a system of normative and empirical premises that lead deductively to a conclusion. More specifically, the basic policy optimizing model involves saying (1) Y is good; (2) X causes Y; and, therefore, (3) adopt X.

There are many ways in which policy-optimizing or evaluation models can be varied or classified. One can talk in terms of (1) whether there are many categories or degrees of Y and X, or simply the categories of present and absent; (2) whether there are many Ys and Xs, or only one Y and one X; (3) whether the relations between X and Y are linear with constant marginal returns, or nonlinear with diminishing marginal returns; (4) whether there are constraints on Y and X so they cannot vary infinitely upward or downward; and (5) whether the relation between Y and X is one that depends on another variable, which may or may not have a known probability of occurring. One particularly meaningful way of classifying policy optimizing models or methods is in terms of the four-part classification that is used in this book. That classification involves (1) finding an optimum choice among policy alternatives; (2) finding an optimum level for a policy requiring moderation; (3) finding an optimum mix in allocating scarce resources; and (4) time-oriented optimizing models.

The book is divided into five parts. The first part deals with general principles of policy optimization. The next four parts correspond to the above four-part classification for policy-optimizing or evaluation models, namely finding an optimum choice, level, mix, or timing. The parts that deal with choice, level, and mix each contain three chapters that provide concrete examples designed to illustrate those models, and then a synthesizing chapter that pulls together the general ideas. Part Five, dealing with time-oriented models, is divided into three chapters; the first emphasizes optimizing models, the second emphasizes predictive models, and the third relates time-oriented models back to finding an optimum choice, level, or mix. Thus the book constantly intersperses general principles and concrete examples. It operates on the principle that one learns new ideas best by (1) being told what is going to be presented; (2) then being given both examples and general principles; and (3) then receiving a summary of what has been presented.

The basic methodology in finding an optimum *choice* among discrete alternatives involves determining the benefits and costs for each alternative, and then determining which alternative produces the most benefits minus costs. This methodology may also involve determining which alternative produces the most total benefits, or the least total costs, where all the effects are stated only in terms of benefits or only in terms of costs. Variations include finding the alternative that gives the highest total benefits provided a total cost constraint is not exceeded, or that gives the lowest total costs provided a minimum benefit level is achieved. The methodology may involve discounting the benefits or the costs by the probability of their occurring. All the examples in Part II are of this kind.

For example, if a government agency is faced with the decision of whether or not to gather some expensive data, a favorable decision runs the risk that, if the data is not used, the effort, time, and money that went into the gathering will have been wasted. An unfavorable decision, however, runs the risk that the data might have been used if it had been gathered. Similarly, a juror in a criminal case runs the risk of voting to convict when the defendant could be innocent, and the opposite risk of voting to acquit when the defendant could be guilty. A would-be criminal may implicitly consider that violating the law risks getting caught and negatively sanctioned, but not violating the law may mean a missed opportunity to obtain the economic or other benefits. In all three situations, an understanding of what is involved in finding an optimum choice may help reach a decision, influence the decisions of others, and predict how decisions are likely to change as a result of changes in the input variables.

The basic methodology in finding an optimum policy *level* involves determining the relation between an increase in the policy and whatever goal one is seeking to optimize. The most interesting optimum level problems tend to involve relations in which doing either too little or too much is undesirable with regard to the policy under consideration. In more quantitative terms, what is involved is determining the functional relation between goal Y and policy X, where that relation produces a valley-shaped total cost curve or a hill-shaped total benefit curve when plotted. What is then involved is determining the value of X when the curve bottoms out if one is minimizing total costs, or reaches a peak if one is maximizing total benefits. The examples in Part III are all of these kinds.

For example, if juries are too large, then it will be difficult for prosecutors to obtain unanimous convictions of guilty defendants. On the other hand, if juries are too small, it may be too easy for prosecutors to obtain unanimous convictions of innocent defendants. An optimum jury size is somewhere between too big and too little. Similarly, if an attorney puts in too much time on a given damage case, much of the time will be wasted when incremental time no longer produces much incremental benefit in terms of (1) increased damage awards if the attorney is representing a plaintiff; or (2) decreased damage awards if the attorney is representing a defendant. If the attorney puts in too little time, however, then the client and the attorney may suffer, whereas additional time could have produced substantial additional benefits in damages awarded and fees received. An optimum time allocation is somewhere between too long and too short. A third example involves prison sentences, where long sentences may mean unduly high and unnecessary holding costs, and short sentences may mean unduly high releasing costs in terms of harm to society that could have been prevented by continued holding. These problems are all capable of being expressed quantitatively, so that the notions of too little and too much can be given more precise meanings.

The basic methodology in finding an optimum *mix* in allocating scarce resources involves first determining the relation between (1) the amount of allocation to each alternative activity or place, and (2) the amount of benefits received. In more quantitative terms, what is involved is determining the functional relation between goal Y and allocations to activity X or place X. When those relations are plotted, they normally produce a positive concave curve for each activity or place where increased allocations produce increased benefits, but at a diminishing rate, or a negative convex curve where increased allocations produce decreased detriments, but also at a diminishing rate. The object is generally to allocate one's scarce resources across the activities or places in such a way as to (1) use all the available budget, while (2) equalizing the marginal rates of return across the activities or places so that nothing is to be gained by switching from one activity or place to another. This kind of allocation recognizes that a good activity or place cannot be given too much because after a while the diminishing marginal rate of return becomes smaller than what can be gained by shifting a dollar or unit of effort to another normally less productive activity or place. The examples in Part IV are all of this kind.

For example, in allocating campaign funds across congressional elections, one does not want to give to a district more than is needed to enable the desired candidate to win. One, however, especially wants to allocate money to those candidates where a small amount may mean the difference between victory and defeat. More complicated campaign allocation involve allocations to alternative activities like mass media versus precinct organization, or allocations to places within a congressional or other election district. There the object is to allocate in such a way as to (1) maximize votes subject to a budget constraint; (2) minimize costs subject to a getting-elected constraint; or (3) maximize votes subject to both a budget constraint and a getting-elected constraint. Another relevant example is how to allocate anticrime dollars across places and activities in order to minimize total crime. One might do so in light of the relations between alternative allocations and crime occurrence. These problems are all capable of being expressed quantitatively so the notion of optimum mix can be given more precise meaning.

Time-optimizing models refer to policy-optimizing models in which delay reduction is the goal to be maximized. Some delay minimization models involve a separate kind of analysis from the general idea of finding an optimum choice, level, or mix. These models include queueing theory, optimum sentencing, and critical path analysis. In queueing theory, one is particularly interested in explaining delay and backlog in terms of the rate at which cases arrive for processing and the rate at which cases are serviced after they arrive. One then uses that information to prescribe ways of getting delay and backlog to desired levels. In government agencies, that kind of optimizing analysis often needs to consider the psychology of both the people being serviced and those doing the servicing, more so than in industrial operations where equipment is often being serviced by other equipment. Optimum sequencing involves arranging the order in which cases will be heard, so as to minimize the average waiting time plus processing time. In government agencies, this kind of optimizing analysis often needs to consider constitutional and equitable constraints more so than in private sector operations. Critical path analysis attempts to find the links in going from start to finish, where effort should be most concentrated to reduce delay. An example might be the time consumed between a preliminary hearing and the trial, which involves preparation by both the prosecutor and the defense, with one side tending to create more of a bottleneck than the other.

In addition to queueing, sequencing, and critical paths, the delay minimization models sometimes involve finding an optimum choice, level, or mix. In that regard, the last chapter brings the analysis back full circle to those important methodologies, although in the specific context of delay reduction models. For example, what is the optimum level of delay or time consumption for the average case of a given type in a court system? If cases are allowed to wait too long before they are completed, then high delay costs may be incurred, such as released defendants disappearing or committing crimes, held defendants spending unnecessarily long pretrial periods in jail, and injured persons having to wait years to recover compensation for their injuries. On the other hand, the speed-up costs to reduce delay may be high, in terms of extra salaries that have to be paid for additional court personnel and possible injustices in terms of premature trials. Similarly, how does one determine an optimum mix in allocating the budget of a court system across judges, prosecutors, public defenders, and other court personnel, in order to get the most total efficiency out of the system in terms of minimizing delay and backlogs? An optimum choice problem might involve how to influence the decisions reached by prosecutors and, to some extent, judges and public defenders, so as to encourage more time-saving and less time-lengthening decisions. This substantive context helps summarize the value of these policy-optimizing models.

This book bears a logical relation to my earlier work. Much of that work involved applying statistical analysis and quasi-experimental methods to determine relations between various outcomes and the characteristics of persons, places, or things, including case outcomes and judges' backgrounds, as in *The Legal Process from a Behavioral Perspective* (Dorsey, 1969). Later work has emphasized outcomes considered socially desirable or undesirable (i.e., goals) and inputs subject to government decisions (i.e., policies), as in *Improving the Legal Process: Effects of Alternatives* (Lexington-Heath, 1975). The present work represents a departure from the earlier work mainly in its emphasis on an optimizing perspective. This perspective takes the information from those statistical or other relations and attempts to use them to arrive at policy decisions that maximize one's goals, i.e., that maximize benefits minus costs. The present work also seeks to generalize beyond the legal process and beyond policy case studies to broader principles that relate to finding an optimum choice, level, or mix.

Many people have cooperated to develop this book, including those who have co-authored various chapters. Marian Neef was especially helpful in developing and drafting many of the optimizing ideas on which this book is based. Other co-authors include David Lamm (Chapter 4), Kathleen Levy (Chapter 7), John McCarthy (Chapter 9), and Nancy Munshaw

(Chapters 13 and 14). Various funding sources also helped cover the expenses involved in producing the relevant research, including the Public Policy Committee of the Ford Foundation, the National Institute of Justice, the Illinois Law Enforcement Commission, and the University of Illinois Research Board. Thanks are also owed to various journals in which earlier versions of some chapters appeared, specifically *Crime and Delinquency, Florida Law Review, Interfaces, Public Administration Review, Public Choice, Society, University of Pittsburgh Law Review,* and the *Washington University Law Quarterly.* The author is also grateful to the many students in his seminars on "Optimizing Alternative Public Policies," "Methods of Policy Evaluation," and "Law, Policy, and Social Science" for the many ideas that they stimulated. As with previous books, he is also grateful to Joyce Nagel for her administrative work in making this book possible. As mentioned on the dedication page, this book is dedicated to the idea espoused by President Jimmy Carter of "Why not the best?" The best is especially difficult to obtain in the realm of government policy, but seeking the best as a goal may still bring substantial practical and theoretical benefits, even if we only get part way there.

POLICY EVALUATION
Making Optimum Decisions

Part I
General Principles
of Policy
Optimization

The purpose of this section is to lay out in a general way the basic policy evaluation methods that will be discussed in Parts 2, 3, 4, and 5. These general methods include (1) finding an optimum choice among discrete alternatives without or with contingent probabilities; (2) finding an optimum level where doing too much or too little is undesirable; (3) finding an optimum mix in allocating scarce resources; and (4) reaching decisions that optimize time. This section is also briefly concerned with the problems of values in arriving at optimum decisions, although these problems, like the above methods, are interspersed throughout the book.

1

Chapter 1
Finding an Optimum
Choice, Level, or Mix

This chapter analyzes some general matters concerning how to arrive at an optimum choice, level, or mix when confronted with alternative policy decisions, especially decisions relating to the legal process. It brings together a variety of ideas into a useful typology of problems. It also synthesizes a variety of optimizing principles with public policy and legal process illustrations.

By "optimum" in this context, we refer to the decision-making alternative or combination of alternatives that will maximize some quantitatively-measured goal or goals. By "choice" we mean a situation involving alternative decisions that fit into discrete categories such as whether to provide counsel for the poor in criminal cases through volunteer counsel, assigned counsel, a public defender, or some combination of the three. By "level" and "mix" we mean a situation involving alternative decisions that fit on a continuum of possibilities such as what level of money to appropriate for a public defender's office in a given county, or what mix of available budget money to allocate between the public defender's office and the prosecutor's office.

By "public policy" we mean governmental decision making that decides on choices, levels, and mixes with regard to controversial alternative ways of doing things. The kind of public policy problems that will be emphasized in this article are those that particularly relate to the procedures whereby courts arrive at decisions but also to procedures of other governmental decision makers and to some substantive problems as well. Given the level of methodological generality, one can easily reason by analogy from the typologies and principles given here to a variety of public policy problems. Our cited examples will often come from more detailed studies that we have made elsewhere, since those are the studies with which we are most familiar and which are most illustrative of the kind of legal policy optimizing to which we are referring.

3

FINDING AN OPTIMUM ALTERNATIVE POLICY IN GENERAL

The methodology of finding an optimum alternative policy in general can be reduced in its most simplified form to a one-sentence rule: Choose the alternative that maximizes net benefits, where net benefits are total benefits minus total costs. This rule can be symbolized as follows: When faced with choosing between X_1, X_2, and so on, choose the X or policy alternative that gives the greatest Y, where Y symbolizes net benefits.[1]

The Y (or NB for net benefits) can be decomposed into various benefits (B_1, B_2, and so on) and various costs (C_1, C_2, and so on). A benefit is an effect of an X alternative that is considered desirable, whereas a cost is an effect of an X alternative that is considered undesirable. Sometimes benefits and costs are referred to generically simply as effects and symbolized Y_1, Y_2, and so on. The overall Y of a given X or alternative represents the sum of the separate Y scores if they are measured with a common unit and can thus be added together. Otherwise, the relation between each X and each Y must either be analyzed separately, or else each Y must be multiplied together rather than added, with exponents indicating their relative value weights.

Given these definitions of benefits and costs, it logically follows that we want to choose policy alternatives that will maximize our benefits and minimize our costs. It is, however, usually impossible to do both simultaneously since doing nothing is likely to be the alternative that will minimize our costs (i.e., bring them down to zero), but it is also the alternative that is least likely to produce any benefits. As well, spending great sums of money or effort may bring substantial or maximum benefits, but only at great cost. Thus, since we cannot have maximum benefits and minimum costs at the same time, a more feasible goal is to try to pick the alternative that will provide the biggest difference between total benefits $B_1 + B_2 + \ldots + B_n$) and total costs ($C_1 + C_2 + \ldots + C_n$) of the alternatives available. This is analogous to a business firm seeking to maximize its profits or the difference between total income and total expenses.

This general rule about maximizing net benefits would be more useful if we were to indicate how it varies in different, general situations. The main typology of situations for methodological purposes is a simple dichotomy between policy problems in which the alternatives have no logical order and policy problems in which the alternatives do have logical order. Policy problems in which the alternatives have no logical order include "yes-no" problems such as whether or not illegally seized evidence should be admissible in court,[2] or whether or not a given defendant should be released or held in jail prior to trial.[3] There is also no logical order among the alternatives where more than two non-numerical categories are involved, such as whether to provide counsel to the poor in criminal cases through a voluntary counsel system, an assigned counsel system, or a public defender system.[4] The number of categories lacking inherent order for a given policy problem can be huge, as in the situation of trying to choose among all the possible ways in which 90 of the downstate Illinois counties could be formed into 18 districts.[5]

Policy problems in which the policy or decisional alternatives do have inherent order include the problem of the optimum number of jurors to have among the alternatives of 6, 7, 8, 9, 10, 11, or 12,[6] or the optimum percent of defendants to hold in jail prior to trial with the alternatives being 1 percent, 2 percent, 3 percent, and so on including all the decimal possibilities between the integer percentages.[7] There is an inherent order where the alternatives involve money or effort expenditures, such as how many dollars to allocate (out of every 100 dollars available) to law reform versus case handling in the Legal Services Program of The Office of Economic Opportunity,[8] or how many dollars to allocate (out of every 100 dollars available) to Illinois, Wisconsin, and other states in order to have a maximum impact on keeping down the national crime occurrence.[9]

Although our overall goal is to choose the alternative that maximizes net benefits, we often use other terminology to mean the same thing. For example, one can talk about legislatively setting bail bonds that will maximize the difference between the probability of pretrial defendants appearing in court (PA) minus the probability of their being held in jail (PH). In that context, PA is like total benefits and PH is like total costs. One can also talk about releasing a percentage of pretrial defendants that will minimize the sum of our holding costs plus our releasing costs. In that context, holding costs can be considered a negative benefit. More specifically, holding costs are the releasing benefits (i.e., the dollars saved by not holding a defendant) which we lose by holding a defendant, and in that sense holding costs are negative-releasing benefits. Thus when we say we want to minimize the sum of our holding costs plus our releasing costs, we are in effect saying we want to maximize our releasing benefits (i.e., minimize our negative-releasing benefits) minus our releasing costs. In other words, costs can be considered negative benefits, and benefits can be considered negative costs. Thus, if we have considered all the relevant effects, we may be maximizing our net benefits even though we only talk about maximizing benefits or minimizing costs.[10]

FINDING AN OPTIMUM CHOICE AMONG DISCRETE ALTERNATIVES

Within the typology of policy problems that involve alternatives lacking inherent order, we can have two kinds of policy problems, namely those that do not involve contingent probabilities and those that do involve them.

Choosing without Contingent Probabilities

A good example of choosing without probabilities is the problem of how to provide legal counsel to the poor in criminal cases. The main alternatives are (X_1) a list of volunteer attorneys, (X_2) assigned counsel generally on a rotation basis from among practicing attorneys in the county, or (X_3) a public defender who is a salaried lawyer hired by the government to represent poor defendants. All other things being equal, the best alternative is the one that is most (Y_1) inexpensive, (Y_2) visible and accessible, (Y_3) politically feasible, and (Y_4) the most likely to result in specialized competence and aggressive representation. A benefit can be defined as being relatively high on one of these goals, and a cost can be defined as being relatively low.

Starting with the goal of inexpensiveness, volunteer counsel and assigned counsel score well. The public defender system is substantially more expensive. On visibility and accessibility all three alternatives are about equal in the sense that arraigning magistrates are expected to inform poor defendants of whatever system the county uses for making counsel available to poor defendants. On political feasibility or acceptability there is not likely to be any great opposition among influential lawyers to the volunteer or public defender alternatives. They are, however, likely to object to the assigned counsel alternative since it forces lawyers against their will to devote time and resources to cases which they may find frustrating and even distasteful. Volunteer counsel is unlikely to result in competent, aggressive lawyers unless substantial fees are paid to the screened volunteers, which is a system that only exists at the federal level. Similarly, assigned counsel tends to result in the appointment of lawyers who may be competent in their specialty, but that specialty is not likely to be criminal law. The public defender system develops competent criminal defense attorneys through specialized, continuous experience although their aggressiveness may be limited by lack of funding and personnel.

The above analysis indicates three relative benefits or advantages for volunteer counsel and one relative cost or disadvantage; two benefits for assigned counsel and two costs; and three benefits for the public defender system and one cost. To resolve the tie between volunteer counsel and the public defender requires giving relative weights to the four goals. If we give more weight to the goals of visibility-accessibility and competence-aggressiveness as a more liberal policy maker might be inclined to do, then the public defender comes out ahead. If we give more weight to the goals of inexpensiveness and political feasibility as a more conservative policy maker might be inclined to do, then the volunteer system comes out ahead assuming that it is capable of providing sufficient counsel to satisfy the constitutional requirements.

This optimizing perspective of listing alternatives, goals, relations, weights and choices may also be applicable to obtaining insights into the best alternatives for resolving other public policy problems. The perspective can be made more sophisticated by using Xs that are not mutually exclusive, thereby introducing combinations of the alternatives such as an X_4 which involves a list of volunteer attorneys for poor defendants who do not like the public defender as is done in the city of Chicago. One can also relate each X alternative to each Y goal by showing the degree of relationship and also the extent to which nonlinear diminishing returns are involved rather than simply whether the relation is relatively positive or negative. In addition, one could indicate the extent to which a relation between an X and a Y is affected by the probabilistic occurrence of an outside event. An example might be that public defenders tend to provide aggressive representation only when they have adequate resources, but the probability of their having adequate resources is roughly .30 in the sense that only about one out of three public defender's offices have funding above an adequate threshold of budget divided by cases, although more exact statistics are currently being developed by the National Legal Aid and Defenders' Association.

Choosing with Contingent Probabilities

The legal process, at least in its judicial aspects, involves a series of choices that are made by the participants on the basis of the probability of the occurrence of some contingent event. For example, the would-be criminal chooses to commit or not commit a crime partly on the basis of the probability of his getting caught and convicted. Similarly the personal injury lawyer accepts a client partly on the basis of the probability of winning the case especially when the lawyer only gets paid if the case is won. Similar probabilistic decisions are faced by arraignment judges, sentencing judges, parole boards, prosecuting attorneys, and insurance company lawyers, although each of these decision makers may be concerned with a different contingent event, different data, and different specific goals to be maximized.

Substantively, we could divide the above situations into criminal case decisional problems or into civil case decisional problems. From a methodological perspective, however, it would be more meaningful to divide those situations into ones that involve a single decision maker trying to make a choice irrespective of anyone else's present choices or interaction, as contrasted to situations involving more than one decision maker whose decisions are influenced by the interactive behavior or decisions of another decision maker.

The one-person decision situation can be illustrated by the bond-setting decision. It involves the contingent event of the defendant appearing in court, and the contingent event of the defendant committing a crime while released. It involves the dichotomous decision of release or hold, and also the numerical decision of what dollar bond to set. The goals or Y scores (associated with each decision and contingent event) can be expressed in non-monetary satisfaction units or in monetary dollar units. The bond-setting problem can be thought of as an individual case-by-case judicial problem, or as a more generalized problem of legislating for types of cases. In addition, the bond-setting problem illustrates distinctions between descriptive models designed to describe how the legal process operates, as contrasted to prescriptive models designed to prescribe how the legal process should operate in order to maximize given goals.[11]

The two-person interacting situation can be illustrated by the process of plea bargaining and out-of-court civil settlements. In plea bargaining, the offers of the prosecutor and the defendant or his defense counsel are partly determined by their perceptions of the probability of a conviction if the case were to go to trial. Similarly, in civil case negotiations, the offers of the plaintiff and the defendant or their attorneys are partly determined by perceptions of the probability of the defendant being found liable if the case were to go to trial. Both the criminal and the civil negotiators will choose between settlement and trial partly on the basis of what the other side offers, unlike the bond setting situation where the defendant does not bargain or make moves with the judge.[12]

The plea bargaining situation is useful not only for illustrating what is involved in making an optimum choice under probabilistic conditions, but also useful for illustrating in a generalized way the sequential steps that are likely to occur from the initial positions of the parties to the final settlement or to a determination that a settlement is impossible. This kind of a sequential analysis may be especially valuable in explaining the occurrence of certain decisions. That kind of sequential analysis, plus the basic decision theory and bargaining models, may also be valuable in analyzing the effect of legal changes and other system changes on the decisional behavior of the participants. By knowing how system changes are likely to affect decisional behavior, system planners can allow for those effects when instituting various system changes such as increased pretrial release, reduced delay, or increased allocation of resources to the participants.

In discussing general optimizing, we emphasized that finding an optimum or alternative policy involves choosing the alternative that maximizes net benefits, where net benefits are total benefits minus total costs. In situations that involve making an optimum choice under probabilistic conditions, that general rule needs to be slightly modified. The modification involves saying: Choose the alternative that maximizes expected net benefits, where expected net benefits are expected total benefits minus total expected costs. In that context, expected total benefits equal the benefits to be received if a contingent event happens times the probability of its happening. Similarly, expected total costs equal the costs to be incurred if a contingent event happens times the probability of its happening. Where there is more than one benefit, each benefit to be received is multiplied by the probability on which it is contingent. Therefore, expected total benefits (or ETB) equals $P_1B_1 + P_2B_2 + \ldots + P_nN_n$, and likewise with expected total costs.

FINDING AN OPTIMUM LEVEL OR MIX ON A CONTINUUM OF ALTERNATIVES

Within the typology of policy problems that involve alternatives having inherent order (such as alternatives involving percentages or dollars), we can also have at least two kinds of policy problems. The simplest kind of policy problems with numerical alternatives is where we have one policy that can be adopted to various degrees, and the problem is one of finding the optimum level or optimum degree to which the policy should be adopted. This problem is illustrated by the optimum percentage of defendants to release prior to trial and the optimum jury-size problem. The other kind of policy problem with numerical alternatives is the problem where we have scarce resources, and we are trying to allocate those resources among activities, places, or other entities so as to maximize our net benefits. This problem is illustrated by the optimum allocation of civil rights effort to six civil rights activities and of anticrime dollars to the 50 states.

Finding an Optimum Level

The legal process tends to be epitomized by U-shaped or valley-shaped cost curves and by bill-shaped benefit curves. This is so both with regard to judicial procedure and the more general problem of the strictness or leniency of legal rules and their application. The due process of fair procedure aspects of the legal process involve a constant struggle between going too far in providing due process and not going far enough. If too much due process is provided, then many guilty persons will go free in criminal cases and liable persons in civil cases, which will mean high total costs to the system at that end of the due process scale. On the other hand, if too little due process is provided, then many innocent persons will be found guilty of wrongdoing in criminal cases and nonliable persons in civil cases, which will mean high total costs to the system at the low end of the due process scale. Somewhere in the middle of that valley-shaped total cost curve, the costs to the system reach a minimum. At that point we have an optimum balance or optimum level of due process.

Similarly, any legal rule can be worded or applied in an overly strict or an overly lenient way. If environmental protection standards become too strict, we suffer unduly high cleanup costs, but if the standards become too lenient, we suffer unduly high pollution damage costs. Similarly, contract law standards can become too strict, thereby interfering with freedom of contract and possibly incurring large societal costs in terms of reduction in the free flow of business. If contract law standards become too lenient, however, then we might encourage large societal costs in terms of exploitation of the side with the lesser knowledge or weaker bargaining power. In tort law, automobile negligence standards could be so strict as to slow traffic almost to a standstill, or so lenient as to paralyze potential drivers and pedestrians from venturing into the streets. Similar problems of doing too much or too little can occur in criminal law, divorce law, housing law, or any field of law. Somewhere between those extremes, however, is an optimum point where a minimum is reached on the sum of the total costs, with or without weights to consider different valuations of each cost.

The optimum level problem can be analyzed with empirical data from the pretrial release situation. If too high a percentage of defendants is held in jail prior to trial, then high holding costs will be incurred with regard to jail maintenance, lost gross national product, and the bitterness that is generated from being held in jail in spite of the fact that one's case results in a dismissal or an acquittal. If too low a percentage of defendants is held in jail prior to trial, then high releasing costs will be incurred with regard to the cost of rearresting defendants who fail to appear for their trials, and the cost of crimes that are committed by defendants prior to trial who would not have committed those crimes if they had been held in jail. The object is to find an optimum percentage of defendants to hold or release prior to trial in order to minimize the sum of the holding and the releasing costs.[13]

Another optimum level problem is the optimum jury size problem. If juries are too large, too many guilty defendants may fail to be convicted; whereas if juries are too small, too many innocent defendants may be convicted. Unlike the percentage-to-release problem, however, virtually no empirical data can be obtained which meaningfully shows for various jury sizes the quantity of defendants who are convicted, let alone the quantity of guilty or innocent defendants. This is so because when the jury size changes in a given state, the type of cases that are decided by jury trials rather than bench trials also tends to change. There is no empirical way of separating out the effect of jury size and case types on changes in the conviction percentages. Therefore, to arrive at an optimum jury size requires a substantial amount of deductive modeling from premises that are acceptable, flexible, empirical, and normative. This kind of model involves probabilistic conditions, but it is basically an optimum level model.[14]

In discussing general optimizing, we emphasized that finding an optimum alternative policy involves choosing the alternative that maximizes net benefits, where net benefits are total benefits minus total costs. In the optimum level situation, we generally convert all the relevant effects into costs and then seek to minimize the unweighted or weighted sum of the costs. One reason for making that conversion is because it is generally easier to obtain cost data than benefit data when dealing with social problems, although an important type of benefit is the dollars-saved (or the negation of the costs) by not having to rearrest a defendant who fails to appear, by not having to lose the gross national product lost by holding a defendant in jail, or by not incurring some other cost. Another reason for expressing effects as costs especially in the optimum level situation, is because doing so emphasizes that the optimum level problem is basically one of minimizing the sum of type 1 errors or costs (where a true hypothesis is rejected, like convicting an innocent defendant contrary to the presumption of innocence), plus type 2 errors or costs (where a false hypothesis is accepted, like acquitting a guilty defendant in accordance with the presumption of innocence).

In spite of the tendency to express optimum level problems in terms of minimizing total costs, they can often be expressed in terms of maximizing total benefits or maximizing certain benefits minus certain costs. For example, we could express the percentage-to-release problem as the problem of finding the percentage to release at which the sum of the releasing benefits (holding costs avoided) plus the holding benefits (releasing costs avoided) will be maximized. We could also express it in terms of finding the percentage to release at which the releasing benefits minus the releasing costs are maximized, or the holding benefits minus the holding costs are maximized, and still arrive at the same solution. The problem of the optimum school integration enforcement level seems to be best stated as finding the level at which we avoid both the lowered integration benefits which are associated with tokenism, as well as the lowered integration benefits which are associated with "white flight" and resegregation, and we thus obtain a maximum point on a hill-shaped total benefits curve. The important thing is that we recognize both overenforcement and underenforcement of any law can cause us to lose benefits or suffer costs including opportunity costs, thereby necessitating a search for the optimum balance or optimum level either with empirical data, deductive models, or a combination of both.

Finding an Optimum Mix

The legal process can be expressed as a series of probabilistic decisions or as an attempt to find an optimum balance of type 1 and type 2 errors. It can also be expressed as an attempt to allocate scarce social resources. This is especially the case with legislative and administrative programs that involve the allocation of funds for various societal purposes. Since money is a scarce resource, the object of these aspects of the legal process is to allocate funds among activities and/or places in such a way as to maximize the total benefits that are obtained where all effects are expressed as benefits (or desirable social indicators like increased longevity) or to minimize the total costs where all effects are expressed as costs (or undesirable social indicators, like disease or crime occurrence). The allocation or optimum mix model also applies to the legal process where non-monetary values are being allocated, such as some measure of effort on the part of civil rights organizations or agencies.

The basic rule for handling the optimum mix problem for allocating scarce resources is to allocate to activities or places in accordance with the budget available and the slopes or marginal rates of return for each activity or place. A slope or marginal rate of return is simply the ratio between a change in output produced for an activity or place and the corresponding change in input or resources expended to that activity or place. If the relation between inputs and outputs is constant or linear, then one would allocate to the activities or places with the largest slopes after satisfying whatever minimum constraints are required. If the relation between inputs and outputs involves diminishing returns or nonlinear relations, then one would allocate to the activities or places until their changing nonlinear slopes are equalized such that nothing could be gained by shifting from one activity or place to another. Under either type of relation, all of the budget should be expended if one wants to maximize benefits without exceeding the budget, but less than all of the budget should be expended if one wants to minimize costs while providing a minimum benefit or satisfaction level.

These general principles can be illustrated with regard to allocating effort among civil rights activities relating to voting, schools, criminal justice, employment, housing, and public accommodations. The problem is one of determining how to allocate the total civil rights effort to those six input activities in order to maximize the total equality improvement. That goal is represented by the collective output activity, as measured by the sum of the improvements obtained in each of the six civil rights fields. The model deals with linear relations for the sake of simplicity and because the range of the data fits a linear model about as well as a nonlinear one. To further simplify the presentation, the optimum mix model can be first presented in the context of finding an optimum mix between only two civil rights activities, namely those that relate to efforts against governmental discrimination and efforts against private discrimination. The model in effect represents a combination of linear regression analysis and linear-programming optimizing. The regression analysis is especially useful for obtaining slopes between each input activity and each output criterion for use in developing an input-output matrix that enables one to see how the outputs would change given various changes in the inputs, or how the inputs would change in order to satisfy changes in the output goals.[15]

The general principles can also be illustrated with regard to allocating dollars among geographical places in order to minimize the national crime occurrence. Here the emphasis is on places rather than activities, which changes the methodology from a single equation (relating the overall output goal to various input activities) into multiple equations (in which the crime occurrence in each place is related to anti-crime dollars spent in that place). The emphasis here is also on diminishing returns, nonlinear relations rather than linear regression and linear programming.[16] In both examples, concern is expressed for obtaining change data or data at more than one point in time, but dollars and anticrime data lend themselves to more precise measurement than effort and antidiscrimination data. Both examples involve an attempt to deal with the crucial problem of controlling for demographic, socio-economic, and other variables which affect crime and discrimination besides antidiscrimination effort or anticrime dollars. Similarly, both examples in differing ways involve an attempt to deal with minimum and maximum political, legal, and economic constraints on the allocation of scarce resources to either activities or places.

In discussing general optimizing, we emphasized that finding an optimum alternative policy involves choosing the alternative that maximizes net benefits, where net benefits are total benefits minus total costs. In the optimum mix situation, we in effect seek that goal by looking at the dynamic benefit-cost ratio of each activity or place to which we are considering allocating our scarce resources. By dynamic benefit-cost ratio, we mean the ratio between a change in benefits and a change in costs in moving from any one point with regard to resources allocated (for that activity or place) to any other point. By observing that benefit-cost ratio, slope, or marginal rate of return and allocating accordingly, we can at least in theory maximize the total benefits we can obtain from our total expenditures. In practice, we may run into considerable difficulty obtaining meaningful data for measuring those ratios, especially in view of our inability to hold constant or statistically control for other variables that may influence the benefits or outputs while changes are occurring in our costs or inputs.

PROBLEMS THAT CAN BE VIEWED AS SIMULTANEOUSLY OR ALTERNATIVELY INVOLVING CHOICES, LEVELS, OR MIXES

In this chapter, we have conceptualized the legal process as a choice model, a probabilistic model, an optimum level model, and an optimum mix model. It is useful to think of each of those models separately since they involve different concepts, methods, and to some extent, different causal and prescriptive theories. Nevertheless, there is considerable overlap among the models since the same problem can often be viewed from more than one perspective and since each model can often be translated into each other model. We previously mentioned that the optimum jury-size problem can be viewed as both a probabilistic model and an optimum level model. The pretrial release problem is an example of a problem that can be viewed from three perspectives. it is a probabilistic problem in the sense that the individual judge is trying to decide whether releasing or holding the defendant produces the highest expected value in light of the probability that the defendant will appear for trial and the costs of making a type 1 error (holding a defendant who would have appeared) versus a type 2 error (releasing a defendant who would not appear). It is an optimum level problem in the sense that the system is trying to arrive at an optimum percentage of defendants to hold in order to minimize the sum of the holding costs and the releasing costs. It is an optimum mix problem in the sense that the system can also be said to be trying to arrive at an optimum mix between defendants who are held and defendants who are released.

The last point illustrates how one model can sometimes be translated into another. Any optimum level problem involving the question of what is the optimum level of due process or enforcement severity can be expressed as an optimum mix problem of finding the optimum mix between type 1 and type 2 errors or between severity and leniency although that conceptualization may be more awkward than the optimum level conceptualization. Similarly, any optimum mix problem can be reduced to an optimum level problem. This is more clearly seen when there are only two activities or two places in which to allocate. Instead of saying what is the optimum mix of 10 dollars between places 1 and 2, we could say, what is the optimum level to allocate our 10 dollars to place 1, given the fact that the more we allocate to place 1, the less we will have to allocate to place 2. If there are three places, then the more we allocate to place 1, the less we will have to allocate collectively to places 2 and 3. This conceptualization, however, may also be more awkward than the optimum mix approach.

To illustrate how the optimum mix and optimum level models can sometimes be virtually interchangeable, one can use the problem of what is the optimum mix betwee a free press and a fair trial in the context of allowing newspapers to report on pending criminal trials where their reporting may tend to prejudice the defendant's case. Expressed in other terms, one is dealing with the problem of what is the optimum level of a free press in that context, or what is the optimum level of a fair trial in that context. The optimum mix perspective tends to appeal to political scientists because of its emphasis on policy tradeoffs in arriving at a solution. On the other hand, the optimum level perspective tends to appeal to econometricians because of its mathematical simplicity, given its emphasis on only one variable.[17]

An interesting combination methodology that combines the optimum mix perspective and the probabilistic perspective is portfolio analysis.[18] It originated in the context of deciding on the optimum mix of stocks to purchase in order to maximize total dividends, profits from resale, or both in light of the probabilistic nature of various dividends to be paid out or various increases occurring in the value of the stock. One researcher has proposed the use of portfolio analysis to determine the optimum mix of prisoners in a prison between, say, armed robbers and burglars, given their differing probabilities of recommitting their crimes and the different costs to society or certain segments within society.[19]

Another set of models that crosses our typologies is that set in which the minimizing of time consumption is the primary consideration. This would include queuing models which inform us how much waiting time and processing time could be saved for court cases by adding additional judges, reducing the time needed for processing an average case, or by reducing the number of cases entering into the waiting lines. Time-oriented models would also include dynamic programming, which could inform us what is the optimum order in which to process cases so as to minimize the average waiting time plus processing time per case. A third kind of time-oriented model is PERT analysis, which can tell us what is the optimum path of alternative processing steps to follow in order to minimize time consumed by the average court case. These three models are prescriptive time-oriented models in the sense that they tell us about means to minimize the anti-goal of delay. Related time-oriented models that are descriptive or causal in nature include time series analysis which relates variables to each other over time, and Markov chain analysis that indicates, in a kind of domino effect, how a change in one variable will affect a series of other variables that are indirectly influenced by the first variable.[20]

VALUE DECISIONS AND POLICY ANALYSIS

One particularly interesting set of issues worth discussing with the problems of optimizing in public policy analysis relate to the role of values in policy analysis. A number of points should be mentioned in this connection. The most basic is the issue of being value free in doing research. By definition, policy analysis at least partly involves seeking to achieve or maximize given values or social goals rather than ignoring them. Policy analysts like other researchers should, however, be value free in the sense of not allowing their values to influence how they record or present information. In fact, the concern for objectivity and replicability in policy analysis research should probably manifest itself in taking extra precautions to keep the bias of researchers from influencing their results given the stronger feelings which generally exist about policy problems, as contrasted to research problems that lack policy implications. These precautions can include drawing upon multiple sources and individuals for cross-checking information, making available raw data sets for secondary analysis, and making assumptions more explicit.

Many policy analysis problems involve taking goals as givens and determining what policies will maximize those goals. The goals, however, may be only intermediate values directed toward achieving other more general values. For example, a policy analysis problem might involve determining how to reduce pretrial jail population (Y). The proposals might relate to methods for increasing pretrial release (X_1) and reducing delay from arrest to disposition (X_2). There might, however, be some policymakers who think the pretrial jail population should be increased (rather than reduced) as a means for punishing arrested defendants who might otherwise escape punishment through plea bargaining or lack of admissible evidence. A second-stage policy analysis could deal with the effect of the pretrial jail experience on reducing crime rates (Z) which can be taken as a higher-level goal. To make policy analysis more manageable between X and Y, one may merely refer to the possibility of doing further research on the relation between Y and Z without actually undertaking it.

Like any research tool (including a calculator or a typewriter), policy analysis can be used for good or evil purposes. A computerized analysis of the effects of alternative legislature redistricting patterns, for example, can be used to facilitate a kind of proportional representation whereby the percentage of districts dominated by Democrats roughly approximates the percentage of Democrats in the state. On the other hand, the same redistricting programs can be used to minimize black representation in a state legislature. Quantitative policy analysis, however, is less likely to be used for purposes that are unconstitutional or for which there is a negative consensus, because policy analysis does tend to make more explicit the values, assumptions, input data, and other parameters used in arriving at the decisions than the more traditional decision making. In the computer redistricting example, one can check the programs and the input data to see what was the basis for the redistricting outputs.

Sometimes people involved in policy analysis may be asked to maximize what they consider to be socially undesirable goals. This brings out the need for policy analysts to choose carefully whom they work for, to try to improve the caliber of those people if they can, to call illegal matters to the attention of appropriate authorities, and to look elsewhere if they are dissatisfied with the goals of their government agency or employer. Normally in a democratic society, elected officials and their political appointees do try to achieve goals that will make them popular and that will be in conformity with the law. Therefore, a policy analyst's desire to do work legally and in the public interest is not so likely to conflict with his or her employer.

Value decisions are particularly relevant to policy analysis in the sense that optimizing solutions are very influenced by the values that are plugged into the analysis. In the redistricting example, the optimum plan is likely to depend on whether the goal is merely to provide an equal population across the districts or as well, to provide such things as proportionality of party representation and competitiveness within districts. Similarly, what constitutes an optimum jury size depends partly on how many guilty people we are willing to acquit in order to save one innocent person from conviction. A tradeoff higher than ten to one may, however, be irrelevant if the maximum reasonable jury size is twelve persons. As another example, the optimum mix of funds in the Legal Services Corporation between law reform and routine case handling may depend on who is evaluating the legal services agencies that constitute the data on which the analysis is based. Lawyer evaluators may tend to give higher ratings to agencies involved in more difficult appellate court precedent-setting cases, but representatives of the poor may give higher ratings to agencies involved in easier but more immediate family, housing, and consumer negotiations. Policy analysts should be particularly concerned with presenting sensitivity analyses in their projects whereby they demonstrate how the optimum would vary when one makes changes in the values being maximized.[21]

SOME CONCLUSIONS

The main thing that all the discussed models have in common is that they are capable of provoking useful insights that might otherwise be missed by viewing policy problems only from other research perspectives. Optimizing models provide comparisons of various forms of optimum behavior with empirical behavior so that one can make policy recommendations to bring the empirical closer to the optimum, or to revise the values attributed to the policy makers in order to bring the alleged optimum closer to the empirical. They also provide insights for understanding the effects on other variables of changing public policies and decisions, and the effects on public policies and decisions of changing other variables. They help to clarify assumptions, goals, alternative means, payoffs from alternative means, contingent probabilities, and other elements essential to understanding more fully the basic simplicities and subtle complexities of the political and legal process.

NOTES

1. Roland McKean, *Efficiency in Government through Systems Analysis* (New York: Wiley, 1958), pp. 25-102. For general works on optimizing methods in public policy analysis, although presenting different perspectives from this article, see Edith Stokey and Richard Zeckhauser, *A Primer for Policy Analysis* (New York: Norton, 1978). Edward Quade, *Analysis for Public Decisions* (New York: Elsevier, 1975); Guy Black, *The Application of Systems Analysis to Government Operations* (New York: Praeger, 1969); Alvin Drake, Ralph Keeney, and Philip Morris (eds.), *Analysis of Public Systems* (Cambridge, Mass.: MIT Press, 1972); and S. Nagel

and M. Neef, *Operations Research Methods: As Applied to Political Science and the Legal Process* (Beverly Hills, Ca.: Sage, 1976).

2. S. Nagel, "Choosing Among Alternative Public Policies" in Kenneth Dolbeare (ed.), *Public Policy Evaluation* (Beverly Hills, Ca.: Sage, 1975), pp 153-74.

3. S. Nagel and M. Neef, *"Bail, Not Jail, for More Defendants,"* 60 *Judicature* 172-78 (1976).

4. S. Nagel, "How to Provide Legal Counsel for the Poor: Decision Theory," in Dorothy James (ed.), *Analyzing Poverty Policy* (Lexington, Mass.: Lexington-Heath, 1975), pp. 215-22.

5. "Computers and the Law and Politics of Redistricting," in S. Nagel, *Improving the Legal Process: Effects of Alternatives* (Lexington, Mass.: Lexington-Heath, 1975), pp. 173-90.

6. S. Nagel and M. Neef, "Deductive Modeling to Determine an Optimum Jury Size and Fraction Required to Convict," 1975 *Washington University Law Quarterly,* 933-78 (1976).

7. S. Nagel and M. Neef, *The Policy Problem of Doing Too Much or Too Little: Pretrial Release as a Case in Point* (Beverly Hills, Ca.: Sage Professional Papers in Administrative and Policy Studies, 1977).

8. S. Nagel, *Minimizing Costs and Maximizing Benefits in Providing Legal Services to the Poor* (Beverly Hills, Ca.: Sage Professional Papers in Administrative and Policy Studies, 1973).

9. S. Nagel and M. Neef, "Allocating Resources Geographically for Optimum Results," *Political Methodology* 383-404 (1976).

10. An alternative conceptualization would involve saying that in some situations we have semantically reduced all effects to positive or negative costs. In those situations, the total benefits are zero, and the net benefits equal the total costs. Similarly, in some situations, we semantically reduce all effects to positive or negative benefits, and the net benefits then equal the total benefits.

11. S. Nagel, M. Neef, and Sarah Schramm, "Decision Theory and the Pretrial Release Decision in Criminal Cases," 31 *University of Miami Law Review* 1433-91 (1977).

12. S. Nagel and M. Neef, "Plea Bargaining, Decision Theory, and Equilibrium Models," 51 and 52 *Indiana Law Journal* 987-1024, 1-61 (1976); and "The Impact of Plea Bargaining on the Judicial Process," 62 *American Bar Association Journal* 1020-22 (1976).

13. See note 7. This study involves benefit-cost data obtained from police chiefs, prosecutors, judges, defense attorneys, and bail officials in 23 cities.

14. See note 6.

15. S. Nagel and M. Neef, *The Application of Mixed Strategies: Civil Rights and Other Multiple-Activity Policies* (Beverly Hills, Ca.: Sage Professional Papers in American Politics, 1976). That study involves civil rights input-output data obtained from NAACP chapter presidents in 31 cities.

16. See note 9.

17. S. Nagel, Kathleen Reinbolt, and Thomas Eimermann, "A Linear Programming Approach to Problems of Conflicting Legal Values Like Free Press Versus Fair Trial," 4 *Rutgers Journal of Computers and the Law* 420-61 (1975). This study involves attitudinal questionnaire data obtained from about 250 police chiefs, prosecutors, defense attorneys, and newspaper editors.

18. William Baumol, *Portfolio Theory: The Selection of Asset Combinations* (New York: McCaleb-Seiler, 1970).

19. Peter Aranson, et al., "Post Conviction Decisions in Criminal Justice" (Research proposal to the Law Enforcement Assistance Administration, 1975).

20. Jack Byrd, Jr., *Operations Research Models for Public Administration*

(Lexington, Mass.: Lexington-Heath, 1975), pp. 115-220; and Haig Bohigian, *The Foundations and Mathematical Models of Operations Research with Extensions to the Criminal Justice System* (North Tarrytown, NY: Gazette, 1971), pp. 171-247.

21. For other discussions of value decisions in policy analysis, see Phillip Gregg, ed., *Problems of Theory in Policy Analysis* (Lexington, Mass.: Lexington-Heath, 1976); Duncan MacRae, Jr., *The Social Function of Social Science* (New Haven, Conn.: Yale University Press, 1976); Gideon Sjoberg, "Politics, Ethics and Evaluation Research," in Guttentag (ed.), *Handbook of Evaluation Research* (Beverly Hills, Ca.: Sage, 1975); Laurence Tribe, "Policy Sciences: Analysis or Ideology?" 2 *Philosophy and Public Affairs* 66-110 (1973); Peter Brown, "Ethics and Policy Research," 2 *Policy Analysis* 325-40 (1976); and S. Nagel (ed.), *Policy Studies and the Social Sciences* (Lexington, Mass.: Lexington-Heath, 1975) (Part VI deals with social philosophy and includes relevant chapters by John Ladd, Eugene Meehan, and Martin Golding).

Part II
Finding An Optimum Choice Among Policy Alternatives

The purpose of this section is to discuss the problems involved in finding an optimum choice among discrete policy alternatives. The first three chapters present concrete examples of situations in which that type of policy evaluation is involved. Those situations include (1) encouraging socially desired behavior, where the would-be wrongdoer has a choice whether or not to do what is socially desired; (2) deciding whether or not data is worth gathering by a government agency, where there are risks of gathering unused data and not gathering needed data; and (3) deciding whether to convict or acquit in criminal cases, where there are risks of convicting the innocent and of acquitting the guilty. Those three chapters are followed by a synthesizing chapter on the general logic of finding an optimum choice, both with and without risk probabilities.

Chapter 2
Encouraging Socially Desired Behavior

The purpose of this short chapter is to bring out the usefulness of a benefit-cost perspective in generating ideas for encouraging socially desired behavior in a variety of different situations. The illustrative situations emphasized are traditional criminal behavior, business wrongdoing, and public officials who do not comply with relevant rules.

In this context, a benefit-cost perspective views the behavior of individuals as being motivated by a desire to maximize their benefits minus costs. Those benefits and costs may be nonmonetary as well as monetary. They may depend on the occurrence or nonoccurrence of some key event such as not getting caught when engaged in wrongdoing.

A benefit-cost perspective can be contrasted with a regulatory one, where socially desired behavior tends to be mandated by government orders, with an emphasis on administrative agencies and courts for enforcement, rather than the manipulation of incentives that make people want to comply. The perspective can also be contrasted with a rehabilitative one, where the emphasis is on the need to change the values of wrongdoers rather than to try to convince them they are acting contrary to their values, or better yet change the situation so their values cause them to want to behave in a socially desired way.

A benefit-cost perspective logically leads to saying that if an individual, group, or society wants to encourage desired behavior, it should think in terms of (1) increasing the benefits of doing the right thing; (2) decreasing the attendant costs; (3) decreasing the benefits of doing the wrong thing; (4) increasing the attendant costs; (5) increasing the probability of being detected and negatively sanctioned if one does the wrong thing; and (6) increasing the probability of being discovered and positively rewarded if one does the right thing.

By thinking in those terms, one can often generate relevant ideas that might otherwise be overlooked, thought of less quickly, or thought of in a less organized way. One can also avoid ideas that may not be so relevant in the sense of not substantially affecting relevant benefits and costs.

There are a variety of ways of classifying the applications of benefit-cost analysis to encouraging socially desired behavior. One is in terms of the subject matter, including criminal behavior, business wrongdoing, and non-complying government officials. A second is in terms of the purpose, including having a deterrence problem for which suggested approaches are needed, or having suggested approaches for which a discussion of their effectiveness is needed, or having suggested approaches for which a discussion of their effectiveness is needed. Another classification involves situations in which the benefits and costs of rightdoing are independent, rather than merely the complements of the benefits and costs of wrongdoing. The situation is complementary if the benefits of rightdoing mainly involve avoiding the costs of unsuccessful wrongdoing, and the costs of the rightdoing mainly involve missing out on the benefits of successful wrongdoing.

TRADITIONAL CRIMINAL BEHAVIOR

Traditional criminal behavior provides a good example of use of the general scheme to suggest and organize approaches for encouraging rightdoing. Since the benefits and costs of rightdoing are complementary here to those of wrongdoing, there are basically only three approaches rather than six. One can (1) increase the probability of being arrested, convicted, and imprisoned, (2) decrease the benefits from successful wrongdoing, and (3) increase the costs of unsuccessful wrongdoing. Each of those three general approaches generates two sets of specific approaches, a relatively conservative or prosecution-oriented set and relatively liberal or defendant-oriented set.

With regard to increasing the probability of being arrested, convicted, and imprisoned, a conservative orientation might emphasize reducing due process restrictions. Thus, one might argue in favor of making arrests, stops, or searches easier on the basis of mere suspicion rather than the higher standard of probable cause of wrongdoing. Similarly, convictions could be made easier by allowing evidence that is based on an illegal seizure, a confession without warnings, or questionable hearsay. Imprisonment upon conviction could be guaranteed by abolishing probation, suspended sentences, and community-based corrections. On the other hand, a more liberal orientation might emphasize increasing the probability of arrest, conviction, and imprisonment by developing more professionalism on the part of police, prosecutors, and other criminal justice personnel. That might include automatic suspensions of police officers who engage in illegal searches on the first occasion and automatic dismissals on the second occasion, especially if illegally seized evidence tends to decrease the chances of obtaining convictions.

With regard to decreasing the benefits of successful wrongdoing, a conservative orientation was reflected in the policies of the Law Enforcement Assistance Administration under Richard Velde. It emphasized what is sometimes referred to as hardening the targets. In the context of store robberies, this might mean developing systems of computerized credit via pushbutton telephones so as to minimize the cash carried in the cash register or by customers. It might also mean building bulletproof glass walls through which sales people transact business with customers in order to decrease the access of a would-be robber to whatever is in the cash register.

A more liberal orientation, although not necessarily mutually exclusive with target hardening, might emphasize decreasing the peer-recognition benefits received by many successful store robbers. More specifically, the typical robber of certain types of stores or the typical mugger may tend to be someone between about ages of 15 and 25 who engages in such behavior at least partly because it brings a kind of prestige from other teenage gang members. Thus, what may help decrease the benefits of successfully knocking over a gas station or a mom and pop grocery store is to change how prestige is obtained among such people. The Office of Economic Opportunity Community Action Program attempted to do that among the Black Peacestone Rangers on Chicago's south side in the 1960s by redirecting their aggressiveness into rent strikes, consumer boycotts, election campaigning, and picketing government agencies. This type of anti-poverty gang work was, however, stopped largely as a result of the negative reaction of Senator McClellan's investigating committee which some people interpreted as being more bothered by this kind of community action than by the robbing and mugging it may have decreased.

On the matter of increasing the costs of unsuccessful wrongdoing, a conservative orientation might emphasize having longer prison sentences, more use of the death penalty, and more severe prison conditions. A liberal orientation, on the other hand, might equally recognize the need for increasing the costs of noncompliance, but instead emphasize a different set of costs, namely, the opportunity costs one suffers as a result of being convicted, and imprisoned, or even just arrested. Middle class business executives do not rob stores or mug people in parks. They probably do not refrain from doing so because of fear of lengthy and severe imprisonment since they would most likely receive probation if a first offense is involved. A more important reason for their restraint is probably the fear of losing the opportunities that are available to them in the middle class business world. What may be needed is to give typical would-be store robbers more alternative opportunities that they risk losing if they are arrested for robbery or other crimes. This may require changing our educational institutions, neighborhood housing patterns, hiring procedures, and other socioeconomic institutions in order to make those alternative opportunities more meaningful. If the teenage gang member did not have more employment opportunities, he would not only suffer greater opportunity costs from getting arrested, but he also would receive less incremental benefits from an extra dollar obtained from a store robbery, and he would also have less need for antisocial peer recognition. Clearly, however, the opportunity costs approach to increasing the cost of noncompliance is a much larger social undertaking than the approach which emphasizes longer and more severe sentences.

One can see from the above example that a benefit-cost model can be suggestive of ideas that might otherwise be overlooked, less emphasized, or be less clearly organized in the absence of such a model. Two caveats however are necessary. First, the model is no substitute for thinking and for understanding the subject matter since the model only provides general categories into which the specific approaches can be placed. Second, the general categories are logically deduced from the model, but the specific approaches reflect value judgments and empirical facts, not deductive logic. In other words, it logically follows that criminal behavior can be reduced by decreasing its benefits and increasing its costs, but target hardening and more severe sentences are not logically more meaningful than changing peer group values and emphasizing social opportunity costs.[1]

BUSINESS WRONGDOING

Business wrongdoing provides a good example of the use of the general scheme when one starts with a set of suggested solutions to a deterrence problem and then analyzes their effectiveness in light of the model. The subfield of business pollution especially lends itself to that approach. A number of incentives have been unsystematically proposed for encouraging compliance with environmental standards. They include pollution taxes, injunctions, civil penalties, fines and jail sentences, tax rewards and subsidies, selective government buying, publicizing polluters, and conference persuasion.

The idea of a pollution tax is often mentioned as an especially effective incentive. Its effectiveness is largely due to the fact that it would directly increase the cost of noncompliance since the tax would be proportionate to the amount of pollution done by the business taxpayer. A common formula with regard to water pollution involves determining the total cost needed to keep a river segment at a given level of water quality, and then assessing each business firm on that river segment a portion of the total cost equal to the ratio between the firm's pollution and the total pollution in the river segment. By reducing its pollution, each firm thereby lowers its tax assessment, and that lowered assessment represents an increased benefit of compliance. The effectiveness of pollution taxes is also enhanced by virtue of automatic monitoring systems which are often a part of such proposals. These systems increase the probability of the above costs and benefits occurring by making the assessment and collection of the tax or fee relatively automatic, as compared to proposals that require more active judicial action to enforce.

Proposed judicial action against polluters tends to be of three kinds: injunctions, civil penalties, and criminal sanctions. Like pollution taxes, the effectiveness of all three tends to depend on how they influence the costs of noncompliance (and the complementary benefits of compliance), and also the probability of those benefits and costs occurring. Injunctions to cease or suspend operation are the most costly to the polluting business firm, but they have the lowest probability of occurring. If an injunction is requested by a government agency, a private group, or an individual, then a judge would normally be quite reluctant to order a steel mill or other manufacturing establishment to shut down in view of the economic damage such a decision might mean to the employees, consumers, stockholders, and the community of the business firm. Civil damages are normally easier to obtain, especially if they are brought under a legal procedure that limits defenses available, such as in workers' compensation actions. Civil damages are, however, normally less costly to the business firm than injunctions, unless a large class action is involved which in turn decreases the probability of success. Criminal penalties in the pollution context are almost exclusively fines, rather than jail sentences. Such fines are easier to obtain than injunctions since they are not so economically disruptive to third parties, but they are more difficult to obtain than civil damages since they involve the more stringent due process standards associated with criminal law. If such fines are imposed, they also tend to be in the middle between injunctions and individual damages with regard to the costs to the polluting firm, although fines can range from low, easily absorbed business expenses, to assessments comparable to pollution taxes, on up to the unlikely possibility of highly punitive fines.

Other proposals place emphasis on decreasing the money saved by noncompliance and simultaneously decreasing the cost of compliance, rather than increasing the cost of noncompliance. Such proposals include tax rewards and subsidies. For example, installing equipment to decrease air, water, and other forms of pollution is normally an expensive cost of compliance. Government policy, though, can ease that cost by providing accelerated business deductions or credits for doing so, or the government can provide outright grants or no-interest, long-term loans to further reduce the cost of compliance. These benefits are likely to occur in such government programs are instituted. In other words, business firms are likely to make the changes if the government in effect makes them cost-free or combines a cost-reducing program with a program that provides enforced penalties for noncompliance. Large government subsidies to private industry, however, may not be so likely to get through the legislative process because of opposition from those who feel business should be doing more on its own, just as pollution taxes are not so likely to get through the legislative process because of opposition from those who feel they are too much of a burden on business.

Other proposals are likely to be less effective than the ones mentioned above because of their lack of influence on the key benefits, costs, and probabilities of the benefits and costs occurring. For example, selective government buying power, in theory, rewards nonpolluters for complying (a benefit of compliance) and makes polluters suffer an opportunity cost (a cost of noncompliance). In practice, however, there are too many polluting firms that are not greatly affected by government purchases. Legislators and government purchasing agents also find it difficult to have pollution criteria override criteria relating to the cost and quality of the products purchased. Similarly, governmental publication of the names of polluters in order to get private consumers to engage in selective buying also has a low probability of the benefits and opportunity costs occurring, especially where the product is not a name brand or not a product bought by ultimate consumers. Conference persuasion is an especially ineffective approach although it was a major part of water pollution enforcement prior to 1972. Merely trying to convince business polluters of the social harm they are doing is not likely to encourage any legally desired behavior since it causes no increase in the costs of noncompliance, decrease in the benefits of noncompliance, or change in the probability of either of those costs or benefits from occurring.

Although pollution is a good example to illustrate the model applied to business wrongdoing, it can also be applied to other forms of business regulation such as consumer fraud, worker safety, product safety, antitrust practices, unfair management or union practices, stock manipulation, and landlord abuses.[2]

NONCOMPLYING PUBLIC OFFICIALS

Noncompliance by public officials can take a variety of forms to which the model can be applied to suggest ideas for encouraging legally desired behavior. A good example where all six elements in the model are applicable is the situation of encouraging criminal court personnel (especially prosecutors and assistant state's attorneys) to make time saving decisions that conclude trials quickly, rather than time lengthening decisions that involve postponements and delay. To increase the benefits of doing the right thing, the system can reward assistant state's attorneys with salary increases and promotions for reducing the average time consumption per case. To decrease the costs of doing the right thing, one could establish a computerized system that informs assistant state's attorneys concerning actual and predicted times at various stages for all cases to minimize the trouble to the attorneys to keep track of cases. They could also be provided with more investigative and preparation resources.

To decrease the benefits from doing the wrong thing, the system can provide for more release of defendants from jail prior to trial so that lengthening the pretrial time will not make the jailed defendants more vulnerable to pleading guilty. By having so many defendants in jail awaiting trial, the prosecutor is benefited by delay, since delay does increase the willingness of such defendants to plead guilty in return for probation or a sentence equal to the time they have already served awaiting trial, rather than wait longer for a trial. To increase the costs from doing the wrong thing, speedy trial rules can be adopted which provide for the absolute discharge of defendants whose cases extend beyond the time limits through no fault of their own. This is a heavier cost than merely releasing the defendant from pretrial detention since an absolute discharge means the defendant cannot be later tried for the incident for which he was being held.

To increase the probability of being detected and negatively sanctioned for delaying cases, the speedy trial rules can allow fewer exceptions such as suspending their application "for good cause" or "exceptional circumstances." These exceptions decrease the probability that the penalty costs will be imposed. To increase the probability of being discovered and positively rewarded if one does the right thing, the same computerized system that easily informs assistant state's attorneys what cases are running beind can also inform the head prosecutor which assistants are doing an especially good job so they will be more likely to receive the salary increases and promotions mentioned above.

On a more general level, one could talk about increasing the compliance of governmental administrators to judicial precedents and legislative statutes. Doing so might involve (1) increasing the probability of being caught and sanctioned; (2) increasing the severity of the sanctions; and (3) decreasing the benefits of continuing the former noncomplying behavior. The probability of being caught and sanctioned can be increased by encouraging citizen suits, as is done to some extent in the fields of environmental protection and equal employment, partly to serve as a check on government agencies in those fields. Whistle-blowers reporting wrongdoing within government can also be protected by civil service rules. Catching wrongdoers is also increased if wrongdoing is clearly defined, as is increasingly occurring in the field of school desegregation by way of guidelines of the Department of Health, Education and Welfare.

The severity of the sanctions to obtain administrative compliance can include reprimands which may not be much of a cost for the average administrator, but can be significant when directed by a court toward an agency lawyer. On a higher level of severity is the sanction of decreasing or blocking appropriations, as has sometimes been done by courts when dealing with racially discriminatory police examination procedures or public-housing site selection. An especially severe sanction might be to hold an administrator in contempt of court subject to a jail sentence, as has occurred with public aid administrators who do not comply with maximum waiting periods for processing public-aid cases. Such contempt sanctions, though, are less effective against officials of public sector unions who lead strikes contrary to federal or state law.

To decrease the benefits of continuing with the former noncomplying behavior may require changing the approval of the constituents of the noncomplying public official. For example, if the official refuses to comply with desegregation orders because of the perception that is what the constituents want, those noncomplying benefits can be decreased by convincing local business interests how detrimental such noncompliance might be to local business expansion. Similarly, if an official refuses to comply because of the perception that noncompliance is what the official's immediate superiors or peers want, then the system should seek to win over these supportive elements. An example is when the Supreme Court or the Department of Justice seems to be talking to police chiefs in order to change police behavior with regard to interrogations and searches. A key benefit from noncompliance is the satisfaction one receives from doing things in their customary way. Courts and legislatures should therefore emphasize successive incremental changes as increasingly has been done to provide counsel for the poor in criminal cases starting with capital punishment cases in the 1930s, some felony cases in the 1940s and 1950s, the rest of the felony cases in the 1960s, and misdemeanor cases in the 1970s.

Numerous other applications of the model could be applied to noncomplying public officials in the judicial, administrative, or legislative realm. For example, one could talk about how to encourage judges to be more sensitive to avoiding errors of holding defendants in jail who would appear for trial if released, as contrasted to errors of releasing defendants who might not appear. A similar sensitivity problem may exist (1) at the police arrest stage; (2) at the decision to incarcerate a convicted defendant or to rely on community-based probation; and (3) at the decision to release on parole. The model can also be applied to discussing how to obtain greater compliance on the part of administrators like school board officials with regard to court desegregation, school prayers, and disciplinary procedures. The model can also be applied to legislators with regard to discouraging corrupt behavior. This type of application may involve a combination of proposals directed simultaneously at legislators, business firms, and bribe-offering individuals, thereby combining all three types of applications dealt with in this chapter.[3]

SOME CONCLUSIONS

From this analysis, one can see that a benefit-cost perspective may be useful for generating, organizing, and analyzing ideas for encouraging socially desired behavior. The perspective merely involves viewing the behavior of individuals as being motivated by a desire to maximize their benefits minus costs of both a monetary and nonmonetary nature, taking into consideration the probability of the occurrence of events on which these benefits and costs depend. From that perspective, one can predict that people will change their behavior if the perception of expected benefits minus costs become greater for the new, over the old, behavior. From that perspective, one can prescribe that if society or public policymakers want to encourage socially desired behavior, they should arrange for such behavior to have a higher perceived expected value than the undesired behavior. What may be needed now are more researchers and practitioners to apply this kind of perspective to a variety of behaviors that are considered undesirable.

NOTES

1. On manipulating benefits and costs to decrease traditional criminal behavior, see Alfred Blumstein (ed.), *Deterrence and Incapacitation: Estimating the Effects of Criminal Sanctions on Crime Rates* (Washington, D.C.: National Academy of Sciences, 1978); Franklin Zimring and Gordon Hawkins, *Deterrence: The Legal Threat in Crime Control* (Chicago: U. of Chicago Press, 1973); Jack Gibbs, *Crime, Punishment, and Deterrence* (New York: Elsevier, 1975); and Gary Becker and William Landes (eds.), *Essays in the Economics of Crime and Punishment* (New York: Columbia U. Press, 1974).

2. On manipulating benefits and costs to decrease business wrongdoing, see Frank Grad, George Rathjens, and Albert Rosenthal, *Environmental Control: Priorities, Policies, and the Law* (New York: Columbia U. Press, 1971); William Baumol and Wallace Oates, *The Theory of Environmental Policy* (Englewood Cliffs, N.J.: Prentice-Hall, 1975); and Richard Posner, *Economic Analysis of Law* (Boston: Little, Brown, 1977).

3. On manipulating benefits and costs to decrease noncomplying public officials, see Harrell Rodgers and Charles Bullock, *Law and General Change: Civil Rights Law and Their Consequences* (New York: McGraw-Hill, 1972); Samuel Krislov and Melcolm Feeley, *Compliance and the Law* (Beverly Hills, Ca.: Sage, 1970); and Stuart Nagel and Marian Neef, *Decision Theory and the Legal Process* (Lexington, Mass.: Lexington-Heath, 1979).

Chapter 3
Deciding Whether Data Is Worth Gathering

Virtually everyone is probably opposed to excessive gathering of data by federal agencies. The key issue on that subject, however, is what is "excessive"? The purpose of this brief analysis is to try to give that concept some operational meaning. The meaning should make sense in light of the expected benefits and costs of gathering or not gathering data. "Expected" benefits and costs refer to the benefits and costs of using (or not using) the data, discounted by the probability of its being used (or not used). In other words, what we have here is a decision problem under conditions of risk or uncertainty. As such, we may gain some substantial insights by analyzing the problem in terms of a simple, decision theory table.

Table 3-1 provides a decision theory table for analyzing a data-gathering problem. There are basically two alternatives available. One either gathers the data, or one does not gather the data. We could, however, make things more complicated by talking in terms of gathering multiple quantities or percentages of data, and thus have many rows on our table. Such an extension can logically be made after clarifying the simpler choice between two alternatives. Similarly, there are basically two outcome possibilities. Either the data gets used in a certain way, or it does not get used. Again, we could later complicate things by talking in terms of multiple uses.

With two alternative decisions and two alternative occurrences, there are four possible outcomes. Two are clearly undesirable or costly, namely to gather the data and not have it used (cell C_g), or to not gather the data when it would have been used if it had been gathered (cell C_n). Two outcomes are clearly desirable or beneficial, namely to gather data which subsequently gets used (cell B_g), and to not gather data which would not have been used if it had been gathered (cell B_n). Of the two undesirable outcomes, it is normally worse to not gather data that would have been used, although sometimes the other undesirable outcome may be worse.

If cell C_n is considered the worse of the two costs, then for convenience we can anchor it at a value of -100. For the sake of consistency, we could then also anchor cell B_n at $+100$ as the better of the two beneficial outcomes. Now all we have to do is determine how many times worse a cell C_n outcome is as compared to cell C_g and we will be able to use the table to operationally define excessive data, i.e., data that should not be gathered.

TABLE 3-1. DECIDING WHETHER OR NOT TO GATHER CERTAIN DATA

ALTERNATE OCCURRENCES

	Data Would Not Be Used (1-P)	Data Would Be Used (P)	Expected Benefits and Costs
Gather the data (g) ALTERNATIVE DECISIONS	C_g Costs of gathering unused data	B_g Benefits of gathering used data	$(B_g)(P)$ $+ (C_g)(1-P)$
Do Not Gather the Data (n)	B_n Costs saved by not gathering unused data	C_n Benefits missed by not gathering used data	$(B_n)(1-P)$ $+ (C_n)(P)$

Abbreviations: P = probability of use; B = benefits; C = costs; g = gathering the data; n = not gathering the data.

Rules for Applying the Above Table:
1. Determine the alternative decisions
   (i.e., what is the data to be gathered or not gathered).
2. Determine the alternative occurrences
   (i.e., what is the potential use that will occur or not occur).
3. Determine the relative costs of C_n to C_g
   (i.e., the ratio of the type 1 to the type 2 error costs).
   a. If C_n is worse than C_g, give C_n a score of -100. Then give C_g a score equal to -Q, where -Q is to -100 as C_g is to C_n.
   b. If C_g is worse than C_n, give C_g a score of -100. Then give C_n a score equal to -Q, where -Q is to -100 as C_n is to C_g.
4. Calculate the threshold probability (or P^*) which equals $C_g/(C_g + C_n)$.
5. Determine whether the perceived probability of use is greater or less than P^*.
6. If P is greater than P^*, gather the data. If less, don't gather the data.

Alternatives to Rules 3 through 6:
3. Determine the probability that the data will be used.
4. Calculate the threshold error cost ratio (or X^*) which equals $P/(1-P)$.
5. Determine whether the ratio C_g/C_n is greater or less than X^*.
6. If C_g/C_n is less than X^* gather the data. If greater, don't gather the data.

If failing to gather needed data in a given situation would be 10 times as bad or as costly as gathering the data and not having it used, then the value of cell C_g on our -100 to $+100$ scale would be -10. Similarly, for the sake of consistency the value of cell B_n would be $+10$.

Now with that information for our hypothetical situation, we can determine the expected values of gathering or not gathering the data. The expected value of gathering the data equals $(+100)$ (P) $+$ $(-10)(1-P)$, where P is the probability that the data will be used, and $1-P$ is the probability that it won't be used. In other words, the expected value of gathering the data equals the benefits and the costs of the gathering, discounted by the probabilities of the benefits and costs occurring. Similarly, the expected value of not gathering the data equals $(+10)(1-P)$ $+$ (-100) (P) which equals the benefits and the costs of not gathering, discounted by their respective probabilities.

What we logically want to do now is to determine how high P has to be before the expected value of gathering the data can exceed the expected value of not gathering the data. To do that, all we have to do is set those two expected values equal to each other and solve for P. Doing so will give us the threshold probability above which we should gather the data (i.e., doing so is not excessive) and below which we should not gather the data (i.e., doing so is excessive or nonrational in a benefit-cost sense). One can show algebraically that the threshold P (or P*) equals $C_g/(C_g + C_n)$ or $10/110$ or .09. In other words, if there is better than a .09 probability that the data will be used, then we should gather it. Otherwise, it's not worth the trouble.

The above analysis can be applied without requiring that the user be capable of translating costs or benefits into dollars, satisfaction units, or any kind of absolute units. All the user has to do is determine which of the two undesirable outcomes is the more undesirable, and the rough ratio of the undesirability of the more undesirable outcome to the less undesirable outcome, taking the facts of the specific situation into consideration. The users then apply the simple formula $C_g/(C_g + C_n)$ to determine the threshold probability, and then they should ask whether the actual perceived probability in this specific situation is greater or less than the threshold probability? If greater, gather the data. If less, don't.

As another quick example, suppose it would be worse to gather the data that is not used because the data is quite expensive and the use to which it would be put is not very momentous. In that situation, cell C_g would be anchored at -100. One would then ask how many times worse is cell C_g than cell C_n? Maybe the answer is 5 times as bad. That means cell C_n has a value of -20. That further means P*, or $C_g/(C_g + C_n)$, is $100/120$, or .83. In other words, under those circumstances, the probability of the data being used would have to be greater than .83 to justify its being gathered. If the data were perceived to have a probability of being used less than .83 and yet it is still gathered, then that would be an example of excessive or non-rational data gathering.

This same type of analysis could also be used to determine what the ratio of the two types of relative error costs has to be in order to justify gathering data. In that regard, one can algebraically show that the formula $C_g/(C_g + C_n)$ is equal to $X/(X + 1)$ where X is the ratio of C_g to C_n. In other words, P* also equals to $X/(X + 1)$. Thus, if the potential data gatherer knows or assumes in advance what the probability of use will be, he can then solve for X to determine what the cost ratio should be to justify gathering the data.

For example, suppose the decision maker feels there is a .50 probability the data will be used. Solving for X in the equation $.50 = X/(X + 1)$, reveals that X has a value of 1.00. That means to justify gathering the data, the cost of not gathering the data (cell C_n) must be at least equal to the cost of gathering the data (cell C_g). Similarly, if the decision-maker feels there is only a .33 probability of the data being used, then X equals .50, meaning the value of cell C_g must be no less than half the value of cell C_n, or cell C_n must be at least twice as costly as cell C_g. A simpler formula for determining this threshold ratio, which algebraically follows from what has been said, merely involves calculating $P/(1 - P)$, or, in the last example, .33/.67, or .50.

This alternative type of analysis provides us with an alternative definition of "excessive" data gathering. It is excessive or nonrational to gather data where the opportunity cost of not gathering data that would be used is less than X* times as great as the cost of gathering unused data. In that definition, X* is the threshold ratio between the C_g and C_n costs when we know or think we know what the probability is of the data being used.

Another use of this type of analysis is to suggest that if we want to make data gathering more rational, we should concentrate on doing one of three things. First, we should try to increase the probability (P) that the data will be used, possibly by increasing its visibility. Second, we should try to decrease the relative cost of gathering data (C_g), possibly by providing for more automatic data-gathering routines. Third, we should try to increase the opportunity costs of not gathering the data when the data could have been used (C_n), possibly by providing more opportunities or ways in which data can serve as inputs into governmental decision making.

Still another set of insights that this type of analysis might generate is a better appreciation of the value of data gathering. That use is harder to justify than the above-mentioned uses which logically follow from the simple logic of the decision theory table. Saying that the table is supportive of data gathering is based on the hypothesis that if the analysis is applied, one will generally discover that the threshold probability (P*) does not have to be very high (relative to reality) to justify most data gathering, given the relative costs of the cell C_n and C_g outcomes. Similarly, the threshold ratio (X^*) of cell C_n to C_g probably does not have to be very high (relative to what is likely in most factual situations) to justify gathering the data in question, given the probability of the data being used.

Often the phrase "expensive paperwork" is used to attack the substance of governmental programs rather than attack the rationality of gathering the data in light of its usefulness to its government program. On the other hand, some people may defend data gathering not because it meets the above-discussed tests, but because they endorse the program of which it is a part even though the data does not get used by the program. It is hoped that this rational decision analysis of when data is worth gathering will help add some rationality to the data gathering discussion.

REFERENCES

Behn, Robert, and Vaupel, James. *Analytical Thinking for Busy Decision Makers.* New York: Basic Books, 1979.

Mack, Ruth P. *Planning on Uncertainty: Decision Making in Business and Government Administration.* New York: John Wiley, 1971.

Nagel S. and Neef, M. *Decision Theory and the Legal Process.* Lexington, Mass.: D.C. Heath, Lexington Books, 1978.

Weiss, Carol H. *Using Social Research in Public Policy Making.* Lexington, Mass.: D.C. Heath, Lexington Books, 1977.

Chapter 4
Voting To Convict or Acquit

This chapter has three purposes. Its initial purpose is to develop a method to determine the values of jurors regarding their propensities to convict or acquit. Its second purpose is to use that method to determine how these propensities differ across types of jurors and cases, and how the propensities influence decisions. Its third and main purpose is to discuss how much propensities can be brought more into line with the legal rules that specify defendants should not be convicted unless they appear to be guilty beyond a reasonable doubt.[1]

In the context of this article "propensity to convict" does not mean a percentage or proportion representing the ratio between conviction votes and opportunities to convict. Instead it refers to a threshold probability of guilt above which a juror will vote to convict, and below which a juror will vote to acquit. In other words, we are referring to a personal value judgment or normative criterion, rather than an empirical or statistical pattern.

For the analysis reported in this article, a method was developed for measuring the propensities of would-be jurors to convict. The measurement system has been applied on a continuing basis using a roughly random sample, mainly of students at the University of Illinois, as part of a series of exercises performed by graduate students and law students in the author's seminar on "Law, Policy, and Social Science." A key purpose of the applications has been to generate ideas for improving the measurement methods, and for developing hypotheses about juror propensities and how they might be brought more into conformity with legal standards. It is hoped that this article will lead to systematic testing of the ideas presented on a more representative sample of would-be jurors.[2]

What juries decide is important not only in the cases that involve jury trials, but even more so because of the influence jury trials have on plea bargaining and out-of-court settlements. Although relatively few cases go to trial, let alone jury trials, that option is always constitutionally available, and it serves to determine the bargaining limits of prosecutors and defense counsel in viewing the alternatives to arriving at a negotiated settlement.

MEASURING THE PROPENSITY OF
A WOULD-BE JUROR TO CONVICT

There are basically three ways one could measure the propensity of a would-be juror to convict. One method would involve observing the decisional behavior of actual or simulated jurors in actual or simulated cases. Such observations reveal that juries unanimously convict 64 percent of the time, unanimously acquit 30 percent, and are unable to reach a unanimous decision 6 percent of the time, according to a study of 3,576 jury trials made in 1955 by the University of Chicago Jury Project. The same project also found that individual jurors vote to convict 68 percent of the time and to acquit 32 percent.[3]

That information, however, does not tell us whether juries or individual jurors have a high or low propensity to convict if we do not know something about the extent to which the defendants appeared to be guilty in those cases. In other words, a 60 percent conviction rate out of 10 cases would reflect a low conviction propensity if all 10 defendants appeared to be guilty, but would reflect a high conviction propensity if all 10 defendants appeared to be innocent. There is no way of knowing how guilty or innocent the defendants in those 3,576 cases appeared to be to the juries, the jurors, or anyone else.

Even if the research design could have been planned so as to ask the jurors not only how they voted, but also how guilty the defendants appeared to be, we still would not be able to measure the jurors' propensity to convict. This is so because the jurors would be likely to report their perceptions in such a way as to justify their voting and vice versa. If cases could be objectively classified on a scale from 0 to 100 with regard to the defendant's appearance of guilt, we still would not be able to measure juror propensities by observing their voting. This is so because if a defendant has a .80 probability of guilt and a juror votes to convict that juror could have a threshold probability of only .10 or .40 or anything under .80. Similarly, if the juror votes to acquit, that juror could have a threshold probability of .95, .87, or anything above .80. We also would not know if the juror perceives the defendant's probability of guilt as being .80 unless we were to tell the juror, and then we would be getting away from the approach of having the juror vote on the basis of the facts in actual or simulated cases.

Thus an approach that involves observing juror behavior is not so meaningful for determining juror propensities in the sense of their threshold probabilities, although observing juror behavior may be an excellent method for other types of jury research. Observing jury behavior also has the disadvantage that it cannot systematically vary the facts and the judicial instructions, and the possible effects of those variations are an important part of this analysis.

A second method for determining the propensity of a would-be juror to convict is the direct or introspective approach of asking would-be jurors how guilty does a defendant have to appear to be before you will vote to convict. The responses to such questions may not be too meaningful given the variety of words used. To provide greater precision one can specify that the respondent should indicate a probability of guilt from 0 to 1.00. Doing so, however, may not give complete precision since each respondent may have a different notion as to what, for example, a .80 probability means. The direct questioning approach, though, has the much greater defect that respondents tend to give responses which they consider socially proper, rather than responses that reflect their true values. Thus respondents, who are aware that the law expects a high guilt probability before a conviction, report that they personally require a high probability before they will vote to convict, whereas that is not true of respondents who think the law expects a lower probability.

Perhaps the best method is one that combines the ease of questioning would-be jurors (as contrasted to the difficulty of observing many actual or simulated trials) with the unobtrusiveness of observing jury behavior unknown to the jurors being observed (as contrasted to the direct questioning method which encourages fudging of answers). This combination method involves asking would-be jurors a series of questions from which one can calculate their threshold probabilities, but where the questions are of such a nature that the would-be jurors do not know how to fudge their answers in order to result in a socially proper threshold probability.

The system of questioning that was used at the University of Illinois involves informing respondents that if they were jurors, they could vote either to convict or acquit, and the defendant could be either innocent or guilty. Thus there are four possible occurrences, namely, (a) one could vote to convict a defendant who is truly guilty; (b) one could vote to convict a defendant who happens to be innocent; (c) one could vote to acquit a defendant who happens to be guilty; or (d) one could vote to acquit a defendant who is truly innocent.

The respondents are then asked which of these four possible occurrences they consider undesirable and which they consider desirable. Most respondents answer that (b) and (c) are undesirable and (a) and (d) are desirable. When we ask, "Of the undesirable occurrences, which is the most undesirable?" Most respondents answer occurrence (b) which involves convicting an innocent defendant. We then ask, "If we position the most undesirable occurrence at −100 on a scale from 0 to −100, then where would you position the other undesirable occurrence?", which is generally voting to acquit a guilty defendant. Respondents are likely to say anything from about −5 to −95.

With that information, we can now easily calculate the would-be jurors' threshold probability for convicting. The formula with the above set of questions is simply $100/(100 + X)$, where the X represents the value the respondent places on the less desirable of the two undesirable occurrences. For example, William Blackstone has written that it is ten times as bad to convict an innocent defendant as it is to acquit a guilty one. Therefore if he were answering these questions consistently with that statement, he would give acquiting a guilty defendant a score of $+ 10$ on a 0 to $- 100$ scale, where convicting an innocent defendant has a score of $- 100$. Thus his threshold probability in ignoring the minus signs would be $100/(100 + 10)$ or $100/110$, which equals .91. This means for William Blackstone the defendant's probability of guilt would have to be greater than .91 before Blackstone would be willing to convict.

The formula thus makes simple sense, although it could also be proved algebraically as resulting in a voting rule that will maximize the expected values of the would-be juror. One could vary the formula to take into consideration the relative value placed on the desirable occurrences, as well as the undesirable ones, but doing so does not generally change the threshold probabilities. One could also vary the questions to make it easier or more difficult for the respondents to see what is likely to be done with their answers. The main variation, however, is to insert alternative factual situations or legal instructions into the questioning process.[4]

HOW PROPENSITIES DIFFER ACROSS
TYPES OF JURORS AND CASES

When the above method for measuring the propensities of would-be jurors to convict was applied at the University of Illinois, it was found that the average threshold probability is only about .55 although there are individual differences. This low average runs contrary to what one might expect, especially since the respondents when directly asked what they thought was a desirable threshold probability tended to come closer to .80 or .90 particularly among the law and prelaw students. The method though does seem to be accurately measuring the true threshold probabilities, and its findings are consistent with other studies that show would-be jurors tend to apply a "mere preponderance of the evidence" standard even in criminal cases, rather than the higher "beyond a reasonable doubt" standard.[5]

One could argue that the threshold probabilities are unduly low (meaning the would-be jurors show an undue willingness to convict) because the would-be jurors are not faced with a real defendant whose liberty is at stake. The would-be jurors, however, are also not faced with a real victim whose presence might cause them to be even more willing to convict. The factual situations were sometimes varied to mention the defendant and the likely sentence. Doing so did result in higher threshold probabilities, but they come down again when the factual situations mention the damage done to the victim or potential future victims.

How might one explain why jurors in criminal cases would apply a standard of guilt that is substantially below the meaning of beyond a reasonable doubt? Perhaps their personal experiences or fears are such that they have more dread of being the victim of a guilty defendant than being wrongly accused of a crime. They might also feel there is no substantial need to let guilty people go free in order to save innocent people from conviction, naively thinking that we can somehow convict all the guilty defendants and free all the innocent ones.

When comparing would-be jurors with different background characteristics, differences in their average threshold probabilities are small. This is true when comparing males with females, business students with liberal arts students, or students with non-students. Similarly, when comparing across types of cases, the differences in the average probabilities are also small, such as when comparing rape, robbery, and consumer fraud cases. If one, however, compares across the background characteristics and case types simultaneously, then some substantial differences do appear. For example, males have higher threshold probabilities than females in rape cases, but they are about the same in cases in general. Similarly, business students have higher threshold probabilities than liberal arts students in consumer fraud cases, but they are about the same otherwise. Having a higher threshold probability means a lower propensity to convict, since one requires that a higher threshold be met before one is willing to convict.

In addition to asking questions designed to calculate the threshold probabilities of student and nonstudent respondents around the University of Illinois, the respondents were also asked to position hypothetical defendants as to their appearance of guilt on a probability scale from 0 to 1.00, and to vote to convict or acquit each such hypothetical defendant. Each respondent could thus be positioned on (1) a threshold probability or value position; (2) a perception of guilt expressed as an empirical probability for a given case; and (3) a decisional propensity as indicated by their individual vote in that case. Consistent would-be jurors tend to vote to convict if the empirical probability is greater than the normative threshold probability, and otherwise to acquit. Many respondents were not so consistent, however, because they were not aware of what their threshold probability was.

An especially interesting occurrence in this preliminary analysis was a rationalization phenomenon, whereby the respondents tend to adjust their perceptions to convict or acquit in accordance with their propensities. For example, some respondents were told that the law requires a .90 probability of guilt before a juror can properly vote to convict (group one). Other respondents were told that the law requires a .75 probability (group two).

The respondents with relatively conviction-prone values who were in the .90-standard group tended to perceive the hypothetical defendants as having a greater than .90 probability of guilt. Those in the .75-standard group on the other hand, tended to perceive the same hypothetical defendants as having a greater than .75 probability of guilt, but not necessarily greater than .90. This tends to indicate that conviction-prone jurors may in effect decide to vote to convict before hearing the facts, and then perceive the facts in light of whatever standards they need to satisfy in order to convict. The same is true of defendant-prone jurors in that those in the group operating under the .75 standard tend to perceive the defendant's guilt as being below .75, whereas equally defendant-prone jurors in the .90 group perceive the same defendant's guilt as being below .90 but not necessarily below .75.

The rationalization phenomenon also involves the respondents tending to adjust their notion of what the law requires in order to be able to vote in accordance with their propensities. For example, some respondents were told that a hypothetical defendant had a .80 probability of being truly guilty, whereas other respondents were told the defendant has a .60 probability of being guilty. The conviction-prone respondents (as indicated by their low threshold probabilities) who were in the .60 defendant group tended to think the law only requires a probability of guilt greater than .50. Those in the .80 defendant group, on the other hand, tended to think the law requires a probability greater than .60, but not necessarily greater than .80. Similarly, the defendant-prone respondents tended to raise their notions of what the law requires high enough to exceed the empirical probabilities that they were given.

The findings concerning the rationalization phenomenon were not as clear-cut as the above description indicates. That description represents a simplification designed to clarify the general tendencies. The important thing is that the sequence of juror decision making may not be (1) to arrive at a standard of guilt; or (2) to perceive how guilty the defendant seems to be; and then (3) vote to convict or acquit depending upon whether the probability from (2) exceeds or goes below the probability from (1). Instead, the sequence may be (1) to arrive at a tentative decision to convict or acquit; (2) to receive a standard of guilt from the court, or anticipate what the standard will be; and then (3) adjust one's perception of how guilty the defendant seems to be so that (1) will be consistent with (2) and (3). The other kind of rationalization may involve (1) arriving at a tentative decision to convict or acquit; (2) perceiving how guilty the defendant seems to be; and then (3) adjusting one's perception of the judge's instructions on the matter of standard of guilt so that (1) will be consistent with (2) and (3). What may often be happening is a combination of both kinds of rationalization. In other words, the perceptions of the defendant's guilt and the perceptions of the judge's instructions may both receive implicit mental adjustments to rationalize preconceived notions of guilt-innocence and thus of the appropriateness of convicting-acquitting. The preconceiving is not necessarily prior to all the facts, but at least prior to the completion of the evidence and the closing arguments.

CHANGING PROPENSITIES
BY JUDICIAL INSTRUCTIONS

The previous part of the analysis tends to indicate that (1) there may be too much divergence between jurors with different backgrounds in certain types of cases; (2) there maybe too little sensitivity to avoiding convictions of the innocent relative to what the law requires; and (3) jurors may be fitting the facts and the law to preconceived decisions, rather than basing their decisions more on the facts and the legal rules. The most important part of the analysis, from the point of view of improving the judicial process, is the part that roughly attempts to determine what some of the effects might be of various types of judicial instruction on those three somewhat disturbing, although inconclusive, findings.[6]

To deal with the problem of diverging backgrounds, an equalizing instruction was developed. The instruction was given to men and women in some rape cases and withheld in others to see what effect it might have on reducing the differences in their threshold probabilities. The wording of the instruction is as follows:

> Social science research tends to show that males are more reluctant to convict rape defendants than females are. When you go into the jury room, if you are a male and you feel reluctant to convict, ask yourself whether your reluctance is based on the facts of the case or on your identifying with the defendant. If you are a female, and you feel relatively willing to convict, ask yourself whether your willingness is based on the facts of the case or on your identifying with the victim.

That type of instruction did result in causing the average male threshold probability of about .70 to go down toward .60, and the average female threshold probability of about .50 to go up toward .60. This seems desirable if we want more uniformity across demographic groups in jury decision making. It would, however, be even more desirable if the uniformity could be at a level closer to the .90 threshold probability, that is generally associated with the standard of beyond a reasonable doubt when judges are asked to translate that standard into a rough probability figure.

To deal with the problem of low threshold probabilities, a series of instructions were tried with some respondents and not others. There were four types of instructions, namely (1) no instruction at all on the meaning of beyond a reasonable doubt; (2) a purely verbal instruction that simply uses the words "beyond a reasonable doubt"; (3) a quantitative instruction that talks in terms of a .90 probability; and (4) the Blackstone quantitative instruction that talks in terms of convicting an innocent person as being ten times as bad as acquiting a guilty person. The results of that analysis are not clear-cut, but they roughly tend to point in the direction of both equalizing and uplifting the threshold probabilities as the instructions move from (1) to (4), as indicated in the simplified data below:

Type Of Jury Instruction	Threshold Probabilities (in rape cases)	
	Males	Females
No instruction	.70	.50
Beyond reasonable doubt	.75	.60
.90 probability	.80	.75
10 to 1 tradeoff	.90	.90

The most difficult instruction to devise is one that will simultaneously stimulate jurors to arrive at a uniform standard, at a high level of sensitivity in avoiding wrongful convictions, and to use the standard along with their perceptions of the evidence to arrive at a consistent decision. Such an instruction might be the following:

> Before voting to convict or acquit, you should decide for yourself what is the probability that the defendant is guilty. By probability in that context, we mean that if the circumstances and evidence in this type of case were to come up about 100 times, how many times out of those 100 do you think the defendant would be truly guilty? Before voting to convict or acquit, you should also bear in mind that our legal system requires a high probability of guilt before we will allow someone to be convicted. By high probability in that context, we mean the evidence should indicate the defendant is so guilty that 90 out of 100 people with this evidence would be truly guilty, or to put the matter differently, our legal system considers it about 10 times as bad to convict an innocent person as it is to acquit a guilty person.

In the pretesting work at the University of Illinois, the above instruction has been tried for understandability. It has not been, however, systematically applied to a variety of situations designed to determine the extent to which it can reduce the rationalization phenomenon, as previously described. What is needed is not more pretesting work with university students, but rather the actual testing of the kinds of ideas presented above on a more random sample of the general population. If such testing shows the suggested instructions can reduce divergence, raise standards, and decrease rationalization, then perhaps those instructions can be tried with real juries.[7]

Although this analysis is mainly a pretest of a way of measuring juror propensities to convict, it does suggest some provocative ideas. First, jurors in criminal cases are generally applying a standard of guilt that is substantially below what judges interpret beyond a reasonable doubt in terms of the probability of guilt needed before one should vote to convict. Second, there may not be much difference across types of jurors or types of cases with regard to propensities to convict, but when certain types of jurors are combined with certain types of cases, substantial differences in the combined categories may appear, such as comparing females in rape cases with males in rape cases.

Third, juror decision making may involve preconceived decisions that strongly influence one's interpretations of the facts and the law, more so than the facts and the law influence one's decisions. Fourth, judicial instructions may be capable of being developed that can (1) substantially raise the standard of guilt which jurors apply, (2) make that standard more uniform, and (3) enable that standard to play a more important role in influencing juror decisions. Actual testing and applying of these ideas can help increase our understanding of jury decision making, and such applications may help make the judicial process more objective, sensitive, and rational.

NOTES

1. For further details concerning the analysis on which this chapter is based see S. Nagel and M. Neef, *Decision Theory and the Legal Process* (Lexington, Mass.: Lexington-Heath, 1979), pp. 187-215; and S. Nagel, David Lamm, and M. Neef "Decision Theory and Juror Decision Making" in Bruce Sales (ed.), *The Jury, Judicial, and Trial Processes* (New York: Plenum, 1980). Thanks are owed Martin Kaplan, David Lamm, and Marian Neef for their helpful comments relevant to this article, and to the Illinois Law Enforcement Commission for its financial assistance.

2. This series of exercises has been conducted in the spring semesters of 1977-79 in the author's graduate seminar. Each seminar averaged about 7 student members. Each of those students interviewed a roughly random sample of 15 other people. There were thus about 20 samples and a total of 300 people interviewed. A more intensive analysis of 183 psychology students as part of an independent study course was conducted by David Lamm who is now a law student at Georgetown University. As mentioned above, the results of those surveys were meant to be a learning experience and to generate suggestive hypotheses for future testing not to be conclusive findings.

3. Harry Kalven, Jr. and Hans Zeisel, *The American Jury* (Boston: Little, Brown, 1966), pp. 56 and 460.

4. For other applications to jury decision making of a decision theory perspective somewhat like this article uses see Alan Cullison, "The Model of Rules and the Logic of Decision" in S. Nagel (ed.), *Modeling the Criminal Justice System* (Beverly Hills, Ca.: Sage, 1971); Michael Fried, Kalman Kaplan, and Katherine Klein, "Juror Selection: An Analysis of Voir Dire" in Rita Simon (ed.), *The Jury System in America: A Critical Overview* (Beverly Hills, Ca.: Sage, 1975); and John Kaplan, "Decision Theory and the Factfinding Process," 20 *Stanford Law Review* 1065-92 (1968).

5. Rita Simon and Linda Mahan, "Quantifying Burdens of Proofs: A View from the Bench, the Jury, and the Classroom," 5 *Law and Society Review* 319-30 1971); and Rita Simon, "Beyond a Reasonable Doubt: An Experimental Attempt at Quantification," 6 *Journal of Applied Behavioral Science* 203-9 (1970).

6. On the art and science of instructing juries, see Bruce Sales, Amiran Elwork,

and James Alfini, "Improving Comprehension for Jury Instructions" in Bruce Sales (ed.), *Perspectives in Law and Psychology* (New York: Plenum, 1978); and N.L. Kerr *et al.,* "Guilt Beyond a Reasonable Doubt: Effects of Concept Definition and Assigned Decision Rule on the Judgments of Mock Jurors," 34 *Journal of Personality and Social Psychology* 282-94 (1976).

7. Charles McCormick's influential *Handbook of the Law of Evidence* (St. Paul, Minn.: West, 1954), pp. 681-85 justifies not defining beyond a reasonable doubt on the grounds that doing so creates more confusion than clarity. The U.S. Supreme Court, however, has recently indicated the need for greater clarity when defining beyond a reasonable doubt. *Taylor v. Kentucky,* 436 *U.S.* 478 (1978).

Chapter 5
Optimum Choice Logic

The general purpose of this chapter is to discuss some of the problems involved in making an optimum choice among discrete policy alternatives. By "discrete policy alternatives" we mean a set of political or governmental choices that have no inherent order, such as releasing or not releasing a defendant prior to trial or choosing among 5,000 legally acceptable ways of redistricting a state legislature. Discrete alternatives can be contrasted with continuum alternatives where the choices do have inherent order, such as deciding an optimum jury size between 6 and 12 jurors inclusively, or deciding how to allocate a 5,000 dollar budget among a variety of places or activities. Twelve jurors is inherently larger than six jurors, and 2,000 dollars given to a place is inherently larger than 1,000 dollars. Continuum decisions are often referred to as optimum level and optimum mix decisions, whereas discrete decisions are simply referred to as optimum choice decisions although both continuum and discrete decisions involve optimum choices. Making decisions with discrete alternatives, however, involves a different and generally simpler logic than making decisions with continuum alternatives.

The basic logic for making optimum decisions with discrete alternatives is to determine the benefits minus costs for each alternative, and then pick the alternative that has the best B–C score. Sometimes the benefits and/or the costs are contingent on the occurrence of an event, and they thus need to be discounted by the probability of the event occurring. Under those circumstances, one should determine the discounted benefits minus the discounted costs for each alternative. Discounting benefits or costs may simply mean determining B and C on the assumption that the event will occur, but then multiplying B and C by the probability of the event occurring. One then picks the alternative that has the best PB-PC score, where each P is a different probability or combination of probabilities. There are also more specialized principles, such as those for (1) discounting the time one has to wait to receive benefits or costs; (2) calculating thresholds for P, B, or C above which one of two alternatives is preferred and below which the other is preferred, and for (3) shortcutting the analysis by eliminating some alternatives for which it is not necessary to calculate benefits and costs.[1]

OPTIMUM CHOICE WITHOUT PROBABILITIES

There are a variety of ways of classifying situations involving the making of an optimum choice without probabilities. One can look at (1) whether or not there are decisional constraints with regard to mutual exclusivity or limited budgets; (2) whether the price and quantity components of the benefits and costs involve interval or binary measurement; and (3) whether the alternatives and goals involve multiple or dichotomous categories.

Decisional Constraints

MUTUAL EXCLUSIVITY

Table 5-1 provides data for a set of five projects. The object is to allocate scarce resources among one or more projects in order to make the optimum use of those scarce resources. For each project, we indicate the benefits for given costs, the net benefits or profitability, and the benefit/cost ratio or efficiency measure. Each project is a lump-sum project in the sense that one can only buy one unit of the project, not multiple units and not fractions of units. That occurrence is more typical of public sector problems than business problems. For example, a typical set of govern-

TABLE 5-1. MUTUAL EXCLUSIVITY AND LIMITED BUDGETS AS DECISIONAL CONSTRAINTS IN OPTIMUM CHOICE WITHOUT PROBABILITIES*

Project	Benefits (in dollars)	Rank	Costs (in dollars)	Rank	B–C (in dollars)	Rank	B/C	Rank
D	4.20	5	3.00	4	1.20	5	1.40	4
E	13.50	1	10.00	1	3.50	1	1.35	5
F	3.50	4	2.00	5	1.50	4	1.75	1
G	9.00	2	6.00	2	3.00	2	1.50	3
H	6.40	3	4.00	3	2.40	3	1.60	2
Totals	36.60		25.00		11.60		7.60	
Averages	7.32		5.00		2.32		1.52	

*Notes to the Figure:

(1)If the projects are mutually exclusive, Project E is the best buy, provided that one can afford the 10 dollar cost.

(2)If the projects are not mutually exclusive, all the projects should be bought provided that one can afford the 25 dollar total cost.

(3)If the projects are not mutually exclusive and one had only 10 dollars available, the best or most profitable combination is G and H, even though they are individually not the most profitable, efficient, effective, or least expensive.

ment projects involving benefit-cost analysis is a set of alternative dams within a river segment. At any given place in the river, it is meaningless to build two duplicative dams, one behind the other or one on top of the other since one dam does all the good that can be done. Similarly, it is meaningless to build half a dam, since the water can flow over half a dam as easily as no dam. Alternative dams are thus not only lump sum projects, but they are also mutually exclusive.

To begin using data from Table 5-1, we can compare Project E or Dam E which has the highest net benefits, with Project F or Dam F, which has the highest efficiency. One basic principle in policy evaluation is to prefer high net benefits over high efficiency. By doing so, we will be better off after that choice is made, assuming other things remain constant. To be more specific, if we invest 10 dollars in Project E, then at the end of the relevant time period we will have the equivalent of 10 dollars in principal and 3.50 dollars in interest, for total assets of 13.50 dollars. If, however, we invest 2 dollars in Project F, then at the end of the time period we will have 2 dollars in principal, 1.50 dollars in interest, and 8 dollars in idle funds, for total assets of only 11.50 dollars. The 8 dollars in idle funds may or may not be able to find an alternative investment opportunity that pays interest at a rate higher than the .75 of Project F or the .35 of Project E. An alternative perspective is to say, if we buy Project E we will have 13.50 dollars in benefits, whereas if we buy Project F we will have 3.50 dollars in benefits plus 8 dollars in unspent funds, for a total of only 11.50 dollars. In other words, we come out behind by going with the more efficient Project F than by going with the more profitable Project E, regardless of whether we view the situation from the perspective of an investor or a consumer. Thus if the projects were mutually exclusive, Project E would be the best buy, provided that we could afford it.

The situation becomes a bit more complicated, but more interesting, if the projects are *not* considered mutually exclusive, so that we can buy more than one project. An example of a set of five nonmutually exclusive lump-sum projects might be five different ways of notifying or reminding released defendants to appear in court. The projects could include (1) sending defendants postcards a few days before their trials; (2) phoning them within that time period; (3) going to their homes; (4) having them report to a court officer within that time period; and/or (5) putting a general notice in the newspaper emphasizing that people who fail to appear for their court dates get arrested. It would not be meaningful to go to their homes twice in that time, or only go halfway to their homes. Deliberately notifying only some of the defendants might be unconstitutional treatment. The data in Table 5-1 could be thought of as applying to those five notification projects rather than to five alternative dams. The benefits would be the dollars saved by not having to rearrest no-shows, as contrasted to the flood damage avoided. If we had an unlimited budget (i.e., a budget of 25 dollars or more) that is capable of buying all the projects, then we would buy all of them since they are all profitable.

LIMITED BUDGETS

Suppose we only have 10 dollars available to spend for those five notification projects. Which ones are the best to buy or invest in? One might think we should use the 10 dollars to buy the first most profitable project, then the second, and so on until we exhaust our 10 dollars. That, however, would be fallacious reasoning since we would then spend all our 10 dollars on Project E for a profit of only 3.50 dollars. By distributing our 10 dollars among other less profitable projects, we could make more total profit. For example, we could buy projects F, H, and D. They would collectively cost us only 9 dollars, leaving 1 dollar left over. Buying those three would include the first and second most efficient projects. More important, the sum of the net benefits for those three projects adds to 5.10 dollars, which is substantially more than the 3.50 dollars we would get by spending our 10 dollars on the single most profitable project. In other words, what is most profitable to do with mutually exclusive lump-sum projects may not be most profitable when the projects are not mutually exclusive.

Although buying F, H, and D with our 10 dollars makes more sense than just buying E, it is still not the most profitable way to allocate our 10 dollars, although it may be a highly efficient way, since it yields 5.10 dollars for an investment of only 9 dollars. It has the defect though of allowing 1 dollar to remain idle that otherwise might be profitably spent. We could use our whole 10 dollars to buy projects G and H. At first glance, that looks irrational, because those projects individually do not score best on benefits, costs, net benefits, or efficiency. At second glance, however, one can see that the G and H combination will produce a total profit of 5.40 dollars, which is higher than one can produce by any other combination of 10 dollars worth of projects, including F, H, and D. More specifically, the G and H combination gives us, at the end of the time period, total assets of 15.40 dollars, which consists of 10 dollars in principal and 5.40 dollars in interest. The F, H, and D combination, on the other hand, gives us at the end of the time period, total assets of only 15.10 dollars, which consists of 9 dollars in principal, 5.10 dollars in interest, and 1 dollar in idle funds.

The general rules that one might derive from this analysis are first, if a government agency is interested in maximizing the good that it does, then it should spend its whole budget, or as much as possible. Second, spend the budget for each of the projects in the order of their efficiency. Those two rules together should lead to an optimum allocation of one's scarce resources among the lump-sum projects, which are often present in governmental decision making.

One might object to the difficulty of measuring both benefits and costs in the same units, especially monetary units. With varying degrees of effort, however, one can usually assign a monetary value to controlling floods, getting the average defendant to show up for a trial date, or obtaining other public sector benefits. The human mind implicitly makes such calculations in deciding whether benefits are worth the costs. Thus, quantifying benefits in terms of cost units is only a matter of making that kind of thinking more explicit. A common alternative is to talk in terms of maximizing benefits subject to a maximum cost constraint, or sometimes mimimizing costs subject to a minimum benefit constraint, rather than maximizing benefits minus costs. These alternatives may sometimes be satisfactory, but they are not as desirable, as is indicated by their inapplicability in deciding between projects E and F if the benefits for those two projects were not both measured in dollars. In other words, 3.5 F units for 2 dollars could be worth more or less than 13.5 E units for 10 dollars, but 3.50 dollars is clearly worth less for 2 dollars, than 13.50 dollars is for 10 dollars. The desirability of maximizing benefits minus costs applies to both business firms and government agencies, although business firms may generally find it easier to measure benefits and costs in dollars as a common unit.[2]

Benefits and Costs As Price Times Quantity

INTERVAL MEASUREMENT ON PRICE AND QUANTITY

Benefits are like total revenue in economics. As such, benefits can be considered as being equal to the value or average price of each unit of benefits, multiplied by the quantity of units. Similarly, costs can be considered equal to the value or average price of each unit of costs, multiplied by the quantity of units. As in economics, price can range over a wide interval, rather than only being a dichotomy of relatively high versus relatively low.

To understand better this type of analysis, it is helpful to have a concrete example. One example is the problem situation of deciding how to decrease the occurrence of illegal searches by the police. One alternative that the courts have adopted is to exclude or throw out illegally obtained evidence from courtroom proceedings in criminal cases, on the theory that doing so will deter the police from using illegal methods to obtain evidence. Prior to 1961, the U.S. Supreme Court allowed the state courts and legislatures to decide themselves whether to adopt this exclusionary rule. In 1961, the Supreme Court in the case of *Mapp v. Ohio* declared that the fourth amendment required that illegally seized evidence be inadmissible in all U.S. criminal cases, at least when objected to by defense counsel.

In 1963, a mailed-questionnaire survey was made of one randomly selected police chief, prosecuting attorney, judge, defense attorney, and ACLU official in each of the 50 states to determine, among other things, their perceptions of changes in police behavior before and after *Mapp v. Ohio*. The experiment was aided by virtue of the fact that 24 of the 50 states had already adopted the exclusionary rule before *Mapp v. Ohio,* and respondents from those states could thus serve as a control group. At that time, 23 had been recently forced to adopt the rule, and respondents from those states could thus serve as an experimental group. Three states had partially adopted it, and they were not used in the analysis.

Table 5-2 shows that 57 percent of the respondents from the control group of states reported an increase in police adherence to legality in making searches since 1961, whereas 75 percent of the respondents from the experimental group of newly adopting states reported an increase. This 18 percentage points difference cannot be readily attributed to a chance fluke in the sample of respondents since there is less than a five out of 100 probability that one could distribute 104 respondents over the six cells in Table 5-2 purely by chance and come out with a + .18 relation. This + .18 relation is also not readily attributable to a misperception of reality on the part of the respondents since there was such a high correlation among the different kinds of respondents from the same state or type of states on the empirical question of police adherence to legality, even though there was great disagreement on the normative question of the desirability of the exclusionary rule. The + .18 relation between newly adopting the exclusionary rule and increased police adherence to legality in searches seems to be largely attributable to the fact that the states that newly adopted the exclusionary rule also disproportionately reported an increase in programs designed to educate the police regarding search-and-seizure law, which in turn correlates highly with increased police adherence to legality. States that already had the exclusionary rule also often underwent an increase in police adherence to legality possibly because of the stimulus of the publicity given in *Mapp v. Ohio,* and because of long-term public opinion trends demanding higher standards of police behavior.

Table 5-2b shows the relation between alternative policies and alternative goals involved in the problem of increasing police adherence to legality when making searches. The top part of Table 5-2b shows that the exclusionary rule (X_1) should be adopted if increased police adherence to legality (Y_a) is one's only goal, since there is a positive relation between X_1 and Y_a. Many judges and others (including Felix Frankfurter in his dissenting opinion in *Mapp v. Ohio)* have argued that criminal and damages actions against the police are more effective than adopting the exclusionary rule as a means of increasing police adherence to legality. The questionnaire asked the respondents how often damages or criminal actions had occurred against the police in their communities for making illegal searches. If one divides the respondents into those relatively few who said there had been at least one such action in recent years versus those who said there had been none, then there is only a + .05 relation between the occurrence of such actions and increased police adherence to police legality. The low relation and the low occurrence of such actions may be attributable to the fact that prosecutors are reluctant to prosecute the

TABLE 5-2. BENEFITS AND COSTS AS QUANTITY TIME PRICE (INTERVAL MEASUREMENT)

5-2a. The Relation Between Adopting the Exclusionary Rule and Increased Police Adherence to Legality in Making Searches

Exclusionary Rule

		Had All Along (Control Group)	Newly Adopted (Experimental Group)	
Police Adherence to Legality	Increase since 1961	57%	75%	+ 18 percentage points difference
	No change	34%	21%	
	Decrease	9%	4%	
	Number of Respondents	48	56	104

5-2b. Alternative Policies and Goals Involved in Increasing Police Adherence to Legality in Making Searches

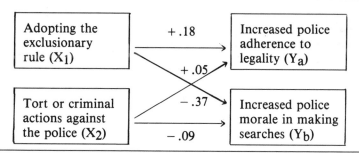

police who have been aiding them, and searched individuals are reluctant to sue because of the time, cost, embarrassment, unsympathetic juries, police discretion, and difficulty of assessing collectible damages. Thus the exclusionary rule (X_1) should be preferred over damages or criminal actions (X_2) if increased adherence to legality (Y_a) is one's only goal (and the decision-maker cannot adopt both policies), since there is a greater positive relation X_1 and Y_a than there is between X_2 and Y_a.

An additional goal one might have in dealing with the problem of increasing police adherence to legality in making searches is the goal of simultaneously increasing police morale, or at least not decreasing it. The mailed questionnaire asked the respondents about changes in police morale before and after *Mapp v. Ohio*. The relation between being a respondent from a state that had newly adopted the exclusionary rule (X_1) and reporting increased police morale (Y_b) in making searches was a $-.37$. The negative relation may be attributable to the fact that when evidence is thrown out that the police have worked hard to obtain through what they may have considered a lawful search, this is demoralizing to their enthusiasm for making future searches. If the relation between X_1 and Y_b had been positive, like the relation between X_1 and Y_a, then it would be easy to decide in favor of adopting X_1. However, since the relation between X_1 and Y_b is negative, one must decide whether that negative relation is enough to offset the positive relation between X_1 and Y_a. The matter is not resolved simply by noting that the X_1 and Y_b relation is greater than the X_1 and Y_a relation. This is so because it is unlikely that one would weigh Y_a and Y_b equally. If the Y_a goal has a weight of 3 times or more than the Y_b goal, then the $-.37$ relation would not be enough to offset the $+.18$ relation in view of the fact that 3 times .18 is greater than 1 times .37. On the other hand, if the Y_a goal has a weight of 2 times or less than the Y_b goal, then the $-.37$ relation would be enough to offset the $+.18$ relation. In other words, if the relation between X_1 and Y_a (times the weight of Y_a) plus the relation between X_1 and Y_b (times the weight of Y_b) is greater than zero, then X_1 should be adopted if Y_a and Y_b are one's only goals.

The most complicated problem situation involves both multiple policies and multiple goals, but even this situation is simple to resolve conceptually after going through the above problem situations. Suppose the weight of Y_a is 3 times greater than the weight of Y_b as determined by a scientific psychological survey of public, legislative, or judicial opinions. Note also that the relation between the occasional occurrence of damages or criminal actions against the police and increased police morale was a $-.09$. Thus, the exclusionary rule (X_1) should be preferred over damages or criminal actions (X_2) if increased adherence to legality (Y_a) and increased police morale (Y_b) are one's only goals (and the decision-maker cannot adopt both policies), since in Table 5-2: $+18 \times 3$ plus -37×1 is greater than $+.05 \times 3$ plus $-.09 \times 1$. In other words, .54 plus $-.37$ is greater than $+.15$ plus $-.09$.

The weight of each goal can be considered a price. The regression coefficients between each policy and each goal can be interpreted like a marginal rate of return (MRR) or a quantity of goal units to be achieved as a result of a one unit increase in the policy. Thus, the total revenue from policy X_1 is equal to P times Q on goal Y_a, and the total cost from policy X_1 is equal to P times Q on goal Y_b. The relation between X_1 and Y_a is a benefit since the MRR or Q is positive, but it is a cost on Y_b since the MRR or Q there is negative. To compare X_1 with X_2, one logically compares the benefits minus costs which each policy produces. Instead of talking in terms of benefits and costs, one could simply talk in terms of effects. Policy X_1 has some positive effects and some negative effects. One can determine the algebraic sum of the positive effects (P × Q for Y_a) and the negative effects (P × Q for Y_b). One can do likewise for X_2, and then compare the net effects of X_1 and X_2 to determine which is better if they are mutually exclusive, or which are profitable if they can both be adopted.

BINARY MEASUREMENT ON PRICE AND QUANTITY

In policy analysis, unlike economics, measurement often tends to be difficult to obtain with more degrees on either quantity or price than simply relatively high versus relatively low. This is the equivalent of binary measurement or of having quantities or values that only fit into two categories. The two categories can be arbitrarily labeled 0 and 1, − and + , or any other pair of labels. Having such measurement is accurate if the relation between X_1 and Y_a is truly greater than the relation between X_2 and Y_a. It does, however, mean losing some information that may or may not be valuable concerning how much greater the first relation is over the second. Similarly, having such measurement is accurate if the value of Y_a is greater than the value of Y_b, although some information is lost concerning how much more valuable Y_a is than Y_b. Fortunately, policy analysis solutions are often insensitive to that unavailable information, since the same solutions would often be reached if the information were available. This is so because policy evaluation solutions typically take the form of X_1 is better than X_2, or X_1 is the best of the policy alternatives. Such statements do not require that we know how much better X_1 is than X_2.

The policy problem of how to provide counsel to the poor in civil cases might be a good example to illustrate how insights can be obtained even when relations are only expressed in terms of direction, rather than magnitude or shape. Three competing alternatives for providing counsel to the poor in civil cases are (1) attorneys who volunteer to be on a list of free attorneys available when poor people have legal problems; (2) attorneys who are salaried by a government agency like the Legal Services Corporation for representing poor people, generally on a full-time basis; and (3) attorneys who represent poor people and are reimbursed for doing so by the government as part of a judicare system analogous to medicare. Four basic goals might be considered in comparing those three policy alternatives, namely being (a) inexpensive; (b) visible and accessible; (c) politically feasible; and providing (d) specialized competence plus reasonably aggressive representation.

For each goal, we can indicate the policy alternative that is relatively more positive, meaning the alternative that most achieves the goal. On being inexpensive, the volunteer system gets a plus, with the salaried attorney and especially the judicare system getting relative minuses. On being visible and accessible, the salaried attorney gets a relative plus, with judicare and especially the volunteer attorney system getting relative minuses. On being politically feasible, both the judicare and especially the volunteer systems create no substantial political problems, and might thus be scored pluses, but the salaried attorney system has had political problems, which gives it a minus. The salaried attorney system, though, tends to result in specialized competence and more aggressive representation which gives it a plus, with minuses to the volunteer and judicare systems on that goal. These relations are summarized in Table 5-3.

With that information, one can say that the volunteer and salaried systems seem to be tied with two pluses apiece. The volunteer system scores well on being inexpensive and politically feasible, whereas the salaried system scores well on being visible/accessible and being specialized/aggressive. To resolve that tie, those goals need relative weights. A conservative evaluator or policy maker would probably place relatively more weight on being inexpensive and politically feasible, and would thus tend to favor a volunteer system. A liberal evaluator would place more weight on being visible/accessible and specialized/aggressive, and would

TABLE 5-3. BENEFITS AND COSTS AS A QUANTITY TIMES PRICE (Binary Measurement)

PROVIDING LEGAL COUNSEL TO THE POOR IN CIVIL CASES

Goals		Weights	Policies and Relations		
			Volunteer (X_1)	Salaried (X_2)	Judicare (X_3)
Y_a.	Inexpensive	less (0)	+	−	−
Y_b.	Visible and accessible	more (1)	−	+	−
Y_c.	Politically feasible	less (0)	+	−	+
Y_d.	Specialized competence and aggressive representation	more (1)	−	+	−
Unweighted sum of pluses			2	2	1
Weighted sum of pluses			2 −	2 +	1 −

+ = Yes, relative to the other alternative policies (or 1)

− = No, relative to the other alternative policies (or 0)

thus tend to favor the government salaried system. Like most policy analysis, no conclusions can be reached without specifying the relative weights of the goals, even if there is agreement on what the goals are. The policy analyst can, however, clarify what policy is best in light of given goals and value weights. The important thing in this context is that insights can sometimes be obtained concerning what policy is best by working with relations between policies and goals that are only expressed in terms of relative direction without specifying the exact magnitude of the relations.

Like the search and seizure problem, the above right-to-counsel problem can be viewed as a problem of determining which policy has the highest score on benefits minus costs, or the highest score by summing algebraically and the weighted positive or negative effects of each policy. Each effect can be expressed as a quantity times price relative to each goal. In this context, each quantity is either a 1 or a zero. For example, on being inexpensive, the volunteer system gets a 1 and the other two policies get zeros. Also, in this context, each value or price is a 1 or a zero. Thus, the value of being inexpensive gets a relative zero to liberals, and a 1 to conservatives. Therefore, each of the three policies (X_1, X_2, and X_3) can be given a total score equal to $(QP)_a + (QP)_b + (QP)_c + (QP)_d$, which shows the benefits or costs which the policy achieves on each of the four goals. The policy which has the highest total score is the best policy, assuming the Q scores are accurate and that one accepts the value of the P scores. One could probably move without difficulty from a binary zero and 1 scoring to a rank-order scoring. The Q scores can then receive ranks of 1, 2, or 3, depending on how well each policy scores relative to the other two policies. The P scores can then receive ranks of 1, 2, 3, or 4, depending on how well each goal scores relative to the other three goals.[3]

Dichotomous and Multiple Policies and Goals

THE MEANINGFULNESS OF DICHOTOMOUS ALTERNATIVES

In making optimum choices, one can talk in terms of the nature of the measurement of the policy-goal relations (Q for quantity or r for relation) and the values of the goals (P for price or w for weight). That measurement can include dichotomies, ranks, or interval measurement. One can also talk in terms of the number of alternatives available when discussing the policies (Xs) or the goals (Ys). A good example might be the policy problem of determining how judges should be selected and for what lengths of terms. There are thus two policy dimensions. One is method of selection, which can be meaningfully dichotomized into selection by the electoral process or selection of gubernatorial appointment. The second dimension is length of term before re-election or reappointment, which can be dichotomized into above or below a national average. There are many goals that one might have in this context, but two that may be especially important are the liberalism/conservatism of judicial decisions in economic policy matters and liberalism/conservatism in civil liberties matters.

One can determine how elected judges differ from appointed judges by comparing (1) elected judges with (2) interim appointed judges, serving on the same state supreme courts hearing the same cases. One can also determine how relatively long-term judges differ from relatively short-term judges by finding state supreme courts where both types of judges are serving simultaneously. If more than two categories were used for method of selection or for length of term, then finding appropriate state supreme courts would be difficult on which those multiple categories might be represented. Comparing judges who are not sitting on the same cases would not be so meaningful, since any differences among them might be due to differences in the cases they hear, rather than to differences in method of selection or length of term.

Applying that kind of analysis to state supreme court judges tends to show that elected judges are more liberal on economic matters than appointed judges, but do not differ substantially on civil liberties matters. That finding holds true even when comparing elected and appointed judges from within the same political party. The explanation might be that elected judges are more likely to come from lower income backgrounds and rise through the party ranks, whereas appointed judges may be more likely to be plucked from prominent law firms partly for their monetary contributions. The analysis also tends to show that long-term judges are more liberal on civil liberties matters than short-term judges, but do not differ substantially on economic matters. The explanation might be that long-term judges are less sensitive to majoritarian pressures which may run contrary to freedom of speech, equal treatment for minorities, and criminal procedure safeguards.

With that information, one can conclude that the best method of selection and length of term depend on one's preferences with regard to liberalism and conservatism in economic and civil liberties matters. More specifically, if one prefers liberal results on both dimensions, the best judges would be elected and long-termers. If one prefers conservative results on both dimensions, the best judges would be appointed and short-termers. If one prefers judges who are likely to be liberal on economic matters but conservative on civil liberties matters, then the best judges might be those who are elected and short-termers. Similarly, if one prefers conservatives on economic matters but liberals on civil liberties matters, then appointing judges for long terms may be the best solution. The important thing from a policy analysis perspective is that one can say some meaningful things about the important issues of how judges should be selected and for what terms, by using a measurement perspective that is no more complex than a simple dichotomy on each of the policy variables and a simple dichotomy on each of the goal variables.

MULTIPLE ALTERNATIVES AND METHODS FOR HANDLING THEM

Discrete choices are not always few in number. In the problem of legislative redistricting, for example, there may be millions of patterns for combining counties or precincts into the desired number of legislative districts in a state. A wasteful approach to handling that problem would be to try every possible pattern and see how it scores on a total-score measure. The total score might be the average deviation between each district's population and the population of the average district. With perfect equality, all districts would have zero deviations, which means they would all have the same population. One could facilitate determining how each pattern scores on that kind of equality measure by arranging for a computer to go through every possible pattern and calculate its equality or inequality score. Even with a computer, the amount of work for a realistic redistricting problem would be prohibitive if all the possible redistricting patterns were checked.

To reduce the number of patterns or alternative policies to be checked on their equality scores, a number of methods can be simultaneously used, such as:

1. Stop the checking when a pattern is found that satisfies a maximum inequality constraint, although doing so will result in a satisfying solution rather than an optimizing one. Such a constraint might be phrased as, no district should have a population that exceeds the average population by more than plus or minus three percent.

2. Do a contiguity check on each pattern before doing the more complicated equality check, and then eliminate any pattern that does not provide for contiguity. By contiguity, we mean that one should be able to go from any place in any district to any other place in the same district without having to leave the district. To check for contiguity requires informing the computer as to which precincts or counties touch each other before any redistricting patterns are tried.

3. Try working with larger geographical units as the building blocks out of which the districts are to be made. The larger the units, the fewer possible patterns there are. Thus, working with counties is better than working with precincts for reducing the policy alternatives, although that might miss some alternative patterns that can provide better equality.

4. Start with the existing pattern as the base from which to create alternative districting patterns, rather than start with some arbitrary random pattern. By starting with the existing pattern, one is likely to be closer to the desired equality than a random pattern would be, and one is also more likely to ease the anxieties of incumbent legislators.

The redistricting problem not only involves numerous or even millions of alternative policies, but also numerous conflicting goals. The goals might include:

1. Equality of Population across districts as measured by:
   a. A maximum allowable inequality constraint like the three percent figure mentioned above.
   b. Minimizing an average deviation from equality, which may conflict with the maximum allowable constraint.
2. Compactness of districts as measured by:
   a. Contiguity as mentioned above, which is a constraint that normally must be satisfied allowing no deviation.
   b. Minimizing an average deviation from the perfect compactness of circular districts, or from having everybody living in one place in each district.
3. Political criteria, such as:
   a. Giving each political party a proportion of the total seats equal to the proportion of party members in the state.
   b. Having competitive districts. This conflicts with the proportionality principle above, which requires having safe rather than competitive districts.
   c. Minimizing disruption to incumbents. This may conflict with all the other goals, but may be politically important.

There are basically three ways of handling multiple goals like the above, either simultaneously, sequentially, or both. The typical approach is to try first to satisfy both the contiguity constraint and the maximum allowable inequality constraint. After doing that and locking the solution in, one can then seek to satisfy political criteria. Another alternative is to create a composite criterion consisting of the product of (1) the average deviation from equality; and (2) the average deviation from compactness; with (3) the equality measure receiving an exponent weight to indicate how much more important it is than the compactness measure. That alternative may have some mathematical significance in terms of developing an optimum districting pattern, but it may lack both legal and political significance. Legally, no matter how low the average deviation is from equality, if there is at least one district that exceeds the maximum allowable constraint, the whole pattern is likely to be declared unconstitutional. Politically, no matter how equal and compact the districting pattern is, the pattern is not likely to be adopted by a state legislature if there are other patterns that can satisfy contiguity and the maximum allowable inequality constraint, which can also give a better break to incumbents and possibly provide some roughly proportional representation.[4]

OPTIMUM CHOICE WITH PROBABILITIES

At least four purposes can be meaningfully present in analyzing optimum choices with probabilities, although those same purposes can apply to other kinds of choices. The purposes consist of (1) making decisions, (2) influencing decisions, (3) predicting decisions, and (4) measuring decisional propensities.

Making Decisions

WITHOUT TIME DISCOUNTING

A good example of where the principles of optimum choice with probabilities are applied is the decision making of personal injury plaintiff lawyers in choosing whether or not to accept a client and whether or not to accept an offer from the other side. The reasoning involved in accepting a client tends to implicitly or explicitly proceed through the following question and answer steps:

1. What damages are likely to be awarded? Suppose that the out-of-pocket medical expenses are 300 dollars for this applicant desiring legal services. By a rough rule of thumb, that means that if the attorney wins the case, about 3,000 dollars in damages will be collected or 10 times the medical expenses. That extra money is awarded by juries to cover lost wages, pain and suffering, and possibly the attorney's one-third fee. Predicting damages awarded from medical expenses can be done more accurately by consulting the loose-leaf service of the Jury Verdict Research Corporation. That service indicates the predicted damages awarded from medical expenses for various types of injuries. The predictions are based on numerous cases which the JVR researchers gather from around the country. The cases are then processed through a statistical regression analysis to develop regression prediction information, which is communicated in simple language to practicing lawyers through the loose-leaf service.

2. What is the probability of winning this case? By a rough rule of thumb, one can use a .65 figure, since that is about the average victory probability in personal injury cases. Predicting victory probabilities can be done more accurately by also consulting the loose-leaf service of the Jury Verdict Research Corporation. The same case samples are used to indicate victory probabilities for various types of cases. A practicing lawyer can combine those probabilities to obtain conditional or joint probabilities, or can simply use them in their raw form by finding the single case-type that best fits his case.

3. What is the expected value to the attorney of this case? If the predicted damages are 3,000 dollars and the predicted victory probability is .65, then the expected value to the plaintiff is 1,950 dollars. The lawyer, however, only gets one-third of what the plaintiff obtains. Therefore, the expected value of the lawyer's fee would be .33 times 1,950 dollars, or 644 dollars.

4. How much are the lawyer expenses likely to be in this case? This requires evaluating how many hours the case will probably consume. The estimated answer might be 20 hours. Unfortunately, there is no loose-leaf service that is helpful on hours consumed for different types of cases, or on the more important matter of relating hours consumed to damages awarded, like relating medical expenses to damages awarded. If such information were available, it could be useful in enabling lawyers to allocate their time better. Answering the expenses question also requires the lawyer to think in terms of how much an hour of time is worth. The answer might be whatever the market rate is, which might be 30 dollars an hour. The lawyer, however, might be willing to work for less than the market rate, where he is having difficulty filling his time with clients at that rate, or where he is receiving nonmonetary satisfaction. In light of those numbers, the hourly expenses for this case would be about 20 hours times 30 dollars, or 600 dollars in variable expenses, which do not include overhead or other variable expenses beside the lawyer's time. For simplicity, we can ignore the fact that those costs are contingent on the case going to trial and should be discounted by that probability.

5. Should the attorney take the case? If the expected value or incremental income is 644 dollars, and the expected incremental expense is 600 dollars, then the case seems worth taking. Cases like this will, on the average, cover the value of the attorney's time and provide something for other case-related expenses plus overhead. The case, however, should be rejected if other cases are available that are even better on benefits minus costs, and the attorney does not have the time for all of them. The important thing for our methodological purposes is that this situation does illustrate how the principles of optimum choice with probabilities can be applied in a practical way to both routine and important decisions. The same reasoning could be applied to cases in which a nonmonetary judgment is involved, such as a criminal prosecution or a civil liberties defense, but then one would have to decide whether the nonmonetary benefits are worth the monetary costs.

TIME DISCOUNTING

The above illustration does not take into consideration that the 3,000 dollars in damages may not be awarded for a few years. There may be no need to consider the future element when deciding whether to accept a client, since the main expenses of working on the case may also not occur for a few years until the case comes to trial. There are, however, many situations where a personal injury lawyer should consider the future element. Considering it means making an adjustment to recognize that 3,000 dollars a few years from now may not be worth as much as 2,500 dollars at the present time, since the 2,500 dollars can be invested so that it might earn interest or a profit, making it worth more than 3,000 dollars in a few years.

For example, suppose a personal injury plaintiff could follow the alternative of going to a federal court (on the jurisdictional grounds that the plaintiff and defendant are from different states), or go to the state court in which the defendant can be sued. Suppose further if the plaintiff goes to the federal court, the case will be heard within one year, and if victorious the plaintiff will collect about 15,000 dollars, but with only a 20 percent chance of winning. If, on the other hand, the case goes to the state court, it will be heard within two years; and the plaintiff, if victorious will collect 10,000 dollars, but with a 40 percent chance of winning. Which alternative should be followed?

The expected value of the federal alternative is 3,000 dollars (i.e., 15,000 dollars discounted by the .20 probability of winning it) without considering the time element, and the expected value of the state alternative is 4,000 dollars (i.e., 10,000 dollars discounted by the .40 probability of winning it). If, however, we take into consideration that one has to wait two years for the 10,000 dollars from the state court, its value substantially decreases. More specifically, the present value of a future amount is calculated by the formula $P = A/(1 + r)^t$ where r is the interest rate that could be obtained by putting money in a savings account for t years. If we assume the interest rate is 6 percent, then the present value of the state's 10,000 dollars two years from now is 8,900 dollars. If we now discount that present value by the .40 probability of achieving it, the expected value of the state case becomes 3,560 dollars. Applying the same formula to the federal case, the present value of its 15,000 dollar award would be 14,151 dollars since 14,151 dollars = 15,000 dollars/(1 + .06)[1]. If we now discount that present value by the .20 probability of achieving it, the expected value of the federal alternative becomes 2,830 dollars which is still less than the state alternative, but not as much less as the difference with time consumption taken into consideration. We, of course, could have offered a hypothetical example where taking time consumption into consideration reverses the rank order as to which is the better alternative.

Another time-discounting application occurs when, for example, the defendant in a civil case is told by a plaintiff that the plaintiff will withdraw his lawsuit if the defendant will pay 3,000 dollars. The defendant figures if the case goes to trial five years from now and the defendant loses, for which there is a 2/3 chance, the plaintiff will be awarded 6,000 dollars. The defendant thus perceives the case as having an expected value of 4,000 dollars. The question then becomes, is the defendant better off paying the plaintiff 3,000 dollars now or 4,000 dollars five years from now? Answering that question involves working with the equation, $A = P (1 + r)^t$, and the current interest rate which we might assume is

.06. The equation thus becomes $A = 3000(1.06)^5$, and A thus equals 4,015 dollars. The defendant would therefore be better off putting his 3,000 dollars into a savings account at 6 percent, waiting 5 years, and then paying 4,000 dollars to the defendant and having 15 dollars left over, than he would be by paying the 3,000 dollars to the plaintiff. For simplicity, we can ignore the fact that the inflation rate may be greater than the interest rate which means the invested money would lose value over time, and that the damages awarded may need to be adjusted upward.

In this illustration, the defendant is comparing a present benefit with a future one, whereas in the other illustration it was a choice for the plaintiff between two future benefits. In this illustration, the defendant (who is paying) is mainly concerned with the future value of a present investment; whereas in the other one, the plaintiff (who is being paid) was mainly concerned with the present value of a future amount. Both are common examples of time-discounting in the legal process. Both have counterparts in numerous public sector situations, where benefits or costs are substantially delayed. The present value of future benefits is often considered by the Army Corps of Engineers in building alternative dams, some of which can be finished sooner than others. The present value of future costs may be a consideration in postponing the burden of supporting a Social Security system, or postponing the suffering from lack of energy conservation. Unfortunately, the present generation may overly discount those future costs.[5]

Influencing Decisions

Another purpose for analyzing optimum choices with probabilities is for understanding and influencing decisions rather than making decisions. Two examples include (1) trying to influence judges to release rather than hold pretrial defendants, when there is doubt about the probability of the defendant appearing in court; and (2) trying to influence prosecutors to make time-saving rather than time-lengthening decisions, when there is doubt concerning the imposition of the rewards or punishments. Each example involves a somewhat different methodological orientation.

WHERE COSTS ARE MISSED BENEFITS, AND
BENEFITS ARE COSTS AVOIDED

The pretrial release problem can be viewed as reaching a decision under conditions of risk, as is shown in Table 5-4. That figure indicates that there are basically two choices available to a judge, namely, to either (1) release the defendant on his own recognizance or low bond; or (2) hold the defendant with no bond or a high bond. Which is the better choice depends on whether the defendant would appear in court if released, or would fail to appear. There are two kinds of errors that could be made. A defendant could be held who would have appeared if he were released (a holding error), or a defendant could be released who fails to appear (a releasing error). The first error is referred to as a type 1 error, because it is the more serious in the eyes of the law. The second error may be less serious legally, but is likely to be considered more costly to judges, since only releasing errors can be detected in individual cases. If the average judge considers a releasing error to be more costly, we can give it a numerical value of -100 in order to have a benchmark for saying something about the relative value of a holding error. Suppose the average judge says he finds a releasing error to be personally twice as upsetting as a holding error. This means a holding error should then have an average numerical value of -50.

If the holding error cost is symbolized as $-A$, then releasing a defendant who does appear can be symbolized $+A$, since releasing a defendant who does appear avoids the holding error cost. Similarly, if the releasing error cost is symbolized $-B$, then holding a defendant who would have failed to appear can be symbolized $+B$, since it avoids the releasing error cost. The expected value of releasing is equal to (1) the expected benefits of releasing plus (2) the expected negative cost, as is shown at the end of the releasing row in Table 5-4. Similarly, the expected value of holding is equal to (1) the expected benefits of holding plus (2) the expected negative costs, as is shown at the end of the holding row. If the expected value of releasing is set equal to the expected value of holding, then by setting those two algebraic expressions equal to each other, one can solve for P with the solution indicating the judge's threshold probability for releasing or holding. Doing that algebra reveals that the threshold probability is simply $B/(A + B)$. That means the average judge, as mentioned above, has a threshold probability of $100/(50 + 100)$, or .67. In other words, for the average judge, the average defendant needs to be perceived as having better than a .67 probability of appearing in order to be released.

In light of that kind of analysis, we can see that in order to move judges toward doing more releasing when in doubt, there are only three alternatives available. One is to increase the probability that the defendant will appear. The second is to increase the holding error cost, and the third is to decrease the releasing error cost. In the figure, specific proposals are offered to influence each of those three variables, which in turn influences the likelihood of judges to arrive at releasing decisions. A similar type of analysis can be applied to other stages in the legal process where the law says, when in doubt decide in favor of the defendant. The decision maker, however, may be more likely to decide against the defendant, because a prodefendant error is likely to be viewed as more costly to the decision maker. This is true of judges deciding to imprison rather than grant probation, of parole boards deciding to retain in prison rather than grant parole, and of judges deciding to convict rather than to acquit. The same kind of analysis can also be applied to influence the would-be criminal into deciding against committing a crime rather than in favor of committing

TABLE 5-4. OPTIMUM CHOICE ANALYSIS FOR INFLUENCING DECISIONS (Where Costs Are Missed Benefits, and Benefits Are Avoided Costs)

INFLUENCING JUDGES TO DO MORE PRETRIAL RELEASING

Probability of Appearance

		Would Appear (P)	Would Fail to Appear (1-P)	Expected Values
Alternative Decisions Available	**Release via ROR or Low Bond**	+ A	Type 2 Error − B	$EV_R =$ (+A)(P) + (-B)(1-P)
	Hold Via No or High Bond	Type 1 Error -A	+ B	$EV_H =$ (-A)(P) + (+B)(1-P)

There are three general approaches to widening the positive difference between EV_R and EV_H:

I. Raise and clarify the probability of appearance (i.e., increase P).
   A. Raise P through better screening and notification.
   B. Clarify P through statistical studies of what percentage of various types of released defendants appear in court.
   C. More vigorously prosecute those who fail to appear.
II. Make more visible the type 1 errors and costs of holding defendants who would appear (i.e., increase A)
   A. Publicize for each judge the percent of defendants held and the appearance percent attained. (Judges vary widely on percent held, but appearance percentages tend to be about 90 percent.)
   B. Make more visible how much it costs to hold defendants in jail.
      1. Jail maintenance
      2. Lost income
      3. Bitterness from case dismissed after lengthy wait
      4. Families on welfare
      5. Increased conviction probability
      6. Jail riots from overcrowding
III. Decrease the costs of type 2 errors of releasing defendants who fail to appear (i.e., decrease 3)
   A. Make rearrest more easy through pretrial supervision.
   B. Decrease the time from arrest to trial.
      1. More personnel, more diversion, and shorter trial stage.
      2. Better sequencing of cases.
      3. Shorter path from arrest to trial.
   C. Decrease pretrial crime committing.
      1. Increase probability of being arrested, convicted, and jailed.
      2. Decrease benefits of successful crime committing.
      3. Increase costs of unsuccessful crime committing.

one. All those examples involve (1) raising and clarifying the probability of some socially desired outcome; (2) increasing the perceived cost of a type of error that society especially wants avoided; and (3) decreasing the perceived cost of an opposite type of error that society is less sensitive to.

WHERE EACH DECISION HAS ITS OWN BENEFITS AND COSTS

The problem of trying to influence prosecutors to make time-saving rather than time-lengthening decisions can also be viewed as reaching a decision under conditions of risk, as is shown in Table 5-5. That figure indicates there are basically two choices in many of the decisions made by prosecutors with regard to moving ahead on a case or delaying action that will dispose of the case. To influence prosecutors toward the time-saving alternative over the time-lengthening one, requires that they perceive the benefits minus costs derived from making a time-saving decision as greater than the benefits minus costs derived from making a time-lengthening decision. Unlike the pretrial release example, the benefits from time-saving are not merely the avoidance of the costs of time-lengthening, and similarly the benefits of time-lengthening are not merely the avoidance of the costs from time-saving. Each of the two decisions has its own benefits and costs independent of the other alternative decision. The key contingent probability in this context is the probability of being penalized for making a time-lengthening decision. The main penalty under the new Speedy Trials Acts is the discharge of the defendant from jail or from prosecution if the time-lengthening exceeds a certain maximum constraint. This penalty, however, is only imposed if the defendant raises the issue and a judge finds the time-lengthening was not justified.

The formula is different here for determining the threshold probability above which the prosecutor would be better off reaching a time-saving decision than a time-lengthening one. However, it can be calculated the same way. It is only a matter of solving for P when the expression for the benefits minus costs of a time-saving decision are set equal to the expression for the benefits minus costs of the alternative time-lengthening decision. Similarly, one can calculate a threshold value for any of the benefits or costs when they are expressed in terms of all the other variables after setting those two expressions equal to each other. The importance of this example, though, is not to aid a prosecutor in calculating a threshold probability or threshold values. Instead, the example is designed to illustrate how thinking in terms of making optimum choices with probabilities can generate ideas for influencing decisions. In other words, the five sets of ideas shown in Table 5-5 might not all have been generated if ways of encouraging time-saving decisions were merely listed without the organized framework which optimum choice analysis provides.

This framework emphasizes a five-part check list that includes: (1) increasing the benefits of rightdoing; (2) decreasing the costs of rightdoing; (3) increasing the cost of wrongdoing; (4) decreasing the benefits from

TABLE 5-5. OPTIMUM CHOICE ANALYSIS FOR INFLUENCING DECISIONS (Where Each Decision Has Its Own Benefits and Costs)

INFLUENCING PROSECUTORS TO MAKE MORE TIME-SAVING DECISIONS

		Alternative Occurrences		
		Being Penalized for Lengthening Time (P)	Not Being Penalized for Lengthening Time (1-P)	**Benefits Minus Costs**
	Time Saving Decision (S)	B_S Benefits from S	C_S Costs from S	B_S-C_S
Alternative Decisions	Time Lengthening Decision (L)	C_L Costs from L	B_L Benefits from L	$(B_L)(1\text{-}P) -$ $(C_L)(P)$

Abbreviations: P = probability of being penalized. B = benefits. C = costs. S = time saving decision. L = time lengthening decision.

To Increase the Likelihood That Time Saving Decisions Will Be Chosen:

I. Increase the benefits from making time-saving decisions (i.e., increase B_S).

For example, reward assistant states attorneys with salary increases and promotions for reducing the average time consumption per case.

II. Decrease the costs of making time saving decisions (i.e., decrease C_S).

For example, establish a computerized system that informs assistant states attorneys concerning actual and predicted times at various stages for all cases to minimize the trouble involved to the attorney in keeping track of cases. Also, provide more investigative and preparation resources.

III. Increase the costs incurred from making time-lengthening decisions (i.e., increase C_L).

For example, provide under the speedy trial rules for absolute discharge of the defendant whose case extends beyond the time limit rather than just release on recognizance.

IV. Decrease the benefits from making time-lengthening decisions (i.e., decrease B_L).

For example, increase release on recognizance so that lengthening the pretrial time will not make the jailed defendant more vulnerable to pleading guilty.

V. Raise the probability of the decision-maker being penalized for lengthening time (i.e. increase P).

For example, allow fewer exceptions to the speedy trial rules such as suspending their application ''for good cause'' or ''exceptional circumstances.''

wrongdoing; and (5) increasing the probability of wrongdoers being penalized. The same kind of analysis can apply where there are three or more alternative decisions, with one especially favored that we want to influence, although we then have more benefits and costs that need to be increased or decreased. Similarly, we can have two or more contingent probabilities that need to be increased or decreased to stimulate favorable decisions.[6]

Predicting Decisions

ESTABLISHING THE DECISIONAL MODEL

A third purpose that can be served from analyzing optimum choice with probabilities is to predict better what decisions are likely to be made given certain likely or contemplated system changes. A good example involves the modeling of the plea bargaining between prosecutors and defense counsel. By plea bargaining we mean an out-of-court settlement whereby the defendant agrees to plead guilty to the original charge or a lesser charge in return for the prosecutor agreeing to reduce the charges or to recommend a sentence perceived as lighter than what the defendant would have received after a trial. A high percentage of all criminal cases are settled through explicit plea bargaining. Explicit plea bargaining involves actual negotiations between the prosecutor and either defense council or the defendant. Implicit plea bargaining involves no negotiations but rather an implicit understanding that if he pleads guilty, the prosecutor will recommend a less severe sentence than if the defendant goes to trial and is found guilty. Because of the importance of plea bargaining in the criminal justice system, it needs to be taken into consideration in order to predict the effects of almost any judicial reform.

A simple but meaningful way of modeling the decision-making in plea bargaining is that shown in the top of Table 5-6. The defendant's best interests will be maximized by accepting the prosecutor's offer of a given sentence if the sentence is less than that which the defendant perceives would be received if convicted by a trial (symbolized S_d), discounted by the probability of being convicted (symbolized P_d), with a bonus added to reflect a settlement that avoids the defendant's costs of going to trial (symbolized C_d). Similarly, the prosecutor's best interests will be maximized by accepting the defendant's offer of a given sentence if the sentence is more than the sentence that the prosecutor perceives the defendant would get if convicted by a trial (S_p), discounted by the probability of being convicted (P_p), with a discount deducted to reflect that defendant's upper limit equals $(SP - C)_d$, and the prosecutor's lower limit equals $(SP - C)_p$. They will reach a settlement if, and only if, the defendant's upper limit exceeds the prosecutor's lower limit. The sentencing level of the settlement (or how high or low the agreed sentence will be) depends on how high or low the numerical values of S, P, and C are.

TABLE 5-6. OPTIMUM CHOICE ANALYSIS FOR PREDICTING DECISIONS

Defense Counsel Strategy:	Prosecutor's Strategy:
1. Accept offer if less than: (perceived probability of conviction) times (sentence if convicted) plus (% bonus to avoid litigation)	1. Accept offer if greater than: (perceived probability of conviction) times (sentence if convicted) minus (% discount to avoid litigation)
2. Otherwise go to trial	2. Otherwise go to trial

Judicial Process Changes that Affect:

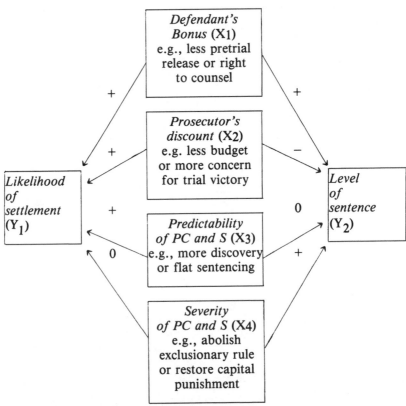

Meaning of symbols

"+" means an increase in X causes an increase in Y, or a decrease in X causes a decrease in Y.

"-" means an increase in X causes a decrease in Y, or a decrease in X causes an increase in Y.

"0" means X is not related to Y. All three types of relations assume other variables are held constant.

DETERMINING THE EFFECTS OF SYSTEM CHANGES ON THE DECISIONS

With that decisional model, we can now predict the effects of a variety of judicial process changes on the likelihood of a settlement being reached and the sentencing level of the settlements that are reached. In order to make those predictions, we need to know how the judicial process changes affect C, P, and S for both the defendant and the prosecutor. Table 5-6 summarizes the various possible relations. They are:

1. Anything that increases the defendant's costs of going to trial, such as less pretrial release or more expensive counsel, will increase the likelihood of a settlement and the level or length of the sentence. Similarly, anything that decreases the defendant's costs of going to trial will decrease the likelihood of a settlement and the level of the sentence.

2. Anything that increases (or decreases) the prosecutor's costs of going to trial, such as changes in the budget or the chances of winning, will increase (or decrease) the likelihood of a settlement. However, if costs go up the prosecutor will then be willing to give a bigger discount that will lower the level of the sentence. Thus, the prosecutor's costs vary directly with the likelihood of a settlement, but inversely with the level.

3. Anything that improves predicting the probability of conviction and the sentence upon conviction should increase the likelihood of a settlement. This is so because if both sides have the same P and the same S, then they are likely to reach a settlement since the defendant's costs move the defendant's upper limit up, and the prosecutor's costs move the prosecutor's lower limit down. Conviction probabilities can be made more predictable if both sides have access to each other's evidence. Sentences can be made more predictable if statutes require judges to give a non-discretionary sentence upon conviction for a given crime. The level of the sentence, however, should not be influenced by improved predictability so long as the improved predictability has not increased or decreased the conviction probability or the likely sentence.

4. Anything that increases the severity of the likely sentence or increases the conviction probability is likely to increase the level of sentence, such as restoring capital punishment or allowing defendants to be convicted with illegally seized evidence. Increasing the severity of S and P, however, should not affect the likelihood of a settlement if both sides are equally perceptive as to how much S and P have increased, since that means the defendant's limit and the prosecutor's limit will equally rise and thereby still allow the same amount of room for a settlement to be reached.

One could expand the model to include any kind of judicial process change, not just the examples given, as long as one can say something meaningful about the effect of the change on C, P, and S of the defendant and prosecutor. The same model could also be used to aid prosecutors and defense counsel in making plea bargaining decisions and to influence them toward accepting each other's offers. The model, however, seems most useful as a predictive model for judicial planning. The previous models that relate to personal injury lawyers, pretrial release, and time-saving can also serve multiple purposes, but they seem especially useful in the context of aiding or influencing decision-making.[7]

Measuring Decisional Propensities

DEVELOPING THE MEASUREMENT SYSTEM

A fourth purpose that can be served by analyzing optimum choice with probabilities is the purpose of measuring decisional propensities. A decision-theory model serves that purpose by asking decision makers questions about how they value various outcomes in order to predict how they would be likely to decide, rather than asking them directly how they would be likely to decide. For example, it would not be so meaningful to ask judges, lawyers, or even lay people how high the probability of guilt has to be before they would vote to convict a defendant. It would not be very meaningful because too many people might answer about .90 since they might know that .90 probability roughly corresponds to the conviction standard of "beyond a reasonable doubt." In other words, they might respond by giving what they consider to be the answer that society or the legal system considers the right answer, rather than indicating how they would actually vote, which they may not even be adequately aware of.

An appropriate system of questioning might involve informing respondents that if they were jurors they could vote either to convict or acquit and the defendant could be either innocent or guilty. Thus there are four possible occurrences: (a) voting to convict a defendant who is truly guilty; (b) voting to convict a defendant who is actually innocent; (c) voting to acquit a defendant who is actually guilty; or (d) voting to acquit a defendant who is truly innocent.

The respondents are then asked which of those four possible occurrences they consider undesirable and which they consider desirable. Most respondents say that (b) and (c) are undesirable, and (a) and (d) are desirable. We then ask, "Of the undesirable occurrences, which is the most undesirable?" Most respondents indicate occurrence (b), which is convicting an innocent defendant. Then we ask, "If we position the most undesirable occurrence at − 100 on a scale from 0 to − 100, then where would you position the other undesirable occurrence?" (voting to acquit a guilty defendant). Respondents are likely to say anything from about -5 to -95.

With that information, we can easily calculate the would-be jurors' threshold probability for convicting. The formula with the above set of questions is simply $100/(100 + X)$, where the X represents the value the respondent places on the less desirable of the two undesirable occurrences.

Wiliam Blackstone, for example, once said that it is 10 times as bad to convict an innocent defendant as it is to acquit a guilty one. If he were answering these questions consistently with that statement, he would give acquiting a quilty defendant a score of -10 on a 0 to -100 scale, where convicting an innocent defendant has a score of -100. Thus, his threshold probability would be $100/(100 + 10)$ or $100/110$, which equals .91. For William Blackstone, the defendant's probability of guilt would have to be greater than .91 before Blackstone would be willing to convict.

APPLYING THE MEASUREMENT SYSTEM

Perhaps the most interesting kind of application of the above measurement system involves applying it to a sample of people, some of whom have been given one set of judicial instructions, and some of whom have been given another set. This can aid in obtaining insights into how different judicial instructions might influence the propensity to convict. Perhaps the most interesting instructions might be those designed to increase the sensitivity of would-be jurors to avoiding errors of convicting innocent defendants and designed to decrease differences among different types of jurors.

There does seem to be a need for developing such instructions because when the measurement system is applied to a sample of fairly knowledgeable and liberal college students, their threshold probabilities for voting to convict tend to be close to about 51 percent, rather than close to about 90 percent which judges tend to associate with the meaning of the legal requirement of only voting to convict when the defendant appears to be guilty beyond a reasonable doubt. If knowledgeable and liberal college students have values that are relatively insensitive to avoiding conviction errors, then the general public may be even less sensitive to such errors, as contrasted to acquittal errors. Similarly, instructions that would decrease differences among types of jurors also seem to be needed because when the measurement system is applied to certain types of people responding to certain types of cases, substantial differences are sometimes revealed. For example, the threshold probabilities of males differ substantially from females in rape cases in the direction that males require a much higher probability of guilt before they will vote to convict, although males and females do not necessarily differ in other cases.

One type of instruction that increases sensitivity to conviction errors is informing the would-be jurors that the legal system expects them to vote for a conviction only when the defendant appears to be guilty beyond a reasonable doubt. That instruction, however, does not substantially decrease the difference between males and females in rape cases, although it does raise both their threshold probabilities. One type of instruction that decreases differences is informing the would-be jurors that decisional studies have shown that (1) male jurors are less likely to convict a rape defendant, (2) female jurors are more likely to convict a rape defendant, and (3) both males and females should be sensitive to whether they are voting in accordance with the facts or in accordance with whether they identify with the male defendant or the female victim. That instruction, however, does not substantially raise the overall threshold probability, although it may raise the female threshold probabiltiy with an offsetting reduction of the male threshold probability. The type of instruction that seems to be capable of both raising low thresholds and equalizing differences across types of jurors is an instruction that informs the would-be jurors that society considers convicting an innocent defendant to be ten times as undesirable as acquitting a guilty defendant, and that jurors should feel about ten times as confident of their accuracy if they to convict as they would if they vote to acquit.

The important point for our methodological purposes is not the substance of these findings in terms of low thresholds, differing thresholds, and how lowness and differences can be reduced. Rather, the point is that a measurement system based on making optimum choices under conditions of risk can reveal underlying values that might otherwise not be as accurately expressed, and that such measurement can then be used to obtain insights concerning would-be jurors in general, different types of would-be jurors, and different types of instructions to would-be jurors. The same kind of subtle, but meaningful, measurement system might also be applied to other kinds of decision making, where individuals vote or decide among discrete alternatives under conditions of risk, and where there is a policy controversy over whether they are applying legal or proper standards in reaching decisions.[8]

SOME CONCLUSIONS

The simple logic which this chapter proposes for solving optimum choice problems involving discrete policy alternatives can be summarized in nine basic rules as follows:

1. Determine the benefits minus costs for each policy alternative, and and then pick the alternative that has the best B-C score (relevant to the beginning of the chapter at pp. 48–51).

2. In calculating the benefits or costs for each policy alternative, bear in mind that the benefits or costs can often be more meaningfully understood by considering them as representing price times quan-

tity, or a relative value-weight times a marginal rate of return (pp. 51–57).

3. In working with alternative policies, it is often meaningful to think in terms of only two alternative choices, although some problems may involve so many policies that special reduction methods need to be adopted to make the choices more manageable (pp. 57–60).

4. In working with goals or effects to maximize (i.e., benefits) or goals to minimize (i.e., costs), it is often meaningful to think in terms of only two positions on a goal (e.g., relatively high versus relatively low), although some problems may involve numerous conflicting goals requiring special methods for handling them simultaneously and/or sequentially (pp. 57–60).

5. Where the benefits or costs are contingent on the occurrence of an event, then the benefits or costs need to be discounted or multiplied by the probability of that event occurring (pp. 61–64).

6. Where the benefits or costs are not received or incurred for some time, they may need to be discounted for the fact that a given benefit or cost later is generally not as beneficial or as costly as the same benefit or cost now (pp. 61–64).

7. Where individuals reach decisions in light of expected benefits minus expected costs, one can encourage the individuals to reach more favorable decisions by seeking to manipulate those benefits, costs, and probabilities (pp. 64–69).

8. Where individuals reach decisions in light of expected benefits minus expected costs, one can predict what decisions will be reached by knowing how changes affect those benefits, costs, and probabilities (pp. 69–72).

9. Where individuals reach decisions in light of expected benefits minus expected costs, one can measure their propensity to reach certain decisions by inquiring how they value certain beneficial or costly outcomes (pp. 72–74).

Many examples can be given for each of those nine rules such as deciding among alternatives relevant to (1) building dams or notifying released defendants to appear in court; (2) increasing police adherence to legality in making searches or providing legal counsel to the poor in civil cases; (3 and 4) selecting judges or redistricting legislatures; (5 and 6) accepting a personal injury client or an offer from the other side; (7) encouraging more pretrial release by judges or more time-saving decisions by prosecutors; (8) predicting the effects of judicial process changes on plea bargaining; and (9) measuring the propensity of would-be jurors to convict. Those examples have emphasized legal policy problems, but examples could be given from a variety of other subject matter areas. Indeed, what may be especially needed in this context is for more political and social scientists to apply these general principles to a variety of subjects. The collective experience of doing so is likely to provide increased benefits and decreased costs for optimum choices among discrete policy alternatives.

NOTES

1. On reaching optimum decisions in general, see Edith Stokey and Richard Zeckhauser, *A Primer for Policy Analysis* (New York: Norton, 1978); Peter Rossi, Howard Freeman, and Sonia Wright, *Evaluation: A Systematic Approach* (Beverly Hills, Ca.: Sage, 1979); Michael White, et al., *Managing Public Systems: Analytic Techniques for Public Administration* (Belmont, Ca.: Duxbury, 1980); and S. Nagel and M. Neef, *Policy Analysis: In Social Science Research* (Beverly Hills, Ca.: Sage, 1979).

2. On benefit-cost analysis as applied to discrete projects, see Mark Thompson, *Benefit-Cost Analysis for Program Evaluation* (Beverly Hills, Ca.: Sage, 1980); Guy Black, *The Application of Systems Analysis to Government Operations* (New York: Praeger, 1968); Roland McKean, *Efficiency in Government through Systems Analysis* (New York: Wiley, 1958), pp. 1-102; Ezra Mishan, *Cost-Benefit Analyis* (New York: Praeger, 1976); and Peter Sassone and William Schaefer, *Cost-Benefit Analysis: A Handbook* (New York: Academic Press, 1978).

3. See any elementary economics textbook on the treatment of total revenue as price times quantity, and the treatment of total cost as average cost times quantity, such as in Paul Samuelson, "Equilibrium of the Firm: Cost and Revenue," in *Economics: An Introductory Analysis* (Hightstown, N.J.: McGraw-Hill, l980). For further details on the study of the relations between the exclusionary rule and increasing police adherence to legality in making searches, see S. Nagel, "Effects of Excluding Illegally Seized Evidence" *The Legal Process from a Behavioral Perspective* (Homewood, Ill.: Dorsey, 1969). For further details on the study of the relations between various goals and alternative ways of providing legal counsel to the poor, see Nagel, "How to Provide Legal Counsel for the Poor: Decision Theory" in *Analyzing Poverty Policy,* ed. Dorothy James, (Lexington, Mass.: Lexington-Heath, 1975).

4. On dichotomous measurement, see M. Dutta, "Dummy Variables" in *Econometric Methods* (Cincinnati: South-Western, 1975). On reducing number of policy or independent variables, see S. Nagel and M. Neef, "Methods of Reducing the Number of Variables and Making Composite Variables" in *Policy Analysis in Social Science Research* (Beverly Hills, Ca.: Sage, 1979). On combining goals, see Allan Easton, *Complex Managerial Decisions Involving Multiple Objectives* (New York: Wiley, 1973). For further details on the study of alternative methods of selecting judges, see S. Nagel, *Comparing Elected and Appointed Judicial Systems* (Beverly Hills, Ca.: Sage American Politics Series, 1973). For further details on alternative methods of legislative redistricting, see S. Nagel, "Computers and the Law and Politics of Redistricting" in *Improving the Legal Process: Effects of Alternatives* (Lexington, Mass.: Lexington-Heath, 1975).   .

5. On making decisions in light of contingent probabilities, see Ruth Mack, *Planning on Uncertainty: Decision Making in Business and Government Administration,* (New York: Wiley, 1971); Wayne Lee, *Decision Theory and Human Behavior* (New York: Wiley, 1971); and Bruce Baird, *Introduction to Decision Analysis* (Belmont, Ca.: Duxbury, 1978). On discounting future benefits or costs in

light of the passage of time, see Ezra Mishan, "Investment Criteria" in *Cost-Benefit Analysis* (New York: Praeger, 1976). For further details on the analysis of the decisions to accept a legal client or to accept an offer from the other side, see S. Nagel and M. Neef, *Decision Theory and the Legal Process* (Lexington, Mass.: Lexington-Heath, 1979), pp. 141-46, 232-35.

6. On the use of probabilistic decision theory to influence or deter decisions, see Lee McPheters and William Stronge (eds.), *The Economics of Crime and Law Enforcement* (Springfield, Ill.: Thomas, 1976). For further details concerning the use of decision theory to influence judges to do more pretrial releasing see S. Nagel and M. Neef, "The One-Person Decision Situation: Bond Setting" in *Decision Theory and the Legal Process* (Lexington, Mass.: Lexington-Heath, 1979). For further details on the use of decision theory to influence prosecutors to make more time-saving decisions, see S. Nagel and M. Neef, "Time-Oriented Models and the Legal Process: Reducing Delay and Forecasting the Future," 1978 *Washington University Law Quarterly* 467-528 (1978).

7. On using decision theory for predictive purposes, see Robert MacIver, "Cause as Incentive" in *Social Causation* (New York: Harper, 1964). For further details on the use of decision theory for predicting the effects of judicial process changes on plea bargaining settlements, see S. Nagel and M. Neef, "The Two-Person Bargaining Situation: Plea Bargaining" in *Decision Theory and the Legal Process* (Lexington, Mass.: Lexington-Heath, 1979).

8. On measuring attitudes in policy-analysis research, see Marlene Henerson, Lynn Morris, and Carol Fitz-Gibbon, *How to Measure Attitudes* (Bevely Hills, Ca.: Sage, 1978). For further details on measuring decisional propensities among would-be jurors, see S. Nagel, Lamm and Neef, "Decision Theory and Juror Decision Making" in *The Trial Process,* ed. Bruce Sales, (New York: Plenum, 1981).

Part III
Finding an Optimum
Level for a Policy
Requiring Moderation

The purpose of this section is to discuss the problems involved in finding an optimum level for a policy where either doing too much or too little is undesirable. The first three chapters present concrete examples of situations in which that type of policy evaluation is involved. Those situations include (1) arriving at an optimum jury size, where juries that are too big are unable to sufficiently convict the guilty and juries that are too small can too easily convict the innocent; (2) arriving at an optimum level of attorney time per damages trial, where too much time will mean that expenses exceed the damages received and where too little time will mean that too little damages are received; and (3) arriving at an optimum length of imprisonment, where excess length incurs unnecessarily high crime-committing costs. These three chapters are followed by a synthesizing chapter on the general logic of finding an optimum level, with a variety of relations between policies and goals.

Chapter 6
An Optimum Jury Size

BACKGROUND ON THE PROBLEM

The U.S. Supreme Court recently made use of some aspects of management science in discussing the constitutionality of juries that contain less than six people. The case was *Ballew v. Georgia*, 98 Supreme Court Reports 1029 (1978).

The management science study was presented as part of an article entitled "Deductive Modeling to Determine an Optimum Jury Size and Fraction Required to Convict," by Stuart Nagel and Marian Neef.[1] This article was written as part of a book entitled *Legal Policy Analysis: Finding an Optimum Level or Mix,*[2] which was written as part of a series designed to describe applications and principles for applying management science and operations research to criminal justice and other policy problems.[3] The Supreme Court became aware of the jury study probably because it was cited by one of the lawyers in the case or one of the clerks to the Supreme Court Justices. It may also have been referred to the Supreme Court as the result of Justice Blackmun's analysis of the relevant literature. He took a special interest in this case, reflecting his background as a magnum cum laude mathematics graduate of Harvard University.

The problem is like an inventory modeling problem. If there are too many jurors, then too many guilty defendants are *not* going to be convicted because the prosecutor has to convince too many people in order to get a unanimous conviction. If there are too few jurors, then too many innocent defendants are going to be convicted because the prosecutor has to convince too few people. Too many jurors is like too much inventory with high spoilage and storage costs, and too few jurors is like too little inventory with high outage costs.

PREDICTING THE CONVICTION EFFECT OF JURY SIZES

Before getting to the question of what is an optimum or even a feasible jury size, one has to somehow determine the relation between jury size and both conviction and acquittal rates. At first glance, one might think an appropriate way to determine that relation would be simply to compare the conviction rates in a state that uses 12-person juries (like Illinois) with a state that uses 6-person juries (like Florida). That approach is likely to be meaningless, however, because any differences we find in the conviction rates may be determined by differences in the characteristics of the law, the people, or the cases in the two states or two sets of states, rather than to differences in their jury sizes.

As an alternative, one might suggest making before-and-after comparisons in a single state or set of states in order to control for those kinds of characteristics which do not generally change so much over a short period of time. If the conviction rate before was 64 percent with 12-person juries, the conviction rate after with 6-person juries might be substantially lower rather than higher, although most criminal attorneys would predict a higher conviction rate with 6-person juries. The conviction rate might, however, fall by virtue of the fact that if defense attorneys predict the 6-person juries are more likely to convict, then they will be more likely to plea bargain for their clients and to bring only their especially prodefense cases before the 6-person juries. Thus, the nature of the new cases, not the change in jury size, would cause at least a temporary drop in the conviction rate, and there would be no way to hold constant the type of cases heard before the new 6-person juries.

As another alternative, one might suggest working with experimental juries all of whom would hear exactly the same case. Half the juries would be 6-person juries and half would be 12-person juries. This experimental analysis, however, has the big defect that it involves a sample of only one case, no matter how many juries are used. Whatever differences or similarities are found may be peculiar to that given case being proprosecution, prodefense, prodivisive, or simply an unrealistic case, and thus a generalization may be valid. What is needed is about 100 different trial cases on audio or video tape, selected in such a way that 64 percent of them result in unanimous convictions before 12-person juries and 36 percent in acquittals or hung juries, as tends to occur in real jury trials. It would, however, be too expensive a research design to obtain and play so many taped trials before a large set of 12-person juries and the same trials before a large set of 6-person juries, especially if the experiment lacks representative realism.

As an alternative to the cross-sectional, the before-and-after, and the simulation approaches, we could try a deductive approach to determine the impact of jury size on the probability of conviction. Table 6-1 shows in a kind of syllogistic form how such a deduction might be made. The basic premise is the fact that 12-person juries tend to convict .64 of the time, and individual jurors on 12-person juries tend to vote to convict .677 of the time. That information has been obtained through a nationwide analysis of jury decisions and individual juror votes conducted by the University of Chicago Jury Project.[4]

TABLE 6-1. IMPACT OF JURY SIZE ON PROBABILITY OF CONVICTION

I. BASIC SYMBOLS

   PAC = probability of an average defendant before an average *jury* being convicted (empirically equals .64 for a twelve-person jury shown to two decimal places).

   pac = probability of an average defendant receiving from an average *juror* a vote for conviction (empirically equals .677 for a juror shown to three decimal places).

II. IMPLICATIONS OF THE COIN-FLIPPING ANALOGY (Independent Probability Model).

   $PAC = (pac)^{NJ}$.

   $.64 = (pac)^{12}$, which deductively means the coin-flipping pac is .964.

III. IMPLICATIONS OF THE BOWLING ANALOGY (Averaging Model)

   $PAC = pac$.

   $.64 = pac$, which deductively means the bowling pac is .640.

IV. WEIGHTING AND COMBINING THE TWO ANALOGIES

   Actual

   pac = [weight (coin-flipping pac) + (bowling pac)] / (weight + 1)

   .677 = [weight (.964) + (.640)] / (weight + 1), which deductively means the relative weight of the coin-flipping analogy to the bowling analogy is .13.

V. APPLYING THE ABOVE TO A SIX-PERSON JURY

   PAC = [weight (coin-flipping PAC) + (bowling PAC)] / (weight + 1)

   $PAC = [.13 (.964)^{6} + (.64)] / 1.13$, which deductively means PAC with a six-person jury is .66.

VI. APPLYING THE ABOVE TO A DECISION RULE ALLOWING TWO OF TWELVE DISSENTERS FOR A CONVICTION

   PAC = [weight (coin-flipping PAC) + (bowling PAC)] / (weight + 1)

   PAC = [.13 (.99) + (.64)] / 1.13, which deductively means PAC with a 10/12 rule is .68.

If jury decision making involved an independent probability model like coin-flipping, then individual jurors would vote to convict .964 of the time in order for 12-person juries to convict .64 of the time. If, on the other hand, jury decision making involved an averaging model analogous to bowling where the 12 pins tend to stand or fall depending on what happens to the average pin, then individual voters would vote to convict .640 of the time in order for 12-person juries to convict .64 of the time.

Since individual jurors actually vote to convict .677 of the time, that means jury decision making is much more like the bowling model than the coin-flipping model, or to be more exact, it is about 1.00 to .13 or 8 to 1 more like the bowling model. We use a weight of 1.00 for the bowling analogy in order to simplify the weights, since we are in effect saying that if the bowling analogy has a weight of 1, then how many more times relative to that base is the coin-flipping analogy worth in explaining the actual .677 individual juror propensity to convict? In other words, we are calculating a weighted average in which the .964 coin-flipping propensity multiplied by its weight is added to the .640 bowling propensity and then divided by the sum of the weights. We know that the weighted average equals .677, and we want to solve for the value of the relative weight of the coin-flipping analogy, which turns out to be .13 when the bowling analogy is 1. If the coin-flipping analogy is set at a weight of 1. then the bowling analogy gets a weight of 8.

With that weight of .13 arrived at through Step IV of Table 6-1, we can now deduce what the probability would be of an average defendant being convicted by a 6-person jury rather than a 12-person jury. Doing so involves raising the .964 individual propensity to convict to the 6th power rather than the 12th. One then recalculates the conviction probability, drawing on the weighted combination of the coin-flipping and bowling models. That recalculated probability for a 6-person jury is a .66 probability for convicting an average defendant. This means if we switch from a 12-person jury to a 6-person jury and everything else remains constant, the conviction rate should rise from 64 percent to 66 percent. We can likewise calculate that the probability will rise from .64 to .68 if a conviction is allowed with only 10 of the 12 jurors voting to convict.[5]

The reason the conviction rate goes up so little when jury size is reduced from 12 to 6 is because jury decision making is more like the bowling or averaging model than it is like the independent probability or coin-flipping model. The reason the conviction rate goes up at all is probably because nonconvicting hung juries decrease with a 6-person jury since holdouts are less likely to have a fellow holdout for reinforcement than with a 12-person jury, and the number of reinforcing supports is more important in maintaining a holdout than the number of opponents within the 6 to 12 range.

FINDING AN OPTIMUM JURY SIZE

Knowing the relation between jury size and conviction rates can in turn be used as input into the empirical premises of an optimizing model designed to arrive at an optimum jury size that minimizes the weighted sum of type 1 errors of convicting the innocent, plus type 2 errors of not convicting the guilty. Figure 6-1 summarizes what is involved in that kind of analysis. The curve of "weighted errors of innocent convicted" was arrived at by using the analysis of Figure 6-1, but operating on the tentative assumption that a 12-person jury would be likely to convict an innocent person only about .40 of the the time rather than .64, and that about 5 out of 100 defendants tried by juries may be actually innocent. It seems reasonable to assume that if the average defendant has a .64 probability of being convicted, then a truly innocent defendant would have something less than a .64 probability of being convicted. We need some tentative figure like .40 for the probability of convicting an innocent defendant to insert into Table 6-1 in place of the .64 for determining the probability of an innocent defendant being convicted with different jury sizes.

The curve of "errors of guilty not convicted" was arrived at with the tentative assumption that a 12-person jury would be likely to convict a guilty person about .70 of the time rather than .64, and that about 95 out of 100 defendants tried by juries are probably actually guilty. It seems reasonable to assume that if the average defendant has a .64 probability of being convicted, then a truly guilty defendant would have something more than a .64 probability of being convicted. We need some tentative figure, like .70 for the probability of convicting a guilty defendant to insert into Table 6-1 in place of the .64 for determining the complementary probability of a guilty defendant not being convicted with different jury sizes. A good check on the .40 assumption for innocent defendants, the .70 for guilty defendants, and the 5 out of 100 defendants being innocent is to make sure those numbers still yield a conviction rate of 64 out of 100, which they do.

The "weighted sum of errors" curve was calculated by simply adding the other two curves after multiplying the points on the first curve by 10 to indicate that convicting the innocent is traditionally considered 10 times as bad as not convicting the guilty, according to William Blackstone.[6] With these tentative assumptions and this analysis, the weighted sum of errors bottoms out at jury sizes between 6 and 8. Justice Blackmun in announcing the Court's decision referred favorably to that analysis in deciding that it was meaningful to allow juries to be smaller than 12 but no smaller than 6.

FIGURE 6-1. IMPACT OF JURY SIZE ON CONVICTION AND ACQUITTAL ERRORS

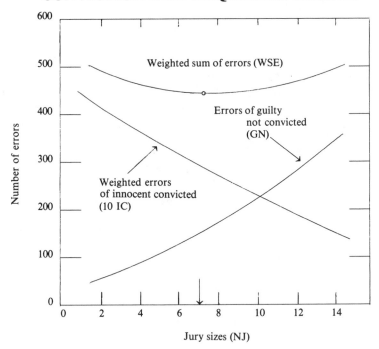

Jury sizes (NJ)

Notes to the Figure:

(1) The number of guilty not convicted (GN) equals the number of guilty subjected to jury trials (G), multiplied by the probability of a truly guilty defendant not being convicted (PGN). G is about 95 out of 100 defendants. PGN is about .30 for a 12-person jury, but decreases with smaller juries.

(2) The number of innocent convicted (IC) equals the number of innocent subjected to jury trials (I), multiplied by the probability of a truly innocent defendant being convicted (PIC). I is about 5 out of 100 defendants. PIC is about .40 for a 12-person jury, but increases with smaller juries.

(3) IC is given a weight of 10 relative to GN, because Blackstone and other influential commentators have said it is 10 times as bad to convict an innocent person as it is not to convict a guilty person.

(4) The weighted sum of errors (WSE) equals (10 IC) plus (GN) for any given jury size.

SENSITIVITY ANALYSIS AND IMPLICATIONS

In his opinion, Justice Blackmun indicated agreement with the analysis in Figure 6-1 and the 10-to-1 tradeoff weight. The model, however, is not particularly sensitive to that tradeoff weight, within the range of 5 to 15 jurors, meaning that the weight cannot be allowed to vary much or one will be outside the feasible region. The model, however, is particularly sensitive to the more subjective assumption that prosecutors operate at a .95 level of confidence on deciding whether a defendant is guilty such that he can be brought to trial. If prosecutors are operating substantially below a .95 level, then one would need larger juries to protect those additional innocent defendants from being convicted. If prosecutors are operating substantially above a .95 level, then one could have smaller juries to increase the probability of convicting those additional guilty defendants.

Thus the optimum jury size depends on what assumption one is willing to make regarding how many jury-tried defendants out of each 100 are truly guilty. People who favor 12-person juries probably perceive the number of innocent jury-tried defendants as being greater than the number perceived by people who favor 6-person juries. Thus the optimum jury size ultimately depends on normative values, rather than observed relations or relations deduced from empirical premises. Nevertheless, the combination of the predictive model of Table 6-1 and the optimizing model of Table 6-1 enable us to see better what is involved in choosing among alternative jury sizes. The same analysis can be applied to choosing among alternative fractions required to convict such as unanimity, a 10/12 rule, or a 9/12 rule.

The same kind of inventory modeling can be constructively applied to a variety of criminal justice problems. For example, what is the optimum percentage of defendants to hold prior to trial in order to minimize the sum of the holding costs like jail maintenance, plus the releasing costs like rearresting those who do not appear in court? Similarly, what is the optimum sentence for various crimes in order to minimize the sum of the incarceration costs from longer sentences, plus the crime-repeating costs from shorter sentences? What also is the optimum bond level for various crimes in order to minimize the probability of holding defendants if the bond is too high, plus the probability of defendants not showing up to retrieve their bond if the bond is too low?

All these problems can benefit from the inventory modeling perspective of management science, where doing too much or too little is undesirable. They can also benefit from the statistical analysis and mathematical modeling associated with management science for determining the relations between goal achievement and either policy increases or decreases. What may be needed is for more management science researchers to apply their skills to such legal policy problems, and for legal researchers to acquire more awareness of management science methods.

NOTES

1. S. Nagel and M. Neef, "Deductive Modeling to Determine an Optimum Jury Size and Fraction Required to Convict," *Washington University Law Quarterly* (1975): 933-78.

2. S. Nagel and M. Neef, "Using Deductive Modeling to Determine an Optimum Jury Size and Fraction Required to Convict," *Legal Policy Analysis: Finding an Optimum Level or Mix* (Lexington, Mass.: Lexington-Heath, 1977), pp. 75-157.

3. S. Nagel and M. Neef, *Decision Theory and the Legal Process* (Lexington, Mass.: Lexington-Heath, 1979); *The Legal Process: Modeling the System* (Beverly Hills, Calif.: Sage, 1977); *Operations Research Methods: As Applied to Political Science and the Legal Process* (Beverly Hills, Calif.: Sage, 1975); and *Policy Analysis in Social Science Research* (Beverly Hills, Calif.: Sage, 1979).

4. Harry Kalven, Jr. and Hans Zeisel, *The American Jury* (Boston, Mass.: Little, Brown, 1966), p. 56.

5. For further details concerning this analysis for arriving at (1) a conviction probability with different jury sizes or (2) an optimum jury size, see S. Nagel and M. Neef, *Legal Policy Analysis,* pp. 75-157.

6. William Blackstone, *Commentaries* (Oxford, England: Oxford University Press, 1965).

Chapter 7
An Optimum Level of
Attorney Time per Case

The purpose of this chapter is to discuss some basic aspects of how attorneys allocate their time to court cases or other types of cases, and especially how they should allocate their time in order to increase their total earnings, or to maximize benefits minus costs. This chapter uses simple principles from modern allocation theory, which has been developed mainly by management science and operations research. It builds on the increasing availability of computerized and other systems for gathering, retrieving, and processing legal case data. It is innovative in its perspective, but it has the potential for being part of an improved mode of analysis and technology in modern law practice.[1]

Suppose for an illustrative example a law firm has two personal injury cases in which it is representing the plaintiffs. Suppose further that case A has a .80 probability of being won, and case B has a .40 probability, although let us leave for later how such information might be determined. For now, a possibly interesting question might be, "How should our hypothetical law firm allocate 100 hours of its time to these two cases?"[2]

HOW NOT TO ALLOCATE

At first glance, one might say:

1. Allocate all our resources to the better case.
2. Allocate 80/120 or .67 of our resources to the better case, and 40/120 or .33 of one's resources to the case less likely to succeed.
3. Allocate as much resources as are needed in order to win both cases.
4. Allocate as little resources to the case less likely to succeed as one might be ethically obligated to do so, and the remainder of one's resources to the better case.
5. Allocate the same amount of resources to case A as has been allocated in the past to the average case of the case A type, and do likewise with case B.
6. Use some other allocation.

All those possibilities lack common sense, as a little careful thought indicates:

1. Allocating all our 100 hours to the better case might be wasteful because we might only need 50 in order to win. If we allocate 100 hours to case A we might also miss the possibility of receiving a judgment from case B and thereby suffer a substantial opportunity cost.

2. Allocating our resources proportionately would mean giving 67 hours to case A and 33 hours to case B, which might represent wasted hours since case A may need less than 67 hours to cross the threshold between being a winner and a loser. Case B may also need more than 33 hours although not necessarily a lot more.

3. Allocating as much resources as are needed to win both cases may be meaningless if by "to win" we mean with a 1.00 certainty since even an infinite number of hours devoted to each case may not be capable of achieving that. The same is true if by "to win" we mean with more than a .50 probability since achieving that for case B may require more than the 100 hours we have available.

4. The fourth alternative of allocating a minimum to the worse case and the rest to the better case would not exceed our hours available (unlike alternative 3) or violate our ethical obligations (unlike alternative 1), but it may represent an excessive allocation to case A and an opportunity cost for case B (like alternatives 1 and 2).

5. The fifth alternative of allocating in terms of past averages has the defect that it assumes what we have been doing on the average in the past has been optimal or rational in allocating our scarce resources.

The answer to our simple hypothetical problem may be that we need more information. For starters, it might help to know what the damage award is likely to be if case A results in a victory, as well as for case B. If the damage award in case A upon a plaintiff victory is 10,000 dollars, then that case can be said to have an expected value of 8,000 dollars (or .80 times 10,000 dollars). If, however, the damage award in case B upon a plaintiff victory is 30,000 dollars, then that case has an expected value of 12,000 dollars (or .40 times 30,000 dollars). Now it looks like case B is the better case. If, however, we apply our five alternative strategies with this new information, we will still come up with the same answers that all five lack common sense for the same reasons.

At this point, one might perceive that we do not need to know the expected value for each case, since this merely reflects a combination of the victory probability and the average damages awarded for cases of that type. Instead, we might need to know the relation between hours allocated and fees received. To obtain that information it would be helpful to know how much damages were awarded in a large quantity of cases that have characteristics similar to those of the cases we are currently considering. Along with the damages awarded information, we would like to know the quantity of billable hours devoted to each case. By "billable hours" we mean hours spent on a case for which a client could be legitimately billed if an hourly rate were being charged, even though the case may be handled on a contingency fee, flat fee, or salaried basis. That kind of information could be shown in a graph like Figure 7-1. Each dot represents a case. By seeing where dots are positioned on the vertical axis, we can tell how much damages were awarded in each case. For many cases there were no damages because they were losing cases in which liability was not established. By seeing where the dots are positioned on the horizontal axis, we can tell how many billable hours were devoted to each case.

FIGURE 7-1. RELATION BETWEEN HOURS ALLOCATED AND DAMAGES AWARDED
(In a Given Type of Case)

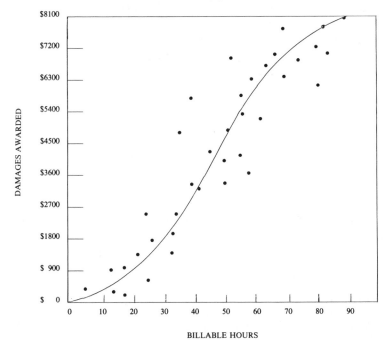

BILLABLE HOURS

After graphing such a set of dots, it might then be appropriate to fit a meaningful curve to the dots in such a way as to minimize the sum of the distances from the dots to the curve. That can be done by a common-sense eyeballing approach or a more sophisticated computerized analysis.[3] One might expect a well-fitting curve to have a kind of S-shape like that shown in Figure 7-1. Such a curve indicates that prior to a certain number of hours, putting in additional time is not likely to raise the damages substantially above zero. In other words, cases tend to require an initial minimum of number of opening hours before additional time can have an effect on the damages received. Similarly, after some number of hours, additional time probably has little effect in increasing the damages awarded. Thus each type of case probably has a bottom range of hours before hours substantially effect damages, and a top range of hours after which the influence of additional hours seem to plateau out.[4]

With that kind of information for case A and case B, one might logically give case A about 75 hours since that is the number of hours roughly corresponding to the upper turning point on the S-shaped curve. We would not want to give the case just 25 hours corresponding to the lower turning point since those 25 hours would be wasted by virtue of the fact that 25 hours only brings us to the point where we first start taking off from a zero damages level. If we devote a number of hours between 25 and 75, then at first glance it looks as if we would be suffering some opportunities costs in the sense of missing the additional damages that could be obtained by putting in some additonal hours. It may, however, be wasteful to devote 75 hours to such a case because the value of 75 hours to us may be greater than the one-third contingency fee corresponding to a 75-hour allocation.

HOW TO ALLOCATE

Figure 7-2 represents an improvement on Figure 7-1 for viewing the time allocation problem. First, it shows the relation between hours allocated and cost to the lawyer, not just damages awarded. A lawyer, like any business firm or individual, is interested not in maximizing income but in maximizing income minus expenses, or benefits minus costs. For the sake of simplicity, we assume here that the only cost is our time and that our time is worth 30 dollars an hour. By 30 dollars an hour we are not referring to the clients' fee (which may be 50 dollars an hour), but rather to the fact that we would be willing to work for as low as 30 dollars an hour.[5]

Second, Figure 7-2 deals with fees received rather than damages awarded. We calculate fees received by taking one-third of the damages awarded in Figure 7-1, since one-third is the usual contingency fee. The

FIGURE 7-2. RELATION BETWEEN HOURS ALLOCATED AND BOTH FEES RECEIVED AND TIME COST (Profit Maximization in Contingency Fee Cases)

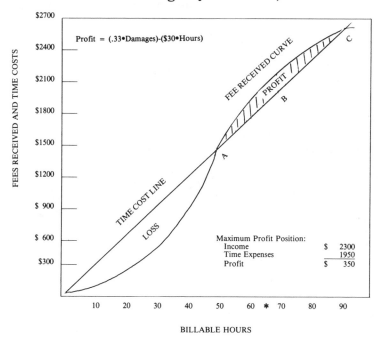

third and most important difference from Figure 7-1 is that with this new information we should now be able to make a more rational decision concerning how many hours to allocate to a case of the type shown in Figure 7-2. The ideal quantity is about 65 hours, rather than the 75 hours where the fee received approaches the maximum. It makes more sense to allocate only 65 hours because that is where the maximum positive difference is between the fee received curve and the time-cost line. At 65 hours, Figure 7-1 shows damages awarded of about 6,900 dollars, and Figure 7-2 shows a one-third contingency fee of 2,300 dollars. At 65 hours, Figure 7-2 also show time expenses of 1,950 dollars at 30 dollars an hour. Operating below or above 65 hours would generally mean taking a loss, or not making as much profit. Billable hours between points A and C are predicted to yield a profit, but at point B (where an asterisk is shown), the profit is at a maximum. Figure 7-1 thus emphasizes how the S-shaped damages awarded curve is derived, and Figure 7-2 emphasizes what to do with such a curve in order to make a profit-maximizing time allocation decision.[6]

When we say 65 hours is the optimum allocation for cases of type A, we do not mean that a lawyer should put in 65 hours on such a case, regardless of what is happening, and then abruptly stop. Similarly, we do not mean that if only 50 hours have been alloted on such a case that a lawyer should throw in an extra 15 hours, regardless of what those 15 hours involve. The 65 hours is only an average optimum that may be meaningfully deviated from in light of aggravating and extenuating circumstances as with flat-sentencing systems. Relevant variables justifying more or less billable hours might include the lawyer's experience, personal cautiousness, and the amount of help from assistants, research tools, and counsel for other parties. Also relevant is the case's difficulty in terms of the quantity of factual and legal issues and the newness of the issues it raises. The way the cases are classified into types, however, is likely to include some general notions of difficulty in that airline crashes are more difficult than dog bites. Although lawyers are generally seeking to maximize fees minus costs, rather than maximizing fees, it is logical to expect a lawyer to spend more time on a potentially big fee case due to the regret of losing such a case, but this is also likely to be considered by the case classification. Although aggravating and extenuating circumstances may influence the extent to which one should deviate from the predicted optimum hours, they should not affect where that optimum generally tends to be for a case with a given set of characteristics.

Figure 7-2 covers those like case A. We can do the same kind of analysis for those like case B. Suppose, however, the optimum number of hours for case B turns out to be about 50 hours given the nature of case B. That would mean that the sum total of both our cases would add to 115 hours, or 15 hours more than the 100 we said we had available. One nice thing about allocating time as contrasted to allocating a fixed budget is that each day or week we get a new time allocation that we can dip into. In other words, over the next two weeks, we can work 65 hours on case A and 15 hours on case B. The week after that, we can finish off the last 35 hours on case B. In this simplified illustration, we are assuming that it is meaningful to concentrate all the time devoted to a case within a single week or two weeks, although in reality the 65 hours or 50 hours may be stretched over a period of months or even years while waiting for other events to occur, such as responses by the other side.

When there is a time conflict between two cases that need working on, it is logical to work on the case that has the closest nonpostponable deadline. If both cases are about equally flexible with regard to impending deadlines, a lawyer might choose to work on the case that will bring in the largest profit so the money can be invested while working on the less profitable case. If both cases are also about equally profitable, lawyers might tend to handle the cases on a first come, first serve basis. Doing so, however, would not be ideal from the point of view of minimizing the average time from acceptance to completion of a case. To minimize this average time, the shortest cases should be taken first, provided that the longer cases are not allowed to exceed a given length of time in light of legal rules and ethical considerations. For example, in our hypothetical situation, if we were to take the 65 hour case first (case A), then the 50-hour case (case B) would have to wait 65 hours to begin its processing. That would mean case B would take a total of 115 hours from the time the client was accepted until the case was completed. If case A takes a total time of 65 hours and case B takes a total time of 115 hours, then the cases average 90 hours apiece from time of acceptance to time of completion, assuming no other distractions occurred along the way. However, if we take the shorter case B first, its total time will be 50 hours. Case A will then have to wait those 50 hours to get started, plus 65 hours of processing time, or a total of 115 hours. But then when we add the 50 hours total time for case B to the 115 hours for case A, we see they will average only about 80 hours apiece rather than 90. This saves about 10 percent for the clients, although the lawyer is still putting in a total of 115 hours. The saving would be even greater if there were bigger differences between processing time of the shorter and the longer cases than just 50 and 65 hours respectively. Table 7-1 shows those relations more clearly.[7]

Although we keep receiving a new allocation of time each week, it does not make sense to say that we should accept an infinite number of cases. For one thing, it does not seem rational to accept unprofitable cases unless, for example, (1) there is some nonmonetary public interest

TABLE 7-1. ALTERNATIVE WAYS OF ORDERING TWO CASES TO MINIMIZE AVERAGE TOTAL TIME

Order Number 1: First Come, First Serve

	Waiting Time	Processing Time	Total Time
Case A	0	65	65
Case B	65	50	115
Totals	65	115	180
Averages	32½	57½	90

Order Number 2: Shortest Case First

Case B	0	50	50
Case A	50	65	115
Totals	50	110	165
Averages	25	57½	82½

cause being served; (2) we are anticipating the unprofitable case will later lead to profitable ones; or (3) there are some educational benefits to be gained. By "unprofitable case" in this context, we mean one in which the fee-received curve does not exceed our time-cost line. This concept of unprofitability enables us to rank incoming cases on their predicted profitability. The most profitable ones have a fee received curve that most exceeds our time-cost line when drawn on the same scale as Figure 7-2. If we were faced with 10 prospective clients simultaneously, we would logically pick the most profitable ones until we use up as much time as we are willing to commit in advance.[8]

We normally, however, do not have 10 prospective clients approach us simultaneously. Rather, they do so sequentially. Under those circumstances, we might be reluctant to accept the first case even though it is predicted to be profitable because we are anticipating an even more profitable case will occur later. That problem is like the lawyer exercising his peremptory challenges in picking jurors. He might be reluctant to use his limited peremptory challenges on the first few jurors because he might be anticipating even worse jurors will come up later in the jury picking process. The best way to handle the sequential client problem might be to say we will accept all profitable cases that exceed a certain threshold. If we wind up accepting too many cases, then we will have to hire help or cut back for a while in accepting new clients. If we wind up accepting too few cases, then we will have to lower our threshold.[9]

VARIATIONS ON THE BASIC APPROACH

Emphasizing Total Caseload and Probabilities

The above approach to allocating attorney time to court cases in effect treats each case mainly as a separate allocation problem. In the language of decision sciences, we are in effect treating the allocation problem as one of finding an optimum level of time to allocate to each case on a case-by-case basis, rather than treating the problem as one of finding an optimum mix for dividing up a fixed budget of time among a set of cases. The optimum level perspective makes more sense for a number of reasons. First, there is probably only a relatively narrow range of hours that could be meaningfully allocated to a given case without going below a minimum ethical threshold or above a maximum wastefulness threshold. That is unlike the allocation of a business firm's budget to various advertising methods where any number of budget dollars could be allocated to each of the methods, since there are no ethical minimums and the plateauing phenomenon is probably not so sharp. Second, time allocation has more flexibility by virtue of the possibility of postponing matters and hiring additional help, as contrasted to the relative inflexibility of the quantity of money allocated to the advertising department of a business firm for a given time period. Third, it is much simpler to think in terms of an optimum level of time to devote to each case (largely out of context of the other cases), than it is to think in terms of having a total amount of time that is to be allocated among many cases.[10]

The above approach also differs from the decision science approach which emphasizes making decisions under conditions of risk or uncertainty. Allocating attorney time is an example of that kind of decision making since each case involves a risk or probability of victory or defeat. The analysis could be modified to take more explicitly into consideration the fact that hours allocated not only influence damages awarded, but also the probability of victory. Doing so, however, would substantially complicate the analysis without a commensurate gain in its usefulness. More specifically, doing so would involve eliminating from Figure 7-1 all the cases in which no damages are awarded, which would shift the curve upward and change its slope but probably not change its S-shape. We would also have to generate a figure similar to Figure 7-1 in which the vertical axis would show victory probabilities ranging from zero to 1.00. All the dots corresponding to the cases would be either at 1.00 or zero, although they would still be above the same billable hours on the horizontal axis, as in Figure 7-1. An S-shaped curve would then be fitted to those dots showing the relation between hours allocated and victory probabilities. We would then create a composite figure by multiplying each point on the Figure 7-1 curve by each point on this new S-shaped curve at each hours mark. That would produce a composite S-shaped curve showing (for each amount of hours allocated) the predicted *expected* damages (which means the predicted damages discounted by the predicted probability of their being received). We could then multiply the points on that composite curve by .33 to take into consideration the one-third contingency fee and have a new more sophisticated expected fee-received curve to work with in Figure 7-2.[11]

Flat Fees and Hourly Rates

Instead of talking about more complicated variations that are sometimes referred to in discussing allocation problems, it may be more useful to talk about even simpler situations than the one used to illustrate the basic approach. The simplest (but very common) situation may be that of the salaried lawyer who receives a set salary per year, or the flat fee case which involves, for example, a charge of 900 dollars for a particular service. Figure 7-3 shows that the optimum allocation of time to such a case would be whatever minimum amount of time will complete the case. Theoretically the optimum is zero hours, since any hours allocated above zero means a reduced profit in the sense of a reduction in the positive difference between the fee received and the time-cost line. The break-even point on a 900 dollars fee is 30 hours figuring time cost at 30 dollars an hour.

FIGURE 7-3. PROFIT MAXIMIZATION IN FLAT FEE CASES

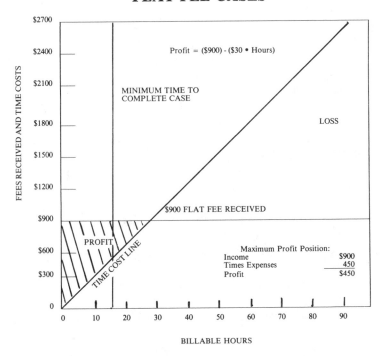

The same situation applies if we think in terms of a 30,000 dollars salary for an attorney working for an insurance company defending personal injury cases, a public defender representing indigent criminal defendants, or an assistant states attorney prosecuting defendants. The 900 dollars would change to 30,000 dollars in the graph, and the break-even point would change from 30 hours to 1000 hours. The concept of minimum time requirement, however, changes when we move from the flat fee case to the salaried attorney. In the flat fee case, the attorney is only expected to complete the case, not to put in any minimum number of hours beyond that. In the salaried situation, attorneys are normally expected to show up at an office for some number of hours per week and weeks per year. Their total working hours may thus add to more than 1000 hours per year, but salaried lawyers may consider their time per hour to be worth less than lawyers paid by the case since salaried lawyers have the security of a salary. Both the flat fee and the salaried lawyers may seek to put in more than the minimum number of hours required to complete their cases and retain their jobs if the additional hours required to complete their cases and retain their jobs if the additional hours are likely to result in increased fees or salary raises. It is, however, quite difficult to determine the relation between hours allocated and client-employer satisfaction or salary raises. Thus the general strategy of trying to minimize one's hours or time cost when being paid a flat fee or a salary may be the best profit-maximizing strategy.

Another simple but common situation is the hourly rate case. Figure 7-4 graphically shows what is involved with regard to the optimum time-allocation in order to maximize the positive difference between fees received and time cost. One can readily see the optimum allocation of time is the maximum time needed to complete the case. Theoretically the optimum time is infinite since the more hours allocated, the more profit, figuring a billable charge of 50 dollars an hour and a time cost of 30 dollars an hour. For each hour there is a 20 dollars profit between revenue and expenses if, for the sake of simplicity, we ignore expenses other than the cost of our time. The more hours we put in, the more profit units of 20 dollars we accumulate, thereby building a larger total profit. For 10 hours the total profit is 200 dollars, whereas for 30 hours the total profit is 600 dollars. At first glance, it looks as if a flat fee case and an hourly rate case would involve diametrically opposed optimum time-allocation strategies, with the former strategy emphasizing time minimization and the latter emphasiz-

FIGURE 7-4. PROFIT MAXIMIZATION IN HOURLY RATE CASES

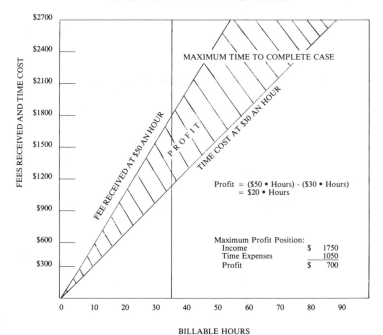

BILLABLE HOURS

ing time maximization. However, if the minimum time to complete the case is close to the maximum time, then in both situations, one may wind up putting in about the same amount of time.[12]

Figures 7-3 and 7-4 could consistently refer to the same case, since it is possible for a case to have a 15-hour minimum time and a 35-hour maximum time. One cannot, however, conclude from that hypothetical data than an hourly rate is more profitable than a flat fee. The extent to which it is or is not more profitable depends on (1) the hourly rate; (2) the flat fee; (3) the maximum time; (4) the minimum time; (5) the actual time; and (6) the value of one's time as reflected by the time cost line. Figures 7-1 and 7-2 are not referring to the same case since the optimum time in Figure 7-2 of 65 hours exceeds the maximum time from Figure 7.4. The profitability of the contingent fee versus the flat fee and the hourly fee depends on the above six elements plus, (7) the relation between the fees received and billable hours as illustrated by the dots and curve in figures 7-1 and 7-2; and (8) the relation between the probability of victory and billable hours as mentioned in the probability variation on the basic approach. With that kind of information one should be able to make decisions not only concerning the optimum hours to allocate, but also the optimum payment arrangement between the contingency fee, hourly rate, flat fee, or some legitimate combination of two or more of those payment arrangements.

As part of the profit maximization strategy, one might say something about setting the amount for the flat fee, hourly rate, or contingency percentage. Back when the bar associations were enforcing fee schedules, those decisions were largely made by a few influential firms or lawyers in an oligopolistic way. Now that there is more competition in fee setting, flat fees and hourly rates may be more determined by the market forces intersecting supply and demand curves. To the extent that law practice is a competitive business, the individual lawyer must operate within the market-determined fees. If the lawyer goes above those fees, clients will be lost. If the lawyer goes below those fees, a loss is likely to be registered. Some law practices may be closer to being monopolistic businesses because they are almost the only firm available in their communities or the only firm specializing in a certain field. They are capable of setting their prices as high as the traffic will bear without an offsetting loss of clients. Regardless of the oligopolistic, competitive, or monopolistic market of lawyers services, the price and the hours allocated would be designed to maximize the positive difference between fees received and expenses incurred, especially time costs, while operating within ethical and other constraints. This general rule operates on the assumption that rational lawyers like rational people in general seek to maximize benefits minus costs in their activities, including nonmonetary benefits and costs.[13]

Lawyers Versus Firms, Society, and Clients

An important variation on this analysis involves talking not in terms of the individual lawyer maximizing benefits minus costs, but rather in terms of the law firm, governmental office, or corporation for which the lawyer might work. If each individual lawyer seeks personal profit maximization, doing so will maximize the profits of the firm if the individual is a sole practitioner, or if the fees that are received become part of the income of a partnership. The interests of a law office with salaried lawyers, however, may not be the same as those of the individual lawyers. For example, a prosecutor's office may have as a collective goal to maximize the number and percentage of convictions, with each conviction weighted by the sentence received and possibly divided by the maximum sentence that could have been received. If individual salaried lawyers in such an office seek to minimize their "billable hours" worked while maintaining at least a minimum quality level, then goal maximizing for the office may not be goal maximizing for the individual because a given lawyer might avoid big cases that are likely to involve after-hours work. Under such circumstances, incentive systems need to be established to get the individual lawyers to internalize the office goals into their benefit-cost considerations. The problem moves up to a still higher level if we talk about how to get both individual lawyers and the groups with which they are associated to internalize societal or public interest goals. That is the subject of other articles having more of a political science or governmental orientation than a management science or economics orientation.[14]

Still another variation on this analysis involves possible conflict between the profit maximization position of the lawyer and the individual client, rather than the firm for which the lawyer works. Under a contingency fee arrangement, the client is better off if the lawyer puts in as many hours as possible, assuming the damages awarded curve keeps rising even if only to a slight extent as shown in Figure 7-1. Even if the curve eventually becomes totally flat, that point is likely to involve more hours than the maximum profit position shown in Figure 7-2. Under a flat fee arrangement, the client is also probably better off the more hours the lawyer puts in, since additional hours should result in higher quality work, at least up to a point. The lawyer receiving a flat fee, however, would prefer to put in as few hours as possible as shown in Figure 7-3. Under an hourly rate arrangement, the client may be better off with few hours provided that the job gets done, whereas the lawyer may be better off in terms of profit with more hours.

Various systems have been proposed to try to reconcile these conflicts. One type of system involves combining different payment arrangements to force the lawyer into a position where maximum profit involves neither trying to stretch work nor shorten it, which is the kind of middling position where the client is usually best off. An example of such a proposed system is the contingent hourly-percentage whereby the lawyer charges an hourly rate, but receives a percentage of the recovery if the recovery exceeds his total hourly fee.[15] Another type of system involves a fee schedule that describes *actual average and maximum* (1) hours; (2) hourly rates; (3) flat fees; and (4) contingency percentages, as contrasted to the now illegal *recommended minimum* fee schedules. The averages could be determined by carefully surveying attorneys, and the maximums could represent the response from the upper 20 percent or other percentage. Regardless of the kind of system that someday might provide client protection from conflict over the allocation of lawyer hours, the lawyer could still follow the general approach and its variations described in this article in order to more nearly maximize benefits minus costs. Having a better understanding of how attorneys can maximize those net benefits is also helpful in developing a governmental or bar association system for regulating payment arrangements and thus time allocation.[16]

Legal aid for the poor is a special kind of attorney-client relationship with regard to payment arrangements and time allocation. Three general kinds of payment arrangements have been tried, namely, volunteer or assigned lawyers who do not generally get paid, salaried lawyers whose salaries are generally paid by the Legal Services Corporation or a public defender's office, and lawyers who are reimbursed by the government for their services on a case-by-case basis analogous to medicare. The volunteer attorney is not working to maximize monetary profits, but rather for the learning experience or the psychological benefits from contributing one's time. The salaried lawyer for the indigent may also have strong non-monetary motivations, although a heavy caseload may prevent the lawyer from allocating as much time per client as hired counsel does. The judicare lawyer is quite expensive when charging on a case-by-case rather than an annual salary basis, even if there is no overcharging to the government. The salaried system now tends to prevail, for both civil and criminal cases, with the exception of cases that can be handled for the poor on a contingency fee basis, and with the exception of federal criminal cases where a regulated reimbursement system operates.[17] Insurance systems are now being increasingly developed for people above the classification of being poor, but not wealthy enough to be able to readily afford individually hired counsel. Attorneys working for such insurance systems may tend to allocate their time like salaried house counsel, rather than like salaried Legal Services Corporation attorneys who tend to be more idealistic.

IMPLEMENTING THE ALLOCATION SYSTEM

What we have presented so far should make sense, at least as a matter of hindsight, even though it might be difficult to develop in response to the question of "How should attorneys allocate time to court cases?" The

Achilles heel of the system is the problem of how to obtain the data for implementing the system, not that it contains any substantially fallacious or unethical reasoning.

An ideal implementation system would be computerized at the three stages of data gathering, retrieval, and processing. With regard to data retrieval, what we would like to have is a business firm compiling data from questionnaires and docket records on thousands of damage cases across the country. For each case, a notation would be made for: (1) billable hours by the plaintiff's attorney; (2) billable hours by the defendant's attorney; (3) damages awarded; (4) the nature of the accident in which the injury occurred; (5) the nature of the injuries; (6) the characteristics of the plaintiff and defendant; (7) the date when and place where the case was decided; and (8) other characteristics of the case that may be relevant to establishing the relation between hours allocated and damages awarded.

If that data set could be made accessible by a computer terminal, the attorneys could ask for all the cases that have whatever combination of characteristics they are interested in. An attorney, for example, could ask for those cases that involve intersection collisions with a whiplash injury by a woman plaintiff. If the attorney gives too much detail in specifying the case characteristics, then too few cases will be received and the request should be redefined. In other words, the system could work similar to the computerized Lexis or Westlaw subscription services for retrieving case citations. Here, however, the attorney does not want citations, but rather to specify the subset of cases to be analyzed. This data set would also involve trial cases, rather than appellate cases, which makes it more like the data compiled by the Jury Verdict Research Corporation. An important difference from their data set, though, would be the fact that the data would indicate billable hours for each side which is not currently compiled by the Jury Verdict people.[18]

After retrieving a subset of cases, the same computer system could then process those cases to determine algebraically or graphically the relation between billable hours and fees received in those cases.[19] The result could be a graph like Figure 7-2 when the system is operated off a computer terminal that provides for graphical output. The time-cost line can be superimposed on the graph if the attorney informs the computer how much his hours are worth in terms of personal cost. If the system merely gives printed output, the attorney could be provided with such information as (1) the general optimum number of hours corresponding to point B on Figure 7-2; (2) the damages likely to be awarded at that optimum number of hours; (3) the range of hours within which a profit is likely to be made corresponding to points A to C in Figure 7-2; and (4) other statistical information such as the equation for the curve and a measure of how well the curve fits the dots. If the computerized system allows for interaction between the attorney and the computer as Lexis and Westlaw do, then the attorney can vary the characteristics of the case and thereby vary the subset of data that gets analyzed. Doing so enables one to see how such variations affect the optimum number of hours and the damages likely to be awarded.

Until a business firm is willing to supply a computerized service or at least a looseleaf binder service, individual attorneys and law firms can try doing the analysis using their own cases and a graphic eyeballing approach, rather than the more mathematical approach of a computer. Such a do-it-yourself approach might involve using index cards to record the kind of data-gathering information mentioned above for each case that will be a part of the data set. One can then retrieve any subset of those index cards corresponding to the type of case one is interested in. Retrieving such a subset is easier if the index cards have some kind of edge notches or colored flags indicating the characteristics of each case. With that subset of index cards, one could then plot dots on a pair of axes like that shown in Figure 7-2, where each dot corresponds to a case. Its position from east to west on the graph indicates the number of billable hours, and the dot's position from north to south indicates the fee received. One can then eyeball an S-shaped curve to the dots trying to provide as good a fit as one can. With that curve, one can see the predicted profitability of cases of that subset-type from the way in which that fee-received curve relates to a predrawn time-cost line reflecting how much per hour one's time is worth. Such a system can be done for a variety of case types. Doing so should provide insights to practicing lawyers regarding the relative profitability of different types of cases.

SOME CONCLUSIONS

The essence of the foregoing allocation model is simply to maximize within each case the positive difference between the fee received and the expenses incurred, especially the time costs, while operating within ethical and other constraints. That strategy involves allocating as little time as possible per case when a flat fee or a fixed salary is involved, and as much time as possible when an hourly rate is involved. In contingency fee cases, that stragey involves allocating a quantity of hours between the minimum and maximum possible. The exact quantity depends on the relation between billable hours and damages awarded (which indirectly determines the fee received), as indicated by analyzing a set of cases that are similar to the case under consideration. Such an analysis can be facilitated by a computerized system of case data gathering, retrieval, and processing or by a do-it-yourself noncomputerized system. The recommended optimum hours from the analysis allows for aggravating and extenuating circumstances. Comparing these optimums across cases can help decide what clients to encourage or accept, as well as improve the allocation of time on accepted cases.

A few years ago lawyers considered the idea of computerized legal searches for case citations to border on science fiction, but it has now become a widespread reality. The next step is to get these computerized data-gathering and retrieval systems to do some processing of the information. A useful first step for such subscription services might be to attempt to relate results to hours allocated. The same systems could also relate results to other case characteristics, but attorneys generally have more control over their hours than over the characteristics of their cases. It is hoped that this article may inspire some experimentation along the lines suggested so law practices could benefit from some of the management science developments that have been so helpful to business firms in allocating their scarce resources. Computerized citation retrieval has lessened some of the drudgery of legal research. Computerized case management has the potential for further expanding the rational use of attorney time.

NOTES

1. For a more detailed analysis of some aspects of the problem of allocating attorney time to court cases and clients, see Chapter 7 in S. Nagel and M. Neef, "Allocating Resources among Court Cases by Legal Counsel" in *Decision Theory and the Legal Process* (Lexington, Mass.: Lexington-Heath, 1979). That analysis treats time allocation mainly as a problem of finding an optimum division of a fixed budget of time among a set of cases, whereas this chapter considers time allocation as more a problem of finding an optimum level of time to allocate to each case on a case-by-case basis. The present analysis also classifies cases mainly in terms of the payment arrangement as contingency fee, flat fee, salaried, or hourly rate cases, whereas the above cited chapter classifies cases mainly in terms of their subject matter as personal injury, criminal, divorce, and other types of court cases.

2. Other studies dealing with time allocation among court cases by legal counsel include criminal justice studies such as, Brian Forst and Kathleen Brosi, "A Theoretical and Empirical Analysis of the Prosecutor," 6 *Journal of Legal Studies* 177 (1977); William Landes, "An Economic Analysis of the Courts," 14 *Journal of Law and Economics* 61 (1971); and Judy Lachman, "An Economic Model of Plea Bargaining in the Criminal Court System" (Unpublished Ph.D. dissertation in the Michigan State University Department of Economics, 1975). In those studies, the time allocation decision is generally only part of a broader economic model of the behavior of prosecutors or the criminal justice system. Like Nagel and Neef, op. cit., they emphasize tradeoffs across cases and the substance of the cases.

Still other studies include personal injury studies, such as F.B. Mackinnon, *Contingent Fees for Legal Services: A Study of Professional Economics and Responsibilities* (Hawthorne, N.Y.: Aldine, 1964); Murray Schwartz and Daniel Mitchell, "An Economic Analysis of the Contingent Fee in Personal Injury Litigation," 22 *Stanford Law Review* 1125 (1970); and Kevin Clermont and John Currivan, "Improving on the Contingent Fee," 63 *Cornell Law Review* 529-639 (1978). These studies do focus on the individual case taken out of the context of the other cases in one's caseload. Like the above criminal studies, however, they are primarily concerned with describing and explaining attorney decision-making using an economic model, rather than trying to improve the efficiency of attorney decision-making using a management science or operations research model.

3. One does not need to know anything about the technical aspects of statistical analysis in order to plot dots and fit a rough S-shaped curve to the dots using an eyeballing approach. On how that might be done more precisely by a computer, see Edward Tufte, *Data Analysis for Politics and Policy* (Englewood Cliffs, N.J.: (Prentice-Hall, 1974), pp. 65-134; and Gordon Hilton, *Intermediate Politometrics* (New York: Columbia University Press, 1976) pp. 186-218. The computer is given (for each case) the damages awarded (the Y score) and the billable hours (the X score). The computer then determines numerical values for the ''b''s in an equation of the form $Y = b_0 + b_1X + B_2X^2 + b_3X^3$. That equation, when plotted by the computer, will appear as an S-shaped curve.

4. An alternative way of conceiving the relation between damages awarded and hours is via a curve that quickly becomes totally horizontal, as contrasted to a curve like that in Figure 7-1 that is always rising at least slightly although at a decreasing rate. See Clermont and Currivan, op. cit., 2. The Clermont-Currivan perspective assumes a flattening of the relation. The type of curve that best fits the empirical reality of actual cases has more than just geometric implications. If the curve does reach a point where it becomes totally flat then one can say that is the point of maximum client recovery which dedicated lawyers should be seeking. If, however, there is no flattening of the curve, then there is no point except at an infinity of hours where the client's interest is maximized. The diminishing returns but nonflat curve does seem more reasonable in light of empirical statistical analyis in other subject matter areas. What is obviously needed is a gathering of the kind of data suggested later in this article to determine the relation between damages awarded and hours allocated in various types of cases.

5. Clermont Currivan, op. cit., assume that if a lawyer charges 50 dollars an hour, he has then incurred 50 dollars in expenses. That assumption is essential to their model which then deduces that lawyers have no incentive to add additional hours under an hourly rate arrangement, because they are only covering their expenses by putting in additional hours. They do recognize that a lawyer, under an hourly rate arrangement, may have an incentive to claim 10 hours were worked when only 8 hours were worked. They do not, however, recognize that a lawyer may have an incentive to work 10 hours when 8 hours could have done the job, since a profit or surplus is made on each additional hour by virtue of the fact that the lawyer is getting paid more than if those hours regularly were free for something else. This does not mean that the attorney can be bargained down from 50 dollars an hour. It simply means that the attorney comes out ahead when working for 50 dollars an hour, i.e., making a net gain of benefits minus costs. A good test to determine the difference between billable charge per hour and the self-perceived time cost per hour might be to ask the attorney how much the 50 dollars per hour would have to be lowered before the attorney would change occupations. Most lawyers would continue to be lawyers even if there were a substantial reduction in the dollars per hour or per year and no reduction in the hourly or annual incomes of other occupations. Changing occupations in this context does not, however, mean shifting to an occupation that requires totally new training like becoming a doctor, or totally new psychological style like becoming an unskilled laborer. It more likely means shifting from one legal specialty to another, from private practice to government or corporate work, from small-town to big-city, from law to business, or similar shifts. The difference between the actual fee and what fee the lawyer would be willing to do similar work for can be considered a producer's surplus.

One could also argue that lawyers, like other wage earners, are under-paid in the the sense that clients, given the benefits received, might be willing to pay more than 50 dollars an hour if they had to. A third perspective says that if the lawyer charges a 50 dollar an hour fee, then the services are worth 50 dollars an hour, because the lawyer would not be asking that rate without the ability to get it. In other words, by devoting an hour to one client the lawyer is suffering a 50 dollar opportunity cost by foregoing 50 dollars that could be received from another client. In the context of the analysis of this article the most reasonable perspective seems to be that lawyers are obtaining a net benefit from every hour worked at the going hourly rate. Otherwise they would be doing something else.

6. To clarify the relation between billable hours and profit, we could superimpose a profit curve on Figure 7-2. Doing so would mean having another column on the vertical axis labeled "Profit," which would have a zero point in the middle, be negative below that point, and positive above that point. The curve would be valley-shaped between zero and 45 hours, reaching bottom at about 30 hours where the biggest loss occurs. The curve would be hill-shaped after 45 hours, reaching a peak at about 65 hours where the biggest profit occurs. There would be three break-even points where the profit curve intersects the zero profit line, namely when billable hours are zero, 45, and 85. After 85 hours, profit goes down continuously as more hours are allocated with little increased damages awarded.

To clarify still further the relation between billable hours and profits, we could recognize that the fee-received or income curve can be expressed as an equation of the form $I = a + b_1H + b_3H^3$, which shows an S-shaped relation between I and H. The value of a, b_1, b_2, and b_3 can be determined from the data in Figure 7-1 using a computerized regression analysis routine, and then multiplying each of the parameters which the computer generates by .33 or whatever the contingency percentage is, since the fee received equals damages-awarded multiplied by the contingency percentage. We could also recognize that the time-cost or expenses line can be expressed as an equation in the form $E = A + BH$, which shows a linear relation between E and H. We know from Figure 7-2 that $A = O$, and $B = \$30$. Net profit (or loss) then becomes $P = a + b_1H + b_2H^2 + b_3H^3 - \$30H$, which represents income minus expenses. That equation can be simplified to $P = a + (b_1 - 30)H + b_2H^2 + b_3H^3$. We can now determine the slope of profit to hours, which is $b_1 - 30 + 2b_2H + 3b_3H^2$. This follows from the rule that if $Y = aX^b$, then the slope of Y relative to X is baX^{b-1}. That slope simplifies to $c + dH + eH^2$, where $c = b_1 - 30$, $d = 2b_2$, and $e = 3b_3$. Setting that slope equal to zero will tell us the value of H when profits either bottom out or reach a peak. Solving for H in the quadratic equation $0 = c + dH = eH^2$ yields two solutions, one where there is a maximum loss at about 30 hours, and one where there is a maximum profit at about 65 hours.

7. On the optimum sequencing of events or cases, see Jack Byrd, Jr., *Operations Research Models for Public Administration* (Lexington, Mass.: Lexington-Heath, 1975) pp. 139-156; and S. Nagel and M. Neef, "Time-Oriented Models and the Legal Process: Reducing Delay and Forecasting the Future," 1978 *Washington University Law Quarterly* 467 (1978).

8. When we say "most profitable" in this context, however, we mean the subset of cases that will collectively yield the most profit. For example, if we have 100 hours available, and the ten prospective cases consist of one 100-hour case that will yield an 11 dollar profit and nine 10-hour cases that will each yield a 10 dollar profit, then the best subset would be to take just the nine 10-hour cases. Doing so will yield a total profit of 90 dollars, whereas taking the one 100-hour case will only yield a total profit of 11 dollars, even though that one case is individually the most profitable. This example assumes our time is worth 30 dollars an hour in all ten cases. The one 100-hour case therefore must involve a total time cost of 3,000 dollars and a fee received of 3,011 dollars. Similarly, the nine 10-hour cases must each involve a total time cost of 300 dollars and a fee received of 310 dollars. Thus they all involve the same hourly rate, but the most profitable case is the one that should be rejected in order to allow more time for taking less profitable cases that will collectively add up to a greater total profit.

9. On the problem of making sequential allocations of peremptory challenges, time, or money, from a limited total quantity, see Steven Brams and M. Davis, "A Game-Theory Approach to Jury Selection," 12 *Trial* 47 (1976); and Howard Raiffa, *Decision Analysis: Introductory Lectures on Choices Under Uncertainty* (Reading, Mass.: Addison-Wesley, 1970).

10. On optimum-level analysis, as contrasted to optimum mix analysis, see discussions of inventory modeling and linear programming in any elementary operations research textbook such as Samuel Richmond, *Operations Research for Management Decisions* (New York: Ronald Press, 1968); Henri Theil et al., *Operations Research and Quantitative Economics: An Elementary Introduction* (Hightstown, N.J.: McGraw-Hill, 1965); and Sang Lee and Laurence Moore, *Introduction to Decision Science* (Princeton, N.J.: Petrocelli/Charter, 1975). For a discussion of optimizing methods with legal process examples, see S. Nagel and M. Neef, *Legal Policy Analysis: Finding an Optimum Level or Mix* (Lexington, Mass.: Lexington-Heath, 1977).

11. On making decisions under conditions of risk or uncertainty, see chapters on that subject in the operations research textbooks in note 10. For a discussion of that optimizing perspective with legal process examples, see S. Nagel and M. Neef, *Decision Theory and the Legal Process* (Lexington, Mass.: Lexington-Heath, 1979). For additional sophistication, we could also discount the fees received, not only by the probability of their being received, but also by the fact that some types of cases take longer to receive fees than others. If a type of case tends to take three years for a settlement or a judgment, then the present value of the fee received need to be divided by $(1 + r)^t$, where r is the interest rate, and t is the number of years one has to wait. See Caroline Dinwiddy, *Elementary Mathematics for Economists* (Fair Lawn, N.J.: Oxford University Press, 1967) pp. 199-216.

12. See note 5 for the questionable alternative perspective that makes no distinction between hourly fees received and time costs. One could superimpose a total profit curve on figures 3 and 4, as described in note 5 above with regard to Figure 7-2. A total profit curve superimposed on Figure 7-3 (flat fee) would be a straight line, reaching a peak profit at zero billable hours, a break-even point at 30 hours, and going continuously downward after that. The equation for such a profit curve or line is $900 - 30(H)$, which represents income minus expenses. A total profit curve superimposed on Figure 4 (hourly rate) would also be a straight line. The break-even point would be at zero billable hours and going continuously upward after that point. The equation for such a profit line is $50(H) - 30(H)$, which represents income minus expenses. It can be simplified to $20(H)$.

13. On the economics of price setting, see any elementary or intermediate economics textbook such as Paul Samuelson, *Economics: An Introductory Analysis* (Hightstown, N.J.: McGraw-Hill, 1972); and William Baumol, *Economic Theory and Operations Analysis* (Englewood Cliffs, N.J.: Prentice-Hall, 1965) pp. 311-37.

14. On internalizing group and societal goals into individual benefit-cost considerations, see "Using Decision Deterrence Theory to Encourage Socially Desired Behavior," which is Chapter 8 in Nagel and Neef, *Decision Theory*. To illustrate the problem of getting individual salaried lawyers to internalize law office goals, that chapter discusses having an incentive system to get assistant prosecutors to move cases faster rather than ask for work-easing continuances. To illustrate the problem of getting a corporation and its house counsel to internalize societal goals, the problem of environmental protection is used.

15. A more sophisticated (but related) alternative involves no fee unless the lawyer wins, but then instead of receiving about one-third of the damages awarded, the lawyer receives payment for his hours at an hourly rate and a percentage of the

amount by which the damages awarded exceeds that hourly payment. Clermont, op. cit.

16. On proposed systems to reconcile the interests of attorneys and clients in allocating time and setting fees, see Murray Bloom, *The Trouble with Lawyers* (New York: Simon and Schuster, 1968); Donald Rosenthal, *Lawyer and Client: Who's in Charge* (New York: Russell Sage, 1974); and Clermont and Currivan, op. cit. The American Trial Lawyer's Association (ATLA) recently proposed a contingency fee system for paying defense counsel in personal injury cases that would increase the conflict between those lawyers and their insurance company clients. The system would involve paying the defense counsel a basic retainer fee. Defense counsel, however, would get a percentage of the damages saved in those cases where the damages awarded are less than predicted. Predicted damages would be determined by doing an analysis similar to that shown in Figure 7-1 except that the key variable would be something like out-of-pocket medical costs, rather than billable hours. Thus suppose the out-of-pocket medical costs are 800 dollars in a given type of case, which normally predicts damages of about 8,000 dollars. If defense counsel succeeds in settling or trying the case with an award of only 5,000 dollars, then defense counsel would be entitled to about one-third of the difference between the 5,000 dollars awarded and the 8,000 dollars normally awarded. The ATLA, which mainly represents plaintiff's lawyers, would like such a system because it would provide defense counsel with an incentive to resolve the cases faster in order to collect the bonus percentage. Such speed would run contrary to the desire of the insurance company clients to keep the money for investment purposes as long as possible. Such a system, however, might cause defense counsel to work harder and thereby reduce the damages enough to make the situation desirable to the insurance companies, but then not so desirable to plaintiff lawyers. See the report on the 1979 ATLA meeting in 65 ABA J. 1301 (1979).

17. On alternative methods for paying lawyers to represent indigent clients or defendants, and how those methods affect the behavior of lawyers, see Arthur Berney, et al., *Legal Problems of the Poor: Cases and Materials* (Boston: Little, Brown, 1975) pp. 499-588; Lee Silverstein, *Defense of the Poor: The National Report* (Boston: Little, Brown, 1975) pp. 499-588; and Nagel, "Effects of Alternative Types of Counsel on Criminal Procedure Treatment," 48 *Indiana Law Journal* 404 (1973).

18. On the computerized data gathering and retrieval systems of Lexis, Westlaw, and related systems, see ABA Law and Technology Committee, *Automated Law Research* (1973), and Diana McCabe, "Automated Legal Research: A Discussion of Current Effectiveness and Future Development," 54 *Judicature* 283 (1971). On the Jury Verdict Research Corporation system, see *Jury Verdict Expectancies Service* (since 1962); *Valuation Handbook Service* (since 1962); and Nagel, "Statistical Prediction of Verdicts and Awards," *Modern Uses of Logic in Law* 135 (1963).

19. See footnote 3 on how a computer can fit a curve to a set of data points where each data point shows the damages awarded and the billable hours for a given case.

Chapter 8
An Optimum Length of Imprisonment

Congress, the state legislatures, the law reviews, and other forums for discussing alternative legal policies are currently debating changes in the traditional system of criminal sentencing. The main debating issue deals with the extent to which judges should have discretion in sentencing convicted defendants. The current consensus seems to be that there is a need for reduced discretion. Liberal commentators and policy makers support reduced discretion partly because they feel discretionary sentencing tends to result in sentencing that is inequitable, due to discriminatory or at least arbitrary differences across judges and cases. Conservatives support reduced discretion partly because they feel traditional discretionary sentencing has led to sentences that are too lenient. With people of diverse ideologies supporting reduced sentencing discretion (or what is often referred to as determinate rather than indeterminant sentencing), the debate has now moved more to the question of what non-discretionary sentences should be promulgated by legislatures and followed by judges.

Determinate sentencing generally means that some policy-making body will arrive at specific sentences for convicted criminals who have committed certain crimes and who have certain prior records. These sentences will then be used by judges in handing down sentences. The sentences are specific in the sense that they do not provide for a range of years within which the judge has substantial discretion in sentencing. They may, however, allow the judge to deviate from the specific sentences by a certain percentage upward or downward where explicitly aggravating or mitigating circumstances are present.[1]

By optimum sentencing in this context we mean specific sentences that a policy-making body has determined to be the best sentences for each crime along with any prior record in terms of maximizing the difference between the benefits of holding people in prison minus the costs of doing so.[2] A simpler way of expressing the same idea is to say that optimum sentences minimize the sum of the costs of releasing people from prison plus the costs of holding them in prison.[3] Optimum sentencing refers to optimum length of sentence for those to be incarcerated, not to whether a convicted defendant should be released on probation, rather than sent to prison. The optimum sentencing problem is thus an optimum level problem along a continuum of alternatives, as contrasted to a dichotomous decision problem with regard to incarcerating versus releasing a defend-ant.[4]

The purpose of this chapter is to discuss alternative ways of arriving at optimum sentences. On a general level, the basic alternatives are either to draw upon empirical data that is relevant to the relation between sentence length and both releasing and holding costs, or to deduce what the optimum sentences should be from certain accepted premises. The first part of this chapter describes a basic model that optimum sentences might attempt to satisfy. The second part uses a statistical induction approach and finds that approach to be incapable of yielding meaningful optimum sentences. The third part uses a deductive approach and finds that approach to be capable of justifying the average sentences as optimum sentences. The chapter then concludes that legislatures, sentencing commissions, or other policy-making bodies should specify the average sentences as determinate sentences and adopt procedures designed to encourage judges to sentence closer to the average.[5]

There is a great deal of prior literature on the subject of determinate sentencing. Most of that literature points to the disparities that exist in sentencing for the same crime and prior record across judges, defendants, places, and time points. Most of that literature also advocates giving less discretion to judges in order to reduce those disparities and sometimes in order to increase the severity of sentencing. Almost none of the literature discusses the idea of optimum sentencing in a benefit-cost sense. A few exceptions mention the idea, but do not attempt to apply it to actual data dealing with the effects of alternative sentences. Nor do they attempt to deduce on a benefit-cost basis what the optimum sentences might be in terms of specific years in prison for various crimes and prior records.[6]

THE BASIC MODEL WITH VARIATIONS

In the March, 1978 issue of *Judicature,* an article appeared suggesting a method for determining optimum sentences based mainly on analyzing the empirical relations between length of sentence and subsequent criminal behavior.[7] The model involves basically three relations, namely the relations between length of sentence and (1) holding costs; (2) releasing costs; and (3) total costs.

The Basic Model

As for the holding costs, there is a positive linear relation between them and length of sentence in the sense that with each subsequent year of incarceration, the holding costs go up one year's worth. Thus the formula or equation for relating holding costs to sentence length would be of the form $HC = A + B(L)$. The value of the "A" is zero, since a zero sentence incurs no holding costs related to that individual defendant, although there may be fixed holding costs in terms of maintaining the prison even if there are no prisoners. The value of the "B" can be considered 1, in the sense that one month of sentence length produces one unit of holding cost. Thus HC = 1(L).

As for the releasing costs, there is a negative convex relation between them and the length of sentence, in the sense that with each year of incarceration, the severity of a defendant's subsequent behavior should go down due to the effects of maturation, deterrence, and rehabilitation, but down at a diminishing rather than a constant rate. Thus the equation for relating releasing costs to sentence length would be of the form, RC = $a(L)^b$. In that equation, the value of the "a" or scale coefficient would be equal to the predicted amount of harm done by a defendant who is released after only one month. The value of the "b" or elasticity coefficient would be a negative number. If the number, for example, were a -2, that would mean that if the length of sentence goes up 1 percent, then the releasing cost comes down 2 percent. The tricky problem in the empirical analysis involves processing data for numerous released convicts to determine what the numerical values are for the "a" and "b" in that equation for various crimes and prior records.

As for the total costs, they simply equal the sum of the holding costs and the releasing costs. Thus the equation for relating total costs to sentence length would be of the form, TC = HC + RC, or TC = 1(L) + $a(L)^b$. That relation when graphed should look like a valley, since it involves summing a positively sloped straight line and a negatively sloped covex curve. The object is to find where that valley-shaped total cost curve reaches bottom. At that point, total costs have been minimized, and the optimum sentence has been found.[8]

The point where the total cost curve reaches bottom is where its slope is horizontal or zero, since before that point its slope is negative, and after that point its slope is positive. To find the point or sentence length where the slope of the total cost curve is zero involves first having a way of algebraically expressing the slope of the total cost curve. Its slope (or ratio of change in TC to change in L) is equal to the sum of the slope of the holding cost line plus the slope of the releasing cost curve. The slope of the holding cost line is B or 1. The slope of the releasing cost curve is $ba(L)^{b-1}$, according to the rules for deriving slopes from equations. Thus the slope of the total cost curve relative to L is simply $1 + ba(L)^{b-1}$.

If we now set that slope equal to zero and find the value of L, we get:

$$1 + ba(L)^{b-1} = 0$$
(Setting the slope of TC equal to zero)

$$ba(L)^{b-1} = -1$$

(Subtracting 1 from both sides)

$(L)^{b-1} = -1/(ba)$

(Dividing both sides by ba)

$L^* = -1/(ba)$ raised to the power $1/(b-1)$

(Raising both sides to the power $1/(b-1)$)

That formula in this highly simplified illustration tells us that if we can determine values for "a" and "b", we can then insert those values into this formula to arrive at an optimum sentence that minimizes the sum of the holding costs and releasing costs.

Expanding on the Basic Model

CONSIDERING DELAY

This basic model is an over simplification in a number of ways of the problem of finding optimum sentences. First, it does not take into consideration that one of the main holding benefits or releasing opportunity costs is the incapacitation factor whereby imprisoned convicts are kept from committing crimes by being imprisoned. In other words, the above formulation of the releasing costs only relates to the severity of the convict's subsequent behavior, not to the extent to which the behavior is delayed due to being in prison and to the "clean" time after getting out of prison. We could symbolize severity with an S, and define it as the number of months in prison that a convict receives subsequent to completing his basic sentence. The basic sentence was previously symbolized with an L, and can be defined as the number of months spent in prison as the basic sentence. Delay can then be symbolized with a D and be defined as L plus C, where C is the number of clean months without known felonious behavior before the S sentence occurs. Thus the new formulation for releasing costs might be $RC = S/D = a(L)^b$. In other words, we are now discounting the severity of the subsequent behavior by the number of months by which it is delayed.

We divide by delay rather than subtract delay from severity because if we subtract, then as delay increases, S minus D decreases at a constant rate and eventually becomes negative when D is greater than S. It does not, however, make sense to have negative releasing costs, since that would mean we are actually getting a benefit out of the subsequent criminal behavior as a result of its being delayed for so long. By dividing by delay, S/D relative to D is a negative convex curve which indicates diminishing returns from increased delay, as contrasted to a negative straight line which indicates constant returns.

A more important relevant matter to justify is why discount for delay by either dividing S by D, or subtracting D from S. One could argue that if the subsequent behavior is an assault, it hurts the person assaulted just as much to get hit on the head in 1990 as in 1985. In other words, the severity to the subjected individual does not lessen because of the date. One could, however, say that John Doe would prefer to get hit on the head in 1990 than in 1985, and thereby delay by 5 years brain injury or other damage. The counter argument to that, though, is that we are comparing an assault to John Doe in 1985 with an assault to Peter Roe in 1990, not necessarily to the same person five years apart. One could, however, selfishly argue that injuries occurring to the present generation should be given more weight than injuries occurring to a future generation. That might make sense if we are talking about the future generation many generations from now. A released criminal, however, is going to do whatever subsequent criminal behavior he does within the present generation. The best argument for discounting for delay is not that the *severity* of any single subsequent act is thereby lessened, but rather because the *quantity* of the subsequent criminal acts is thereby lessened. In other words, the longer the delay occurs, the smaller the number of subsequent crimes the convict is likely to commit during the remainder of his lifetime. Thus if a convict delays five years after his L-length sentence before committing his S-severity subsequent crime, then one can predict longer intervals between his crimes than the convict who only delays one year. If the intervals are longer, the number of crimes will be fewer and the total severity will be less, assuming a normal lifetime of about 70 years.

WEIGHTING THE COSTS

A second way in which the basic model is an oversimplification is that it treats a month-of-severity cost as being equal to a month-of-incarceration cost, and (now in our expanded model) equal to a month-of-delay benefit. Simply because the three variables of L, S, and D are all measured in months does not mean their measurement units have equal importance. A 1910 penny, for example, does not have the same value as a 1980 penny in the rare coin market, although they are both pennies. To take into consideration that a severity-month is a more important cost than an incarceration-month or a delay-month, we can square S in our formulation of the releasing costs. The revised formulation would thus be $RC = S^2/D = a(L)^b$. We raise S to the exponent 2 to show that it is twice as important as D rather than multiply S by 2 because $(2S)/D$ is the equivalent of $2(S/D)$. In other words, there is no way that the S/D ratio knows whether the 2 as a multiplier is multiplying S or is multiplying S/D. By squaring S, we clearly indicate severity has twice the importance of delay. Then when we calculate the total costs as being $TC = HC + RC$ or $TC = 1(L) + S^2/D$, we are in effect saying that a severity-month has a weight of two, and both a delay-month and a length-month have relative weights of one apiece. These weights seem reasonable but we can later try other weights to see what effects they have on the optimum sentences.[9]

An alternative weighting might say that the importance of delay should depend on the severity of the crime that is being delayed. That might involve a set of weights like $S^2/D^{.3S}$. These weights indicate that the weight of delay is not 1, but rather it is three-tenths of whatever the value of S is. At first glance, such a weighting system sounds appealing, although it might be quite difficult to determine what the .3 figure should really be. More importantly, however, the weight of delay should not depend on the severity of the subsequent criminal behavior, but only on the quantity of the subsequent criminal behavior. The severity of the behavior is the same whether it occurs 10 or 5 years after release, but if it occurs 10 years after, then the quantity of occurrences will be less over the lifetime of the defendant. This means that the total severity of the sum of the separate criminal acts will also be less.

Another alternative weighting system might say that since society spends about 2.5 times as much on police as it does on corrections, society must consider the releasing costs (which police try to decrease) as being worth 2.5 times the holding costs (which corrections people are responsible for). That reasoning, however, is fallacious since society might actually consider a holding cost unit to be twice as valuable as a releasing cost unit. Society, for example, might like to have 20 HC units and only 10 RC units, and yet spend only 100 dollars for HC and 250 dollars for RC because HC units are 5 dollars apiece and RC units are 25 dollars apiece. One also cannot determine the value to people by knowing the price of a product since price is determined by supply and demand, whereas the value of something valuable like air and water could have a low price because the supply is relatively plentiful in spite of its high demand.

Still another alternative might involve working with the previous average sentences as if they were optimum sentences and working backward to determine the weight of severity to delay that would justify those sentences as being optimum. This alternative uses judicial behavior to deduce implicit judicial values. It is partly used later in this chapter, where assigning S an exponent weight of 2 relative to D results in the previous average sentences being considered optimum.

CONTROLLING FOR PRIOR RECORD

A third way in which the basic model is an oversimplification is that it assumes a negative relationship between length of sentence (L) and the releasing costs (S in the original formulation, and now S^2/D). More specifically, we have been assuming that as the length of sentence increases, the severity of the subsequent behavior decreases due to maturation, deterrence, and/or rehabilitation. We are now further assuming that as the length of sentence increases, the delay of the subsequent criminal behavior also increases due to (1) the tautological fact that one component of D is L since D equals L plus C; and (2) the assumption that longer sentences produce more clean time (C) as well as less severity (S) because of maturation, deterrence, and/or rehabilitation. If L relates negatively to S and positively to D, then L should relate negatively to RC since RC now equals S^2/D.

L, however, is likely to have a spurious positive relation with S, and a spurious negative relation with D, if we do not control for prior criminal record. The reason why L is likely to relate positively to S is because convicts with bad prior records (R) are likely to receive longer sentences (L) even when the crime is held constant, and they are likely to commit more severe subsequent crimes (S), as measured by subsequent sentences. The reason why L is likely to relate negatively to C is because convicts with bad prior records (R) are likely to receive longer sentences (L), and they are likely to have shorter periods of clean time after being released from prison (C).

In order to hold prior record constant, we need to redefine our releasing costs as $RC = S^2/D = a (L)^{b_1}(R)^{b_2}$. In other words, we are now making releasing costs a function or a dependent variable of two independent variables, namely L and R rather than just L. In this context, the dependent variable of S^2/D can be referred to as a goal variable, since it is something that is desirable to reduce, although our overall goal is to reduce TC. The independent variable of L can be referred to as a policy variable, since it is a variable that is subject to governmental manipulation, and it is the variable we are trying to optimize. R can be referred to as a control variable since we are seeking to statistically control for it in order to make b_1 meaningfully negative, although R can also enter into the optimizing formula later. The b_2 shows for a one percent change in R, how much of a percent change occurs in RC. That change in RC should be a positive change, since as prior record increases, S should go up, and S is the key component of RC because S is squared. Part of that increase will, however, be offset since R has a positive relation with L, and a negative relation with C, but L may constitute more of D than C does. Like L, S, and D, prior record can also be measured in months. It requires no normative weight, though, since it is not a component of a goal variable. The "a" in this new way of relating releasing cost to sentence length represents the amount of predicted releasing cost (expressed in months) for a convict who has a one month length of sentence (L = 1) and a one month prior record (R = 1).

THE NEW OPTIMUM SENTENCE LENGTH

The next logical thing to do is to determine the formula for optimum sentence length (L*) in light of our expanding on the basic model. As before, the optimum sentence is where a valley-shaped total cost curve reaches bottom. Total cost is still defined as HC plus RC. In algebraic terms, that means $TC = 1(L) + S^2/D$, or $TC = 1(L) + a(L)^{b_1}(R)^{b_2}$. Given that new definition of total costs, what is the slope of TC relative to L? The answer is $1 + b_1a(R)^{b_2}(L)^{b_1-1}$. In other words, the slope of TC relative to L is the the slope of HC relative to L, plus the slope of RC relative to L. The second slope follows the basic rule of slopes that if $Y = aX^b$, then the slope of Y relative to X is baX^{b-1}.

Given that slope of TC relative to L, what is the value of L when that slope is set equal to zero? That is the same as saying what is the value of L when the valley-shaped TC curve bottoms out or has a horizontal zero slope? The answer is derived as follows:

$1 + b_1 a(R)^{b_2}(L)^{b_1-1} = 0$

$b_1 a(R)^{b_2}(L)^{b_1-1} = -1$

$(L)^{b_1-1} = -1/(b_1 a(R)^{b_2})$

$L^* = -1/(b_1 a(R)^{b_2})$ raised to the power $1/(b_1 - 1)$

This formula tells us that if we can meaningfully determine values for "a" and "b" (either through statistical induction or logical deduction), we can then insert those values into this formula (or further variations on it) in order to arrive at optimum sentences that minimize the sum of the holding costs and releasing costs for various crimes and prior records. In the next section, we discuss some statistical induction methods for doing that. In the subsequent section, we discuss some logical deduction methods.

EMPIRICAL RELATIONS AND OPTIMUM SENTENCES

In order to test the empirical meaningfulness of the expanded basic model, we need some data for a substantial number of cases or convicts involving various crimes. The data should show for each convict (1) The length of prison term for the immediate crime (L); (2) The length served for whatever subsequent felony was committed (S); (3) The length of delay between committing the subsequent crime and the time the prison term began for the immediate crime (D, where $D = L + C$); and (4) The length of time in prison before imprisonment for the immediate crime (R). Such data is available from the Federal Bureau of Prisons for about a thousand cases. The records for each convict were analyzed for about 18 years after being released from prison to determine their subsequent known criminal behavior. With that data, we should be able to determine the empirical relations between S^2/D and both L and R, and also other relevant relations.[10]

Applying the Data to the Expanded Basic Model

EXPRESSING THE RELATIONS NUMERICALLY

Table 8-1 shows the results of that empirical analysis. It indicates that we have within the data a substantial number of cases for the federal crimes of vehicle theft, narcotics offenses, burglary or larceny, robbery or kidnap, fraudulent check or counterfeiting, income tax or embezzlement, nonrobbery assault, and moonshine. The data allows us to break down the crimes further, but this set of categories should be illustrative. Those are the most general categories used in coding the Federal Bureau of Prison's data.[11]

TABLE 8-1. EMPIRICAL RELATIONS AND OPTIMUM SENTENCES

CRIME	N	a	b_1	b_2	r
Vehicle Theft	313	9.49	- .20	.02	.03
Narcotics Offense	125	213.75	-1.05	-.35	.26
Burglary or Larceny	130	2.17	- .13	.18	.08
Robbery or Kidnap	28	.17	.82	.01	.27
Fraud Check or Counterfeiting	63	.26	.50	.35	.18
Income Tax or Embezzlement	25	2.80	.57	-.38	.33
No-Robbery Assault	37	19.82	- .58	.24	.21
Moonshine	104	6.85	- .24	.06	.04

CRIME	L^*	L^* (R = 10)	L^* (R = 100)	Comments
Vehicle Theft	$1.91(R)^{.01}$	2	2 +	b_2 is almost zero
Narcotics Offense	$53.85(R)^{-.26}$	51	30	b_2 is negative
Burglary or Larceny	$.21(R)^{.21}$	0	1	b_1 is almost zero
Robbery or Kidnap	$-.14(R)^{.01}$	0	0	b_1 is positive
Fraud Check or Counterfeiting	$-.02(R)^{.55}$	0	0	ditto
Income Tax or Embezzlement	$-.17(R)^{.28}$	0	0	ditto
Non-Robbery Assault	$24.67(R)^{.31}$	50	103	b_1 & b_2 are high
Moonshine	$1.68(R)^{.06}$	2	2 +	b_1 & b_2 are low

Notes to the table:
(1) b_1 shows the relation between releasing costs (S^2/D) and length of sentence (L).
(2) b_2 shows the relation between releasing costs and prior record (R) in the equation, $S^2/D = a(L)^{b_1}(R)^{b_2}$.
(3) N is the number of cases.
(4) r is the multiple correlation coefficient between S^2/D and both L and R together.
(5) L^* is the optimum sentence in light of those relations and the specified prior record. $L^* = -1/(b_1 a(R)^{b_2})$ raised to the power $1/(b_1 - 1)$.

Let us analyze the 313 cases that involve vehicle theft as a particularly illustrative example of what is involved in Table 8-1. In order to determine numerical values for the a, b_1, and b_2, we insert into a computer for the 313 cases the scores that each case received on the four above-mentioned variables of L, S, D, and R, along with a set of standard statistical routines for doing regression analysis, like those contained in the SPSS statistical package.[12] Then one simply informs the computer to in effect plot in three-dimensional space the 313 dots. The three dimensions are S^2/D on the height axis, L on the length axis, and R on the width axis. The computer then implicitly (although not explicitly) draws a three-dimensional negative convex curve (that looks like a children's slide) designed to best fit among these dots. Best fit means minimizing the squared distances from the dots to the curve or slide. The computer then reads out an equation that says the best fitting curve to those dots is $RC = 9.49(L)^{-.20}(R)^{.02}$, as indicated in row 1 of Table 8-1. That best fit, however, is not a very good fit, since the dots are spread widely around the curve rather than being on it, as indicated by the low multiple correlation coefficient shown on the right side of row 1 of Table 8-1.[13]

With that numerical information from the top of Table 8-1, we can now calculate an optimum sentence for vehicle theft cases. The optimum sentence, algebraically speaking, as previously shown, is $L^* = -1/(b_1a(R)^{b_2})$ raised to the power $1/(b_1 - 1)$. If we insert into that formula the numerical values for a, b_1, and b_2, and then simplify the result by doing the arithmetic, we get $L^* = 1.91(R)^{.01}$. If we now apply that simplified formula to a hypothetical convict with a prior record of 10 months, we get a recommended sentence of 2 months in prison, and just slightly more than that for a hypothetical convict with a prior record of 100 months.

LACK OF MEANINGFULNESS IN THE RELATIONS

The recommended sentence for vehicle theft comes out fairly low because the b_1 or elasticity coefficient of sentence length related to releasing costs is a rather low .20, although not as close to zero as the b_1 for burglary/larceny. If b_1 is low, the data is in effect telling us that there is not much of a saving of releasing costs from holding convicts in prison for long periods of time. The recommended sentence does not increase substantially when the prior record is increased from 10 to 100 because the b_2 or elasticity coefficient of the prior record is an especially low .02. If b_2 is low, the data is in effect telling us that convicts with long prior records are not much worse in terms of their releasing costs than convicts with relatively short prior records. Thus the negative direction of b_1 makes sense and also the positive direction of b_2, but the combined magnitudes of a, b_1, and b_2 may not make sense in terms of the size of the recommended sentences which they lead to.

The pattern of not making much sense also shows up on most of the other crimes or rows in Table 8-1. For example, with 125 narcotics offense cases, b_2 comes out negative. This means that the worse the prior record, the better the defendant behaves after being released from prison. It further means that defendants with worse prior records in narcotics cases should be given shorter sentences than defendants with better prior records, since the ones with worse prior records have lower releasing costs. In the burglary/larceny category, the b_1 elasticity coefficient is so low that there is virtually no benefit from holding such convicts in prison in order to reduce the releasing costs. The ultimate extreme is in the robbery/kidnap, checks/counterfeiting, and tax/embezzlement cases. In those cases the longer the sentence, the worse the subsequent behavior, even when prior record is held constant. If those b_1s are accurate (at least in direction if not magnitude), then such convicts should not be held in prison at all. Holding them in prison in general just increases both the releasing costs and the holding costs. Thus the total costs for those three categories of crimes are constantly going up as length of sentence goes up, instead of bottoming out when the falling marginal-releasing costs intersect the rising marginal-holding costs.

The results for nonrobbery assault represent a problem opposite to that of vehicle theft. The b_1 for nonrobbery assault is negative as one would think all the b_1s would be. Similarly, the b_2 is positive as one would think all of them would be. The problem, however, is that their magnitudes may seem too large to have face validity (i.e., common-sense meaningfulness) in terms of the recommended sentences to which they lead. When R equals 10, L* equals 50 months or over 4 years; and when R equals 100, L* equals 103 months or almost 9 years. The 50 months may not seem so out of line, but the 103 months seems rather high considering that the average sentence for all the nonrobbery assault cases was only 3.5 years, although the average prior record was only 6 months in view of the large proportion of the nonrobbery assault defendants who had no prior record. The last crime is the distinctively federal one of moonshine or making liquor without buying the federal tax stamps. For that crime, the recommended sentences are quite low since both b_1 and b_2 are low. Moonshine may, however, be the least serious of the eight crime categories. That is also reflected in the fact that the average moonshine sentence tends to be only 1 year, although the prior record is close to 3 years of previous imprisonment, a large part of which may be previous moonshine offenses.

Of the eight crime categories, the recommended sentences may only make sense for nonrobbery assault and maybe moonshine, with vehicle theft running a distant third, and the other five in effect outside the region of feasibility. Perhaps, however, the basic model can be improved further in light of these empirical relations and the available data. We now turn to what some of those further improvements might be.

Alternative Data-Based Applications of the Model

ADDITIONAL CONTROL VARIABLES

One improvement might be to control for variables in addition to prior record. Perhaps there are other variables that correlate well with both L and S and/or both L and C, thereby causing a spurious positive b_1 which would otherwise be negative if those variables were controlled for. Similarly, there may be spurious b_2 negative relations due to variables that relate to both R and S. An additional example of the first kind of control variable is prior job length. Job length should have negative causal relation with subsequent crime severity (S) and a negative causal relation with sentence length (L). Those two negatives, however, might make for a spurious positive b_1 relation between sentence length and subsequent severity. Another example of the second kind of control variable is age. Older defendants have a negative causal relation with subsequent crime severity (S) because as convicts get older, they become less capable of pursuing criminal careers. Older defendants, however, are more likely to have longer prior records (R) because they have been around longer. The positive relation with S and the negative relation with R may cause a spurious b_2 negative relation between S and R, if age is not controlled for.

That kind of thinking leads one to change the RC equation to $S^2/D = a(L)^{b_1}(R)^{b_2}(J)^{b_3}(A)^{b_4}$. The J stands for prior job length, and the A stands for age at time of sentencing, i.e., the beginning of L. With that more sophisticated multivariate regression equation, one might think that the likelihood of b_1 being negative and b_2 being positive would be improved. With that equation, one can still use the same L* slope formula of $b_1a(R)^{b_2}(L)^{b_1-1}$. Doing so in effect sets J and A both equal to 1 for optimizing purposes, although now b_1 and b_2 should be different since we are controlling for job length and age. In other words, we can control for J and A without having to use those characteristics in the optimizing formula. The results of this more sophisticated analysis, however, turn out to worsen rather than improve the kind of analysis which appears in Table 8-1. Apparently what happens is that the relations among the four predictor variables get so complicated with their intercorrelations that some of the regression coefficients tend to go wild, especially the "a" or scale coefficients. Age does have an interesting positive relation with severity in the checks/counterfeiting cases, where older defendants are more likely to be involved, and a strong negative relation with S in narcotics offenses where younger defendants are more likely to be involved.

CHANGING THE WEIGHTS

Another improvement on the basic model might be to change the relative weights of severity, delay, and sentence length. We have been working with S^2, D^1, and L^1. Maybe as a result, the recommended sentences have generally come out too low. This seems to be true of all the crimes with the exception of nonrobbery assault. To increase the recommended sentences, perhaps all we have to do is increase the weight of the releasing costs relative to the holding costs. We could do that by cubing S rather than just squaring S. The result, however, is to increase the number of b_1s that come out positive, contrary to the model. The reason seems to be that part of the negative relation between L and S^2/D is due to L correlating positively with D since D is L plus C, and D in turn correlates negatively with S^2/D. However, if S is cubed rather than squared, this dilutes the influence of D in S^3/D, and thereby decreases the likelihood that there will be a negative relation between RC and L.

CHANGING THE FIT BETWEEN RC AND L

In addition to changing the predictor variables and the weighting, we can also experiment with changing the method of fitting a curve to the dots. For example, instead of using a curve of the form $RC = a(L)^b$, we could use a curve of the form $RC = a + b \text{ Log } (L)$. Working with the logarithms of L has the effect of drawing a curve, rather than a straight line, to the dots representing the relation between L and RC, where RC is still defined as S^2/D. That approach is referred to as a semi-log function because only the independent variable is logged, as contrasted to curves of the form $RC = a(L)^b$, which are generally referred to as power functions, because the independent variable is raised to a power. The semi-log curve has the advantage of simplicity, since with that relation, the slope of RC relative to L is simply b/L, according to the rules governing slopes. Thus the slope of TC relative to L would be $1 + b/L$. If we set that slope equal to zero to find the value of L where TC bottoms out, then we get (1) $0 = 1 + b/L$; (2) $0 = L/L + b/L$; (3) $0 = (L + b)/L$; (4) $0 = L + b$; and therefore (5) $L^* = -b$.

The trouble with that method of curve fitting in this context, however, is that it does not provide any meaningful way of both controlling for the prior record, and also using the prior record in the optimizing formula. The semi-log approach can control for the prior record by working with the formula $RC = a + b_1 \text{ Log } (L) + b_2(R)$. There is no need to log the prior record since we are not hypothesizing a diminishing or increasing returns relation between prior record and RC. That reformulation should increase, but not guarantee, the likelihood that b_1 will be negative, rather than a spurious positive. The slope of RC relative to L, however, is still b_1/L, meaning prior record will not enter into the optimizing formula because it is added to L in the equation, rather than multiplied by L. A multiplicative term could be inserted so that the equation reads $RC = a + b_1 \text{ Log } (L) + b_2(R) + b_3(R) (\text{Log } L)$. The slope then becomes $b_1/L + b_3R/L$ with R retained, and L^* then becomes $-b_1 - b_3R$. There is, however, no substantive justification for adding a third term, which in effect says there is a special relation between the releasing costs and the combination of the prior record and the sentence length, separate from the effect of the prior record on RC and the sentence length on RC. Working with that reformulation also produces an inconsistency between b_2 and b_3. We want b_2 to be positive to show that bad prior records produce high releasing costs. We want b_3 to be negative so bad prior records will result in longer recommended sentences in the optimizing formula. However, b_3 is likely to have the same sign as b_2, since b_3 is more influenced by the stronger relation between R and RC than the weaker relation between L and RC.[14]

CHANGING THE FIT BETWEEN TC AND L

Another method of curve fitting that may produce more desirable numerical results, but with a lack of substantive justification, is the quadratic function approach. It involves a curve of the form $Y = a + b_1X + b_2X^2$. When plotted, that kind of an equation produces either a valley-shaped curve or a hill-shaped curve. The curve fitting for RC that we have been working with only produces convex or concave curves that change slope, but do not change direction. The quadratic function approach would be applied to TC, not to RC. More specifically, we might conceive of TC in terms of LS^3/D^2, or as $L + 3S - 2D$. Either conceptualization indicates that TC varies directly with L and S and inversely with D. Either one also indicates that we consider S to be three times as important as L and that we consider D to be twice as important as L, although the first considers diminishing returns and the second has a constant returns approach. We could then relate either conceptualization as the dependent variable in an equation of the form $TC = a + b_1(L) + b_2(L)^2 + b_3(L)(R)$. That approach yields an L* equation of the form $L^* = (-b_1 - b_3R)/2b_2$. It also yields a set of numerical coefficients in which the recommended sentences will more often, but not always, be in the right direction in terms of recommended sentences greater than zero, and longer recommended sentences for defendants with greater prior records.

The quadratic function approach, however, seems impossible to justify in terms of the substance of the variables and their generally known or assumed relations. The interaction term designed to control for the prior record and to have the prior record enter into the optimizing formula has no substantive justification here or in the semi-log approach. More important, the conceptualizations of TC run contrary to the basic ideas that TC is defined as HC + RC. HC in turn is defined as L multiplied by the absolute cost (or at least raised to the power of the relative cost) of holding someone for one month. RC should also be defined as (1) S times the cost to society of one month of bad behavior (2) divided by D times the benefit to society of one month of delay, although those cost figures can be relative exponents instead of absolute multipliers. The quadratic approach is somewhat like defining the releasing costs as R/L and then relate

R/L to $a(L)^{b_1}(R)^{b_2}$. By definition, that formulation should provide us with consistently negative b_1s and consistently positive b_2s. That formulation, however, is meaningless, since RC is not R/L.

The problem might be that no tinkering approach will work that involves statistical regression analysis whereby we seek to inductively relate some formulation of releasing costs to length of sentence. The fault may not be in the data, although we might get more meaningful results from larger samples and better measurement of the variables. The data, however, probably does accurately reflect the relations or nonrelations between subsequent criminal behavior and sentence length. The fault may also not be in the basic model, but in trying to apply it by statistical induction whereby one fits curves to numerous data points. That general approach may be incapable of yielding meaningful regression coefficients in view of the complicated ways the relevant variables relate to each other, which cannot be adequately controlled for the way chemists control the relations among chemicals. The same kind of research problem occurs when social science researchers attempt to relate homicide rates to capital punishment. There are simply too many confounding and unmeasured variables operating simultaneously for an interplace analysis, a time series, or a combination analysis, and one cannot perform a pure experiment by arranging for a random group to be subjected to capital punishment. What then can one do under these circumstances to arrive at optimum sentences for various crimes and prior records? The answer might be some type of deductive approach whereby we begin with certain accepted premises, preferably ones that have empirical validation, and then deduce from those premises what the optimums ought to be, rather than rely on unreliable statistical regression coefficients.

THE AVERAGE AS THE OPTIMUM

One could arrive at determinate sentences by simply codifying the previous averages for each crime. That would have the benefit of reducing the disparities that otherwise exist across judges, defendants, and places within a given state, ethnic groups, and other ways of grouping cases. The usual justification for codifying the previous averages is simply because they are readily available, not because they are considered to be optimum in terms of minimizing the sum of the holding costs and the releasing costs. Perhaps, however, they actually may be optimum if we are willing to assume that the average sentence for a given crime represents the collective good judgement of a set of judges in those cases from which the average was calculated. In other words, maybe those judges collectively, although not individually by judge or by case, implicitly arrive at optimums, even though they do not explicitly make any statistical or mathematical analysis. This part of the chapter is designed to explore in what sense the basic model can be used to consider the average as the optimum. By average sentence in this context is meant the average amount of time actually served by a defendant who is sent to prison for a given crime. In that sense, the averages represent the collective wisdom of not just the judges, but also the legislators who establish the legal constraints within which the judges operate, and the parole boards and prison administrators who modify the sentences imposed in determining the sentences actually served.

Common Sense Reasonableness

There are occurrences in the prior analysis that lead one toward working with the average sentence per crime, although those occurrences do not prove that the average is the optimum. For example, in the power function approach, the optimum is $L^* = [-1/(b_1 a(R)^{b_2})]$ raised to the power $1/b_1 - 1$). With that formulation, what happens when a convicted defendant has no prior record? The mathematical answer involves inserting a zero in place of R, which causes the fraction in brackets to be equal to $1/0$, assuming b_1 is negative and b_2 is positive. The ratio $1/0$ yields an infinitely large quotient, since the size of the quotient keeps increasing as the denominator gets smaller until it reaches infinity when the denominator becomes zero. We thus have infinity raised to a negative power, again assuming b_1 is negative. That exponentiation yields one divided by infinity, which is the equivalent of zero. Thus the formula tells us that if defendants have no prior record, they should receive a zero sentence. This recommendation lacks reasonableness, since we feel that defendants committing a serious crime should be imprisoned even if it is their first crime. The question then becomes what sentence should be received if the formula is incapable of recommending any sentence other than zero when R is zero. A logical answer is to have a decision rule that says if R is zero, then the convicted defendant gets the average sentence that has been handed down for that crime to defendants who have no prior record. If, however, we adopt that decision rule for defendants with no prior record, then we might wonder why we do not adopt a similar decision rule for defendants with some prior record. Those defendants would then receive the average sentence given to defendants who had some prior record, or to those who had the same R score.

Another occurrence that leads toward working with the average sentences per crime and per prior record is the analysis of the optimums in Table 8-1. What happens there is that we look at the optimum recommended figures for each crime, and we have a tendency to say that some seem reasonable and some seem unreasonable. More important, we have a tendency to say implicitly or explicitly that reasonableness depends on what the previous average has been. If, however, we are going to use those averages to judge the validity of our alleged optimums, then we are in effect saying that the averages are the optimum or close to them. The situation may be like a psychologist who tries to develop a new IQ test and judges the validity of the test by how well the scores correlate with scores on the Stanford-Binet IQ test. If the Stanford-Binet test is such a good criterion to use in judging IQ tests, then why not just use the Stanford-Binet so long as it is applicable.

There are situations where we can justify the statistical optimum over the average, but the sentencing situation may not be one of them. A related example of where the statistical optimum makes more sense than the actual average is in determining the optimum percentage of defendants to hold in jail prior to trial. An optimum percent was calculated by obtaining data from numerous cities concerning their holding costs (HC), releasing costs (RC), and actual percentages of defendants held in jail prior to trial (%H). The numerical parameters for two regression equations were then determined of the form, $HC = A(\%H)^B$, and $RC = a(\%H)^b$. Total costs thus equal $A(\%H)^B + a(\%H)^b$ and the slope of total costs to percent held equals $BA(\%H)^{B-1} + ba(\%H)^{b-1}$. Setting that slope equal to zero and solving for %H yields an optimum %H of about 4 percent. The actual average, however, is 27 percent. One can justify the 4 percent as being a more meaningful optimum than the 27 percent on the grounds that the 4 percent reflects societal costs, whereas the 27 percent mainly reflects the cost considerations of the individual judges deciding whether to release or hold defendants. The individual judges do not personally bear the incarceration costs, the lost income costs, or the bitterness costs that relate to holding defendants in jail. Rather, the individual judges are more concerned with the embarrassment of a released defendant not appearing in court or committing a crime while released, even though the objective probabilities of those events occurring may be rather low.[15]

In the sentencing context, however, judges do seem to be sentencing in accordance with what they implicitly perceive the societal holding and releasing costs to be. Thus there is less of a gap between individual and societal benefit-cost considerations in post-conviction sentencing as contrasted to pretrial release, and that kind of discrepancy cannot justify accepting the optimums of Table 8-2 (or a similar table) over the actual averages. A general principle seems to be that working with a benefit-cost perspective is more effective for achieving societal goals when (1) alternative policies can be meaningfully related to those goals, and (2) existing decisions tend to reflect individual goals, with the individual goals generally being in conflict with the societal goals. An averaging approach is more effective when either of those criteria is absent.

Incapacitation and General Deterrence

A mathematical or deductive justification for using the average as the optimum should take into consideration the empirical realities which the statistical analysis has revealed. The main empirical reality seems to be that there is virtually no reliable relation between length of sentence (L) and severity (S) or delay (D) of subsequent criminal behavior, when holding prior record (R) constant. This statement is not the same as saying there is no relation at all. That would be untrue since there are some patterns in Table 8-1. For example, in three-fourths of the crime categories, there was a positive relation (b_2) between prior record and S^2/D, and in more than half the crime categories there was a negative relation (b_1) between sentence length and S^2/D. That kind of consistency, however, is not good enough on which to base a sentencing system. Even when the direction of the coefficients seems reasonable, the magnitudes may sometimes be unreasonably high or low. Given the unreliability of the direction and magnitude of the coefficients, one can possibly conclude that the statistical relation between sentence length and postsentence behavior is too unreliable to be part of a valid sentencing system.

This may amount to saying that within the range of the actual cases, there may be very little maturation, deterrence, or rehabilitation. There is no question that if 90-year-olds are released from prison, they will be less capable and less likely to engage in vehicle theft, narcotic offenses, burglary, or the other crimes, as compared to 25-year-olds. Defendants, however, are not kept in prison from age 25 to age 90. In the vehicle theft cases, for example, the average defendant went to prison at age 24 and stayed for a year and a half. He was thus released while still in his mid-twenties which does not allow for much maturation. As far as deterrence is concerned, his perception of the unpleasantness of going to prison may have been changed in the direction that it is not as unpleasant as he originally thought it would be. Deterrence also means that the defendant upon being released is supposed to have a more socially desirable notion of the benefits of legal activities relative to criminal activities. Having an additional prison record may, however, decrease the legal opportunities available, and prison may increase the ability of the ex-convict to successfully pursue a criminal career as a result of learning from fellow convicts. Rehabilitation means little unless it is capable of substantially changing an ex-convict's future job opportunities in a favorable direction, which prison seldom does.

Although maturation, deterrence, and rehabilitation may not be reliably effective, imprisonment can still be justified on two grounds. One ground is incapacitation or a custodial justification, whereby one recognizes that at least during the time convicted defendants are held in prison, they cannot engage in the socially detrimental behavior for which they were convicted, at least not against people outside the prison. This might be referred to as a safety-deposit-box theory of imprisonment, not in the sense that convicts are valuable and need to be kept locked up to keep them from being stolen, but rather in the sense that outsiders are valuable and need protection against theft. The second ground is general deterrence of other people (other than the convict) who may be deterred by knowing people go to prison for criminal behavior, as contrasted to specific deterrence in the sense of decreasing the subsequent criminal behavior of the convicted individual. Neither of those two grounds are adequately considered in the statistical regression approach. General deterrence is not considered at all as a releasing cost. Incapacitation gets lost in talking about subsequent criminal behavior, rather than the criminal behavior that otherwise might occur while the convict is in prison, although subsequent behavior was defined as behavior subsequent to the start of incarceration until a postrelease felony. A mathematical deductive justification should consider both incapacitation and general deterrence. A big advantage of deductive analysis is that it often can meaningfully consider such factors that cannot be so readily measured as part of a statistical analysis.[16]

Mathematical Justification

REFORMULATING RC AS M/L

The above analysis is leading to a reformulation of the concept of releasing costs that will be closely related to the basic model, but will not use statistical regression coefficients. First let us reiterate that our formulation of the holding costs still makes sense, namely that $HC = 1(L)$. This equation simply says that for every month of imprisonment, the holding costs go up one holding cost unit, monetary unit, or however the holding costs are measured. A new, more meaningful way to now define releasing costs might be $RC = M(L)^{-1}$. M symbolizes the mean or average sentence length for the crime under consideration. M is the equivalent of the "a" coefficient in the basic model, and -1 is the equivalent of the "b" coefficient. $RC = M(L)^{-1}$ is also the algebraic equivalent of $RC = M/L$, but we can write the equation the first way to show its relation to the basic model, and for ease in finding the RC slope. What, however, does this new formulation mean in common-sense terms, and in terms of incapacitation and general deterrence?

The simplest situation involves a defendant who receives the minimum possible prison sentence under our measurement system, which is one month in prison, since judges do not give prison sentences less than a month where felonies are involved. If L is 1, the equation becomes $RC = M$. That equation tells us the costs will be the equivalent in harm to society of the average severity of the crime for which the defendant was convicted. We are in effect saying that if the average defendant were released, there is a good chance the same crime would be committed over again or a crime of similar severity. The best way to measure how much society is harmed by a given crime is to determine what the average sentence is that society inflicts upon people who commit the given crime. Society expresses these values mainly through judges and the legislation they apply. Most judges are elected or are appointed by elected governors or presidents, with the consent of elected senators or legislators. Thus they roughly represent society's values, especially if one talks in terms of the average sentence for a given crime across many judges and many cases. This kind of averaging tends to balance judges who are overly severe and those who are overly lenient. By saying M represents the likely harm, we are saying that incapacitating the defendant may prevent that harm from occurring. We are also saying that the judges collectively give an average sentence of M because they perceive another kind of releasing cost, namely the opportunity cost in terms of the lost general deterrence if they do not give such a sentence. Thus, M represents the likely harm from the minimum sentence of 1L both in terms of lost incapacitation and lost general deterrence.

The next situation to discuss in order to clarify the equation RC = M/L is the situation where the sentence is greater than one month, i.e., where L moves up to two, three, etc. With each successive month in lengthening the defendant's sentence, the releasing costs go down by one month. Thus, if the average sentence for a given crime is twenty-four months (M), then if a given defendant receives a one-month sentence (L), the releasing cost (RC) is twenty-four. If the defendant is given a two-month sentence, the releasing cost is twelve. For a three-month sentence, it is eight, and so on. The releasing costs thus go down as the defendant's sentence lengthens because that kind of delay decreases the number of subsequent crimes the defendant is likely to commit by shortening the remainder of his criminal career. The releasing cost, however, cannot reach zero unless L reaches infinity which is the equivalent of the defendant passing into the hereafter.

WEIGHTING SEVERITY AND FINDING OPTIMUM LENGTH

One defect in the above analysis is that it implies that M and L are of equal importance. In other words, it implies that the releasing cost due to lost incapacitation and lost general deterrence is equal in importance to one month of delay due to being incarcerated. Society, however, would probably consider the numerator in the ratio M/L to be at least twice as important as the denominator, which can be shown by squaring M. That improvement results in changing the equation to RC = M^2/L. We can now define the total costs as TC = $M^2(L)^{-1}$ + (L), or TC = M^2/L + 1L. The slope of the total costs relative to L thus becomes $-M^2/L^2 + 1$.

If we now set that slope equal to zero to find where total cost bottoms out, we get the following:

$-M^2/L^2 + 1 = 0$ (Setting the slope of TC equal to zero)

$-M^2/L^2 = -1$ (Subtracting 1 from both sides)

$M^2/L^2 = 1$ (Multiplying both sides by -1)

$L^2/M^2 = 1$ (Inverting both sides)

$L^2 = M^2$ (Multiplying both sides by M^2)

$L^* = M$ (Taking the square root of both sides)

The above analysis proves that the average or mean sentence per crime is the optimum sentence if one is willing to accept the reasonable premises from which that conclusion is deduced. Those premises are (1) the releasing cost from a minimum sentence is equal to the average severity to society of the original crime, as indicated by the average sentence; (2) the releasing cost is discounted by the length of the sentence, since longer sentences decrease the opportunities for subsequent crimes; and (3) reducing severity is twice as important as the benefit of a month of delay or the cost of a month of incarceration.[17]

ALTERNATIVE WAYS OF REDEFINING RC

An alternative way of arriving at a similar conclusion is to think of the holding costs as being 1L, and the releasing costs as being PM^2. P stands for the probability that released convicts will commit a crime with a severity of the average sentence given to the crime which they committed (M). We continue to square M to show that severity is twice as important as the probability that such a crime will be committed. We are in effect discounting the predicted criminal behavior by the probability of its occurring. We should, however, note that the probability goes down as time passes, i.e., as the length of sentence is extended. Thus, P bears a relation to L of the form $P = a(L)^b$, where b is a negative number indicating that there is a negative convex relation between P and L. We can, therefore, substitute $a(L)^b$ for P in defining the releasing costs as $RC = a(L)^b M^2$. However, since b is a negative number, that expression is algebraically equal to $M^2/(aL^b)$, with b as a positive number. Thus, TC equals $M^2/(aL^b) + L$, which is quite close to our previous formulation of $TC = M^2/L + L$, The big defect in this new formulation is not just that it is redundant to the previous simpler formulation, but rather that it reintroduces statistical induction by bringing back in the unreliable regression coefficients of ''a'' and ''b''.

Another alternative way of arriving at a similar conclusion is to think of the numerator of the releasing costs as being S or S^2. Doing so attempts to recognize that the harm done by releasing a defendant may not be equal to the average severity of the crime previously committed, but rather equal to the severity of the defendant's subsequent criminal behavior. S, however, is a function of M in the sense that if we know how severe the immediate crime was, we should be able to predict something about what the subsequent criminal behavior is likely to be. Thus, S can probably be expressed as $S = a(M)^b$ with b being a positive number to show that there is a positive increasing, constant, or decreasing relation between S and M. If we use that formulation, then total cost becomes $TC = a(M)^b/L + L$. We can still square M to show its relative importance to a delay-month and an incarceration-month. TC thus becomes $TC + aM^{2b}/L + L$, which is quite close to our previous formulation of $TC = M^2/L + L$. As with the other alternative formulation, this alternative is not only redundant to the simpler formulation, but it again reintroduces the unreliable regression coefficients of "a" and "b".

Empirical Averages

AVERAGE SENTENCE AND SPREAD BY PRIOR RECORD

After determining that the average sentence may be considered the optimum sentence, it seems logical to show what the average sentences are for each of the eight crime categories by prior record, as in Table 8-2. It indicates for each crime category what the mean or average sentence was for defendants with no prior record or with some prior record, using the same Federal Bureau of Prison's data that was used for Table 8-1. The total sample size for each crime in Table 8-2 is larger than the total sample size in Table 8-1, because some cases that are usable in Table 8-2 cannot be used in Table 8-1 for lack of information on S and D which is relevant to Table 8-1. We could have provided for more crime categories and more prior record categories if more cases were analyzed. Fortunately for research purposes, but unfortunately from a societal perspective, there are plenty of federal criminal cases on which sentencing data is compiled by the Administrative Office of the U.S. Courts. That additional data might be especially relevant to determining the average or optimum sentences for additional crimes and for breaking apart burglary/larceny, robbery/kidnapping, and the other multiple crime categories in Table 8-2.[18]

One especially interesting aspect of the data used to generate the top part of Table 8-2 is the great diversity of sentences for each crime, even when all the defendants have no prior record. For example, the average defendant in vehicle theft defendants with no prior record received a sentence of 15 months, but 35 percent of those 80 defendants were more than 25 percent above that average, and 18 percent of the 80 defendants were more than 25 percent below that average. The 25 percent figure is used because it is frequently mentioned as an upper and lower threshold for allowing judges to consider aggravating and mitigating circumstances under determinate sentencing. Thus, if determinate sentencing were being applied to the vehicle theft defendants who had no prior record, then more than half of them would receive a lower or higher sentence than they did receive. The same is true of almost half the defendants in fraud check/counterfeiting, burglary/larceny, and robbery/kidnapping, and it is true of more than one-third of the defendants in moonshine, nonrobbery assault, and narcotics offenses, although the tax/embezzlement defendants are treated with more uniformly low sentences. A much higher percent of the cases would be outside the upper and lower threshold of 15 percent were used as the threshold figure rather than 25 percent, and if this analysis were applied to all defendants including those who do have a prior record.

The diversity seems even greater if one calculates the average devia-

TABLE 8-2. AVERAGE SENTENCE BY CRIME AND BY PRIOR RECORD

Crime Category	No Prior Record M_0	N_0	Some Prior Record M_1	N_1
Vehicle Theft	15	(80)	21	(261)
Narcotics Offense	20	(43)	27	(89)
Burglary or Larceny	16	(41)	21	(99)
Robbery or Kidnapping	37	(17)	71	(15)
Fraudulent Checks or Counterfeiting	16	(13)	22	(55)
Income Tax Evasion or Embezzlement	10	(19)	30	(6)
Nonrobbery Assault	38	(28)	46	(12)
Moonshine	10	(33)	13	(73)

Crime Category	L^*	L^* (R = 10)	L^* (R = 100)	r
Vehicle Theft	$14(R)^{.11}$	18	23	.33
Narcotics Offense	$18(R)^{.10}$	23	29	.36
Burglary or Larceny	$13(R)^{.09}$	16	20	.28
Robbery or Kidnapping	$22(R)^{.26}$	41	74	.53
Fraudulent Checks or Counterfeiting	$15(R)^{.07}$	17	20	.21
Income Tax Evasion or Embezzlement	$9(R)^{.24}$	16	-28	.52
Nonrobbery Assault	$32(R)^{.03}$	34	36	.07
Moonshine	$8(R)^{.13}$	11	15	.46

Notes to the table:
(1) Prior record is expressed in terms of months of previous imprisonment.
(2) The numbers in parentheses indicate the number of cases on which those averages are based.

tion in months or other time units for those who are above or below the thresholds. For example, the vehicle theft defendants who are more than 25 percent above the 15-month average received an average sentence of 61 months which is more than 400 percent above the 15-month average. Similarly, the vehicle theft defendants who are more than 25 percent below the 15-month average received an average sentence of 4 months, which is only 27 percent of the 15-month average. Most of the other crimes involved even bigger ratios between the upper average and the overall average, and between the overall average and the lower average. Those measures of diversity when crime and prior record are held constant do tend to indicate the need for more uniformity in sentencing.

PREDICTING SENTENCE LENGTH FROM PRIOR RECORD

A better way to handle the relation between prior record and sentence length is to develop a regression equation like that shown under L* in Table 8-2. In the vehicle theft cases, for example, doing so involves inserting into a computer two items of information for each of the 261 cases in which the defendant had some prior record. One item is the sentence the defendant received (L), and the second item is the defendant's prior record (R), both expressed in months of imprisonment. With that information and a standard nonlinear or power-function program, the computer is capable of generating a meaningful scale coefficient (i.e., "a") and elasticity coefficient (i.e., "b") relating L to R. All the defendants for a given crime are used to calculate those coefficients, but the bottom of Table 8-2 should only be applied to defendants with some prior record. The top of Table 8-2 should be applied to defendants with no prior record, since applying the bottom of Table 8-2 will result in a recommendation of a zero sentence for defendants with a zero prior record.[19]

A nonlinear power function is used rather than a linear or constant returns approach because prior record relates positively to length of sentence in a diminishing returns way, such that sentences are not increased proportionately as prior records increase. With a hand calculator, one can easily insert into the power functions under L* any prior record expressed in months in order to obtain a predicted or optimum sentence length. For example, if a convicted vehicle theft defendant has a prior record of 10 months, the predicted or optimum sentence is $15(10)^{.11}$, which is 19 months as indicated on row 1.

These predictions or optimums in Table 8-2 are much more reliable than those in Table 8-1 as indicated by a number of criteria. First, the dots represented by the cases when graphed cluster closely to the positive-concave, diminishing-returns curves, as indicated by the relatively high correlation coefficients. That can be seen by comparing the "r" column of Table 8-2 with the "r" column of Table 8-1. Second, there are non-zero sentences recommended for every crime. Third, in every instance, the categories of defendants with some prior record receive longer sentences than those with no prior record. None of those three criteria are satisfactorily met by the approach that attempts to relate S^2/D to L and R in Table 8-1, as contrasted to simply relating L to R in Table 8-2.

SUBSTANTIVE MEANINGS ACROSS CRIMES

There are some interesting substantive findings in Table 8-2. First, although prior record within a given crime category is a relatively good predictor of sentence length, the relation is not very steep. This means that although the case dots may be on the curve, it is a rather flat curve, which means that sentences do not go up very much as prior records go up. The relation is not only rather flat, but it gets even flatter as prior record worsens. A point is never reached, however, where having a long prior record results in a reduced sentence compared to those with a short prior record, except when using prior record categories that have an unreliably small number of cases. Second, the crimes differ concerning how much of a difference prior record makes. A good way to see that is to observe how much M changes when one goes from no prior record to some prior record, or how much L* changes when one goes from R = 10 to R = 100, or the size of the elasticity coefficient in the L* formula. The smallest change is in fraudulent checks, which may indicate that judges do not feel very disturbed if a bad-check passer has previously been a bad-check passer, since it is almost an expected recurrence. On the other hand, a repeater with regard to robbery or kidnapping is taken more seriously, and the sentence is likely to be doubled as a result of having a prior record in that category. The tax/embezzlement category has too few repeater cases to reliably interpret its pattern (only six), as does nonrobbery assault (only twelve).

The most interesting substantive findings may be comparing crimes not with regard to the sentencing on recommitting a crime, but rather the sentencing on the initial offense. In that sense, the crime categories seem to fall into three groups. The lowest consists of moonshine and tax/embezzlement (M = 10). The relatively light sentencing treatment for those crimes may reflect the victimless nature of moonshine and a white-collar bias in tax/embezzlement cases. The highest categories consist of robbery/kidnapping and nonrobbery assault (M equals 37 and 38 respectively). These crimes are dangerous crimes against persons on which society places a high negative value. The middle categories consist of crimes against property, such as vehicle theft, burglary/larceny, and checks/counterfeiting. They are not as physically dangerous as the high-sentence crimes, but clearly not semitolerated like the low-sentence crimes. Narcotics offenses can range from tolerated marijuana matters to large-scale and physically dangerous heroin matters. This three-part rank order seems reasonable, but we cannot say it is reasonable or optimum simply because it represents actual averages. The reasonableness of the values implicit in that ranking depends ultimately on the holding costs (which are roughly the same per month for each crime) and the releasing costs. The releasing costs, however, may be meaningfully measured by taking into consideration what the average sentences are, along with the above-mentioned premises with regard to (1) discounting those averages by the passage of time, and (2) considering those averages to be twice as important to reduce as the other cost variables.

SOME CONCLUSIONS

The previous analysis leads to three types of conclusions, namely research needed, substantive policy recommendations, and policy analysis implications.

Research Needed

The research needed could include improvements with regard to both Tables 8-1 and 8-2. Perhaps a more sophisticated data analysis for Table 8-1 could generate meaningful regression coefficients between crime severity and length of sentence and also between crime severity and prior record. By "more meaningful" we mean (1) showing negative relations between S and L; (2) showing positive relations between S and R; (3) defining S to consider the harm a released defendant can do, discounted by the extent to which the harm is delayed; (4) explaining large portion of the variation on S; and (5) resulting in magnitudes for the recommended sentences that have some face validity or common-sense reasonableness. This, however, may be impossible given the nature of the real world regarding how those variables actually relate to each other.

As an alternative research design, one might explore the question of arriving at an optimum choice between the decision to imprison and the decision to release on either supervised probation or a suspended sentence, rather than the optimum level problem of how long should the imprisonment be. Arriving at an optimum in-out choice involves determining for each individual case (1) the probability that the defendant will commit a subsequent felony if released during the time period when the defendant would otherwise be in prison; (2) the relative harm (A) that is done by making an error of imprisoning the defendant for that time period when no felony would have been committed if the defendant were released; and (3) the relative harm (B) that is done by making an error of releasing the defendant for that time period if a felony would have then been committed. One can show that the optimum decision under those circumstances is to imprison if P is greater than $A/(A + B)$ and to release if P is less than $A/(A + B)$. For example, if under the circumstances it is considered twice as bad to make a Type B error as a Type A error, and we fix the relative value of the worst error at 100, then the value of $A/(A + B)$ is $50/(50 + 100)$, or .33. That means the probability should be greater than .33 of a subsequent felony during the time period under consideration in order to justify imprisoning rather than releasing the defendant. Research, however, is needed on how one can meaningfully make those relative value determinations and probability predictions for specific defendants, average defendants, or defendants of various kinds. Perhaps there may be substantial deterrent value in the decision to imprison or not, even though there does not seem to be a meaningful pattern with regard to the relation between length of imprisonment and subsequent deterrence.[20]

Further research can improve on Table 8-2 by considering many more crimes. It could use some variables in addition to prior record to more accurately predict sentence length. Such additional variables, however, should be those that can be constitutionally considered in giving different sentences for the same crime. They might include (1) being a juvenile versus being an adult; (2) having multiple charges versus a single charge; and (3) being willing to plead guilty versus being found guilty after a bench or jury trial. The additional variables could not include race, sex, economic class, urbanism, or other variables that may have good predictive power, but cannot be constitutionally considered as part of a sentencing system. Even so, it might be quite interesting to do a kind of simulation analysis, whereby one determines what the recommended sentences would be if those variables were considered, and what the sentences would be if those variables were not considered or not allowed to be considered. A good predictor of crime performance (such as prior record) could constitutionally be used even if it correlates with race, sex, etc., just as a good predictor of job performance (such as a test score) can be used even if it correlates with race, but race itself cannot be constitutionally used as a sentencing criterion.[21]

Policy Recommendations

This logically leads to the substantive policy implications. If one wants to reduce discrimination or disparities along race, sex, class, and other lines or simply reduce random disparities across defendants, judges, and places, one can do so by legislating that the previous averages shall be the future sentences. The legislation can provide that judges can go above or below those sentences by a given percentage, where there are explicit aggravating or mitigating circumstances. The legislature can also provide that the sentence imposed should be twice the average sentence served to allow a day off for each day of good behavior.

As of now, determinate sentences like sentences in general tend to be arrived at by legislatures through a kind of political horse-trading. One legislator on the relevant drafting committee may feel especially concerned about the need for more severe sentences in rape cases. Another legislator may feel especially concerned about the need for less severe sentences in marijuana possession or consenting sex cases. Still other legislators may have strong feelings on embezzlers, consumer fraud, or other matters. The resulting sentence recommendations may involve each legislator making some concessions in order to obtain the type of sentences especially desired. Perhaps, however, the legislators should use the previous average sentences per crime and per prior record category as the starting point in their negotiations. The negotiating process can be defended on the grounds that the previous averages may not reflect current values. Individual legislators, however, may also not reflect current values but their personal feelings (and/or those of interest groups) and the coincidence of being on an important drafting committee. This, however, is almost an inherent aspect of the legislative process. Discussing how to make legislators more representative, or how to decrease the power of senior legislators or key committees is beyond the purpose of this chapter.[22]

It is also beyond the purpose of this chapter to discuss in detail whether a determinate-sentencing system ought to be adopted, as contrasted to what the determinate sentences should be. This broader adoption subject is discussed in the literature referred to in the introductory paragraph of this chapter. One might note, however, that the more obvious benefits of determinate sentencing include (1) the elimination of arbitrariness at the parole board level if there is no longer a provision for parole board reductions (although a safety valve may need to be provided for governors to pardon and to commute executions); (2) the reduction of arbitrariness at the judicial level if the sentencing range is narrowed; (3) the elimination of a prosecutor's punitive recommendation of a particularly severe sentence after a defendant who dared go to trial has been found guilty; and (4) the reduction of some plea bargaining abuses by taking sentences out of the realm of bargaining (although maintaining the fixing of the charges and whether or not to prosecute). Decreasing absolute discretion at those levels does mean increasing the relative discretion of the legislature to control sentencing decisions. In doing so, however, legislators tend to think in the abstract when they are assigning a sentence to a crime, whereas parole boards, judges, and prosecutors assign sentences to specific individuals whose irrelevant racial, class, personality and other characteristics may influence those sentences. The main disadvantage of determinate sentencing is that it decreases the flexibility of judges to consider special circumstances that go beyond the plus or minus 25 percent for aggravation or mitigation.[23]

If the legislature or a sentencing commission does not want to make the previous averages obligatory on the judges (but rather discretionary), then devices can be developed to encourage (but not require) the judges to sentence closer to those previous averages. Such devices or incentives can include (1) publicizing the average sentences among judges or the public and how deviant each judge is from the averages; (2) requiring judges who want to deviate from an average sentence to write an opinion justifying their deviation; (3) requiring judges who want to deviate in a specific case to call in two other judges to jointly decide the case or at least to confer; and (4) allowing for automatic or easier appeals when a sentence deviates from the average.

Using the previous averages can be justified not simply because they are readily available and understandable, but because a case can be made for saying that they represent a type of optimum sentences. They can be considered optimum in a mathematical sense that defines an optimum sentence as the sentence where marginal or incremental benefits equal marginal or incremental costs. This is the same as saying, L^* is where the sum of the holding costs and the releasing costs have been minimized. The average sentences can also be considered optimum in a less economic, more political sense by emphasizing that those averages across judges and cases collectively represent a combination of (1) representative normative values concerning the harm done to society by different crimes and incarceration costs, and (2) empirical perceptions concerning the likelihood that the average defendant, if release, will recommit a similar crime or that other people will be encouraged to do so. Those previous average sentences actually represent the collective wisdom of legislators and parole boards, not only judges.

This does not mean that the previous average sentences are optimum because they are known by an omniscient being who can accurately predict the behavior of each individual defendant and the average defendant. They also may not be optimum as known by an omnibenevolent being who has perfect values, since optimum sentencing is a combination of facts and values. Nevertheless, the previous averages can be considered to be about as optimum as we can humanly get. One might, however, reasonably argue that we can humanly improve upon those previous averages. The above-mentioned research needs may facilitate such improvements by clarifying (1) relations between sentence length and subsequent behavior, and (2) the variables that influence those previous averages.

Optimizing Methods

On a still higher level, the previous analysis may have important implications with regard to the concepts and methods of optimizing. In the sentencing context and in numerous other substantive contexts, there are two kinds of optimizing. One kind involves finding an optimum policy through the use of benefit-cost accounting, statistical regression analysis between goals and alternative policies, or other inductive reasoning processes working with large data sets and attempting sophisticated measurement of the relevant goal variables and policy variables. This kind of optimizing might be called explicit or disaggregated optimizing. A second kind involves arriving at an optimum policy by policy makers or decision makers rather than researchers through a kind of holistic or gestalt approach that implicitly, but not explicitly, considers social values and perceived facts. This kind of optimizing might be called implicit or aggregated optimizing. These alternative and supplementary approaches closely correspond to the terms rationalism and incrementalism in policy analysis, although rationalism seeks to emphasize arriving at an optimum all at once by considering various policies and goals, and incrementalism emphasizes arriving at an optimum through trial and error steps. Both approaches could involve statistical and deductive analysis. In this sentencing context, a more meaningful distinction might be whether the sentences are justified by showing the benefits-costs of each sentencing alternative, or are justified by showing that that is how things are generally done.

It is desirable to make explicit the existing policies in any substantive context so that people will be informed of what to expect. It also seems desirable to make explicit the process whereby policies are arrived at, so that people can know in a democratic society how to influence policies and how they are influenced. It may not be so necessary, however, in all situations to try to disaggregate the benefits and the costs and to relate them statistically or in an accounting fashion to the alternative policies. Explicit optimizing may often be virtually impossible, or worse it may lead to ignoring or de-emphasizing important but not so readily measurable variables in the relations. Explicit optimizing may also often be unnecessary in situations where the individual goals of the decision-makers are not in conflict with societal goals. A deductive analysis that seeks to better understand average decisions and how they might be implicitly optimum might often be a more productive kind of policy analysis than statistical regression analysis or benefit-cost accounting. Perhaps we need to give more credit to how well the human mind works in making policies and decisions without explicitly doing any calculations, at least when we average many human minds together in many cases.

APPENDIX 8-1. GLOSSARY OF TERMS IN OPTIMUM SENTENCING LEVELS

See the list of formulas in Appendix 8-2 for how various concepts are calculated.

Symbol	Represents	Page First Appearing
BASIC VARIABLES (all measures in months)		
L	Length of basic sentence served.	111
S	Severity of sentence subsequent to completing the basic sentence.	113
C	Clean-time, or months of no felonious behavior subsequent to completing the basic sentence.	113
D	Delay of subsequent sentence from the start of the basic sentence to the start of the subsequent sentence, where $D = L + C$.	113
AGGREGATE OF COST VARIABLES		
HC	Holding cost, or the cost of holding a convict in prison for one month.	111
RC	Releasing cost, or the cost of releasing a defendant from prison in light of S and D.	112
TC	Total cost, or $HC + RC$, with some consideration for the relative weights of the differing measurement units.	112
PARAMETERS OF THE RELATIONSHIP BETWEEN LENGTH AND COSTS		
A	The holding cost if a convict is held in prison for zero months, with the relation $HC = A + B(L)$, where $A = 0$.	111
B	The increase in holding cost as a result of a one-month increase in sentence length.	111
a	The releasing cost or amount of harm done by a convict who has been released after only one month, with the relation $RC = a(L)^b$.	112
b	The percentage increase in harm done as a result of a one-percent reduction in sentence length.	112
CONTROL VARIABLES (all measured in months)		
R	Prior record as indicated by months of sentences previously served before the basic sentence.	116
A	Age at beginning of basic sentence.	121
J	Duration of longest job held prior to basic sentence.	121
OPTIMUM SENTENCE LENGTH		
L*	Optimum sentence length to minimize $HC + RC$,	113

in light of the relations between length and
HC, RC, and TC.

AVERAGE AS OPTIMUM

M	The mean or average sentence length for a given crime.	128
P	The probability that a released convict will commit a crime with a severity of the average sentence given to the crime which he already committed.	130

MISCELLANEOUS SYMBOLS

N	Number of cases in a crime category.	118
r	The correlation between one variable and another, or a measure of how well a relation-equation fits data.	118
Y	Any dependent variable, or variable being predicted to.	117
X	Any independent variable, or variable being predicted from.	117

APPENDIX 8-2. BASIC FORMULAS IN OPTIMUM SENTENCING LEVELS

See the glossary of terms in Appendix 8-1 for the definition of the symbols.

Formula	Represents	Page First Appearing
THE BASIC MODEL		
1. $HC = A + B(L)$, or $HC = 1(L)$	Holding costs related to sentence length.	111, 112
2. $RC = a(L)^b$	Releasing costs related to sentence length.	112
3. $TC = HC + RC$	Total costs related to holding costs and releasing costs.	112
4. $TC = 1(L) + a(L)^b$	Total costs related to sentence length.	112
5. $1 + ba(L)^{b-1}$	The slope of TC relative to L, given equation 4.	112
6. $L^* = -1/(ba)$ raised to the power $1/(b-1)$	The optimum sentence length, given expression 7 set equal to O.	113
EXPANDING ON THE BASIC MODEL		
7. $RC = S^2/D = a(L)^{b_1}(R)^{b_2}$	Releasing costs related to sentence length and prior record, with releasing costs defined as severity squared discounted by delay.	116

MISCELLANEOUS FORMULAS

21. $Y = aX^b$	Y related to X to show a one-directional curved-relation, like the left or right side of a hill or valley.	117
22. baX^{b-1}	The slope of Y relative to X, given equation 21.	117
23. $Y = a + b_1X + b_2X^2$	Y related to X to show a two-directional curved-relation, like a valley or a hill.	123
24. $b_1 + 2b_2X$	The slope of Y relative to X, given equation 23.	
25. $X^{-b} = 1/X^b$	Any variable raised to a negative exponent equals the reciprocal of the variable, with the denominator raised to the same exponent but positive in sign.	129

APPENDIX 8-3: INCORPORATING GENERAL DETERRENCE INTO THE RELEASING COSTS CURVE

What may be needed as part of a future research project dealing with optimum sentencing is to add an expression to our basic equation which will take into consideration the relation between sentence length and (1) general deterrence as well as (2) specific deterrence-incapacitation-maturation-rehabilitation. We can thus talk about general and specific releasing costs. The general releasing costs relate to the effect of length of sentence on deterring the general public from crime committing. The specific releasing costs relate to the subsequent crime-committing of the convicts themselves.

As of now, our releasing costs equation is basically $S^2/D = a(L)^{b_1}(R)^{b_2}$, but that equation only considers specific releasing costs. We need to determine the parameters for the relation between crime rates and sentence length using the United States as of different points in time as the units of analysis, rather than using individual convicts as the units of analysis. More specifically, we could use data for the United States as of 1980, 1979, and so on back through about 1960. The data would basically consist of two items of information for each year. One item would be the average sentence length for that year for the crime we are analyzing, such as federal larceny. That kind of information might be available from the Federal

Bureau of Prisons. As an alternative, we could use the average sentence handed down for each year (rather than actually served), and divide by two on the assumption that the sentences which judges give are roughly twice what defendants actually serve. The sentences handed down by federal judges for each year are available from the reports or the raw data of the Administrative Office of U.S. Courts or the Federal Judicial Center. The second item of information would be the larceny crime rate for each of those years, which is relevant to the dependant variable. In order to express all the variables in terms of the same units of measurement, namely months, we could multiply the number of crimes by the average sentence for each year. We would then have crime months or crime severity (S) as the dependent variable, and sentence months or length (L) as the independent variable.

If, however, we do a regression analysis of the form, $S = a(L)^b$, we are not likely to obtain a negative exponent on the right side of the equation (showing that long sentences have a negative influence on crime rates) for two reasons. First, even if sentence length reduces crime rates, crime rates probably have a stronger influence on increasing sentence length. In other words, if federal larceny is increasing, this probably causes judges to feel more upset about its occurrence and to react by handing down more severe sentences. That tends to convert what otherwise would be a negative relation into a positive one. Second, both crime rates and sentence length may be influenced by other variables that cause them to rise and fall together. For example, a conservative presidential administration may stimulate or reflect public opinion and judicial opinion that is oriented toward more severe sentences. Likewise, a conservative administration may place more weight on reducing inflation than on reducing unemployment and discriminatory practices, which in turn may generate some additional criminal behavior. To get at both the reciprocal causation and the spurious causation, we can work with a more sophisticated regression equation of the form, $S_t = a(L_{t-1})^{b_1}(S_{t-1})^{b_2}$. By relating sentences of the prior year (L_{t-1}) to crime severity of the subsequent year (S_t), we reduce the extent to which crime severity causes sentence length, rather than vice versa. By holding constant crime severity of the prior year (S_{t-1}), we thereby indirectly hold constant all variables that influence crime severity with the exception of sentence length. The result should be to obtain a more meaningful negative value for b_1 than we otherwise would.

To combine the specific and the general releasing costs, we sum the two together to obtain an expression of the form $a(L)^{b_1}(R)^{b_2} + A(L_{t-1})^{B_1}(S_{t-1})^{B_2}$. To avoid confusion, the parameters for the general releasing costs are shown as capital letters. To express the total costs, we add the holding costs expressed in sentence months (L) to those two releasing costs. We then express the slope of total costs to sentence length using the rules previously mentioned for expressing slopes. The slope of TC to L is $b_1 a(R)^{b_2}(L)^{b_1-1} + B_1 A(S_{t-1})^{B_2}(L)^{B_1-1} + (L)$. We can then set that expression equal to zero to find the optimum value of L when total cost bottoms out. Doing that means inserting the computer-generated numerical values for a, b_1, b_2, A, B_1, and B_2. To get a numerical value for optimum L would also mean inserting the defendant's prior record expressed in months (R) and last year's crime rate severity for federal larceny (S_{t-1}). Solving for L in that equation would involve reiterative guessing, whereby we try different values on a programmable calculator until we obtain a value for L that causes the left side of the equation to be equal to zero.

Carrying out the above suggested research may provide some useful insights. The relations between sentence length and general releasing cost (or general deterrence) may, however, be at least as lacking in acceptable meaningfulness as the relations between sentence length and specific releasing costs. Thus, although the above research may substantially improve the analysis, the results may still fall short of the acceptable meaningfulness that can be obtained by averaging the sentences across judges and cases.

NOTES

The author acknowledges the helpfulness of Anne Schmidt of the National Institute of Justice and Daniel Glaser of the University of Southern California in providing him with the Federal Bureau of Prisons' data referred to in this chapter. Thanks are also owed to Eli Noam of the Columbia Graduate School of Business and Jameson Doig of the Princeton Woodrow Wilson School of Public Affairs for their helpful comments concerning this chapter.

1. On determinate sentencing in general, see A. Dershowitz, *Fair and Certain Punishment* (Hightstown, N.J.: McGraw Hill, 1976); D. Curtis, *Toward a Just and Effective Sentencing System: Agenda for Legislative Reform* (New York: Praeger, 1977); and R. Singer, *Just Desserts: Sentencing Based on Equality and Dessert* (Cambridge, Mass.: Ballinger, 1979).

2. On optimum sentencing, see Brian Forst, William Rhodes, and Charles Wellford, "Sentencing and Social Science Research for the Formulation of Federal Sentencing Guidelines," 7 *Hofstra Law Review* 355-78 (1979); Peter Aranson, "The Simple Analytics of Sentencing," in Gordon Tullock and Richard Wagner (eds.), *Policy Analysis and Deductive Reasoning* (Lexington, Mass.: Lexington-Heath, 1978); and S. Nagel, M. Neef and Thomas Weiman, "A Rational Method for Determining Prison Sentences," 61 *Judicature* 371-75 (1978). All three articles discuss the concept of optimum sentencing, but they do not offer data analysis applying the concept.

3. There are four different ways we could define optimum sentence, all of which are algebraically equal. They are (1) maximize the positive difference between holding benefits and holding costs, (2) maximize the positive difference between releasing benefits and releasing costs, (3) maximize the sum of the holding benefits and the releasing benefits, and (4) minimize the sum of the holding costs and the releasing costs. We choose the fourth alternative because it is easier to work

with sums than with differences, and because in the crime context, it is easier to work with costs than benefits. In other words, it is easier to talk about minimizing crime occurrence than it is to talk about maximizing crimes prevented.

One can prove that alternatives 1, 2, and 3 are equal to alternative 4 by noting that two negatives make a positive. More specifically, if we start with the first alternative, MAX (HB − HC), and we negate both sides of that expression, we get MIN (−HB + HC). Holding benefits, however, are just the releasing costs avoided. Thus, if we negate HB, we get RC. That is the same as saying MAX (HB − HC) equals MIN (RC + HC). Similarly, if we start with MAX (RB − RC) and negate both sides, we get MIN (−RB + RC), which equals MIN (HC + RC). This is so since the releasing benefits are just the holding costs avoided by releasing a defendant. Thus negating RB yields HC. If we start with MAX (HB + RB) and negate both sides, we get MIN (−HB − RB), which again equals MIN (RC + HC) for the above reasons.

On optimizing in general, see Samuel Richmond, *Operations Research for Management Decisions* (New York: Ronald, 1968), especially 3-126; and Michael Brennan, *Preface to Econometrics: An Introduction to Quantitative Methods in Economics* (Cincinnati: South-Western, 1973), especially pp. 1-192 and 308-52. On optimizing in a public policy context, see Michael White, et al., *Managing Public Systems: Analytic Techniques for Public Administration* (Belmont, Ca.: Duxbury, 1980), especially pp. 245-59 and pp. 278-90; and Edith Stokey and Richard Zeckhauser, *A Primer for Policy Analysis* (New York: Norton, 1978), especially pp. 139-42. On optimizing in a legal policy context, see Gary Becker and William Landes (eds.), *Essays in the Economics of Crime and Punishment* (New York: Columbia, 1974); S. Nagel and Marian Neef, *Legal Policy Analysis: Finding an Optimum Level or Mix* (Lexington, Mass.: Lexington-Heath, 1977), especially pp. 1-158.

4. The literature on whether a given defendant is a good enough risk to release includes Daniel Glaser, *The Effectiveness of a Prison and Parole System* (Indianapolis: Bobbs-Merrill, 1964), pp. 287-310; McEachern & Newman, "A System for Computer-Aided Probation Decision-Making," *Journal of Research in Crime and Delinquency* (1969) pp. 184-98. There are also other dimensions to optimum sentencing besides length of sentence, such as (1) whether a convicted defendant is to be placed in a maximum, medium, or minimum security prison, (2) whether the sentence is served completely in prison or with some provision for work-release on weekdays, during the day, or toward the end of the sentence, with imprisonment on weekends, during the night, or toward the beginning of the sentence; (3) which prison the defendant is assigned to within a given security category; and (4) what kind of routine the defendant is subjected to while in prison. Those decisions are generally made by prison administrators or parole-probation departments, rather than judges. One could attempt to optimize those decisions (like the length decision) by gathering and analyzing data relevant to the benefits and costs of each alternative.

5. Another rare but important dimension on the issue of optimum sentencing is whether or not to impose capital punishment, where a capital crime is involved. One could analyze that problem by either (1) attempting to determine under what circumstances the benefits of capital punishment outweigh the costs and under what circumstances the contrary is true, or (2) attempting to determine under what circumstances capital punishment is actually imposed and when it is not. The first approach corresponds to Section II of this article, and the second approach corresponds to Section III. For an example of the second approach, see Baldus, "Quantitative Methods for Judging the Comparative Excessiveness of Death Sentences," in M. Saks & C. Barron (eds.), *The Use/Nonuse/Misuse of Social Research in the Courts* (Cambridge, Mass: ABT, 1980), pp. 83-94. In the discussion

of the Baldus paper at page 97, I advocate trying a benefit-cost perspective, which partly led to the development of the present chapter.

6. See notes 1 and 2 regarding the prior literature on determinate sentencing and optimum sentencing.

7. Nagel, Neef & Weiman, *supra* note 2. That article provides a more elementary treatment of the basic model, but it does not get into variations or actual data. It also recommends the idea that the optimum may not be the average, but it does so only on intuitive grounds.

8. If the basic model were to fit reality perfectly, we would have a set of curves like the following:

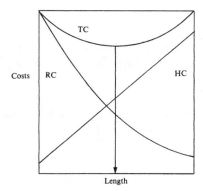

The HC curve is linear positive. The RC curve is convex negative. The TC curve has a two-directional valley-shape, with the arrow showing approximately where it bottoms out. Nagel, Neef, & Weiman, *supra* note 2, for a more detailed, but simple, description of those curves.

9. Instead of thinking of the weighting system as giving severity a relative weight of 2. and giving both delay and length base weights of 1, we can think of the weighting system as giving RC and HC equal weight, with S twice the weight of D. These two conceptualizations are equal algebraically, although the first can be symbolized $S^2/D^1 + L^1$, and the second can be symbolized $1(S^2/D) + 1(L)$. The second conceptualization is similar to defining the goal to be minimized in determining an optimum jury size. That goal is defined as minimizing the weighted sum of the type 1 errors of innocent defendants convicted (IC), plus the type 2 errors of guilty defendants not convicted (GN). The type 1 errors were considered to be 10 times as undesirable as the type 2 errors, relying on William Blackstone's criterion. The goal was thus symbolized as 10(IC) + 1(GN). The weight of 10 is used as a multiplier since only addition and no division is involved. On the jury-size problem, see S. Nagel and Marian Neef, "Deductive Modeling to Determine an Optimum Jury Size and Fraction Required to Convict," *Washington University Law Quarterly* 933-78 (1975). On the general matter of combining goal variables into a composite goal, see S. Nagel and Marian Neef, *Policy Analysis: In Social Science Research,* (Lexington, Mass.: Sage, 1979), pp. 105-32.

10. Previous studies that have used the Federal Bureau of Prisons data include Howard Kitchener, Anne Schmidt, and Daniel Glaser, "How Persistent Is Post-

Prison Success?'' 41 *Federal Probation* 9-15 (March, 1977); and Daniel Glaser, *The Effectiveness of a Prison and Parole System* (Indianapolis: Bobbs-Merrill, 1964).

11. To obtain a better understanding of the variables used in this analysis, one might note the average score across crimes expressed in months for L, S, C, and R. For length of sentence, the average is 22 months, with a low of 12 months for moonshine and a high of 51 months for robbery/kidnap. The importance of those average sentence-lenths is discussed below. For severity of subsequent behavior, the average is 26 months, with a low of 4 months for moonshine and a high of 35 months for vehicle theft. These averages include convicts who scored zero on subsequent felonious behavior. For clean time after getting out of prison until committing a subsequent felony or until the follow-up study ended, the average is 62 months, with a low of 46 months for vehicle theft and a high of 92 months for tax/embezzlement. Convicts who did not commit a subsequent felony are recorded as having clean time equal to 216 to 228 months since that was the length of the follow-up study. If we just examine those convicts who did commit a subsequent felony, the clean time tends to be about 24 months since 55 percent of the subsequent felonious recidivism occurs within two years and 80 percent within five years. Only about 60 percent of the convicts committed subsequent felonies within the 18-19 year follow-up period, with a low of 24 percent for tax/embezzlement and a high of 77 percent for vehicle theft. For prior record, the average was 25 months, with a low of 6 months, for nonrobbery assault and a high of 47 months for fraud check/counterfeiting. The percent of convicts who had no prior record was 41 percent, with a low of 23 percent for vehicle theft and a high of 76 percent for tax/embezzlement.

12. Norman Nie, et al., *Statistical Package for the Social Sciences* (New York: McGraw-Hill, 1975), especially pp. 320-397; Hubert Blalock, *Social Statistics* (New York: McGraw-Hill, 1972), especially pp. 361-472; and William Rich, Michael Saks, Paul Sutton, and Todd Clear, ''Modeling the Sentencing Process: An Examination of Empirically Based Sentencing Guidelines'' (Law and Society Association annual meeting, 1980).

13. To obtain a better understanding of the relations among the variables using this analysis, one might note that the six correlation coefficients among the four key variables are (1) $+.15$ for the influence of prior record on sentence length; (2) $-.16$ for the influence of prior record on subsequent clean time; (3) $+.09$ for the influence of prior record on subsequent crime severity; (4) $-.03$ for the influence of sentence length on subsequent clean time, although that slight negative becomes almost perfect zero when prior record is statistically held constant; (5) $+.07$ for the influence of sentence length on subsequent crime severity, although that slight positive moves toward zero when prior record is statistically held constant; and (6) $-.27$ for the relation between subsequent crime severity and subsequent clean time. One general point to note is that the relations among the variables are generally weak, although somewhat higher when crime is held constant.

14. An alternative way to try to hold prior record constant and still have it enter into the sentence-recommending process is to split the defendants into those who have below average or no prior record, and those who have above average or some prior records. We would then obtain for each subset on a given crime, the numerical parameters for the semi-log curves of the form $RC = a + b_1 Log (L) + b_2(R)$. Each subset would have a different L*, although both L*s would be equal to $-b_1$ of their respective curves. That method, however, requires that the b_1 for the subset with no prior record be negative and smaller than the b_1 for the subset with some prior record. Otherwise the defendants with no prior record would get longer recommended sentences. There is, however, no substantive justification for that difference between the b_1s.

15. The problem of determining the optimum percent of defendants to hold in jail prior to trial is discussed in S. Nagel, Paul Wice, and M. Neef, *Too Much or*

Too Little Policy: The Example of Pretrial Release (Beverly Hills, Ca.: Sage, 1977). A shorter version appears as "Determining an Optimum Percentage of Defendants to Release Before Trial: Applying Inventory Modeling Concepts to Legal Policy Problems," 6 *Journal of Criminal Justice* 25-34 (1978).

16. Statistical researchers have attempted to determine statistically the relation between sentencing severity and crime rates as a measure mainly of general deterrence and, to a lesser extent, incapacitation. See, for example, Blumstein & Nagin, "On the Optimum Use of Incarceration for Crime Control," 26 *Operations Research* 381 (1978); Greenberg, "Crime Deterrence Research and Social Policy," in S. Nagel, *Modeling the Criminal Justice System* (1977), 281-296, and *Deterrence and Incapacitation: Estimating the Effects of Criminal Sanctions on Crime Rates* (Blumstein ed., 1978). The relation is difficult to establish because as sentencing severity changes across places or over time, other changes also occur that cannot be sufficiently controlled for statistically, such as urbanism, population changes, and industrialization. It is especially difficult to separate out the effect of general deterrence versus incapacitation, even if one could establish that longer sentences causally relate to a lower crime rate. No researcher has attempted to combine statistically an analysis of general deterrence, incapacitation, specific deterrence, maturation, and rehabilitation. This is partly because the units of analysis for examining general deterrence tend to be states or time periods, and the units of analysis for examining the other processes tend to be individual defendants, although both types of analysis may have sentence length as the causal variable and crime as the effect variable.

17. One raises M to the second power rather than multiply it by 2, because multiplying $(M)(1/L)$ by 2 is the equivalent of multiplying $(1/L)$ by 2, since the placement of the 2 as a multiplier rather than an exponent has no effect on which of those two variables is multiplied by 2. A 2 is used rather than a 2.5 or a 1.8, because we do not have enough information to use decimals rather than whole numbers. One can accurately say that if we give ranks of 1 and 2 to severity and delay, severity would be ranked more important, which means a rank of 2, and delay would be ranked less important, which means a rank of 1. The normative weight of 2 is only an approximation and thus when one says that "The average may be the optimum in determinate sentencing", one is in effect saying that "The average may approximate the optimum in determinate sentencing." How one might improve upon the average is discussed later in the concluding section on "Policy Recommendations." In the concluding section on "Research Needed," one might also note the usefulness of surveying legislators or the public to determine the relative value they place on being subjected one month from now to an assault that generates a two-month sentence versus being subjected to an assault two months from now that generates a one-month sentence. Increasing the size of the exponent does not make the empirical relations more meaningful, as indicated in the previous section on "Changing the Weights." Varying the exponent from 2 upward or downward within a narrow range also does not substantially affect the deductive analysis, which tends to show that the optimum length is equal to the mean or average length. If the exponent or normative weight is considered to be 2, the L^* equals or approximates M raised to the power 2/2, or simply M. If the exponent is considered to be X, then L^* equals or approximates M raised to the power X/2.

18. Instead of showing the average or mean score by crime and by prior record, we could show the median score. The mean, however, is more customary since it takes all the cases into consideration, whereas the median is only concerned with the middle case. Thus, with three cases, we could have sentences of 1, 10, and 11, or 9, 10, and 20. In both situations, the median is 10 months. In the first situation, however, the mean is 7.33, and in the second situation the mean is 13. The median does have the advantage over the mean in that if we predict that everybody is at the

median, we will minimize the sum of the absolute deviations between predicted scores and actual scores. If, however, we predict everybody is at the mean, we will minimize the sum of the squared deviations, which makes less common sense, although most statisticians prefer squared deviations. That, however, is a technical matter which does not substantially offset or add to the loss of information from using the median. The median is also often used where a few isolated cases can distort the mean, as where we have 10 cases with a one-month sentence, and one case with a 1,000-month sentence. The typical case there is more a one-month case (which is the median) rather than a 92-month case (which is the mean). Sentencing, however, does not seem to be so skewed like that. The same principles, though, for saying "The average may be the optimum," can be applied to saying, "The median may be the optimum."

19. If the regression approach of predicting sentences from prior record is used, then an allowance could still be made for aggravating and mitigating circumstances. One would do so by calculating the predicted sentence length from prior record by using a formula of the form $a(R)^b$, like that given in the lower left of Table 8-2. One then simply determines the upper and lower 25 percent thresholds. For example, if a vehicle theft defendant has a 20-month prior record, the predicted or optimum sentence would be $14(20)^{.11}$. Raising 20 to the power .11 with a hand calculator yields the number 1.39, since 20 raised to the 1.00 power is 20, and 20 raised to the 0 power is 1. We then multiply 1.39 by 14 and get 19 months. The upper threshold is 25 percent above 19, or 1.25 times 19, which is 23.75. The lower threshold is 25 percent below 19, or .75 times 19, which is 14.25. That kind of information could be supplied to a judge, as part of the presentence report that deals with aggravating and mitigating circumstances. If this kind of regression prediction approach seems too complicated, one can predict from the average for each prior record category or interval, as is done in the upper part of Table 8-2. One can also demonstrate how deviant the present sentences are from these regression predicted sentences by determining the percentage of cases that are above or below the 25 percent threshold and by how much.

20. For a discussion of this kind of optimum choice or in-out decision, see S. Nagel and M. Neef, *Decision Theory and the Legal Process* (Lexington, Mass.: Lexington-Heath, 1979). This type of decision is particularly involved when a judge decides to hold or release a defendant prior to trial. It is also involved when a prosecutor or defense counsel decides whether or not to go to trial, and a juror decides whether to vote to convict or acquit. In determining the relative value of a Type A error to a Type B error, one should take into consideration not just the prison maintenance costs but also the harm to society's sense of justice that is associated with unnecessarily imprisoning someone. In this context, however, we are only talking about defendants who have been convicted and who are presumably guilty, rather than imprisoning an innocent or unconvicted defendant, as may occur at the pretrial detention stage. One should also take into consideration the general deterrence factor such that releasing a defendant on probation may encourage others to commit similar crimes or at least miss the opportunity of discouraging others. The cost of supervising a defendant on probation should be added to the Type B costs, but the supervision probably reduces these costs by decreasing the defendant's likelihood to do harm. To decrease what some might consider excessive use of probation, the legislature could specify that probation can only be considered for defendants who have no prior record.

21. Related research is currently being conducted as part of the development of sentencing guidelines. Leslie Wilkins, *Sentencing Guidelines: Structuring Judicial Discretion* (Washington, D.C.: LEAA, 1978); and Don Gottfredson et al., *Guidelines for Parole and Sentencing* (Lexington, Mass.: Lexington-Heath, 1978). Sentencing guidelines, however, are usually not classified as a form of determinate

sentencing, because the legislature or sentencing commission does not specify specific sentences but rather specifies sentencing criteria that are partly subjective and generally nonmandatory. The criteria may involve working with charts that score the characteristics of the defendant and the crime in order to arrive at specific sentences.

22. On the nature of the legislative process in arriving at sentences, see John Heinz, et al., "Legislative Politics and the Criminal Law," 64 *Northwestern University Law Review* 277-358 (1979); Sheldon Messinger and Phillip Johnson, "California Determinate Sentencing Statute: History and Issues" in Sanford Kadish (ed.), *Determinate Sentencing: Reform or Regression?* (Washington, D.C.: LEAA, 1978); George Cole, "Will Definite Sentences Make a Difference?" 61 *Judicature* 58-65 (1977); and Richard Berk, et al., *A Measure of Justice* (New York: Academic Press, 1977).

23. On the effects of judicial sentencing discretion on disparities along dimensions of race, class, urbanism, and region, see S. Nagel and Robert Geraci, "Effects of Judicial Sentencing Discretion" (Annual meeting of the Law and Society Association, 1980).

Chapter 9
Optimum Level Logic

The purpose of this chapter is to show how virtually any public policy problem can be solved through simple logic and algebra once the relation has been established between the goal to be achieved and various policy levels. By an "optimum policy level problem" is generally meant a problem in which doing either too much or too little on a policy is undesirable in the sense of producing unduly decreased benefits and/or increased costs.[1]

A typical optimum level problem might be one in which a government agency is concerned with how strongly to enforce a set of regulations relating to pollution, crime, delay, consumer protection, or other matters. If enforcement is pushed too far, there may be heavy enforcement costs of both a monetary and nonmonetary nature. On the other hand, if enforcement is allowed to be too lenient, there may be considerable damage costs in terms of the kind of damage that can be done by pollution, crime, or other negative social indicators. The object is generally to arrive at a policy level where the sum of the enforcement costs plus the damage costs is minimized. At that point, benefits minus costs are maximized in terms of enforcement benefits (i.e., damage costs avoided) minus enforcement costs, or damage benefits (i.e., enforcement costs avoided) minus damage costs. Although a typical policy level problem may involve a valley-shaped total cost curve or a hill-shaped total benefit curve, such problems also can involve one-directional relations between policies and goals. Here the object is to obtain as much of the policy as possible within economic and other constraints, assuming the policy relates positively to a desirable goal.

To simplify the discussion, the set of symbols that we will frequently use is defined as follows:

Y = the degree of overall goal achievement. It may represent a composite of subgoal achievements. It may represent total benefits, total costs, or benefits minus costs.

Y_1 = the degree of goal achievement on one of the subgoals of the overall goal. It too may represent a composite, and it can also be a benefit or a cost. The Y_1 curve also means the curve that is positively sloping between Y and X.

Y_2 = the degree of goal achievement on a second subgoal of the overall goal. It is generally an opposite type of benefit or cost in the sense that if Y_1 increases when X increases, then Y_2 generally decreases, and vice versa. It can also be opposite in the sense that Y_1 is a benefit from increases in X, and Y_2 is a cost; or Y_1 is a cost, and Y_2 is a benefit. The Y_2 curve also means the curve that is negatively sloping between Y and X.

X = the degree of policy input for achieving the overall goal.

X* = the optimum degree of policy input for maximizing the overall goal where Y is a benefit, or for minimizing the overall goal where Y is a cost.

Y* = the overall goal achievement when the degree of policy input is at an optimum (and likewise with Y^*_1 and Y^*_2).

a or A = the Y-intercept of the scale coefficient in a linear or nonlinear equation relating Y to X. Lower case letters refer to one kind of cost or benefit (Y_1), and upper case letters refer to another opposite kind of cost or benefit (Y_2).

b or B = the slope or other regression coefficient in a linear or nonlinear equation relating Y to X. In this context, subscripts 1, 2, and 3 refer to other such coefficients in the same Y to X equation, rather than to other sub-goals.

W = the relative value-weight of Y_1 versus Y_2 where they are not both measured in the same units.

The discussion begins with the simplest situations which may be almost too simple. They are presented, however, because they are used to build more complex situations that one normally would think could not be solved by simple logic and algebra, but only by a more sophisticated knowledge of calculus or nonlinear programming routines. This chapter does not explicitly use calculus reasoning or symbols, although the proofs of some statements do require calculus. One, however, can use those statements without a previous background in calculus or any awareness of what the calculus proofs might involve. There might be some optimum level situations that this chapter has not included, but they are probably too uncommon to be worth including. The author, however, welcomes learning of such situations so as to be able to further extend this logical approach to the analysis of optimum policy levels.

ONE-DIRECTIONAL RELATIONS BETWEEN A POLICY AND A GOAL

The simplest optimum level situation is one in which adopting more of a given policy consistently produces more of a given goal, or consistently produces less of a given goal, although not necessarily at a constant rate. If that type of relation were graphed with Y on the vertical axis and X on the horizontal axis, the graph might show a positively sloping diagonal line, or a negatively sloping diagonal line. Each of these lines not only moves in one direction but each also moves at a constant rate. They however, do, slope as contrasted to a perfectly horizontal or perfectly vertical line, neither of which has a definable slope.

An example of a one-directional linear relation between a policy and a goal might be the relation between the policy of restricting newspaper reporting concerning pending criminal trials (X) and the goal of assuring defendants a fair trial in being free of prejudicial newspaper reporting (Y). In that example, as X increases, Y increases although not necessarily at a constant rate.[2]

Graphing the relation between Y and X could also show various types of smooth curves that move in one direction, but at a decreasing or increasing rate. Such curves can take four shapes, namely: (1) A positive-concave curve that is steep up and then flattens out, like the left side of a hill; (2) a positive-convex curve that is flat at first and then steep up, like the right side of a valley; (3) a negative-convex curve that is steep down and then flattens out, like the left side of a valley; and (4) a negative-concave curve that is flat at first and then steep down, like the right side of a hill. All these curves are steep at one end and plateau out at a diminishing rate at the other end.

The S-shaped curve is the third type of one-directional relation that often occurs in relating goals to policies. Variations on S-shaped curves all are steep at the beginning and the end, but plateau in the middle, or they plateau at the beginning and end, but are steep in the middle. Such curves can also take four shapes, namely: (1) a positive S-curve that is steep up, flattens out, and then steep up again; (2) a positive S-curve that is flat at first, then steep up, and then flattens again; (3) a negative S-curve that is flat, steep down, and then flattens again; and (4) a negative S-curve that is steep down, flattens, and then steep down again.

Regardless whether straight lines, diminishing-returns curves, or S-shaped curves best shows the relation between goal achievement and adopting more of a given policy, the decision rules are fairly simple for determining the optimum policy level. They are as follows:

1. If Y is a benefit (and there is a positive relation), or if Y is a cost (and there is a negative relation), then adopt as much of X as is possible within the economic, legal, political, or other constraints under which one is operating.

2. If Y is a benefit (and there is a negative relation), or if Y is a cost (and there is a positive relation), then adopt as little of X as is possible within the constraints under which one is operating.

TWO-DIRECTIONAL RELATIONS BETWEEN A POLICY AND A GOAL

A two-directional relation between a goal and a policy when graphed produces a hill-shaped curve or a valley-shaped curve. Such curves are generally obtained by combining two one-directional relations such as a positive-convex cost curve (Y_1) and a negative-convex cost curve (Y_2) which produce a valley-shaped total cost curve (Y). Sometimes, however, it is meaningful to relate a goal to a policy using a type of relation which is inherently hill-shaped or valley-shaped without involving a combination of one-directional curves. The most common type of curve like that is a quadratic curve which algebraically is of the form:

$$Y = a + b_1X + b_2X^2 \tag{1}$$

An example of a two-directional relation between a policy and a goal might be the relation between school integration (Y) and busing levels (X). School integration can be measured by determining the extent to which the black student percentage in each school deviates from the overall black student percentage in the district. Busing levels can be measured by determining how much money is spent per student for busing, or how many miles the average student is bused with an adjustment to take into consideration the total size of the district if comparisons are going to be made across districts. The relation between busing level and integration may be a hill-shaped relation. When busing is relatively unused, there may be relatively little integration. As the busing level increases, school integration may also increase up to a point. Beyond that point enough "white flight" may occur so that the increased busing has fewer whites to integrate, with a resulting decrease in integration. The policy problem can thus be viewed as finding the peak or tipping point on that hill-shaped curve.[3]

The numerical values for a, b_1, and b_2 in Equation 1 can be determined through a statistical analysis in which data is obtained on Y and X for many places at one-point-in-time, for many time-points in a single place, or by a combination of both approaches. The numerical values for the parameters of this equation and for other equations relating Y to X can also sometimes be determined by carefully asking knowledgeable people what they perceive the parameters to be and then averaging their responses. By knowing the numerical parameters for other related equations, one can also sometimes deduce what the parameters should be for the equation in which one is interested. Under certain circumstances, it might also be reasonable to assume certain values for the parameters, as where one assumes that when $X is zero, Y is also zero.[4]

If we have a meaningful relation like that shown in Equation 1, then we can easily arrive at an optimum level of X which will maximize Y (if it is a benefit), or minimize Y (if it is a cost). Doing so first requires determining the slope of the relation between Y and X. Since Equation 1 generates a hill-shaped or valley-shaped curve, the slope is not constant. If a hill is involved, the slope is positive at first, then zero where the hill reaches a peak, and then negative where the hill is going down. Similarly, if a valley is involved, the slope is negative at first, then zero where the valley reaches bottom, and then positive where the valley is going up. Thus the slope of Y relative to X depends partly on X.

To find the slope of Y relative to X requires applying two rules governing slopes. Rule 1 says, if the relation between Y and X is of the form, Y = a + bX, then the slope is b. Rule 2 says, if the relation between Y and X is of the form $Y = aX^b$, then the slope is baX^{b-1}. This baX^{b-1} is the slope of any of the straight lines that could be drawn tangent to the curve which would be produced by plotting $Y = aX^b$. Applying those two rules to Equation 1 involves recognizing that the equation is like a combination of three equations, namely: (1) $Y = a$; (2) $Y = b_1X$; and (3) $Y = b_2X^2$. The slope for the first equation is zero following Rule 1, since the slope of a constant is horizontal and thus has no slope. The slope for the second equation is b_1, also following Rule 1. The slope for the third equation is $2b_2X^{2-1}$, following Rule 2. That slope simplifies to $2b_2X$. Putting those three slopes together gives us $b_1 + 2b_2X$ which is the slope of Y relative to X for all of Equation 1.

What now do we do with that information? The logical thing to do is to set that slope equal to zero, and then solve for X. By doing that, we are recognizing that we want to know the value of X when Y hits a peak on a hill-shaped curve or hits bottom on a valley-shaped curve. At either of those two points, the slope of Y relative to X is zero. Setting that slope equal to zero, and solving for X, involves the following steps:

1. $b_1 + 2b_2X = 0$
2. $2b_2X = -b_1$ (Subtracting b_1 from both sides)
3. $X^* = -b_1/2b_2$ (Dividing both sides by $2b_2$)

The third step tells us that the optimum value of X is $-b_1/2b_2$. That means that if we can determine the numerical values for b_1 and b_2, then we will be able to maximize benefit Y or minimize cost Y by adopting X at the $-b_1/2b_2$ level.

COMBINING ONE-DIRECTIONAL RELATIONS TO MAKE A TWO-DIRECTIONAL RELATION

In General

As mentioned in the beginning of this article, the most common optimum level problem is one in which a total cost or total benefit curve is determined by combining two subgoal curves. Each subgoal curve is likely to involve a one-directional relation, and the combination is likely to involve a two-directional relation like a hill-shaped curve or a valley-shaped curve. There are various ways of classifying such relations. One dimension relates to whether we are (1) adding opposing costs; (2) adding opposing benefits; or (3) subtracting costs from benefits. Another dimension relates to whether we are combining (1) linear relations; (2) nonlinear relations that proceed at an increasing or decreasing rate, but not both; or (3) nonlinear relations that are S-shaped. A third dimension relates to whether the optimum level on the overall goal can be found (1) through a decision rule without solving an equation; (2) through an equation where X can be made to stand by itself on the left side of the equals sign; or (3) through an equation that requires reiterative guessing of values for X until the optimum value is found.

As for the first method of classification, the combination of two one-directional relations may involve adding two opposing costs as, for example, where one sums (1) a holding cost curve, showing the relation between (a) the percentage of defendants held in jail prior to trial and (b) holding costs, including the cost of incarceration, lost gross national product, and some amount to consider the bitterness generated by being held in jail without being found guilty; plus (2) a releasing cost curve, showing the relation between (a) the percentage of defendants held in jail and (b) the releasing costs, including the cost of crimes committed by released defendants and the cost to rearrest no-shows. The combination may also involve adding two opposing benefits as for example, where one sums (1) an acquittal accuracy curve showing the number of innocent defendants acquitted (Y_1) as jury sizes (X) increase since larger juries are less likely to convict under a unanimity rule; plus (2) a conviction accuracy curve showing the relation between the number of guilty defendants convicted (Y_2) as jury sizes (X) decrease since smaller juries are more likely to convict under a unanimity rule. The combination may also involve subtracting cost relation from a benefit relation as, for example, where one subtracts (1) an S-curve showing the relation between the probability of being held in jail (Y_1) and various dollar bond levels (X), from (2) an S-curve showing the relation between the probability of appearing in court (Y_2) and various dollar bond levels (X).[5]

Which of these three types of combinations to use is largely a matter of semantics, since they are all interchangeable depending on whether one talks about (1) achieving benefits; (2) missing benefits that could have been achieved; (3) incurring costs; or (4) avoiding costs. In the analysis which follows, the examples will emphasize combinations that involve adding what might be called type 1 costs to type 2 costs in order to obtain a total cost curve. It is easier to work with addition than with subtraction, and policy problems generally or often involve trying to decrease negative social indicators like crime, pollution, disease, and jury errors. One, however, can reword the rules which follow to cover examples in which the combinations involve summing benefits or subtracting costs from benefits.

Another meaningful way of classifying combinations is not in terms of whether they involve adding costs, adding benefits, or subtracting costs from benefits, but rather in terms of whether the one-directional relations are linear or nonlinear. Within the nonlinear relations, it is helpful to know whether the one-directional relations involve curves that move at an increasing or decreasing rate (like diminishing-return curves), but not partly at a decreasing rate and partly at an increasing rate (like S-shaped curves). Curves that move at a decreasing or increasing rate, but not both, can be classified in terms of the form of their equations as being semi-log functions, power functions, or exponential functions, each of which will be defined shortly. That kind of classification is useful for informing one how to express the slope of the relation between Y and X in a combination curve regardless whether it is a total-cost, total-benefit, or benefit-minus-cost curve.

Table 9-1 uses equation form to show 15 common optimum level situations where one-directional relations are combined. There are five types of one-directional relations that one may be likely to encounter in public policy analysis. One is linear and four are nonlinear. Of the nonlinear, three involve decreasing or increasing returns but not both, and one involves both. Going from the northwest corner of the table toward the southeast, the combinations move from the easier to the more difficult along the main diagonal, which consists of situations 1, 3, 6, 10, and 15. The numbering of the combinations or situations is also roughly from the simpler to the more difficult, but trying to keep together those relations that involve similar equations. Each situation above the main diagonal is duplicated below it. Each situation involves a combination of two relations or equations. We sometimes use the word function or curve, instead of equation or relation. In that context, a function is the right side of an equation with Y on the left side. A curve is the equation plotted.

TABLE 9-1. COMMON OPTIMUM LEVEL SITUATIONS WHERE ONE-DIRECTIONAL RELATIONS ARE COMBINED

	Linear	Semi-Log	Power	S-Shape	Exponential
Linear	1	2	4	7	11
	D	A	A	A	A
Semi-Log	2	3	5	8	12
	A	D	A	G	G
Power	4	5	6	9	13
	A	A	A	G	G
S-Shape	7	8	9	10	14
	A	G	G	A	G
Exponential	11	12	13	14	15
	A	G	G	G	G

Solution by: D = Decision Rule; A = Analytic Solution; G = Reiterative Guessing

The easiest combinations are those in which an optimum policy level can be determined by a decision rule like the two rules mentioned above in discussing a one-directional relation between a policy and a goal. Of the 15 situations, there are only two such situations, and they are designated by a D in the lower right-hand corner of their cells. Easy solutions, but not quite as easy, are those in which X can be made to stand by itself on the left side of an equation with numerical parameters on the right side, like the situation described above in discussing a two-directional relation between a policy and a goal. There are seven such situations. They are designated in a table by an A for analytic solution. The relatively more difficult situations require reiterative guessing to determine an optimum value of X, although those guesses can be quickly checked with a programmable calculator against fairly simple criteria so that even those solutions are not difficult. There are six such situations designated by a G in the table. Even they can be avoided by expressing relations between policies and goals through the use of simpler relations where they are applicable.

Linear Relations

The first situation in Table 9-1 involves combining two linear relations. One relation might show how holding costs go up when the percentage of defendants held in jail prior to trial goes up. The other relation might show how releasing costs go up when the percentage of defendants held in jail goes down. The first relation might be graphed as a positively sloped diagonal line (Y_1), and the second relation might be graphed as a negatively sloped diagonal line (Y_2). If one then sums these two lines, one obtains a total cost curve that is also a diagonally sloped straight line. It is positively sloped if the first relation has a steeper slope than the second relation, and it is negatively sloped if the opposite is true. In other words, if the first linear relation is expressed as:

$$Y_1 = a + bX, \tag{2a}$$

and the second relation is expressed as:

$$Y_2 = A + BX, \tag{2b}$$

then the sum of those two relations will be positively sloped if b is greater than B, and negatively sloped if the opposite is true.

In view of the fact that combining two linear relations results in a linear total cost curve, the decision rules that apply to one-directional relations between a policy and a goal also apply here. This means that:

1. If b is greater than B, this tells us that Y_1 cost curve is steeper than the Y_2 cost curve, and that total cost will be a positively-sloped line. More important, it tells us to adopt X to as small a

degree as possible since the more X we adopt, the more the total cost increases.

2. If B is greater than b, this tells us that the Y_2 cost curve is steeper than the Y_1 cost curve, and that the total cost will be a negatively sloped line. More important, it tells us to adopt X to as large a degree as possible, since the more X we adopt, the more the total cost decreases.

Such a combination of straight lines may fit some policy situations. It, however, may be a generally unrealistic situation for two reasons. First, it ignores diminishing returns in the sense that if an increase in X causes an increase in Y_1 costs, then as X goes down Y_1 should also go down, but at a diminishing rate. Similarly, if a decrease in X causes an increase in Y_2 costs, then as X goes up, Y_2 should go down, but at a diminishing rate. One, however, may find linear relations to be present over short intervals on an X policy variable. Second, working with a combination of straight lines may be politically unrealistic, as well as lacking empirical reality. These combinations tend to result in solutions that say X should be zero percent or 100 percent where X is a percent, or that X should be negative or positive infinity where X has a complete range of numbers. Solutions like that may be too extreme to be meaningful. For example, where we are talking about the optimum percentage of defendants to hold in jail prior to trial, we can predict in advance that an all-linear approach will result in an optimum point (where total costs are minimized) of zero percent or 100 percent, which means unrealistically recommending that no one be held or that everyone be held.

Semi-Logarithmic Relations

To improve the realism of the way we relate costs (or benefits) to policy levels, we can work with semi-logarithmic equations of the form:

$$Y = a + b \operatorname{Log} X \tag{3}$$

The numerical values for a and b can be determined for that equation (or any of the other equations in this chapter) by using statistical regression analysis, questioning of knowledgeable people, deductive reasoning, or reasonable assumptions, as was mentioned in discussing two-directional quadratic relations. If b is a positive number, then when Equation 3 is plotted, it will generate a positively-sloped diminishing returns curve that is steep up at first and then flattens out. If b is a negative number, then when Equation 3 is plotted, it will generate a negatively-sloped diminishing returns curve that is steep down at first and then flattens out. Semi-log curves are useful for relating costs or benefits to policies where one wants a curve rather than a straight line, but an especially simple curve in terms of the easy slope rule that is associated with a semi-log curve.

If we combine a semi-log relation and a linear relation, we get an equation of the form, $Y = a + bX + A + BX$. Given that equation, the slope of Y relative to X is $(b) + (B/X)$. The first part follows from Rule 1, which says, if $Y = a + bX$, then the slope is b. The second part follows from Rule 3, which says, if $Y = a + b \log X$, then the slope of Y to X is b/X. Therefore, if we set that slope equal to zero in order to find where the combination total-cost curve bottoms out, we would go through the following steps:

1. $(b) + (B/X) = 0$

2. $B/X = -b$ (Subtracting b from both sides)

3. $X/B = 1/-b$ (Inverting both sides)

4. $X^* = B/-b$ (Multiplying both sides by B)

This tells us that in Situation 2, the optimum value for X is $B/-b$, since that value will minimize total costs. If the goals were worded differently, $B/-b$ would maximize total benefits, or maximize benefits minus costs.

Saying $X^* = B/-b$ actually means that if we sum a linear curve and a semi-log curve, we will obtain either a hill-shaped or a valley-shaped summation curve, and the peak or bottom of that curve will occur where X equals $B/-b$. A hill-shaped summation curve results from a positively-sloped semi-log curve and a negatively-sloped line where the hill shows total benefits. A valley-shaped summation curve results from combining a negatively sloped semi-log curve and a positively sloped line. It is that kind of combination relation which we want to emphasize in analyzing the combination relations, namely those that result in valley-shaped summation curves.

The next situation in Table 9-1 is Situation 3 which involves combining a positively-sloped semi-log curve and a negatively-sloped one. Doing so produces an equation of the form $Y = a + b \log X + A + B \log X$. One can, however, show such a combination of two semi-log curves like the combination of two straight lines produces a one-directional total costs curve or total benefits curve. The easiest way to show that is by substituting any values for a, b, A and B, and then allowing X to move up from .001 to 1,000. Doing so reveals that Y is constantly increasing or decreasing, although at a decreasing rate, but never changing direction. Thus, Y never reaches a peak or a bottom. It is therefore meaningless to determine the slope of the above equation, set that slope equal to zero, and then solve for X, since there is no point where the slope of Y relative to X is zero. The optimum value of X under these circumstances must be determined by a decision rule analogous to the decision rule for determining the optimum X value when combining two straight lines. The appropriate decision rule is:

1. If b (the positive coefficient) is greater in magnitude than B (the negative coefficient), then as X increases, Y will also increase. Therefore, adopt as little X as possible, assuming Y is a cost rather than a benefit.

2. If B is greater in magnitude than b, then as X increases, Y will decrease. Therefore, adopt as much X as possible, assuming Y is a cost.

3. If b and B are both positive, then as X increases, Y will increase; and if b and B are both negative, then as X increases, Y will decrease. We should then act accordingly with regard to the degree of X to adopt.

Power Function Relations

Many relations between costs (or benefits) and policies are shown by equations of the form:

$$Y = aX^b \tag{4}$$

The "a" or scale coefficient represents the value of Y when X is 1. The "b" or elasticity coefficient represents the percent that Y changes when X changes 1 percent. Unlike semi-log curves which can only be positive concave or negative convex, power functions can be positive concave (if b is greater than zero, but less than 1), linear (if b is 1), positive convex (if b is greater than 1), or negative convex (if b is less than 0). Power function curves are useful for relating costs or benefits to policies where one wants to allow for all those possibilities, and when one wants the easy interpretation of the b or elasticity coefficients.

In Situation 4, we combine a linear relation with a power function relation. The straight line can be a positively sloping cost, and the power function can be a negative convex cost. Another alternative that will yield a valley-shaped total cost curve is for the straight line to be negatively sloping, and for the power function to be positive convex. Under either situation, the combination yields an equation of the form, $Y = a + bX + AX^B$. Given that equation, the slope of Y relative to X is $b + BA(X)^{B-1}$. Setting that slope equal to zero and solving for X involves the following steps:

1. $b + BA(X)^{b-1} = 0$

2. $BA(X)^{B-1} = -b$

3. $(X)^{B-1} = -b/BA$

4. $X^* = -b/BA$ raised to the power $1/(B - 1)$

Thus, if we have an optimum policy level problem involving a combination of a linear cost and a power-function cost and we can determine the numerical values of b, B, and A, then all we have to do find the optimum X level is insert those values in the above formula in step 4.

In Situation 5, we combine a semi-log cost curve with a power function cost curve. That means a negative convex semi-log curve with a positive convex power curve. Such a combination has the form, $Y = a + b \log X + AX^B$. Its slope is $(b/X) + (BAX^{B-1})$. Setting that slope equal to zero to find the value of X when Y bottoms out involves:

1. $(b/X) + (BAX^{B-1}) = 0$

2. $BAX^{B-1} = -b/X$

3. $(X)(X)^{B-1} = -b/BA$

4. $X^{1+(B-1)} = -b/BA$

5. $X^B = -b/BA$

6. $X^* = -b/BA$ raised to the power $1/B$

That formula can be used to find a peak or a bottom for any combination of a semi-log curve and a power curve, although the only combination that will yield a valley-shaped curve is a negative-convex semi-log curve and a positive-convex power function.

In Situation 6, we combine a positively sloping power function and a negatively sloping one in order to obtain a valley-shaped total cost curve. The combination curve is thus an equation of the form, $Y = aX^b + AX^B$. Such an equation has a slope of the form, $baX^{b-1} + BAX^{B-1}$. Setting that expression equal to 0 and solving for X yields:

1. $baX^{b-1} + BAX^{B-1} = 0$

2. $baX^{b-1} = -BAX^{B-1}$

3. $(X)^{b-1}/(X)^{B-1} = (-BA)/(ba)$

4. $(X)^{(b-1)-(B-1)} = (-BA)/(ba)$

5. $(X)^{b-B} = (-BA)/(ba)$

6. $X^* = (-BA)/(ba)$ raised to the power $1/(b - B)$

Summing two power functions to obtain a total cost curve or a total benefits curve is especially common in policy analysis. It is also common to subtract a cost curve from a benefits curve, where both are power functions. The formula in step 6 applies to either kind of addition. If the combination involves subtraction, then the combination equation is simply $Y = aX^b - AX^B$. The two slopes then have a minus sign between them instead of a plus sign, and in the sixth step showing X^*, there is no minus sign to the right of the equals sign.

A common variation on the power function is to work with an equation of the form $Y = c + aX^b$. The advantage of that variation is that it enables one to show that when nothing is spent on X (or X is operating at the zero level), then there are still fixed benefits or costs obtained. Determining the value of c may involve inspecting the dots of a scattergram to determine "c," and then using $Y - c$ as the dependent variable in a statistical regression analysis to determine "a" and "b." Doing that, however, has no effect on the optimizing procedure since c is a constant, and thus the slope of $Y = c + aX^b$ is baX^{b-1}, just as much as it is when $Y = aX^b$. The same is true if a constant "c" is added to an exponential relation of the form $Y = ab^x$. There is already a constant "a" in a linear, semi-log, quadratic, and S-shaped relation.

S-Shaped Relations

In policy analysis, many relations between policies and either benefits or costs can be best shown by equations of the form:

$$Y = a + b_1X + b_2X^2 + b_3X^3 \qquad (5)$$

Equations like that are especially useful for policies that have little effect at first, then a substantial effect, and then plateau out. An example might be the level at which bail bonds are set (as the policy variable, X) and the probability of defendants being held in jail (as a cost variable that we would like to hold down, Y_1). As the bond level goes up, the probability or percentage of defendants held in jail stays low, at least while the bond level is going up at a low level. At some point, however, increases in the bond level do result in substantial increases in defendants being held in jail. At another point, the bond level becomes so high that virtually everyone gets held in jail, as being unable to meet the bond level. At that point, increases in the bond level have little effect on increases in the percentage of defendants held in jail.

If we combine a positively sloped S-shaped curve with a negatively sloped straight line, we get an equation of the form, $Y = a + bX + A + B_1X + B_2X^2 + B_3X^3$. One can think of the negatively-sloped straight line as representing the probability of nonappearance in court for trial, which is a kind of cost curve that goes down when the bond level goes up. The slope of that combination valley-shaped curve is an expression of the form, $b + B_1 + 2B_2X + 3B_3X^2$. That expression simplifies to $c + dX + eX^2$, where $c = b + B_1$, $d = 2B_2$, and $e = 3B_3$. To solve for the value of X, when that valley-shaped curve hits bottom, we set that expression equal to zero. Doing so, however, yields a quadratic equation that is more easily solved by a formula than by trying to get X to stand by itself, on the left side of the equation. The formula for solving a quadratic equation in the above form is:

$$X^* = [-d \pm (d^2 - 4ce)^{.5}]/2e \tag{6}$$

To use this formula, we simply insert the numerical values of the parameters for the two curves, namely a, b, B_1, B_2, and B_3, after they have been translated into the symbols c, d, and e. After making those insertions, we will obtain two solutions for X^*. One will indicate where the combination curve reaches a peak of maximum costs, and the other will indicate where the combination curve reaches a peak of maximum costs, and the other will indicate where the combination curve reaches a bottom of minimum costs. It is, of course, the value of X where the curve reaches bottom that interests us. If, however, we were summing two benefit curves, or dealing with the difference between a benefits and a cost curve, then we would be interested in knowing the value of X where the combination curve reaches a peak.

In Situation 8, we combine an S-shaped curve with a semi-log curve. As in Situation 7, the S-shaped curve could relate the probability of being held in jail to alternative bond levels, and the semi-log curve could relate the probability of nonappearance to the bond levels. The equation representing that combination is, $Y = a + b \log X + A + B_1 X + B_2 X^2 + B_3 X^3$. The slope for that equation is $b/X + B_1 + SB_2 X + 3B_3 X^2$. If, however, we set that expression equal to zero and try to solve for X, we will find that it is algebraically impossible to get X to stand by itself, on the left side of the equals sign. The quadratic equation formula is also no help, since it requires that all the exponents be either zero, 1, or 2, with no decimal or negative exponents. The first addend in that slope is the algebraic equivalent of bX^{-1}, which involves a negative exponent. To solve for X when the above slope is set equal to zero might best be done on a programmable calculator. We would insert into the calculator the numerical values for b, B_1, B_2, and B_3, and show how they are related to each other in the above slope expression. In place of X in that expression, we would use whatever we insert as a guess into calculator storage register No.1. We then insert a guessed value into that storage register, push the start button, and observe the display to see what value the expression has with that guess. If the value of the expression is above zero, we try a lower guess. If the value of the expression is below zero, we try a higher guess. Only a few seconds of calculation are required between guesses until our guessing is able to make the expression equal to zero. The guess at that point is the optimum value of X because it is X when the slope of Y is zero, indicating in this context that Y has reached the bottom of a valley-shaped total cost curve.

In Situation 9, we combine an S-shaped curve with a power function. That combination yields an equation like $Y = aX^b + A + B_1 X + B_2 X^2 + B_3 X^3$. The slope for that equation is $baX^{b-1} + B_1 + 2B_2 X + 3B_3 X^2$. Setting that slope equal to zero and solving for X requires the same kind of reiterative guessing approach as in Situation 8. The subsequent tenth situation, however, can be solved through the analytic solution method. It involves summing two S-shaped curves, one that might represent the probability of being held, with the second representing the probability of nonappearance. Nonappearance may be graphed as a negatively sloping S-shaped curve, in the sense that at low bond levels there is a *high* probability of nonappearance, until some point is reached when it becomes worthwhile to show up in order to get one's bond money back, rather than treat the small bond forfeiture as a substitute for a fine. At extremely high bond levels, there may be a continuously *low* probability of nonappearance, at least in misdemeanors or traffic violations, since the average defendant is probably as likely to appear to collect a 20,000 dollar bond as a 25,000 dollar bond. The equation which represents the sum of two such S-shaped functions has a form like Equation 5, with lower-case letters for its parameters added to a similar equation with upper case letters. The slope of such an equation looks like the slope of the quadratic equation for Situation 7, except $c = b_1 + B_1$, $d = 2b_2 + 2B_2$, and $e = 3b_3 + 3B_3$. Also like Situation 7, the solution for X when that slope is set equal to zero requires the use of the quadratic formula given in Equation 6.

Exponential Relations

In policy analysis, some relations between policies and costs or benefits are best expressed by an exponential curve. Such curves have the form:

$$Y = ab^X \tag{7}$$

The numerical parameters can be arrived at through a statistical analysis by obtaining scores for persons, places, or things on the Y variable and the X variable, and then inputting that data into a regression analysis with just the dependent variable logged. For a power function, one logs both Y and X; whereas for a semi-log function, one just logs the X variable. The numerical parameters may also be obtained by deductive mathematical reasoning, as in the policy analysis problem of finding an optimum jury size. In that problem, X is the number of jurors to be solved, b is the probability that an average juror will vote to convict, and the "a" coefficient is relative normative weight that one places on obtaining accurate convictions versus accurate acquittals. In an exponential function, the unknown or the policy level to be found is an exponent, whereas in a power function the unknown policy level is the base which is raised to a power.

Situation 11 combines a linear function with an exponential function. The positive exponential function might show that as the number of jurors increases, the errors of guilty defendants who are not convicted increases at an exponential rate, since it is much more difficult to obtain a unanimous conviction with more jurors. The straight line would be negatively sloped in the opposite direction and show that the number of errors of innocent persons being convicted goes down as the number of jurors increases, since the number of defendants convicted in general goes down as the number of jurors increases. Such a pair of relations when combined generates an equation of the form $Y = a + bX + AB^X$. To find the slope for that equation requires Rule 4. The previous three rules dealt with a linear relation, a power function, and a log function. The S-shaped curve required no new rule, since it is a combination of linear and power-function terms. Rule 4 says that if $Y = ab^X$, then the slope of Y relative to X is $(LN b)(ab^X)$. The expression LN b means find the natural logarithm of b, which can easily be done on an inexpensive calculator. The common logarithm of 100 is 2, since 100 is 10 squared. The natural logarithm of 100 is 4.61 since 100 is e (or 2.72) raised to the power 4.61. Knowing Rule 4 enables us to determine that the slope of the combination equation is $b + (LN B)(AB^X)$. Setting that slope equal to zero and solving for X involves the following steps:

1. $b + (LN B)(AB^X) = 0$

2. $(LN B)(AB^X) = -b$

3. $(AB^X) = -b/(LN B)$

4. $B^X = -b/[(LN B)(A)]$

5. $Log(B^X) = Log\{-b[(LN B)(A)]\}$

6. $X(Log B) = (Log -b) - Log[(LN B)(A)]$

7. $X(Log B) = (Log -b) - [Log(LN B) + Log A]$

8. $X(Log B) = (Log -b) - Log(LN B) - Log A$

9. $X^* = [(Log -b) - Log(LN B) - Log A]/Log B$

Optimum policy-level formulas similar to that one were actually used to arrive at a tentative optimum jury size between 6 and 12. That analysis was favorably referred to by the U.S. Supreme Court in the case of *Ballew v. Georgia*, 435 U.S. 233 (1978).

The rest of the situations numbered 12 through 15 can easily be developed by combining the separate equations for an exponential function and a semi-log function (Situation 12), a power function (Situation 13), an S-Shaped function (Situation 14), and another exponential function (Situation 15). All four of those situations generate slopes that require the reiterative guessing approach in order to solve for X when the slopes are set equal to zero. That reiterative guessing will indicate the numerical value X should have in order to minimize the sum of Y_1 plus Y_2. By slightly varying the analysis, one can also determine the numerical value of X in order to maximize the sum of Y_1 and Y_2 (where they are benefits rather than costs), or maximize $Y_1 - Y_2$ or $Y_2 - Y_1$ (where one is a benefit and the other is a cost).

OTHER COMBINATIONS

The other main combination that has a reasonable likelihood of occurring in policy analysis involves a combination of a one-directional relation (like any of the five just discussed) and a two-directional relation (like a quadratic relation in the subsequent section). An example of this type of combination might be finding an optimum school busing level where we are concerned with two goals. One goal is that of integration (Y_1), as measured by the average deviation between the black student percentage of each school and the black student percentage in the district. A second goal (although a negative one) might be the dollar costs (Y_2) at various busing levels for fuel, drivers and equipment. The first goal might be related to busing levels by way of a hill-shaped quadratic relation of the form, $Y = a + b_1X + b_2X^2$, as previously discussed. The second goal might be related to busing levels as a positively sloped linear, semi-log, power, S-shaped, or exponential function. The object of the analysis analysis is to find the busing level that maximizes the Y_1 benefit minus the Y_2 cost.

One problem in this analysis, which often occurs in any kind of optimum level analysis, is how to measure Y_1 and Y_2 in the same units so that Y_2 can be meaningfully subtracted from Y_1, or how to develop a coefficient to indicate the relative importance of a one-unit increase in integration versus a one-unit increase in busing costs. Although the problem is frequent, it seems more obvious here because we are combining two substantially different kinds of curves and because it seems almost unethical, inequitable, or unconstitutional to assign a dollar value to increases in integration. The problem arises whenever two goals are combined which may be measured in different units, or even when the same units have different meanings. An example of the latter situation is where we combine conviction errors (Y_1) and acquittal errors (Y_2) in arriving at an optimum jury size. They are both measured in "errors," but a conviction error clearly does not have the same meaning as an acquittal error. Even in the simple one-directional linear relation of the form, $Y = a + bX$, there may be a problem of combining goals since Y may be a composite of various subgoals.

This measurement problem may not be as difficult as it at first seems for at least three reasons. First, people deal with this kind of problem almost every day in satisfactory ways as when, for example, a shopper decides to buy a can of beans for 1 dollar, rather than two cans of asparagus for 1 dollar. In doing so, the shopper is in effect saying that one can of beans has more value than two cans of asparagus. That implicitly involves some kind of value scale on which beans and asparagus can be compared. Shoppers are also capable of deciding between one can of beans at 1 dollar and two cans of asparagus at more or less than 1 dollar. Putting integration units (measured in percentage points) and busing costs (measured in 1,000s of dollars) on roughly the same scale should not be so much more difficult. Second, psychologists and economists have been studying the problems of combining goals, and they have developed simple and not-so-simple methods for doing so. Third, to do the combining does not necessitate that integration percentage points be converted into dollars, that busing dollars be converted into percentage points, or that both units be converted into something else like utility or satisfaction units. All one needs to make the combination meaningful is to get agreement or an average opinion of relevant people on how many times more or less is the relative value of a one-unit increase in integration versus a one-unit increase in busing costs.[6]

A more concrete example can help clarify the problem, especially how it might be resolved through the relative-value approach. Suppose we have three schools in a district, and one is 10 percent black, the second is 20 percent, and the third is 30 percent black. The average black percentage is thus 20 percent, which is the same as the percentage of black students in the district if each school has the same population. The first school deviates from the average by 10 percentage points, the second school by zero, and the third school also by 10, for an average deviation of 20/3 or 7 percentage points. If we subtract those 7 percentage points from 100, we can meaningfully say that this district is 93 percent integrated, although we would have to explain how the 93 percent was calculated. If busing costs are measured in 1,000 dollar units, then the measurement question becomes how many times more than 1,000 dollars in government expenditure is it worth to the community or district to move from 93 percent integrated to 94 percent integrated.

Perhaps a survey of relevant people to that question might produce an average response of 10. If so, then when it comes time to subtract predicted Y_2 from predicted Y_1 in order to calculate Y, we would use an equation like $Y = 10Y_1 - Y_2$. If Y_1 is a quadratic function and Y_2 is a linear function, the equation can also be expressed as $Y = 10(a + b_1X + b_2X^2) - (A + BX)$. Inserting 10 for W (or weight) does not complicate the analysis. It simply means that the a, b_1, and b_2 get multiplied by 10. We can also ignore the 10 and consider that $a = 10a$, $b_1 = 10b_1$, and $b_2 = 10b_2$. To be more sophisticated, we can also recognize that the weight of 10 may not be a constant. In other words, W may be 10 when we move from 93 percent and 94 percent, but less than 10 when we move 97 percent to 98 percent. If W moves down as the integration percentage (P) moves up, the relation might have the form, $W = aP^b$, with b being a negative number. If so, then we would substitute $a(P)^b$ for the W of 10 in the above equation.

To combine such a weighted quadratic relation with a linear relation is no problem in light of the previously described procedures. We simply note that given those two relations, the slope of Y relative to X is $b_1 + 2b_2X - B$. If we set that slope equal to zero, we get:

1. $b_1 + 2b_2X - B = 0$

2. $2b_2X = B - b_1$

3. $X^* = (B - b_1)/2b_2$

That third step indicates that if one can determine those numerical parameters for B, b_1, and b_2, then by inserting them into that equation, one can determine an optimum busing level that will maximize the integration benefits minus the busing costs. If, however, that analysis shows X^* will yield an integration score of only about 40 percent, then that X value might be outside the feasible region in the sense that the Supreme Court may not tolerate an integration percentage that low. The Supreme Court has specified maximum deviations in legislative redistricting cases, but it has not yet indicated precise constraints or outer limits in school integration cases.

To combine a weighted quadratic-relation with a semi-log, power, S-shaped, or exponential busing cost-relation involves basically the same kind of reasoning. The combination with a semi-log cost-curve, however, leads to a slope equation of the form, $b_1X + 2b_2X^2 - B = 0$, which is best solved by the quadratic formula. Similarly, when one combines a quadratic and an S-shaped relation, and then sets the slope of the combination equal to zero, one also obtains an equation that is best solved by the quadratic formula. When one combines either a power function or an exponential function (to represent the relation between busing levels and busing costs) with a quadratic function (to represent the relation between busing levels and integration), one gets the kind of equation which can only be solved by reiterative guessing after setting the slope of the combination equal to zero.

One might ask how it is possible to have so many different relations between busing costs (Y_2) and busing levels (X). If busing levels are measured in terms of dollars spent per student, then the relation between Y_2 and X would have to be linear, since Y_2 would equal the number of students times X. If, however, busing levels are measured in terms of miles per student, we could have a positively sloped diminishing-returns curve between Y_2 and X. In other words, busing costs could keep going up as the number of miles increases, but at a diminishing rate since many of the costs are fixed costs for equipment, rather than variable costs like fuel. With this subject matter, however, an S-shaped curve does not seem meaningful since it requires costs to move up at a decreasing rate and then at an increasing rate, or to move up at an increasing rate and then a decreasing rate. Neither of those occurrences seems to fit the realities here, although these occurrences may apply to other policy analysis problems.

In discussing optimum policy-level problems, one might also ask about curves that are more than two-directional, including curves that have more than one bend as in a business cycle curve. Those curves may be quite meaningful when relating time (on the horizontal axis or as the independent variable) to changes in either a social indicator goal (Y) or to changes in a policy (X) (on the vertical axis or as the dependent variable). These curves, however, do not seem to fit any relations between a social indicator goal (as a dependent variable) and a policy (as an independent variable). One partial exception might be that when two of the curves previously discussed are combined together, the result may be an S-shaped curve on its side. Such a curve goes down to a bottom, up to a peak, and then down again, or else up to a peak, down to a bottom, and then up again. That type of combination curve can, for example, occur when a positively sloped S-shaped curve is combined with a negatively sloped straight line. The result may be a combination curve that has both a bottom indicating minimum costs and a peak indicating maximum benefits. Both points, as previously mentioned, can be found through the use of the quadratic formula. One simplifying reality about policy analysis, as compared to natural science or pure mathematics, is that there are so few curves that do realistically fit policy analysis data. It also helps that those curves can be expressed as variations on linear regression analysis and as curves for which slopes can easily be determined.

With regard to other combinations, it may be quite reasonable to have an optimum level problem in which the valley-shaped total cost curve or hill-shaped total benefit curve is generated by combining more than two curves. For example, in the optimum speed limit problem of Duncan MacRae (mentioned in note 1 above), three curves are combined to generate a valley-shaped total cost curve. They are (1) time saved as a benefit which is a negative convex power function; (2) operating costs including fuel which is a positive-linear function; and (3) accidents cost which is also shown as a positive-linear function. All three subgoal variables are measured in dollars which eases the goal-combining problem. Other optimum level problems could conceivably involve any number of benefit curves and cost curves that are algebraically and geometrically summed to get a total curve with a bottom or a peak. One, however, might sum the cost curves to get a total cost curve, sum the benefit curves to get a total benefit curve, and then get a net benefits curve by subtracting the total costs curve from the total benefits curve. One might also sum the positively sloping cost curves, sum the negatively sloping cost curves, and then sum these two opposite cost curves to get a total cost curve, or do similarly where all the effects are expressed in terms of benefits like the time saved rather than time lost. Once one obtains the total curve that has a bottom or a peak, the slope of its equation can be set equal to zero, and a solution found for X which will indicate the optimum policy level.

POLICY EVALUATION

SOME CONCLUSIONS

The simple logic and algebra which this chapter proposes for solving optimum policy-level problems can be summarized in three sets of rules, dealing with equations, slopes and optimization. With regard to curve-fitting equations, the rules indicate the type of equation one should or could use for showing certain types of relations between goals and policies. The rules are as follows:

1. If the relation increases or decreases at a constant rate, the equation should read, $Y = a + bX$, or variations on that relation with control variables.

2. If the relation increases or decreases at an increasing or decreasing rate, but not both, the equation should read:

   a. $Y = a + b \text{ Log } X$, when we want simplicity in expressing a diminishing returns slope.

   b. $Y = aX^b$, when we want a coefficient that will relate a percentage change in Y to a one percent change in X.

   c. $Y = ab^X$, when the subject matter is such that it makes sense for the policy variable to be an exponent.

3. If the relation produces a valley-shaped or hill-shaped curve without combining relations, the equations should read, $Y = a + b_1X + b_2X^2$.

4. If the relation increases or decreases at both an increasing and a decreasing rate roughly in the shape of an S, the equation should read $Y = a + b_1X + b_2X^2 + b_3X^3$.

There are other comparative reasons for using these various equations in policy analysis, but these are probably the most frequent ones.

With regard to slopes, the rules are:

1. If $Y = a + bX$, then the slope of Y relative to X is b.

2. If $Y = a + b \text{ Log } X$, then the slope is b/X.

3. If $Y = aX^b$, then the slope is baX^{b-1}.

4. If $Y = ab^X$, then the slope is $(LN\ b)(ab^X)$.

5. If $Y = a + b_1X + b_2X^2$, then the slope is $b_1 + 2b_2X$.

6. If $Y = a + b_1X + b_2X^2 + b_3X^3$, then the slope is $b_1 + 2b_2X + 3b_3X^2$.

Rules 5 and 6 are combinations of rules 1 and 3.

With regard to optimization, the rules are:

1. If a curve showing the relation between degrees of policy adoption

(X) and either total benefits, total costs, or benefits minus costs (Y) is a straight diagonal line or a one-directional curve, then adopt as much or as little as possible of the policy within the constraints depending on whether moving up or down on the policy is desirable.

2. If the curve showing the relation between degrees of policy adoption (X) and either total benefits, total costs or benefits minus costs (Y) is a valley-shaped or hill shaped curve, then adopt the policy up to the point where one reaches the minimum on the valley shaped curve or the maximum on the hill-shaped curve. Doing so involves:

   a. Expressing the relation between X and Y as a quadratic equation of Type 3 above, or a combination of any two of the above equations.

   b. Determining the slope of that equation or combination of equations.

   c. Setting that slope equal to zero, and

      (1) solving for X by getting X to stand by itself on the left side of the equation, or

      (2) solving for X by using reiterative guessing with a programmable calculator.

With that set of six equations, four slope rules, and three optimization rules (linear, analytic solution, and reiterative guessing), plus the numerical parameters from a statistical, deductive or other analysis, one should be able to arrive at an optimum policy level through simple logic and algebra. Obtaining those numerical parameters, including relative value weights, is not easy. The work involved in obtaining them, however, should be more meaningful if one knows better what is going to be done with that kind of numerical information after it has been obtained. Too often in policy analysis, data is gathered for what is intuitively viewed as an optimum policy-level problem, where doing too much or too little would be undesirable, but the data gatherers may only have in mind showing the extent to which a given policy has achieved its intended goals. Such data gathering and analysis may miss the opportunity to go further and say something about what might be the optimum policy level under various normative constraints and empirical coefficients. It is hoped that this chapter will help clarify what is involved in optimum policy-level analysis so that more policy-relevant data gatherers will apply their data to developing optimum policy-level models.

NOTES

1. On the general methodology of optimum level analysis, see Michael Brennan, *Preface to Econometrics* (Cincinnati: South-Western, 1973), pp. 111-92; Samuel Richmond, *Operations Research for Management Decisions* (New York: Ronald, 1968), pp. 40-124; and William Baumol, *Economic Theory and Operations Analysis* (Englewood Cliffs, N.J.: Prentice-Hall, 1978), pp. 1-71. The examples in these three books are, however, all from business situations rather than governmental policy situations.

The governmental policy analysis literature tends to slight optimum level analysis. For example, the popular book, Edith Stokey and Richard Zeckhauser, *A Primer for Policy Analysis* (New York: Norton, 1978) only mentions the important problem of arriving at an optimum policy level (where doing too much or too little is undesirable) on pp. 140-1 out of its 356 pages. There is no mention at all in such books as John Gohagan, *Quantitative Analysis for Public Policy* (Hightstown, N.J.: McGraw-Hill, 1980); Christopher McKenna, *Quantitative Methods for Public Decision Making* (Hightstown, N.J.: McGraw-Hill, 1980); and Edward Quade, *Analysis for Public Decisions* (New York: Elsevier, 1975). Of the many policy analysis books published from 1975 through 1980, the one with the most material on the subject, although the treatment is still quite shallow, is Michael White, et al., *Managing Public Systems: Analytic Techniques for Public Administration* (Duxbury, 1980), pp. 278-90. But also see the excellent case study of "The Optimum Speed Limit" in Duncan MacRae and James Wilde, *Policy Analysis for Public Decisions* (Belmont, Ca.: Duxbury, 1979), pp. 133-56.

Earlier, more abbreviated attempts than this present chapter to develop a logic and algebra for optimum policy-level analysis include S. Nagel, "Finding an Optimum Mix or Optimum Level for Public Policies," in Frank Scioli and Thomas Cook (eds.), *Methodologies for Analyzing Public Policies* (Lexington, Mass: Lexington-Heath, 1975), pp. 79-87; and S. Nagel and M. Neef, "A Simplified Approach to Solving Optimum Level Problems," in *Policy Analysis: In Social Science Research* (Beverly Hills, Ca.: Sage, 1979), pp. 157-59.

2. On the free press, fair trial example, see S. Nagel and M. Neef, *Legal Policy Analysis: Finding an Optimum Level or Mix* (Lexington, Mass.: Lexington-Heath, 1977), pp. 281-316.

3. On the school busing example, see Gary Orfield, *Must We Bus?* (Washington, D.C.: Brookings, 1978).

4. On determining the numerical parameters (for the equations given in this chapter)through the use of statistical regression analysis, see Jacob Cohen and Patricia Cohen, *Applied Multiple Regression/Correlation Analysis for the Behavioral Sciences* (Hillsdale, N.J.: Erlbaum, 1975), especially pp. 212-64; Don Lewis, *Quantitative Methods in Psychology* (Iowa City: U. of Iowa Press, 1966), especially pp. 51-136; and Edward Tufte, *Data Analysis for Politics and Policy* (Englewood Cliffs, N.J.: Prentice-Hall, 1974), especially pp. 65-134.

In seeking the perceptions of knowledgeable people, one could ask such questions as, "If X is zero, what do you think the value of Y would tend to be?" for determining "a" in $Y = a + bX$; or "If X increases by one unit, then by how many units do you think Y would tend to increase or decrease?" for determining "b". One could also ask such questions as, "If X is one unit, what do you think the value of Y would tend to be?" for determining "a" in $Y = aX^b$; or "If X increases by one percent, then by how much of a percent do you think Y would tend to increase or decrease?" for determining "b".

A deductive approach to determining the numerical parameters might involve knowing the relation between X and Z and the relation between Z and Y, and then deducing the relation between X and Y, or deducing the parameters from a purely mathematical model as in the jury size example discussed later under exponential equations. See S. Nagel, "Deductive Modeling in Policy Analysis," in *Policy Analysis: In Social Science Research* (Beverly Hills, Ca.: Sage 1979), pp. 177-96. On the making of assumptions to arrive at the numerical parameters, see S. Nagel and M. Neef, *Legal Policy Analysis: Finding an Optimum Level or Mix* (Lexington, Mass.: Lexington-Heath, 1977, pp. 232-34, and pp. 242-43.

The numerical parameters should reflect causal relations between the goals and the alternative allocations, not just spurious correlations. On causal analysis, see Hans Zeisel, *Say It With Figures* (New York: Harper and Row, 1968); Hubert Blalock, *Causal Influences in Non-Experimental Research* (Chapel Hill: U. of North Carolina Press, 1964); and S. Nagel and M. Neef, "Determining and Rejecting Causation," in *Policy Analysis: In Social Science Research* (Beverly Hills, Ca.: Sage, 1979), pp. 69-102.

5. On the example of determining an optimum percentage of defendants to hold in jail prior to trial, see S. Nagel and M. Neef, *Legal Policy Analysis* (Lexington, Mass.: Lexington-Heath, 1977) at pp. 1-74. On the example of determining an optimum jury size, see the same book at pp. 75-158. On the example of determining an optimum dollar-bond level in pre-trial release, see S. Nagel and M. Neef, *Decision Theory and the Legal Process* (Lexington, Mass.: Lexington-Heath, 1979), pp. 1-70.

6. On the methodology of combining goals, see J.P. Guilford, *Psychometric Methods* (New York: McGraw-Hill, 1954); Allan Easton, *Complex Managerial Decisions Involving Multiple Objectives* (New York: Wiley, 1973); and Peter Gardiner and Ward Edwards, "Public Values: Multiattribute Utility Measurement for Social Decision Making," in Martin Kaplan and Steven Schwartz (eds.) *Human Judgement and Decision Process* (New York: Academic Press, 1975).

Part IV
Finding an Optimum Mix in Allocating Scarce Resources

The purpose of this section is to discuss the problems involved in finding an optimum mix in allocating scarce governmental or political resources. The first three chapters present concrete examples of situations in which this type of evaluation is involved. These situations include (1) allocating political campaign funds across a set of elections, such as 435 congressional elections by a national congressional campaign committee or five state-wide elections in a given state and election year; (2) allocating campaign funds across activities like media versus organization, or across places like counties within an election; and (3) allocating anticrime dollars across places like cities or states, or across activities like police, courts, and corrections. Those three chapters are followed by a synthesizing chapter on the general logic of allocating scarce resources, with a variety of relations between goals and alternative allocations.

Chapter 10
Allocating Campaign Funds across Elections

The main purpose of this chapter is to try to provide a practical and theoretical model for allocating campaign expenditures within a geographical area which has multiple electoral districts in order to maximize the utility of each dollar spent by the organization or candidate doing the spending. As such this chapter is part of the growing literature which attempts to make political campaigning more scientific.[1] The chapter, however, presumes no knowledge more sophisticated than simple arithmetic and some algebra. More technical matters are left to the footnotes.

The example generally used in the chapter is the Democratic Congressional Campaign Committee trying to decide how much money to allocate among the 435 congressional districts.[2] As one of many other alternatives, one could use a gubernatorial campaign trying to decide how much money to allocate to each county in a given state, or a city machine trying to allocate funds among its ward committeemen. Whatever is presented in this chapter from the view point of Democratic Party strategy could also be applied by analogy to Republican Party strategy.

A secondary purpose of this chapter is to generate ideas for a model for rationally allocating other kinds of expenditures or revenue sharing among geographical districts besides political campaign expenditures. For example, if a federal agency were seeking to allocate education funds among the states or a state agency were seeking to allocate antipollution funds among its counties, then a rational allocation model using different variables, but a similar methodology, might be applicable. As such this chapter is also designed to be part of the growing literature which attempts to provide a better understanding of rational policy making[3] and rational law making.[4]

This chapter will first discuss how one might calculate the amount to spend in a district in order to produce a minimum victory margin. Then it will discuss how to rank each district regarding the worthwhileness of spending the money needed to produce within it a minimum victory margin by looking to closeness, importance, switchability, and turnout improvability in each district. Next certain miscellaneous matters are considered like combining worthwhileness criteria, introducing unquantified criteria, considering district boundary changes, handling primaries, allocating among activities rather than districts, and allocating to can-

180 POLICY EVALUATION

didates on the same ticket. Finally the geographical campaign allocation problem is compared with the problem of allocating governmental expenditures among geographical districts.

CALCULATING THE AMOUNT TO SPEND IN A DISTRICT

The Basic Formula with Variations and Alternatives

The basic formula for calculating the amount of campaign dollars to spend in a given district is:

$$\text{Votes Obtained} = a + b\,(\text{Dollars Spent}) \tag{1}$$

In the above formula, a equals the amount of votes which are likely to be obtained if nothing is spent by the candidate. The b equals the likely ratio between an increase in dollars spent over the increase in votes obtained. The numerical value of a and b can be derived by feeding into a computer (along with what is known as a regression program) information on how many votes were obtained and how many dollars were spent by as many congressional candidates in the last election as one can obtain information on.[5]

The *Congressional Quarterly* periodically publishes data on money spent and votes obtained by congressional candidates. Money-spent data can also be obtained through confidential questionnaires from party committees sent to past candidates within the party.[6] Campaign-spending data can be obtained for the 1972 congressional districts and candidates under the new 1972 reporting act from the Clerk of the U.S. House, the Secretary of the U.S. Senate, the Common Cause Organization, and from the secretaries of state in the 50 states.

With the above basic formula, one can determine the number of votes that will be likely to be obtained for a given number of dollars spent, as $V = a + b(D)$. One can determine the number of dollars needed to be spent in order to obtain a given number of votes, as, $D = (V - a)/b$. If in the latter formula[7] one wants to determine D (number of dollars to spend), then V (votes to obtain) should equal about 51 percent of the total votes expected to be cast in a two-candidate contest possibly with a few percentage points for insurance.[8]

One can assume the total votes that will be cast will be approximately the same as the total cast in (1) the last congressional election which accompanied a presidential election if the next congressional election is also presidential; or in (2) the last nonpresidential congressional election if the next congressional election is nonpresidential. As a more complicated alternative, one can predict the total votes cast by extending a trend line from past elections.[9]

The numerical value of a and b in the main formula above can be derived separately from congressional campaign data for different regions of the country (e.g., North and South), since costs per vote do differ by region. The numerical value of a and b can also be derived separately for incumbents and challengers, since incumbents can get votes with fewer dollars than challengers can.[10] The degree of competitiveness of the districts might also be considered in view of the fact that candidates in more competitive districts spend more than candidates in the less competitive districts, and yet the more competitive candidates win by smaller margins.[11] Competitiveness may be indirectly covered by region since northern districts tend to be more competitive than southern ones in general elections.

Other supplementary variables can be added to the regression prediction of votes obtained from dollars spent (in addition to region and incumbency) if they improve the predictive relation. These additional variables can be inserted directly into the regression equation so the equation would then have a form like:

$$V = a + b_1(D) + b_2(Region) + b_3(Incumbency) \tag{2}$$

where b_1, b_2, and b_3 represent the computer-calculated weights of dollars-spent, region, and incumbency respectively in determining votes obtained.[12] Region could be given a dichotomous score of two for South and one for North. Incumbency could be given a score of two for being an incumbent and one for being a challenger. As an alternative, the additional variables can be used to break the main equation into types of equations, for example, by grouping the districts by region and the candidates by incumbency so that separate regression equations can be determined from each grouping.[13]

To further improve the predictability of the relation between dollars spent and votes obtained, one might also consider the phenomenon of diminishing marginal returns. Thus more money may bring more votes, but only up to a point and then the incremental expenditure of money may not equal the incremental gain in votes. The formula that best describes such a relation is probably a logarithmic regression formula rather than either a linear regression formula (like formula 1) or a linear multiple-regression formula (like formula 2). The logarithmic variation simply involves substituting $b(\log D)$ for $b(D)$ in formulas 1 and 2. One then solves for D by determining the antilogarithm of $(V - a)/b$ or the antilogarithm of $(V = a - b_2X_2 - b_2X_3)/b_1$ where X_2 and X_3 correspond to region, incumbency, or other supplementary variables.[14]

As an alternative to predicting votes-obtained from dollars-spent by using a regression equation, one could calculate the *average* number of dollars or cents spent per votes-obtained (with certain types of candidates). If one then wants to predict how many dollars a candidate needs to obtain a given number of votes, one just multiplies (1) the appropriate dollars-per-vote figure by (2) the total votes needed. This method, however, is defective mainly because it fails to consider that dollars and votes are not directly proportional (i.e., the b ratio between an increase in dollars-spent over the increase in votes-obtained is not equal to 1, and the a value is not equal to zero).[15]

The above formulas assume that the candidate on the other side will spend about the same amount as our candidate. If the candidate on the other side is known to be unwilling or unable to spend commensurately, then our spending can be reduced accordingly. If the other candidate is known to be willing and able to spend substantially larger amounts, then our spending may have to be increased accordingly if that is possible and worth the effort.

The above regression formulas (for estimating the number of dollars needed to obtain a given number of votes in a certain type of election) are based on past experience with similar elections. These formulas assume that the money in the election under consideration will be spent efficiently, or at least not any more wastefully than the average past election from which one is trying to generalize. Efficient spending on a given election means spending for those activities that will roughly maximize one's votes up to the point of obtaining a winning majority. The use of quantitative analysis to aid in choosing electoral activities *within* a given district is briefly discussed below after further discussing the use of quantitative analysis to rationally allocate funds *between* districts.

All-Or-Nothing Allocation versus Proportionate Allocation

If (1) the number of dollars to spend is calculated as above for each congressional district; and (2) the districts are ranked in terms of a combination of closeness, importance, switchability, and turnout improvability; and (3) G equals the grand total of dollars available to be spent over all the districts, then allocate G so as to provide the D needed for the first district, the second district, and so on until G is used up. This means all the money will go to places where it can do the most good as determined by the rank order of the districts, and no money will go to places where it can do the least good.

A certain minimum number of dollars per capita may have to be allocated to each district or to some districts, no matter how low it is ranked in order to preserve party structure and morale for future elections or to preserve good will with an important incumbent.[16] Similarly, the D allocated to any higher-ranked district can be reduced to the extent there are funds available from sources other than G. One can also allocate one-third of the D at a first stage in the campaign; a second one-third at a second stage; and a last one-third at the final stage. The rank order of the districts can then be recalculated at each stage.

The above method of geographical allocation, which is emphasized in this chapter, might be referred to as the all-or-nothing approach since it involves (1) trying to give enough money to the most highly ranked districts so the favored congressional candidate can get *all* the votes needed to get elected but no more than that; and it involves (2) giving the most lowly ranked districts *nothing* or nothing above a certain minimum. This approach can be contrasted with a proportionate approach which involves giving money to each geographical district in proportion to the district's combined scores on closeness, importance, switchability, and turnout improvability.

The proportionate approach is particularly applicable to allocating funds among counties in a single governor election. Each county can get an amount equal to the total state dollars available times the ratio between the county's target population and the state's target population. The county's target population for a Democratic gubernatorial candidate is equal to the Democratic population of the county, plus twice the estimated number of switchable voters (see the section below on measuring switchability), plus the estimated number of new voters capable of being turned out (see the section below on measuring turnout improvability). Switched votes are doubled because, unlike new voters, they not only add to the candidate being supported but they also take away from the other candidate, although they may cost more than twice as much to obtain. The state's target population is equal to the sum of the county target populations.

A more sophisticated version of this three-voter-types approach could take into consideration the fact that the costs are generally least for preserving past Democratic votes, middling for getting out new votes, and most for switching votes. Such a system would require knowing or estimating the regression equation between (1) dollars spent for preserving, creating, or switching favorable voters; and (2) votes preserved, created or switched, or at least knowing or estimating the average cost per vote preserved, switched, or created. One would then seek to obtain the total votes needed to win by concentrating first on activities or functions related to preserving votes, then creating votes, and then switching votes (see below).[17] After doing so, one could then arrive at the cost of the total votes needed and then (1) meet all-or-nothing of this cost under the all-or-nothing system for allocating to congressional districts; or (2) meet a proportion of this cost for allocating to counties depending on (a) the total state funds available and (b) the ratio of the county's target population to the state's target population.

DETERMINING THE RANK ORDER OF THE DISTRICTS

The next four subsections of this chapter will deal with four different criteria for ranking the worthwhileness of each district as a place in which to spend campaign money. The criteria will then be combined into a single composite criterion in order to apply the all-or-nothing or the proportionate allocation method.

The Criterion of the Closeness of a District

The closeness of a district refers to how close a district is to shifting from the incumbent to the challenger. The object here is to define the concept of closeness in terms of numerical operations in order to give it quantitative precision. The closest possible election is one in which each of the two major political parties gets 50 percent of the two-party vote. Thus a good measure of closeness would simply involve determining the absolute difference (i.e., regardless whether the difference is positive or negative) between 50 percent and the predicted percentage the Democrats will get in the forthcoming election.

There are three ways of estimating the predicted Democratic percentage of the two-party vote. One way is to simply use the Democratic percentage in the last congressional election. Another method is to extend to the next election a trend line which is algebraically (by a computer) or geometrically (by a ruler) fitted to points which show Democratic percentages in at least two previous congressional elections. A third method involves asking local knowledgeable persons to estimate the predicted Democratic percentage on the basis of whatever they consider relevant, and then averaging their predictions. If more than one of these three methods is used, the result of the multiple methods can also be averaged, giving an overall predicted Democratic percentage.

After this overall percentage is subtracted from 50 percent, the absolute difference can then be subtracted from 100, giving an overall closeness score. The absolute difference from 50 percent is used because a difference of X percent over 50 is equal in closeness to X percent under 50. The subtraction from 100 is done so that when closeness is higher, the closeness measure will go up instead of down. For example, if the predicted Democratic percentage is 65 percent, then the closeness score is 85; and if the predicted Democratic percentage is 45 percent, then the closeness score is 95.

The concept of closeness only applies to allocating funds among congressional or other elections, and not among counties in a state gubernatorial election or other intraconstituency units in a statewide or citywide election. This is because the county votes are summed in determining the winning candidate for governor. A candidate is thus not a total loser if less than 51 percent of a certain county's vote is obtained; nor a wasted surplus winner if one obtains substantially more than 51 percent of a certain county's vote.

The Criterion of the Importance of a District

The importance of a district refers to how much difference it would make in terms of Democratic party goals or especially interest group goals if there was a shift from the incumbent to the challenger in the district. The object here is also to operationally define the concept of importance to give it quantitative precision. A good measure of importance would simply involve determining the absolute difference between (1) the average ideological score of the 435 congressmen and (2) the incumbent's ideological score.

Ideological scores can be those used by the Americans for Democratic Action, the *New Republic*, the Americans for Constitutional Action, Guttman scaling by the researcher, or those obtained from other sources or by other methods.[18] Ideological scores are generally represented by a percentage showing the quantity of a congress member's votes that were favorable to the evaluating group's viewpoint divided by the member's total vote on about ten selected issues. The average ideological score represents the sum of the scores of all congress members divided by the number of congress members. The absolute difference is used because an incumbent X percent *above* the average desirable ideological score is just as important to *retain* in Congress, as an incumbent X percent *below* the average ideological score is to *remove* from Congress.

As an alternative or supplement to the above way of determining the importance of a district, one can determine the absolute difference between the ideological score of the incumbent and the ideological score of the challenger. If the challenger has not served in a scored legislative body at about the same time as the incumbent, then the challenger's ideological score can probably be determined only by asking local knowledgeable persons how the challenger would have voted or will vote on the issues involved or by asking the challenger directly. The absolute difference is used because the bigger the gap between the ideology of the incumbent and challenger regardless of the direction of the gap, the more important a shift would be from the incumbent to the challenger.

An overall importance score for a district could also consider the incumbent's seniority expressed in years in Congress. Similarly, the overall score could consider the importance of the incumbent's committee memberships. This could be expressed as a simple dichotomy of important versus not so important, or be refined into three or four categories. What categories in which to put certain committee memberships could be decided by the congressional campaign committee or the organization that is doing the campaign financing in light of its interests.

Four measures of district importance have been given above with regard to the incumbent's seniority, and the incumbent's committee memberships. An overall importance score can be arrived at by multiplying those four subscores together. They cannot be simply summed and divided by four (as four percentages could be), since they do not each involve a zero to 100 percentage as did the three suggested measures of district closeness.

In dealing with congressional or legislative districts, each district contributes the same number of representatives to the total legislature, where there are single-member districts, or approximately the same number of representatives per capita, where there are multiple-member districts. In dealing with counties in a gubernatorial election or states in a presidential election, however, outcome importance should be measured almost completely in terms of the county population (in a gubernatorial election) or the state electoral college votes (in a presidential election). Some additional subjective importance (like a multiplier of 1.2) can be given to those counties or states, if any, whose pre-election day straw votes or early returns are likely to influence other counties or states.

The Criterion of the Voters' Switchability in a District

The switchability of a district refers to the likelihood that Democrats in the district may vote Republican or vice versa, regardless how close to or far from the predicted 50 percent closeness level the district might be.[19] One way to give this concept quantitative meaning is simply to determine the absolute difference between the Democratic percentage of the two-party vote in the last election and the Democratic percentage in the next-to-last election. This provides a crude measure of change between the last two elections. If more elections are used, calculate an average switchability score by summing the absolute differences for each pair of elections and dividing the number of pairs. The absolute difference is used because an X percentage increase in the Democratic vote is just as much of a switch as an X percentage decrease.

For a more sophisticated way of measuring switchability, one could determine the absolute difference between the actual Democratic percentage in the last election and the predicted Democratic percentage, taking into consideration the background characteristics of the voters in the district. This is done by developing an equation in the form:

$$\text{Predicted Democratic Percentage} = a + b_1X_1 + \ldots + b_nX_n \qquad (3)$$

In the above formula, a equals the Democratic percentage which will be obtained regardless of the characteristics of the voters. Each b equals the ratio between an increase in the Democratic percentage over the increase in each X characteristic. The numerical values of a and b can be derived by feeding into a computer (along with the previously mentioned regression program) information on what the Democratic percentage was and what the aggregate background characteristics of the voters were for as many congressional districts in the last election on which one can find information.

Relevant aggregate background characteristics or Xs for each district obtainable from census data might include such items as the percentage of the population employed in agriculture, the percentage of the nonwhite population, the average income or an indirect measure of economic status, the average school grade completed, percentage of Catholics, and whether the district is in the North or South. With the above formula 3, one can determine the predicted Democratic percentage for any district by simply inserting the background characteristic scores for the district into the formula. If this second measure of switchability is used, then it can be averaged with the first simpler measure since they both are expressed as the difference between two percentages.

It would also be useful in determining the switchability of districts to have the percentage of voters who did not vote a straight party ticket in the last congressional election and information on intensity of party preferences obtained from public opinion polls. This kind of information, however, is not readily available across congressional districts. Similarly, it would be helpful to have census data on how the background characteristics of the voters have changed since the last election, but this kind of data is generally not available for time periods shorter than ten years.

The Criterion of the Turnout Improvability in a District

Turnout improvability refers to the likelihood that new voters can be brought out to vote in favor of the Democratic or liberal candidate in our hypothetical allocation problem. It is assumed that if all other variables are held constant additional turnout will usually favor Democratic and liberal candidates, since the poor, the young, and blacks tend to have relatively low turnout and to vote Democratic or liberal.[20] One can calculate a turnout improvability score (as a switchability score was calculated) by determining the absolute difference between the percentage of persons eligible to register or vote who actually voted in the last election and a similar percentage for the next-to-last election. This provides a crude measure of turnout improvability or changeability between the last two elections.

A more sophisticated alternative or supplement would involve determining the absolute difference between the actual turnout percentage in the last election and predicted turnout percentage, taking into consideration the background characteristics of the voters in the district. The procedure for calculating a predicted turnout percentage is the same as the procedure described above for calculating a predicted Democratic percentage, except turnout percentages for the districts rather than Democratic percentages are fed into the computer to arrive at the numerical values of a and b in formula 3.

Another turnout measure could involve calculating the difference between the turnout percentage for each district and an average turnout percentage for all the districts. This is a comparison across space instead of over time. One could have done the same thing when determining the switchability of a district by calculating the difference between the Democratic percentage for each district and an average Democratic percentage for all the districts. One, however, would expect the turnout percentages to be more alike across districts than the Democratic percentages.

Instead of thinking in terms of gross turnout improvement, one could think in terms of turnout improvability for Democratic groups minus the turnout improvability for Republican groups. Democratic groups are people with background characteristics normally associated with the Democratic party, and similarly for Republican groups. Data for determining such a *net* turnout improvability score, however, is not generally available as contrasted to data for determining a *gross* turnout improvability score for each district.

ADDITIONAL CONSIDERATIONS IN ALLOCATING CAMPAIGN EXPENDITURES

In order to rank the districts on the worthwhileness of each district with regard to spending money on it, one should determine an *overall utility* score which represents a combination of the district's score on closeness, importance, switchability, and turnout improvability. This overall utility score can be symbolized:

$$U = C \times I \times S \times T \tag{4}$$

If one wishes to weigh C, I, S, and T differently, then give each term an exponent to indicate its relative weight. For example, if some of the above elements are evaluated by the congressional campaign committee as being twice as important as others, those elements should be squared and the other elements should have no exponent.[21]

After using the above formulas to rank order the districts in terms of the worthwhileness of each district for spending money in it, one can *subjectively adjust* the rankings to consider unquantified but important bits of information. For example, if a certain district is held by an incumbent who is the head of a committee and defeating the incumbent would mean a new committee head who is far better or worse ideologically (regardless of the ideological difference between the incumbent and the challenger), then this district should be moved upward or downward to some subjective extent.

It is relatively easy to determine the past vote, turnout, or background characteristics for a congressional district whose *boundaries* have not changed. If the boundaries have changed, then determining a past vote, turnout, and background characteristics for a congressional district might involve summing the figures for subdistrict units like counties or wards. If a subdistrict unit has been split between two new congressional districts, one may have to estimate how many voters to assign from the split unit to each new congressional district, depending on where geographically the split occurred and on whatever information is available concerning the split portions of the subdistrict unit.

The same basic formulas as formulas 1, 2, 3, and 4 above can be applied to allocating funds in a Democratic *primary* by substituting conservative Democrat versus liberal Democrat wherever the above formulas talk about Republican versus Democrat. Similarly in a Republican primary, substitute conservative Republican and liberal Republican. A congressional campaign committee would normally not be likely to finance one Democrat against another, but a nonpartisan interest group might wish to do so.

This chapter has discussed rationally allocating campaign expenditures among electoral districts, but related formulas could also be presented with regard to rationally allocating campaign expenditures among different *activities* or functions, like canvassing versus media within a district or group of districts.[22] To obtain the basic data necessary, questionnaires can be sent by the congressional campaign committee to past candidates at least from within its own party asking, for example, how many votes did the candidate obtain, how much money was spent on canvassing organization (C), and how much money was spent on mass media coverage (M).[23] This data from a number of congressional candidates can be used by a computer to solve the numerical value of the a and the two bs in the formula: Votes Obtained $= a + b_1C + b_2M$.[24] To obtain the ideal mix of organization and media dollars, one feeds the following into a computer:

1. The above formula with the numerical values of the a and bs inserted. For example, $V = 50,000 + 1.4C + .8M$.

2. The maximum number of dollars available for spending on both canvassing and media. For example, $C + M \leq 20,000$ dollars.

3. The minimum number of votes to obtain. For example, $V \geq 100,000$.

4. An indication that none of the variables can be less than zero. For example, $V \geq 0; C \geq 0; M \geq 0$.

5. An instruction to minimize $C + M$ at a given V or to maximize V at a given $C + M$.

6. A linear optimizing program available at most university computing centers.[25]

Linear programming could also be used to allocate expenditures among different geographical areas, not only among different activities. Doing so, however, requires having data at more than one point in time for each of the districts for votes-obtained and dollars-spent. Each time point instead of each district then becomes the unit of analysis. The regression equation (analogous to the formula mentioned above in discussing the application of linear programming to choosing among activities) then becomes: Number of Districts Won $= a + b_1X_1 + b_2X_2 + \ldots + b_nX_n$ where X_1 is the number of dollars to spend in district one and also for X_2 on up to X_n. With instructions like those numbered 2 through 6 above, the computer is then capable of telling us what is the optimum way to allocate our money among the districts in order to maximize the number of districts won without exceeding our total national budget. Such an approach emphasizes those districts which have switched from our side to the other or vice versa in the election years for which we have data. Such an approach indirectly considers the closeness, switchability, and turnout improvability that is likely to switch the results. Each district or X score could be given an additional weight to show its importance in terms of the voting record of the incumbent.[26]

After determining how much to allocate to various districts and activities, one should seek to get the most for the money spent on each activity. Here is where traditional *campaign strategy* manuals and articles can be especially helpful.[27] They often provide useful information on how to make the best use of canvassing organization and mass media.

Another different, but related, campaign allocation problem is how to allocate party funds among candidates or *contests on the same ticket.* For example, how much should be allocated to the race for governor, attorney general, and secretary of state in a statewide election year. This problem is more analogous to the allocation among districts than to the allocation among different activities. The problem can be resolved more rationally if one can estimate the relation between dollars-spent and votes-obtained as with the congressional example. Then the above three or more contests on the same ticket can be ranked in terms of predicted closeness and the importance of a victory, also like the congressional example. Voter switchability and turnout improvability should be about the same for each of those contests since the constituency is held constant. The total available funds would then be allocated to the contests in light of their rank order, taking into consideration alternative funds and the minimum allocation needed for preserving morale.

Allocating campaign expenditures among electoral districts, diverse activities, or among candidates has traditionally been done in an unsystematic manner involving hunches, unexplicit values, and trial and error, as well as some systematic data processing. It would be interesting to apply the same kind of allocation model described in this chapter to a large set of congressional elections from 1974 or 1972 using a variety of different goals to maximize and data to input. One would then compare the optimum allocations generated by the model with the actual allocations of the candidates, and then attempt to explain the variance between those *optimum and empirical allocations.* Obtaining and explaining these allocations is a massive project in itself, but it is hoped that the ideas generated by this model will stimulate others to follow that line of empirical research and/or to develop improvements on the basically deductive model, as well as stimulate more effective use of the limited campaign dollars available.

By way of summary, it might be said that the basic model contains essentially one normative premise, namely that dollars should be spent in those election districts where they will do the most good in winning elections, and one empirical premise, namely that votes-obtained bears a positive relation to dollars-spent. The basic conclusion, which is in effect deduced from the premises, is that dollars should be allocated to those districts that combine the highest closeness, importance, switchability, and turnout improvability in order to allow those districts to cross the predicted threshold of votes needed for victory by the desired candidate.

BROADER IMPLICATIONS FOR GOVERNMENTAL EXPENDITURE ALLOCATION

Differences from Campaign Allocation

If a federal agency were seeking to allocate funds among its counties, then a rational model that maximizes the utility of the dollars-spent should also be followed.[28] Such a model, however, might have a number of important differences from the campaign allocation model presented above.[29]

First, the normative goal is not to maximize votes, although legislators have been empirically known to pressure administrators and each other to spend more money in their legislative districts in order to help the legislators get re-elected, rather than focusing on the special needs of their districts. The accepted normative goal, however, is more likely to maximize the average gain to the recipient entities times the number of recipient entities (e.g., educational advancement per average individual, or cleaner air per average air quality region).

Second, many government expenditure programs are directed toward individual or family benefit rather than area benefit. Thus if the per family income in a ten-family state is 5,000 dollars, but it is based on one family having a 50,000 dollar income and the other nine having no income, then that first state needs more federal welfare aid than a ten-family state with every family having a 3,000 dollar income, even though the average family income in the second state is lower. In campaign allocation, as in antipollution allocation, however, one is concerned with areawide measures of effectiveness.

Third, one can sometimes eliminate funds from some areas in allocating campaign expenditures on the ground that the desired candidate is a hopeless loser or a sure winner. On the other hand, for humanitarian and political reasons, one cannot so easily eliminate government funds from an area on the basis that it is so badly off as to be a hopeless rathole into which to pour money, or that it is so well off that it will, in an enlightened way, not expect to get any return on its taxes. This requires some kind of a proportionate approach, rather than an all-or-nothing approach (as defined earlier).

Fourth, there is a precise threshold of success in campaign allocation, namely achieving 51 percent of the two-party vote. Anything less than that is almost as bad as zero percent, and anything more than that is wasted. However, in federal aid to education like most federal aid programs, there is no accepted threshold up to which all school districts should be raised. Similarly, a district cannot be said to be overeducated if there are jobs available appropriate to the education level obtained.

Fifth, in campaign allocation one starts with a total sum of money to be divided among 50 states or other electoral districts. In allocating other governmental expenditures, one may total the needs of the 50 states (possibly each discounted by a certain percentage) in order to arrive at the total sum of money which would be appropriated by Congress. In other words, campaign allocation tends to start from the top and trickle down, whereas some government expenditure programs start from the bottom and roughly add upward.

Similarities to Campaign Allocation

In spite of the differences in campaign allocation and government spending allocation, there are important similarities. They both involve deciding how much money should be spent over a set of geographical areas to obtain the most total benefit. They should both take population into consideration where geographical areas of unequal population are being considered (like states or counties rather than congressional districts). They should both take importance or need into consideration. They should both consider whether, with some extra funds, each geographical area is reaching up to some minimum threshold level. They both tend to consider how much money can be raised locally to supplement the funds which might be allocated from above.

The exact considerations in rationally allocating government expenditures depend on the subject matter of the spending program. Thus somewhat different calculations—worthwhileness variables, and additional allocation considerations analogous to the campaign spending model—would be used depending on whether the program involves aid to education, welfare, antipollution, or some other social goal. It is, however, hoped that the ideas presented in this campaign allocation chapter will generate further ideas for developing related models for rationally allocating government expenditures among geographical districts in those other specific programs.[30]

It is further hoped that the allocation model presented here will have both practical and theoretical significance. It will have practical significance if it gets used, in modified form, by those involved in making geographical allocation decisions. The model will have theoretical significance if it gets used by those seeking a better understanding of allocation decisions, with the model serving as (1) an idea-generating model or as (2) a model to compare with empirical data on the actual making of allocation decisions.

NOTES

1. Political campaigning is making increasing use of mathematical, statistical, and computer techniques to predict voter responses to various stimuli, to do scheduling, and for other planning activities. See James Perry, *The New Politics: The Expending Technology of Political Manipulation* (New York: Clarkson Potter, 1968) pp. 148-70; Robert Agranoff (ed.), *The New Style in Election Campaigns* (Raleigh, N.J.: Holbrook Press, 1972); Robert Chartrand, *Computers and Political Campaigning* (Rochelle Park, N.J.: Spartan Books, 1972); Ronald Totaro, *How to Conduct a Political Campaign with the Systematic Analysis Study System* (New York: Vantage, 1971); Gerald Kramer, "A Decision Theoretic Analysis of a Problem in Political Campaigning" in *Mathematical Application in Political Science*, II (Dallas, Tx.: Arnold Foundation, 1966); and *Politeia*, the quarterly of the American Association of Political Consultants.

2. For an empirical analysis on how congressional campaign committees currently allocate funds among candidates (rather than an optimizing analysis of how they could), see Kevin McKeough, *Financing Campaigns for Congress: Contribution Patterns of National-Level Party and Non-Party Committees, 1964* (Los Angeles: Citizens Research Foundation, 1970) pp. 109-11. McKeough finds national campaign committees tend to favor incumbents, competitive districts, and low-cost rural districts.

Studies of the effects of the electoral college for choosing the president sometimes deal with how a presidential candidate might best allocate expenditures among the states. Steven Brams and Morton Davis, "Resource Allocation Models in Presidential Campaigning: Implications for Democratic Representation," and Eric Uslaner, "Pivotal States in the Electoral College," both in Lee Papayanopoulos (ed.) *Democratic Representation and Apportionment: Quantitative Methods, Measures, and Criteria* (New York: New York Academy of Sciences, 1973), and also Claude Colantoni, et al., "Campaign Resource Allocation under the Electoral College," *American Political Science Review* (1974), pp. 141-61. The peculiarities of the electoral college system, however, make it difficult to generalize these models to expenditure allocation in other campaigns or noncampaign governmental expenditures.

3. Guy Black, *The Application of Systems Analysis to Government Operations* (New York: Praeger, 1968); Philip Morse, *Operations Research for Public Systems* (Cambridge, Mass.: M.I.T. Press, 1967); and Thomas Goldman (ed.), *Cost-Effectiveness: New Approaches in Decision-Making* (New York: Praeger, 1967).

4. Louis Mayo and Ernest Jones, "Legal Policy Decision Process: Alternative Thinking and the Predictive Function," 33 *George Washington Law Review* 318-456 (1964); and S. Nagel, "Optimizing Legal Policy," 18 *U. of Florida Law Review* 577-90 (1966).

5. On regression analysis, see Hubert Blalock, *Social Statistics* (New York: McGraw-Hill, 1960), 273-85; and N. Draper and H. Smith, *Applied Regression Analysis* (New York: Wiley, 1966). Instead of fitting an equation to the dollars-spent, votes-obtained data by the ordinary regression method, one could use related methods for a possibly better fit like the maximum likelihood, limited information, or two-stage least squares methods. William Baumol, *Economic Theory and Operations Analysis* (Englewood Cliffs, N.J.: Prentice-Hall, 1965), pp. 214-17, 228-30, 237-49. The latter method might be helpful for separating out the independent effect or slope of campaign dollars on subsequent votes as contrasted to the effect of increased votes on stimulating increased campaign dollar contributions.

6. On campaign expenditure reporting in general, see Herbert Alexander,

Regulation of Political Finance (Los Angeles: Institute of Government Studies and Citizens Research Foundation, 1966). Some campaign expenditure data for Senate and House candidates in the 1970 elections is given in *Congressional Quarterly*, "Dollar Politics: The Issue of Campaign Spending" (Washington, D.C.: Congressional Quarterly, Inc., 1971), pp. 62-72. Data for radio-TV spending for Senate, House, and governor candidates is given in Federal Communications Commission, *Survey of Political Broadcasting* (Washington, D.C.: FCC, 1971). Related data for the 1972 and 1974 congressional elections is also available from the *Congressional Quarterly* and the Federal Communications Commission, with more detailed data available from the secretary of state in each state under the Federal Election Campaign Act of 1971. See especially *The Annual Statistical Report of Contributions and Expenditures Made During the 1972 Election Campaigns for the U.S. House of Representatives,* 93rd Congress, 2d Session, Document 93-284, 1198 pages, April, 1974, GPO Stock Number 5271-00402, cost $11.40; and Document 93-284 Part II, 175 pages, June, 1974, GPO, cost $2.10.

7. The formula for determining D is *not* $D = A + BV$, where A = the Y intercept and B equals the slope (with D as an endogenous variable and V as an exogenous variable). This is not the correct formula because we are not asking, "How many votes in a previous election will generate how many dollars in a subsequent election?" Instead we are asking, "Given the number of votes we need to win and given the relation between dollars as an exogenous variable and votes as an endogenous variable, how many dollars do we need to achieve the needed number of votes?"

8. For empirical data (rather than mathematical formulas) on the positive correlation between dollars spent and votes obtained, see Alexander Heard, *The Costs of Democracy* (Chapel Hill: U. of North Carolina Press, 1960), pp. 24-34; William Crotty, "Party Effort and Its Impact on the Vote," 65 *American Political Science Review* 439-50 (1971); Paul Dawson and James Zinser, "Broadcast Expenditures and Electoral Outcomes in 1970 Congressional Elections," 35 *Public Opinion Quarterly* 398-402 (1971). On television dollars spent and percentage of votes obtained, Herbert Alexander found little relation in 1960-62, but he did not control for being a Republican which may have correlated positively with TV spending and negatively with victory. Herbert Alexander, "Broadcasting and Politics" in Kent Jennings and Harmon Zeigler (eds.), *The Electoral Process* (Englewood Cliffs, N.J.: Prentice-Hall, 1966).

9. On projecting or extending trend lines, see Margaret Hagood and Donald Price, *Statistics for Sociologists* (New York: Holt, 1952), pp. 160-87. One can also use a computerized regression analysis to predict (1) the percent of registered voters who will vote by looking at (2) the background characteristics of the voters in the district. This predicted percentage can then be applied to the number of registered voters to determine the total votes expected to be cast.

10. Charles Jones, "The Role of the Campaign in Congressional Politics," in Jennings and Zeigler, op. cit.

11. *Congressional Quarterly, op. cit.*, pp. 11-14, 19-27.

12. Instead of using a purely additive model in formula 2 above, greater predictability might be obtained from multiplying two of the variables and their b-weights together in addition to adding them. This is so if the variables have a joint relation with votes obtained such that neither variable alone is important but together their impact is substantial. Blalock, op. cit. pp. 463-64; and Walter Burnham and John Sprague, "Additive and Multiplicative Models of the Voting Universe: The Case of Pennsylvania 1960-1968," 64 *American Political Science Review* 471-90 (1970).

13. Technically speaking this is the problem of analysis of variance (or covariance) versus regression analysis, or the problem of fractionation (or partitioning) versus partial correlation. For further detail, see Blalock, op. cit., pp.

234-39, 329-33; Draper and Smith, op. cit., pp. 243-62. By fractionating the sample, one reduces the sample size for each regression, but fractionation is a more meaningful means of holding constant region and other intervening variables than the partial correlation method which is built into the multiple regression analysis, provided the samples are still substantial. Fractionation also reduces the number of variables and the compounding intercorrelations among them.

14. On curvilinear regression, see Hagood and Price, op. cit. note 7, pp. 442-47; Blalock, op. cit., pp. 351-54; Draper and Smith, op. cit., pp. 263-303. On how to read a table of logarithms in order to determine the antilogarithm or number which corresponds to a given logarithm, see Hobart Sommers, *Living Mathematics Reviewed* (Chicago: Wilcox & Follett, 1943) pp. 213-317.

15. Predicting from averages rather than regression equations is compared in J.P. Guilford, *Fundamental Statistics in Psychology and Education* (New York: McGraw-Hill, 1956), pp. 362-66.

16. In addition to a minimum constraint per district, there may also have to be a maximum constraint per district to keep a few districts from excessively consuming nearly all the money. Such a constraint is, however, probably unnecessary since one ranks the districts by worthwhileness and allocates to the most worthwhile first.

17. See notes 22 through 25 and the corresponding text.

18. On techniques for positioning legislators on ideological scales which are more sophisticated than the box scoring or simple percentaging used by the ADA and ACA, see John Wahlke and Heinz Eulau, *Legislative Behavior: A Reader in Theory and Research* (New York: Free Press, 1959), pp. 388-413.

19. A district can have high switchability among its voters but low closeness, as where the district goes 25 percent Democratic, 40 percent D, and 10 percent D over three congressional elections. A district can have high closeness but low switchability as where the district goes 49 percent D, 49 percent D, and 49 percent D over three congressional elections. Similarly, a district can be high on both closeness and relatively high on switchability as where the district goes 45 percent D, 55 percent D, and 45 percent D. Finally, a district can be low on both criteria as is the case of a district that goes 35 percent D, 35 percent D, and 35 percent D. Switchability refers to voters in the district switching the party for which they vote, not to districts switching from a Democratic to a Republican congress member or vice versa.

20. Lester Milbrath, *Political Participation* (Chicago: Rand McNally, 1965) pp. 110-42; Robert Lane, *Political Life* (New York: Free Press, 1964) pp. 46-52, 220-34; Bernard Berelson et al., *Voting* (Chicago: U. of Chicago Press, 1954) pp. 327-37.

21. Similarly, the subcomponents of C, I, S, and T can be weighted (1) by exponents if the subcomponents are multiplied or (2) by multipliers if the subcomponents are added. If multiplier-weights are used, the divisor should equal the sum of the multiplier weights in arriving at an average score. David Miller and Martin Starr, *Executive Decisions and Operations Research* (Englewood Cliffs, N.J.: Prentice-Hall, 1960) pp. 161-65.

22. For empirical data on how campaign money is allocated to different activities, see David Adamany, *Campaign Finance in America* (Belmont, Ca.: Duxbury Press, 1972) pp. 84-125; and Heard, op. cit., pp. 387-99.

23. From the overall expenditure data for each district (mentioned in note 6 and the corresponding text), one can subtract the FCC radio-TV figures (M) to obtain a rough measure of canvassing expenditures (C).

24. To consider the phenomenon of diminishing returns, use the logarithmic variation of this formula. See note 13 and the accompanying text. An alternative logarithmic variation that lends itself to the use of a linear regression computer formula is $V = a(C)^{b_1}(M)^{b_2}$ or $\log V = \log a + b_1(\log C) + b_2(\log M)$.

25. On linear and other forms of optimum programming among activities, see Miller and Starr, op. cit., pp. 158-61, 400-6, 190-209; and William Baumol,

Economic Theory and Operations Analysis (Englewood Cliffs, N.J.: Prentice-Hall, 1965) pp. 70-102. For a more impressionistic optimizing model than the linear programming approach, see Steve Hanson, "Media, Mix, and Computers" (mimeographed paper included in the transcript of a two-day 1970 seminar presented by the American Association of Political Consultants on "Information Systems, Computers, and Campaigns"). For further related detail, see S. Nagel, "Choosing among Alternative Public Policies", in Kenneth Dolbeare, *Public Policy Evaluation* (Beverly Hills, Ca.: Sage, 1975). One could apply the same linear programming allocation to activities preserving past favorable voters, creating new favorable voters, and switching voters from the other side.

26. As an alternative related conceptualization, we could determine for each district a regression equation of the form $Y = a + bX + cZ$ where Y is the number of votes obtained by the Democratic candidate or other desired side, X is the number of dollars spent for that side in the district, and Z refers collectively to other determinants of either votes or the dollars-votes relation like incumbency and region. The b and c are slopes of Y with regard to X and Z respectively. The units of analysis here are two or more time points for the district. The districts are then ranked by the size of their b slopes which are their marginal rates of return.

The disadvantage of this linear or nonlinear marginal return approach is that a district may have a high marginal rate of return but still be a bad place in which to spend dollars because, for example, (1) the desired candidate is already likely to be a winner and spending will just increase the margin of votes from 55 percent to 65 percent, or (2) the desired candidate has so far to go, from 25 percent to 51 percent. In other words, the marginal return approach does not consider district closeness, nor does it consider district importance. It does, however, reflect voter switchability and turnout improvability, and it could be used to replace or supplement those measures.

For further detail on the marginal rate of return approach including its modified use to consider the above mentioned constraints, see S. Nagel and M. Neef, "Finding an Optimum Geographical Allocation for Anti-Crime Dollars and Other Government Expenditures" (paper presented at the 1975 annual meeting of the Midwest Political Science Association).

27. For example, Dan Nimmo, *The Political Persuaders; the Techniques of Modern Election Campaigns* (Englewood Cliffs, N.J.: Prentice-Hall, 1970); Joseph Napolitan, *The Election Game and How to Win It* (1971); Paul Van Riper, *Handbook of Practical Politics* (New York: Row Peterson, 1960); Movement for a New Congress, *Vote Power: The Official Activist Campaigner's Handbook* (Englewood Cliffs, N.J.: Prentice-Hall, 1970).

28. When operations research or systems analysis people talk about spatial optimization, they do not mean optimizing expenditures among geographical areas. They mean how to locate warehouses or field offices so as to minimize distances from users. See Black, op. cit., pp. 109-16.

29. On approaches to allocating federal grants-in-aid to states and communities, see George Break, *Intergovernmental Fiscal Relations in the United States* (Washington, D.C.: Brookings, 1966), pp. 128-9; Deil Wright, *Federal Grants-in-Aid: Perspectives and Alternatives* (Washington, D.C.: American Enterprise Institute, 1968); and Commission on Intergovernmental Relations, *Twenty-Five Grants-in-Aid Programs* (Washington, D.C.: Government Printing Office, 1956).

30. There is a substantial literature on the geographical allocation problem in the field of education, some of which is useful in generating more general ideas. McKinsey and Company, *Allocating Educational Funds to the Community School Districts* (New York: N.Y.C. Bd. of Ed., 1970); Arthur Wise, *Rich Schools, Poor Schools: The Promise of Equal Educational Opportunity* (U. of Chicago Press, 1968); and John Coons *et al., Private Wealth and Public Education* (Cambridge, Mass.: Harvard U. Press, 1970).

Chapter 11
Allocating Campaign Funds across Activities and Places

The purpose of this brief chapter is to present some general principles with regard to rationally allocating campaign expenditures across activities and places. The chapter is particularly concerned with describing how modern methods of operations research and management science can be used to make campaign allocations more effective in winning votes and more efficient in saving money, while at the same time satisfying legal and political constraints.

These methods are applicable at the national, state, or local level. National and statewide campaign committees, however, may be in the best position to put these methods to good use since they generally have better access to a broader data base, more knowledgeable researchers, and better research facilities. The chapter avoids technical discussion as much as possible by approaching the subject from a consumer's perspective rather than from the perspective of one who is likely to be doing the data gathering and processing.

ALLOCATING ACROSS ACTIVITIES

To illustrate some of the problems involved in allocating campaign expenditures across activities, suppose the Democratic or Republican national congressional campaign committees are interested in advising the local campaign committees how they should allocate their funds between media dollars (i.e., TV and radio) and precinct organization dollars (nonmedia), to obtain at least 51 percent of the two-party vote without exceeding the local campaign budget.

This type of activity-allocation question can be answered by going through the following steps:

1. Obtain the relevant raw data for a set of congressional districts in a recent congressional election year.
   a. The radio-TV expenditures can be obtained from the Federal Communications Commission.
   b. The total expenditures can be obtained from the Federal Election Commission.
   c. The total votes received by each candidate can be obtained from the Congressional Quarterly.

2. Record on an IBM card the following information for each major party candidate, with one card per candidate:

   a. Radio-TV or media dollars spent ($M).

   b. Nonradio-TV or precinct dollars spent ($P), which represents the difference between total expenditures and $M.

   c. Percent of the two-party vote obtained (%V).

   d. Whether the candidate was an incumbent or a contender.

   e. Whether the candidate was a member of the majority or minority party according to the election returns in the congressional election preceding the one being used.

3. With that set of IBM cards, we can now determine the relative importance of media dollars versus precinct dollars for various types of candidates such as:

   a. Nonincumbents from the minority party running against nonincumbents from the majority party.

   b. Nonincumbents from the majority party running against nonincumbents from the minority party.

   c. Incumbents running against nonincumbents.

   d. Nonincumbents running against incumbents.

   The candidates are classified as incumbents or nonincumbents, and as candidates of the majority or minority party because those two characteristics especially influence the effect of dollars on votes.

4. Determining the relative importance of $M and $P involves working with the IBM cards for the category of candidates in which we are interested. The cards are fed into a computer along with a prepackaged statistical prediction program (available at nearly all computing centers) to determine the numerical values of a, b_1, and b_2 in an equation of the form $\%V = a(\$M)^{b_1}(\$P)^{b_2}$. That equation can be interpreted as follows:

   a. The "a" represents the percent of the two-party vote the candidate is likely to receive if only one unit $M and $P are spent.

   b. The b_1 indicates the effect on %V of a one percent increase in $M, holding constant the effect of $P and one's status as a nonincumbent or a minority party candidate.

   c. The b_2 indicates the effect on %V if a one percent increase in $P, holding constant the effect of the other variables.

   This equation also takes into consideration that $M and $P may increase %V, but at a diminishing rate of increase as additional votes become harder to get.

5. With this type of equation, one can now arrive at a few simple

rules for optimally allocating a campaign budget between $M and $P in order to maximize %V. They are as follows:

a. Give to $M a proportion of the budget equal to $b_1/(b_1 + b_2)$.

b. Give to $P a proportion of the budget equal to $b_2/(b_1 + b_2)$.

c. Before giving to $M and $P, reduce the budget by whatever minimum, if any, has to be given to $M and $P in light of the smallest amounts previously needed to win.

d. Do not give to $M or $P an amount that will exceed whatever the legal constraints might be.

6. The same general method can be used to make allocation decisions between two or more other alternative activities, provided data can be obtained from records or questionnaires concerning how much candidates previously allocated to those activities and the votes they received. Variations on the method are also available for minimizing expenditures while still obtaining 51 percent of the two-party vote.[1]

ALLOCATING ACROSS PLACES

To illustrate some of the problems involved in allocating campaign expenditures across places, suppose a statewide campaign committee for governor or senator is interested in deciding how much of their total funds to allocate among the counties or other districts within the state to maximize the percent of the two-party vote for their candidate. Alternative illustrations might involve allocating across congressional or state legislative districts in order to maximize the percentage of legislative seats won.

Allocating across places might best be handled by going through the following steps:

1. Create a set of IBM cards for each district, with each card corresponding to one previous election. On each card record the following raw data:

    a. The total campaign expenditures for the candidate from one's party, adjusted for inflation in order to provide comparability across election years ($C).

    b. The percent of the two party vote obtained by the candidate from one's party (%V).

2. Feed the cards from each district into a computer along with a prepackaged statistical prediction program (available at nearly all computing centers) to determine the numerical values of a, b_1, and b_2 in the equation of the form, $(\%V)_t = a + b_1 \text{Log} \$C_t + b_2(\%V)_{t-1}$. That equation can be interpreted as follows:

a. The "a" represents the predicted percent of the two-party vote that a candidate will receive who spends one monetary unit at a time t and who received no votes at time $t - 1$.

b. The b_1 represents the increase in the percent of the two-party vote a candidate is predicted to receive as a result of a ten monetary-unit increase in campaign expenditures.

c. The b_2 represents the effect on %V of variables other than $C which influence %V. We are in effect holding constant the prior two-party vote percentage and indirectly whatever influences it other than $C.

3. With that type of equation, one can now arrive at a few simple rules for optimally allocating a campaign budget across the districts. Those rules are as follows:

a. Give to each district in proportion to its b_1 coefficient. That means we sum all the b_1 coefficients that are positive, and then we divide the b_1 for the first district by that sum to determine its share of the budget. Then we divide the b_1 for the second district by that sum to determine its share, and so on.

b. Before allocating the budget in proportion to the b_1 coefficients, reduce the total budget by the sum of the minimums given to each district in order to maintain morale or for other reasons. Any district that has a negative b_1 coefficient gets no more than its minimum.

4. The same general method can be used to make allocations across places where a vote from Place 1 is worth as much as a vote from Place 2, which is the case when both places are in the same district. Variations on the method are also available where 51 percent of the two-party vote is needed to win in the district. Then votes above or below that figure represent wasted votes. Taking that into consideration would mean allocating to each place in proportion to their b_1 coefficients, but with no place receiving a $C value that will cause its $V to substantially exceed or fall below 51 percent.[2]

These allocation methods are widely used in allocating budgets across alternative activities and places in business decision making designed to maximize sales or profits. The same methods can be used in political campaigns to maximize votes or elections won within an available budget. Business procedures are increasingly being used in political campaigns, although not necessarily allocation procedures. The main reasons why they have not been used are probably a lack of awareness on the part of campaign strategy committees and a lack of data for applying the methods. It is hoped that this brief chapter will stimulate interest in (1) obtaining further details for applying the methods described, and (2) adding to the shared experiences in using those methods.

NOTES

1. For further details on optimally allocating across campaign activities, see Edie Goldenberg and Michael Traugott, "Resource Allocations and Broadcast Expenditures in Congressional Campaigns" (unpublished paper available from the authors at the Center for Political Studies, University of Michigan, 1979), Gerald Kramer, "A Decision-Theoretic Analysis of a Problem in Political Campaigning," in *Mathematical Applications in Political Science* (Arnold Foundation of Southern Methodist University, 1966), and S. Nagel with M. Neef, *Operations Research Methods: As Applied to Political Science and the Legal Process* (Beverly Hills, Ca.: Sage, 1977), especially pp. 10-19.

2. For further details on optimally allocating campaign expenditures across places, see Joel Barkan and James Bruno, "Operations Research in Planning Political Campaign Strategies," 20 *Operations Research* 925-941 (1972), Philip Kotler, *Marketing Decision Making: A Model Building Approach* (New York: Holt, 1971), and chapters 10 and 12 in this book.

REFERENCES

Attempts to optimally allocate campaign expenditures assume that expenditures make a difference in votes obtained. There are now a considerable number of articles confirming and discussing various aspects of that relation, such as the following:

Achen, Christopher. "A New Estimator for Issue Voting, Nonrandomized Experiments, and the Effects of Campaign Expenditures." Paper presented at the annual meeting of the American Political Science Association, 1979.

Bental, Benjamin, Uri Ben-Zion, and Yair Moshel. "Money in Politics: An Empirical Study." Paper presented at the annual meeting of the Public Choice Society, 1977.

Ben-Zion, Uri and Zeev Eytan. "On Money, Votes, and Policy in a Democratic Society." 17 *Public Choice* 1-10, 1974.

Blydenburgh, John. "An Application of Game Theory to Political Campaign Decision Making." 20 *American Journal of Political Science* 51, 1976.

Cook, W., et al. "Models for the Optimal Allocation of Funds over N Constituencies during an Election Campaign." 20 *Public Choice* 1-16, 1974.

Crain, William and Robert Tollison. "Campaign Expenditures and Political Competition." 19 *Journal of Law and Economics* 745-71, 1976.

Crotty, William. "Party Effort and Its Impact on the Vote." 65 *American Political Science Review* 429-50, 1971.

Dawson, Paul and James Zinser. "Broadcast Expenditures and Electoral Outcomes in the 1970 Congressional Elections." 35 *Public Opinion Quarterly* 398-402, 1971.

Deegan, John. "The Effects of Campaign Expenditures in Nonpartisan Elections." Mimeographed paper, 1977.

Giertz, Fred and Dennis Sullivan. "Campaign Expenditures and Election Outcomes." 31 *Public Choice* 1977.

Glantz, Stanton, Alan Abramowitz and Michael Burkart. "Election Outcomes: Whose Money Matters?" 38 *Journal of Politics* 1033-38, 1976.

Jacobson, Gary. "Practical Consequences of Campaign Finance Reform: An Incumbent Protection Act?" 24 *Public Policy* 1-32, 1976.

_____. "The Effects of Campaign Spending in Congressional Elections," 72 *American Political Science Review* 469-91, 1978.

Johnston, R. "Resources Allocation and Political Campaigns: Notes toward a Methodology." 5 *Policy and Politics* 181-200, 1976.

––––––. "Campaign Spending and Votes: A Reconsideration." 33 *Public Choice* 83-92, 1978.

Lott, William and P.D. Warner III. "The Relative Importance of Campaign Expenditures: An Application of Production Theory." 8 *Quality and Quantity* 99-106, 1974.

Palda, Kristian. "The Effect of Expenditure on Political Success." 18 *Journal of Law and Economics* 745-71, 1976.

Silberman, Jonathan. "A Comment on the Economics of Campaign Funds." 25 *Public Choice* 69-77, 1976.

Silberman, Jonathan and Gilbert Yochum. "Campaign Funds and the Election Process." Paper presented at the Public Choice Society Meeting, 1977.

Taylor, A. "The Effect of Party Organization: Correlation Between Campaign Expenditures and Voting in the 1970 Election." 20 *Political Studies* 329-31, 1972.

Tullock, Gordon. "The Purchase of Politicians." 10 *Western Economic Journal* 345-55, 1972.

Welch, William. "Money and Votes: A Simultaneous Equation Model." Paper presented at the Public Choice Society Meeting, 1977.

Welch, William. "The Economics of Campaign Funds." 20 *Public Choice* 83-97, 1974.

Welch, William. "The Effectiveness of Expenditures in State Legislative Races." 4 *American Politics Quarterly* 333-56, 1976.

Chapter 12
Allocating Anticrime Dollars across Places and Activities

The purpose of this chapter is to discuss the provocative methodological problems of how to use information on social indicators (like crime rates) and governmental expenditures to attempt to arrive at an optimal allocation of those expenditures.*

Those problems include how to relate in a causal way the social indicators to the expenditures, and how to use those relations to allocate to places and activities, separately and simultaneously. The chapter describes the relevant issues, criteria, and defects in the prior literature. It provides a concrete example dealing with the reallocation of the 1973 budget of the Law Enforcement Administration Agency so as to minimize predicted 1974 crime in light of the 1968 through 1972 crime and expenditure data across 10 large U.S. cities. By "optimally allocating" in this context, we mean making use of the quantitative methods of operations research, management science, and related fields in order to allocate anticrime dollars across places and activities in such a way as to obtain as much improvement as possible regarding crime occurrence and other desired outcomes.

The references that follow this chapter contain a number of items relating to optimum allocation in general, and also optimum allocation in the anticrime context. Although these items are relevant, they generally have a number of defects that limit their applicability, including the items previously written by the co-authors of this chapter. These defects include the following:

1. Allocating either to places or to activities, rather than creating a methodology that considers the interrelations of both types of allocations.

2. Data that relate either to subject matters other than criminal jus-

---

*The author gratefully acknowledges the helpful suggestions of Eli Noam of Columbia University, Judith Liebman and Wayne Davis of the University of Illinois, and Wesley Skogan of Northwestern. They represent backgrounds in law/economics, operations research, and political science, respectively, all of which are relevant to the interdisciplinary topic of optimally allocating anticrime expenditures.

tice and law enforcement or that use only hypothetical criminal justice figures.

3. Allocating to only a few places or activities at a time, rather than the more realistic problems that involve many places and many activities.

4. Emphasized use of linear statistical routines that are unrealistic in light of the principle of diminishing returns, which tends to be present in relating allocations to results.

5. Occasional use of simultaneous equation-solving methods or non-linear programming routines. These methods, however, are quite difficult to apply especially in the absence of sophisticated computer software and personnel.

6. They do not adequately control for variables other than anticrime dollars which also influence crime occurrence. Nor do they control for the reciprocal relation between crime and anticrime dollars.

ISSUES THAT NEED TO BE RESOLVED

Measuring Crime and Anti-Crime Expenditures

CRIME

The *Uniform Crime Reports* provide the best data for cities, states, and the nation, although they do represent an underreporting of crime. There is, however, an almost perfect correlation between the UCR crime scores of cities and the victimization survey scores of cities. Thus the allocations should remain roughly the same regardless of the type of scores used. This is especially so since the cities are not being compared with regard to their quantity of crime, but rather with regard to the relation between their quantity of crime and their quantity of anticrime expenditures. Also the influence of underreporting is further reduced by using multiple time points and controlling for prior crime which indirectly controls for city size and other variables which influence crime.

ANTICRIME EXPENDITURES

The LEAA *Expenditures and Employment Data* surveys provide the best data available for cities, states, the nation, and such general activities as police, courts, and corrections. A defect in the data, however, is that it does not provide a more detailed breakdown of activities. On the other hand, one would not expect a detailed activity (like money spent for notifying released defendants of trial dates) to relate in a substantial way to so general a social indicator as the *Uniform Crime Reports*. Instead one would be more likely to relate trial notification expenditures to an indicator like the percent of court appearances. However, by evaluating each activity against its own criterion, rather than (at least implicitly) to a common criterion, one cannot make optimum decisions concerning how much of a given budget to allocate to each activity.

ALTERNATIVE GOALS AND ACTIVITIES

The above analysis emphasizes that an optimum quantitative allocation methodology requires a common goal criterion across the activities and places being compared. Such a criterion is not always available for all levels of generality. Thus, one might use crime occurrence as the criterion at the highest level of generality. However, in comparing dollars spent for pretrial notification, screening and supervision, one might use appearance percentages as the criterion. In doing so, one might relate appearance percentage to dollars spent for each of those three activities over a series of time points in order to calculate the marginal rate of return for each of those three activities.

Relating Crime to Anticrime Expenditures

THE PROBLEMS

The key problems in relating a goal criterion to the effort variables are (1) how to control for other variables that influence the criterion and possibly the effort expended; and (2) how to control for the fact that the goal achievement may have a substantial influence on effort, rather than the other way around. Thus a positive relation is generally observed between increases in anticrime expenditures and increases in crime. This positive relation may be due to (1) a spurious correlation whereby a variable like urbanism causes both crime and anticrime expenditures to increase together; and (2) a reverse causation whereby increases in crime cause increased anticrime expenditures, more so than increases in expenditures cause decrease in crime.

A SOLUTION

Controlling for other variables in the regression analysis between crime and anticrime expenditures does not generally convert the positive relations into negative relations. The method that does generally work involves relating crime for a given year (Y_t) to anticrime expenditures for the prior year (X_{t-1}), while holding constant crime for the prior year (Y_{t-1}). Holding constant prior crime has the effect of holding constant variables that influence crime other than anticrime expenditures. By relating crime to prior (rather than present) expenditures, we also decrease the reverse relation involving the influence of crime on expenditures, rather than expenditures on crime.

APPROACHES THAT DO NOT WORK

Controlling for other variables becomes quite clumsy if one attempts to include the major variables that can influence both crime and anticrime expenditures. These include urbanism, demographic characteristics, and deterrence characteristics for each city. Demographic characteristics can include race, income, and age level. Deterrence characteristics include sentencing severity and the crime clearance rate. It is much simpler and the results are more meaningful to only control for prior crime which indirectly controls for whatever causes crime.

Working with one-point-in-time data tends to be meaningless for arriving at a marginal rate of return for each city. One could calculate a kind of benefit/cost ratio by dividing crime by dollars for each city as of 1972. Doing so, however, would not tell us anything about the extent to which crime gets reduced as a result of an increase in anticrime dollars. Doing so also falsely implies that if one has ten crimes for 2 dollars, then one would have five crimes for 1 dollar.

Instead of using crime as the dependent variable or goal variable to be minimized, one could conceivably use unexplained crime, which is crime that cannot be explained by prior crime. To calculate that dependent variable, we determine the parameters for the regression equations $Y_t = a + b(Y_{t-1})$. With those parameters we can now determine the predicted crime for each year since we know how much crime there was in the previous year. The difference between predicted crime and actual crime is the unexplained crime (Y'). That then becomes the dependent variable in a regression equation of the form $Y' = aX^b$. The marginal rate of return for each city can then be calculated by the formula baX^{b-1}, which is the slope of Y' relative to X when $Y' = aX^b$. That method, however, will not work because there is virtually no unexplained crime for anticrime dollars to explain, since prior crime accounts for nearly all of the variation of a subsequent crime. The reason anticrime dollars have no explanatory power is because their explanatory power is already figured in by virtue of the positive correlation that anticrime dollars have with prior crime.

Allocating Expenditures to Activities and Places

ACTIVITIES

With the above regression parameters, one can arrive at a crime-minimizing allocation of expenditures to activities by allocating in proportion to the elasticity coefficient of each activity, with nothing more than the minimum allocated to activities that have a positive elasticity coefficient. This can be shown to be algebraically equal to the distribution, which equalizes the marginal rates of return across all the activities such that there is nothing to be gained by shifting dollars from one activity to another. In other words, it makes sense to invest our first dollar in the activity that has the generally steeper slide between crime and anticrime expenditures, but to shift our second or subsequent dollar to the less steep activity when the first activity begins to plateau out. The total crime from the expenditures on the two activities will hit the bottom of a valley-shaped curve when (1) the total budget is spent, and (2) the marginal rates of return (or the slopes) on the respective slides are equal.

PLACES

With the above regression parameters for each place or city, there is no proportionality formula that algebraically gives the same results as equalizing the marginal rates of return across the cities. A meaningful proportionality formula involves allocating to each city in proportion to its elasticity coefficient and scale coefficient. The elasticity coefficient given by the regression analysis shows the percentage by which crime is likely to be reduced in a city as a result of a one percent increase in anticrime expenditures. The scale coefficient represents the quantitative level of crime on which the city is operating. In other words, we are allocating to each city in proportion to the product of its a and b coefficients from an equation of the form $Y = aX^b$ for each city, since the marginal rate of return for each city is baX^{b-1}. Doing so approximates the exact optimizing solution, but does not equal it. For a somewhat closer approximation, one could allocate in proportion to the scale coefficient and the square of the elasticity coefficient, since the elasticity coefficient figures twice in the MRR for each city.

PLACES-APPROACHES THAT DO NOT WORK

Other approaches for allocating to places work substantially less well. For example, one alternative to using a proportionality formula is to use a nonlinear programming routine or a simultaneous equation-solving routine. Those allocation alternatives involve access to a computer, tend to be quite complicated, and often produce answers which result in getting stuck in an allocation other than the optimum allocation. This is especially so as the number of places increases.

Another approach involves the concept of suboptimization, whereby we try to find an optimum level of dollars to allocate to each city, out of the context of the other cities and the total budget. By each city arriving at an optimum level, the total allocation across the cities may be at an aggregate optimum. For an individual city to arrive at an optimum level of anticrime expenditures would first involve determining an optimum crime rate. To do that would mean determining the crime-damage costs for various crime rates, and the crime-enforcement costs for various crime rates. The damage costs for various crimes could possibly be assessed by looking at the money stolen and damages awarded in comparable personal injury cases. The optimum crime rate then would be the rate where the sum of those two costs is minimized. The enforcement costs at that optimum level, however, may be so high that when we add these costs figures across a set of cities, the sum is more than the total budget available. Under those circumstances, we could allocate to each city in proportion to their optimums, but calculating those individual optimums may be quite difficult if not impossible. The same is true if we try to suboptimize each activity.

Another approach involves abandoning the idea of having a separate regression equation for each city that relates crime to anticrime expenditures while holding constant prior crime. Instead, one could use a single equation in which total crime for the set of cities involved is the dependent variable. One could then have a set of independent variables corresponding to the anticrime expenditures of each city. This information could be obtained for a number of years in order to calculate the elasticity coefficients for each of the cities in that multiple city equation. One could then allocate to the cities in proportion to their elasticity coefficients, which would involve a provably optimum allocation, provided that the elasticity coefficients make sense. We may, however, run into the problem that if we have more cities than years, then we will have more variables than units of analysis, and it will be impossible to determine the elasticity coefficients. This problem can be handled by allocating to regions and other groupings and then allocating to cities, so as never to have an equation with more variables than time points. Unfortunately, in this context, the coefficients are quite arbitrary, because they depend on the coincidence of whatever other cities happen to be simultaneously included, and there is too much confusing interaction between the variables to understand what the coefficients mean, even if prior crime is held constant.

SUPPLEMENTARY QUALITATIVE APPROACH

A completely different approach to allocating to both activities and places might involve a verbal qualitative approach rather than a numerical quantitative approach. A verbal qualitative approach could take the form of asking people knowledgeable about each place or activity, how efficient is the activity or place in terms of what those involved could do or would be likely to do if they were given some extra money, possibly as compared to other activities or places. Essentially we would be asking for a qualitative marginal rate of return that would be hard to quantify, but this approach may be a useful and essential supplement to the quantitative approach described in this chapter, and vice versa.

ACTIVITIES AND PLACES TOGETHER

One can first allocate to anticrime activities like police, courts, and corrections in accordance with the above activity procedure. Then within those activity allocations, allocate to the cities in accordance with the above places procedure. An alternative involves allocating first to places and then within each place to the three or so activities. A third alternative involves allocating half the budget to activities (and then suballocating those allocations to places), and the other half to places (and then suballocating those allocations to activities). A fourth alternative involves some split other than half and half in light of the relative power or marginal rate of return of an activity allocation versus a geographic allocation, as determined by a regression analysis in which crime is related to two types of allocations.

DETERMINING THE TOTAL BUDGET AMOUNT TO ALLOCATE

To determine how much to budget for a set of activities related to a common goal, one can determine the regression relation between the goal and how much has been budgeted in the past, yielding a regression equation of the form $Y = aX^b$. One can determine an optimum level of Y by using optimum level analysis associated with operations research and then solve for the corresponding budget amount, X. Instead of finding an optimum level on Y, one can simply insert last year's Y figure, on the theory that we would be be pleased to do no worse than last year. In this context, Y is national crime occurrence, X is anticrime expenditures, holding constant prior crime, with years as the unit of analysis.

MINIMIZING EXPENDITURES WITHIN A CRIME CONSTRAINT

The above discussion assumes that we are trying to minimize crime within a budget constraint. In time of budget cutbacks, there may be a more-than-normal tendency to think in terms of minimizing expenditures within a crime constraint. Under either situation, we could allocate to activities in proportion to the elasticity coefficients in an equation of the form $Y = a(P)^{b_1}(J)^{b_2}(C)^{b_3}$, where P, J, and C represent expenditures for police, judiciary, and corrections respectively. Similarly, we could allocate to places in proportion to their scale and elasticity coefficients where each place has an equation of the form $Y = aX^b$ where X represents the place's anticrime expenditures. When seeking to minimize crime subject to a grant total budget (G), we would thus allocate to activity "i" in accordance with the formula $(b_i/\Sigma b)(G)$, and allocate to place j in accordance with the formula $a_j b_j/\Sigma ab)(G)$.

If, however, we are seeking to minimize expenditures subject to a crime constraint, we could use last year's total crime (Y_{t-1}) as the crime constraint not to be exceeded. We then solve for X in the equation $Y_{t-1} = aX^b$, and substitute X for G in the formula for allocating to activities or places. If X is less than the grand total budget available, we will be spending less than the budget while getting crime down to approximately Y_{t-1}. This method is not an exact solution because there may be inconsistencies between $Y = aX^b$ and $Y = a(P)^{b_1}(J)^{b_2}(C)^{b_3}$ even though $P + J + C = X$, and because the proportionality method provides an exact solution only when allocating to activities rather than places.

CRITERIA FOR AN OPTIMUM ALLOCATION METHOD

Many criminal justice agencies are frequently faced with making decisions as to how to allocate their funds, personnel, or effort among various places or activities to obtain a maximum return on their investment. A methodology is needed whereby such criminal justice decision makers can meaningfully use the statistics that have been compiled with regard to crime rates, due process, or other goal indicators to aid in making such allocation decisions. The research that is proposed here is designed to help develop such a methodology. It draws upon the techniques of business administration and marketing research to reach decisions on allocating the funds of business firms among various places or activities in order to maximize the firm's profits.

The methodology's criteria should include the following:

1. The methodology should emphasize the use of existing or readily obtainable data such as the *Uniform Crime Reports*, the annual LEAA *Expenditure and Employment Data*, and appellate court reviews of police, trial courts, and corrections. The crime data may, however, have to be adjusted in light of what is known from the victimization surveys, and the expenditure data may have to be supplemented with questionnaire information to provide greater detail concerning the activities for which expenditures have been made.

2. The methodology should be capable of controlling for other variables that influence the occurrence of crime in addition to anticrime expenditures so that the relations between past crime and past anticrime expenditures will more accurately reflect causal relations.

3. The methodology should recognize the diminishing-returns relationship between anticrime expenditures and crime occurrence, since additional effort expended in fighting crime may produce an additional reduction in crime. However, this will probably occur at a diminishing rate since it becomes increasingly difficult to eliminate the more profitable and firmly entrenched crime.

4. The methodology should arrive at allocations that are close to optimum, in the sense of equalizing marginal rates of return across different places and different activities, so there is nothing to be gained by shifting limited funds or effort from one place to another or from one activity to another.

5. The methodology should be simple enough to apply so that criminal justice personnel making allocation decisions can use it as a routine supplement to their regular decision-making processes without having any specialized technical skills or access to computer facilities and software.

6. The methodology should take into consideration that minimum amounts may have to be provided various places and activities regardless of their efficiency in reducing crime or achieving other goals.

7. The methodology should be capable of handling problems that involve either maximizing a goal subject to a budget constraint, or minimizing expenditures subject to a minimum level of goal achievement.

8. The methodology should be capable of handling problems that involve allocating to places first and then suballocating to activities, activities first and then suballocating to places, or to places and activities simultaneously.

9. The methodology should be flexible enough to be able to handle a composite goal consisting of crime reduction (as measured by past or future *Uniform Crime Reports*), due process improvement (as measured by appellate court reversals of criminal cases), and other goal indicators.

10. The methodology should be just as meaningful in terms of allocations at the federal, state, or local levels, or allocations by legislatures or administrative agencies.

11. The methodology should be useful in making initial allocation decisions or revised allocations, and in comparing optimizing allocations with actual ones. This comparison is especially useful in order to obtain a better understanding of how the optimum needs to be determined to come closer to the actual, and vice versa.

SPECIFIC ANTICRIME ALLOCATION EXAMPLES

General

To illustrate the general methodology, the authors obtained relevant data on a random sample of ten of the thirty largest U.S. cities, namely Boston, Cincinnati, Dallas, Houston, Kansas City, Milwaukee, New Orleans, Pittsburgh, San Francisco, and Seattle. The main relevant data consisted of the total crime occurrence figures for each city for the five years 1968 through 1972 obtained from the *Uniform Crime Reports*, and the total anticrime expenditure figures for each city for the same years obtained from the LEAA *Expenditure Data*. In 1973, the total anticrime expenditures for all ten cities was 349 million dollars. Of that total, 41 million dollars consisted of LEAA money. The object of the analysis is to show how that LEAA money could have been allocated to be more effective in reducing crime for the subsequent year of 1974 in light of the data for the previous years 1968 through 1972. In other words, if one had 41 million dollars in LEAA money as of 1973, how might one allocate the money to those ten cities in light of that data to obtain a maximum return on one's investment?

Some of the rough tentative results are shown in the following tables. Table 12-1 indicates how the dollars might be allocated to the 10 cities. Those optimum or improved allocations do result in less crime than the actual allocations. There, however, is not much room for the LEAA allocations to influence crime since so much of the actual and optimum allocations are determined in this example by non-LEAA anticrime expenditures. Table 12-2 indicates how the 349 million dollars might be allocated to police, judicial, and corrections activities. Other such tables are being developed for allocations to activities within cities, to cities within activities, to cities and activities simultaneously, and for allocations which involve other minimums, goals to optimize, and regression coefficients.

Allocating to Places

The first step in arriving at these allocations involves determining the marginal rate of return for an anticrime dollar expended in each city, and the marginal rate of return for an anticrime dollar expended on each activity. To obtain the marginal rate of return for an anticrime dollar awarded in Boston, we compute the regression parameters for the equation $Y_t = a(X_{t-1})^{b_1}(Y_{t-1})^{b_2}$. In that regression equation, Y represents crime in thousands, and X represents anticrime dollars in millions. The parameters are based on five units of analysis for the city of Boston, namely the years 1968 through 1972. Both the Y scores and the X scores for Boston for each year are logged before making the regression run in order to take nonlinear diminishing returns into consideration. Y at time t is related to X at time $t - 1$ in order to take into consideration that crime tends to reflect anticrime expenditures of the previous year more than of the present year. Crime for the previous year is held constant in relating crime to anticrime dollars because doing so tends indirectly to hold constant the variables other than anticrime dollars which influence previous crime and thus probably present crime. Performing that simple regression analysis on the Boston data yields the equation $Y_t = 12.47(X_{t-1})^{-.28}(Y_{t-1})^{.59}$.

With the above information, we can know from elementary calculus and operations research that the marginal rate of return for an incremental dollar spent in 1973 in Boston is $(-.28)(12.47) (X)^{-.28-1.00}(39)^{.59}$ which simplifies to $-30.32(X)^{-1.28}$. In terms of algebraic symbols (particularly those numbers used in Appendix 3), these expressions equal $b_1a(X_{t-1})^{b_1-1}(Y_{t-1})^{b_2}$, which simplifies to $b_1A(X_{t-1})^{b_1-1}$, since A equals $a(Y_{t-1})^{b_2}$. Sometimes in this paper, the scale coefficient refers to "a" and sometimes to "A", but one should be able to tell from the context which scale coefficient is meant.

A marginal rate of return can be similarly computed for each city. The amount of money which should be allocated to each city in light of this data should be approximately proportional to the product of the exponent and the multiplier in each of those marginal rates of return. This is so since the exponent or elasticity coefficient, before subtracting 1.00, represents

TABLE 12-1. ALLOCATING ANTICRIME DOLLARS TO CITIES

City	Minimum $ (M)	Actual $ (X)	Optimum $ (X*)	$ Difference (Act.-Opt.)	Crime from (Actual $) (Y)	Crime from Optimum $ (Y*)	Crime Diff. (Act.-Opt.)
1. Boston	54	67	54.11	13	33	35	-2
2. Cincinnati	19	21	22.21	1	19	18	1
3. Dallas	26	32	26.19	6	37	40	-3
4. Houston	29	34	29.02	5	57	58	-1
5. Kansas City	26	26	28.29	-2	12	11	1
6. Milwaukee	35	37	35.00	2	22	21	1
7. New Orleans	22	27	22.00	5	36	33	3
8. Pittsburgh	18	21	18.62	2	22	24	-2
9. San Francisco	59	62	93.29	-31	24	14	10
10. Seattle	20	22	20.27	2	22	23	-1
TOTAL	308	349	349.00	0	284	277	7

All dollars are in millions for 1973. All crimes are in thousands for 1974.

Minimum $ = Non-LEAA dollars. Actual $ = Non-LEAA + LEAA dollars. Optimum $ or X* = Minimum $ + $41(A_ib_i/\Sigma\ Ab)$.

1974 Predicted Crime = $a(X_{73})^{b1}(Y_{73})^{b2}$ from Actual 1973 $. 1974 Predicted Crime = $a(X^*_{73})^{b1}(Y_{73})^{b2}$ from Optimum 1973 $.

See text for further details

TABLE 12-2. ALLOCATING ANTICRIME DOLLARS TO ACTIVITIES

Activity	Minimum $ (M)	Actual $ (P,J,C)	Optimum$ (P*,J*,C*)	$ Difference (Act.-Opt.)	Crime from Actual $ (Y)	Crime from Optimum $ (Y*)	Crime Diff. (Act.-Opt.)
1. Police	252	285	292	-7	216	215	1
2. Judicial	35	40	35	5	3	3	0
3. Corrections	21	24	22	2	3	3	0
TOTAL	308	349	349	0	222	221	1

All dollars are in millions for 1973. All crimes are in thousands for 1974.

Minimum $ = Non-LEAA dollars. Actual $ = Non-LEAA + LEAA dollars. Optimum $ = Minimum $ + 41 ($b_i \lessgtr b$).

1974 Predicted Crime from Actual 1973 $ = $a(P_{73})^{b1}(J_{73})^{b2}(C_{73})^{b3}(Y_{73})^{b4}$.

1974 Predicted Crime from Optimum 1973 $ = $a(P^*_{73})^{b1}(J^*_{73})^{b2}(C^*_{73})^{b3}(Y_{73})^{b4}$.

See text for further details.

the percent by which crime is likely to be reduced in each city as a result of a one percent increase in anticrime expenditures. The multiplier or scale coefficient (before multiplying by $-.28$ or b_1) represents the level of crime on which each city is operating, such that it is better to invest in a city with a 5 percent yield on a 100 crime base than a city with a 10 percent yield on a 20-crime base, since the first city will generate a 5-crime reduction and the second city will generate only a 2-crime reduction.

With the above principles and marginal rates of return we can develop a reasonably optimum allocation of our 349 million anticrime dollars among the ten cities by first giving to each city a minimum which represents its own money rather than the LEAA money. Next we allocate the remainder of the anticrime dollars (which can be symbolized G) to each city in accordance with the formula $X_i^* = G(a_ib_i/\Sigma ab)$, where X_i^* equals the optimum incremental allocation to city "i", "a'" equals the scale coefficient times b_1 of city "i," and "b" equals the elasticity coefficient minus 1.00. This formula is only applied to those cities that have negative elasticity coefficients. Any city that has a positive elasticity coefficient should only receive the minimum allocation since an incremental dollar does not seem to result in a reduction in crime in those cities. However, by holding constant the previous year's crime, most of the elasticity coefficients become negative.

Allocating to Activities

To obtain the marginal rate of return for an anticrime dollar expended on the police we compute the regression parameters for the equation $Y_t = a(P_{t-1})^{b_1}(J_{t-1})^{b_2}(C_{t-1})^{b_3}(Y_{t-1})^{b_4}$. In that regression equation, Y represents crime; P represents dollars spent on the police; J represents dollars spent on judicial activities; and C represents dollars for corrections. The parameters are based on 50 units of analysis consisting of five years for each of the ten cities. All the variables are logged to take nonlinear diminishing returns into consideration, and also logged to consider the delayed effect of anticrime dollars on crime. Crime for the previous year is again held constant to indirectly get at other variables other than anticrime dollars which influence crime. Performing that simple regression analysis on the data yields the equation $Y_t = 1.86(P_{t-1})^{-.07}(J_{t-1})^{.001}(C_{t-1})^{-.001}(Y_{t-1})^{.89}$.

One can prove algebraically that the optimum allocation to each activity (in light of the above equation and elementary calculus) can be determined by the formula $X_i^* = G(b_i/\Sigma b)$, where X_i^* equals the optimum incremental allocation to activity "i," and b equals the elasticity coefficient of activity "i." There is no need to consider the scale coefficient "a", since all the activities share the same scale coefficient. Similarly they share the same Y_{t-1}, although its presence influences the values of b_1, b_2, and b_3 particularly by generally making them negative rather than positive. This

X_i^* formula is only applied to activities which have negative elasticity coefficients. An activity with a positive coefficient should only receive the minimum allocation, which is equal to an estimate of what the cities spent on that activity independent of LEAA. This estimate assumes LEAA spent its 41 million dollars on police, judicial, and corrections in the same proportions as the cities did.

Comparing Optimum and Actual Allocations

After these optimum allocations are determined one can compare them with the actual allocations to see how much crime they would produce in light of the previously computed regression equations relating crime to anticrime dollars. One can also compare the optimum with the actual allocations to see how the computing of the optimum and actual allocations can be improved. It should be especially noted that once the regression parameters are computed through a standard regression analysis program, all the criminal justice decision maker needs to arrive at these tentative optimums is a desk calculator, given the simplicity of the formulas involved.

The optimum allocations differ from the actual in allocating to *cities* possibly because some cities are more vigorous or politically influential in applying for funds than others (like Boston) or some cities may not be recognized for the high marginal rate of return that they have (like San Francisco). The optimum may differ from the actual in allocating to *activities* largely because the optimum only considers crime occurrence as a goal (which favors police) rather than due process (which favors courts). The optimum and actual allocations may also differ since the optimum is based on only five time points and the actual is based on only one time point. With data over a longer period of time, the two types of allocation might be closer. The crime difference is low between the optimum and actual allocations for either places or activities because the marginal rates of return for anticrime expenditures are low, and because the LEAA only has 41/349, or 12 percent of the total anticrime dollars to allocate.

SOME CONCLUSIONS

Each year a great deal of anticrime money is allocated by the federal government to states, cities, and activities. Most police money is raised by city taxes to be allocated among police precincts. Most court money is raised by state taxes to be allocated among counties, and most corrections money is also raised by state taxes to be allocated among prisons. Within all levels of government and all branches of government, frequent decisions are made allocating anticrime money or effort. Political and social scientists can study those allocations to determine who gets what, when, how and why. More specifically, they can experiment with alternative allocation methodologies to see how they effect various criteria and outcomes. They can also seek to determine through interviewing, questionnaires, and data analysis how allocations are made and what variables correlate with them. That kind of political and social science research should increase our understanding of the causal forces behind these important decisions, and possibly result in making the allocation process more effective in achieving its goals.

APPENDIX 12-1. DATA FOR ANTICRIME ALLOCATION

(Crimes are in 1,000's, and Expenditures are in $1,000,000's)
(See end of appendix for explanations.)

PLACES AND YEAR (t)	CRIMES (Y)	ACTIVITIES Police $(P)	Judicial $(J)	Corrections $(C)
1. Boston				
1973	53	40	10	5
1972	39	35	8	5
1971	43	37	8	4
1970	38	29	7	5
1969	35	29	7	4
1968	33	25	6	4
1967	25	23	6	3
2. Cincinnati				
1973	29	14	3	1
1972	21	12	2	1
1971	22	13	11	1
1970	17	13	2	1
1969	13	12	1	1
1968	12	11	1	1
1967	9	9	1	1
3. Dallas				
1973	70	24	2	½
1972	45	21	2	½
1971	46	22	1	½
1970	50	17	1	½
1969	42	14	1	½
1968	24	14	1	½
1967	20	13	1	½
4. Houston				
1973	82	24	2	2
1972	60	21	2	1
1971	59	22	1	1
1970	60	18	1	½
1969	58	18	1	½
1968	48	16	1	½
1967	38	14	1	½

5. Kansas City

1973	32	(18)	(1)	(1)
1972	24	17	1	1
1971	28	14	1	1
1970	29	12	1	1
1969	32	13	1	1
1968	25	12	½	1
1967	23	11	½	1

6. Milwaukee

1973	31	(29)	(1)	(½)
1972	21	22	1	½
1971	22	27	1	½
1970	20	25	1	½
1969	19	23	1	½
1968	17	22	½	½
1967	17	18	½	½

7. New Orleans

1973	35	(15)	(4)	(3)
1972	30	14	4	3
1971	35	13	4	2
1970	35	14	4	2
1969	28	14	4	1
1968	27	15	3	1
1967	25	11	3	2

8. Pittsburgh

1973	26	(16)	(1)	(½)
1972	24	17	1	½
1971	26	19	1	½
1970	28	20	1	½
1969	32	16	1	½
1968	32	14	½	½
1967	23	13	½	½

9. San Francisco

1973	58	(34)	(10)	(6)
1972	47	33	8	7
1971	58	30	8	7
1970	57	27	8	6
1969	54	26	8	6
1968	47	23	6	6
1967	39	22	5	6

10. Seattle

1973	40	(15)	(1)	(1)
1972	26	16	1	1
1971	27	17	1	1
1970	31	15	1	1
1969	35	14	1	1
1968	25	12	1	1
1967	20	11	1	1

Notes to Appendix 12-1.

1. Inflation multipliers used for P, J, and C before doing the regression analysis were:

.799 for 1972
.824 for 1971
.860 for 1970
.911 for 1969
.960 for 1968
1.000 for 1967

The above dollar amounts, however, are not adjusted for inflation.

2. The boxed-in numbers for each city show the data base used in doing the regression analyses. The data base involves lagging P, J, C, and X by one year as independent variables with Y as the dependent variable.

3. The circled numbers for each city show the actual P, J, and C 1973 expenditures to be compared with the optimum P, J, and C 1973 expenditures developed via the regression and optimizing analyses.

4. All numbers are rounded to integers except expenditures less than $500,000 which are rounded to $500,000 rather than $0.

APPENDIX 12-2. REGRESSION ANALYSIS FOR ANTICRIME ALLOCATION

Places	Scale Coef. (a)	Elasticity Coef. of $X_{t-1}(b_1)$	Elasticity Coef. of $Y_{t-1}(b_2)$	Variance Explained (R^2)	Crime in 72 (Y_{72})	$A = (a)(Y_{72})^{b_2}$
1. Boston	12	- .28	.59	75%	39	108
2. Cincinnati	3	-1.07	1.70	95%	21	497
3. Dallas	9	- .36	.70	68%	45	130
4. Houston	9	- .07	.51	87%	60	73
5. Kansas City	26	-1.05	.83	66%	24	365
6. Milwaukee	3	.14	.45	77%	21	13
7. New Orleans	3	.39	.36	33%	30	10
8. Pittsburgh	155	- .69	.05	87%	24	181
9. San Francisco	54	-1.25	1.13	87%	47	4175
10. Seattle	24	- .53	.48	44%	26	115

Notes to Appendix 12-2:

1. The three coefficients correspond to a, b_1, and b_2 in an equation for each city of the form $Y_t = (a)(X_{t-1})^{b_1}$, where Y is crime and X is anti-crime expenditures.

2. When Y_{t-1} is not included in the equation, the elasticity coefficients of the anti-crime expenditures tend to be positive rather than negative, and the variance explained is substantially lower.

3. These regression results are based on the data from Appendix 12-1. The results (especially A and b_1) become the input for creating Table 12-1 in accordance with the formulas given at the bottom of Table 12-1.

4. The regression results when expenditures are recorded by police, judiciary, and corrections are: scale coefficient = 1.86; elasticity coefficient of police expenditures = .07; judicial expenditures = .001; corrections expenditures = -.001; and crime from the previous year = .89. The percent of variance explained is 89%.

APPENDIX 12-3. GLOSSARY OF TERMS IN ANTICRIME ALLOCATION

Symbols for either expenditures or crime can refer to a single city or a set of cities unless they have a subscript that indicates reference to a given city. The X or X* symbol can either refer to total expenditures or serve as a general symbol for police, judicial, or corrections expenditures, depending on the context. Unless indicated otherwise, crime symbols refer to the base year 1974 or to any year, whereas expenditure symbols refer to the prior year 1973 or to any prior year.

ACTUAL EXPENDITURES
X   Anticrime expenditures
P   Police expenditures
J   Judiciary expenditures
C   Corrections expenditures
X1   Anticrime expenditures for city 1 or activity 1

OPTIMUM EXPENDITURES
X*   Optimum anticrime expenditures
P*   Optimum police expenditures
J*   Optimum judiciary expenditures
C*   Optimum corrections expenditures

CRIME SYMBOLS
Y   Actual crime or predicted crime
Y*   Crime when expenditures are optimum
Yp   Predicted crime
Y'   Crime unexplained by prior crime

TIME PERIOD
t   Base year (1974) or any year
t-1 Previous year

REGRESSION EQUATION PARAMETERS
a   Scale coefficient in an equation of the form $Y = aX^b$. It represents the value of Y when X is one.
b   Elasticity coefficient in an equation of the form $Y = aXb$. It represents the ratio between a percentage change in Y and a one percent change in X.

a   Y-intercept in an equation of the form $Y = a + bX$. It represents the value of Y when X is zero.

b   Slope in an equation of the form $Y = a + bX$. It represents the ratio between a change in Y and one unit change in X.

A   Product of (a) and (Y_{t-1}).

MISCELLANEOUS SYMBOLS

M   Minimum allocation to be given to a place or an activity.

G   Grand total budget available for allocating, after the minimums have been allocated.

i   The ith place or activity, i.e., any place or activity.

APPENDIX 12-4. BASIC FORMULAS IN ANTICRIME ALLOCATION

Allocation formulas below only deal with two cities or activities, but they can be extended to deal with more cities or activities. In allocating to places or activities, the minimums should be allocated first before applying the formulas given below, or the minimums should be included as part of the nonlinear programming constraints.

I.   RELATING CRIME TO ANTICRIME EXPENDITURES

A. Cross-Lagged Analysis

1. Places
$$Y_t = a(X_{t-1})^{b1}(Y_{t-1})^{b2}$$

2. Activities
$$Y_t = a (P_{t-1})^{b1}(J_{t-1})^{b2}(C_{t-1})^{b3}(Y_{t-1})^{b4}$$

B. Residual Analysis
$$Y_p = a + b(Y_{t-1})$$
$$Y' = Y_p - Y$$
$$Y'_t = a(X_{t-1})^{b}$$

C. Multi-City Equation
$$Y_t = a(X_1)^{b1}(X_2)^{b2}(Y_{t-1})^{b3}$$

II. ALLOCATING EXPENDITURES TO TWO PLACES

A. Minimizing Crime (Y) Subject to a Budget Constraint (G)

1. Proportionate Approach
$$X_i^* = \{(A_i b_i)/(\Sigma\ Ab)\}(G)$$

2. Nonlinear Programming
Minimize crime which equals $(AX^b)_1 + (AX^b)_2$
Subject to $X_1 + X_2 \leq G$

3. Simultaneous Equations
$$(bAX^{b-1})_1 = (bAX^{b-1})_2$$
$$G = X_1 + X_2$$

B. Minimizing Expenditures (X) Subject to Crime Constraint (Y_{t-1})

1. Proportionate Approach
$$X_i^* = \{(A_i b_i)/(\Sigma\ Ab)\}(X)$$
Where $X = (Y_{t-1}/a)^{1/b}$

2. Nonlinear Programming
   Minimize expenditures which equal $X_1 + X_2$
   Subject to $(AX^b)_1 + (AX^b)_2 \leq Y_{t-1}$

3. Simultaneous Equations
   $(bAX^{b-1})_1 = (bAX^{b-1})_2$
   $Y_{t-1} = (AX^b)_1 + (AX^b)_2$

III. ALLOCATING EXPENDITURES TO TWO ACTIVITIES

A. Minimizing Crime (Y) Subject to a Budget Constraint (G)
   1. Proportionate Approach
      $X_i^* = (b_i / \Sigma\, b)\, (G)$
   2. Nonlinear Programming
      Minimize crime which equals $A(X_1)^{b1}(X_2)^{b2}$
      Subject to $X_1 + X_2 \leq G$
   3. Simultaneous Equations
      $b_1 A(X_1)^{b1-1}(X_2)^{b2} = b_2 A(X_2)^{b2-1}(X_1)^{b1}$
      $X_1 + X_2 = G$

B. Minimizing Expenditures (X) Subject to a Crime Constraint (Y_{t-1})
   1. Proportionate Approach
      $X_i^* = (b_i / \Sigma\, b)(X)$
      Where $X = (Y_{t-1}/a)^{1/b}$
   2. Nonlinear Programming
      Minimize expenditures which equal $X_1 + X_2$
      Subject to $A(X_1)^b(X_2)^b \leq Y_{t-1}$
   3. Simultaneous Equations
      $b_1 A(X_1)^{b1-1}(X_2)^{b2} = b_2 A(X_2)^{b2-1}(X_1)^{b1}$
      $Y_{t-1} = a(X_1)^{b1}(X_i)^{b2}$

APPENDIX 12-5. AN ALTERNATIVE CAUSAL AND OPTIMIZING ANALYSIS

A basic alternative way of relating crime to anticrime expenditures involves a logarithmic curve fitting rather than a power function curve fitting. Instead of working with power curves of the form $Y = aX^b$, we then could work with logarithmic curves of the form $Y = a + b \operatorname{Log} X$. That simply means having a computer arrive at the numerical values for the "a" and "b" by working with actual Y and the log of X, rather than the log of both Y and X. In the anticrime context, it means working with the log of anticrime expenditures and prior crime (the right-side variables) and the unlogged values of subsequent crime (the left-side variable), yielding equations of the form $Y_{t-1} = a + b_1 \operatorname{Log} (X_{t-1}) + b_2 \operatorname{Log} (Y_{t-1})$. The direction of the b values should normally be the same regardless of whether power functions or log functions are used. They should generally be negative convex for anticrime dollars (to show diminishing returns from incremental dollars) and positive for prior crime.

The advantage of using this type of curve fitting is that it lends itself to a very simple optimizing approach. For example, suppose we have two cities with log relations of the form $Y_1 = a + b \log X_1$, and $Y_2 = A + B \log X_2$. This means that the marginal rate of return for the first city for an incremental dollar is b/X_1, and for the second city B/X_2. Thus if we want optimally to allocate a grant total budget (G) across the two cities, we would solve the following pair of equations simultaneously: $X_1 + X_2 = G$ and $b/X_1 = B/X_2$. The first equation says spend all the money, and the second says equalize the marginal rates of return. Solving for X_1 in the preceding pair of equations yields $b/(b + B)$ times G, and solving for X_2 yields $B/(b + B)$ times G. The budget available should thus be allocated to each city in proportion to its logarithmic regression coefficient. Doing so provides an exact solution to the optimizing problem, as contrasted to the approximate solution associated with power curves rather than logarithmic curves.

If we apply the above analysis to the data given in Appendix 12-2 in order to generate coefficients such as those shown in Appendix 12-3, then we find the direction of all the b values is the same for both the power fit and the logarithmic fit, although for one city the b value of prior crime becomes negative rather than positive. Of particular importance is the fact that the percentage of the variance explained tends to be quite similar for both types of curve fitting. The variance explained is greater for six cities using the power fit, greater for three cities using the log fit, and the same for one city. Summing those differences yields an average difference of only three percentage points. Thus there was no substantial sacrifice in goodness of fit by using the log fit.

If we use the revised figures from Appendix 12-3 to recalculate the figures in Table 12-1, we find some interesting results. The new optimums involve giving more money to some cities than the old optimums, and less money to other cities. One can, however, feel more confident about the meaningfulness of the new optimums, since they represent an exact optimizing solution. Of particular importance is the fact that the new optimums result in a substantially larger difference between 1974 predicted crime from actual dollars (340 crimes) and 1974 predicted crime from optimum dollars (315 crimes), a difference of 25 crimes (in thousands). The power fitting method generates a difference in Table 12-1 of only 7 crimes. Thus the log fitting method not only seems to be simpler and more exact, but also more effective in achieving predicted crime reduction.

The power fitting method is, however, simpler and more exact when allocating to activities. Under these circumstances, a simple and exact solution is arrived at by allocating to the activities in proportion to their elasticity coefficients. Both approaches involve basically the same issues of how and whether to measure crime and anticrime expenditures, how to relate crime to expenditures in order to deal with spurious and reciprocal causation, and how to allocate expenditures in light of the criteria mentioned in this chapter and in the allocation examples. Together they represent especially useful methods in the tool kit of policy analysts interested in the optimum allocation of scarce resources across places and activities.

APPENDIX 12-6. A MULTIATTRIBUTE UTILITY APPROACH TO ANTICRIME ALLOCATION

As a substantially different approach to anticrime allocation one might ask, What are the attributes or characteristics of cities that should get more federal money to fight crime than other cities? The attributes are likely to be of two kinds: those that relate to the need for money and those that relate to the ability to use it efficiently. Need attributes might be population size, crime occurrence, or wealth of the city. These attributes are similar to allocating income in accordance with need, in which each family receives an income in accordance with the number of people in the family, disease occurrence or other variables that require expenditures, and how much wealth or other income the family already has.

An ability attribute in the anticrime context might include the quality of the police recruitment system measured on a one-to-ten scale. This would be analogous to allocating income on the basis of ability or potential contribution, whereby those with more education or intelligence are allocated higher incomes, anticipating that they will put the money to better use or that such a system will stimulate them to get more education. Ability can also refer to applied ability, not just potential ability. In the anticrime context, this might refer to the scoring of cities by knowledgeable people on how well they have been actually fighting crime. This would be analogous to allocating income to people in terms of how much they have actually been contributing to the betterment of society or the economy as measured by marketplace factors or by a national planning commission.

Once an appropriate set of allocation attributes has been determined, one might then ask, What does one do with that information? Suppose we only want to allocate on the basis of population between two cities. City A has 40 people and City B has 10 people. If we have $200 to allocate, we would logically give 40/50, or 80%, to City A, and 10/50, or 20%, to City B. We would not give everything to City A because we recognize the phenomenon of diminishing returns or diminishing utility. This means that City A may have more need or ability in general than City B, but the two-hundredth dollar given to City A is likely to produce less need satisfaction or goal achievement than the first dollar given to City B. We thus allocate proportionately, as if we were allocating in accordance with nonlinear elasticity coefficients rather than in accordance with linear slopes. This simple kind of analysis can be extended easily to more than two cities. We simply allocate to each city in accordance with the ratio between its population and the total population of all the cities, or in accordance with the ratio between its attribute score and the sum of the attribute scores of all the cities.

Suppose we want to work with two attributes such as population and crime. Suppose further that City A has 90 crimes and City B has 60 crimes. If we are only allocating in accordance with crime, City A would receive 90/150, or 60%, of the $200 and City B would receive 60/150, or 40%, of the $200. Since we are allocating in accordance with two attributes, each of which has equal weight, the logical thing to do is to compromise between the $160 that City A would receive in accordance with the population allocation and the $120 that it would get in accordance with the crime allocation. That is, with these two attributes, City A should receive $140, and City B sould get $60. This simple kind of analysis can be extended easily to more than two attributes by simply determining how much each city would be allocated using the proportional allocation for each attribute separately. We then arrive at an average allocation for each city by averaging across those differing attribute allocations. Each attribute should be scored so that a high score indicates a desirable characteristic.

Suppose our two attributes are not equally important. More specifically, suppose a survey of legislators, public opinion, or some other relevant group determines that crime is twice as important in allocating as population is. In this situation, we simply figure that City A would receive 80% of the budget, if population were the only criterion, and 60% of the budget two times, if crime were the only criterion with a weight of two. What that means is that we sum 80%, 60%, and 60%, divide by three, and obtain 67%. In other words, if the two attributes were weighted equally, City A would get 70%, but since crime is given a weight of two, City A only gets 67% and City B gets 33%, rather than just 30%. In more general terms, we allocate to each city by summing the weighted percentage scores and dividing by the sum of the weights. The weights should not only consider the relative importance of each attribute, but also the measurement units used and the other attributes that are present. Thus an income attribute measured in $1 units would get a smaller weight than one measured in $1,000-units. Likewise, crime would get a greater weight if population were not also included as an attribute, since crime occurrence and population size are closely related.

The most difficult aspect of a multiattribute approach involves determining the relevant attributes and how they should be weighted. The need attributes are generally determined through (1) the legislative process, (2) the judicial process, where constitutional equal protection issues may be involved, and/or (3) the administrative process, where administrative agencies have been delegated authority to make such decisions. Need attributes and their weights can also be determined by surveying relevant people, deducing from other related allocation procedures, or making assumptions and then determining how the allocations are influenced by alternative assumptions. Ability attributes and their weights can be determined by the same methods. In addition, though, one can use a relational analysis, whereby proposed ability attributes are correlated with such goals as crime occurrence per capita to see how much empirical regression weight they have in such relations.

The next most difficult aspect of using a multiattribute approach involves scoring the cities, states, or activities on each attribute. Sometimes this is quite easy as with an attribute such as population. Sometimes it is more difficult as with an attribute such as crime, which involves more reporting problems. Sometimes it is even more difficult as with an attribute such as quality of the police recruitment system. Scoring systems for attributes such as the last one, however, can be developed through the aid of knowledgeable insiders and people experienced in measuring performance or psychological variables. Once the attributes and their weights have been determined and the cities have been scored, the multiattribute allocation system is quite simple to apply.

How is a multiattribute approach likely to compare with the marginal analysis approach that we have been using? The marginal analysis approach seeks to relate benefits to alternative allocations. It then arrives at an optimum allocation in light of (1) the regression coefficients of each place or activity and (2) certain minimum equity constraints. The minimum constraints are like need attributes and involve the same problems in determining them. Marginal analysis produces more effective or goal achieving allocations when we are confident that the regression coefficients are capturing the true causal relationships between benefits and alternative allocations. That confidence is often difficult to achieve, since there are problems of reciprocal causation and spurious causation that are difficult to control for. Under such circumstances, a multiattribute approach may be more meaningful, especially if the attributes, the weights, and the scoring can be agreed upon by those whose opinions are considered relevant. The best test of these two basic approaches to optimum or effective allocation is to try them both and see how they compare on goal achievement. Trying them may involve either simulations such as those used in this chapter or actual randomized experiments or unrandomized quasi-experiments.

Table 12A summarizes what is involved in a multiattribute utility approach to anticrime allocation.

TABLE 12A. DATA FOR ILLUSTRATING THE MULTIATTRIBUTE APPROACH TO ANTICRIME ALLOCATION (Budget = $200)

City	Attribute Score	Percentage	Allocation ($)	Unweighted Average Allocation ($)	Weighted Average Allocation ($)
One Attribute: Population As an Example					
City A	40 people	80	160		
City B	10 people	20	40		
Total	50 people	100	200		
Two Attributes: Population (Weight = 1) and Crime (Weight = 2)					
City A	90 crimes	60	120	140 (70%)	133 (67%)
City B	60 crimes	40	80	60 (30%)	67 (33%)
Total	150 crimes	100	200	200 (100%)	200 (100%)

General Symbols and Formulas

Symbols
X_i^* = Optimum amount to give City i
G = Grand total available to allocate
S = Raw attribute score
P = Attribute score expressed as a percentage of the sum of the scores
W = Relative weight of each attribute

Formulas
One attribute: $X_i^* = (G)(P)$, where $P = S_i/\Sigma S$
Two or more attributes unweighted: $X_i^* = (G)(\Sigma P/N)$
Two or more attributes weighted: $X_i^* = (G)[\Sigma(WP)/\Sigma W]$

REFERENCES

Optimum Allocation in General

Bardach, Eugene. "The Truth about The Spending Service Cliche." Unpublished paper. U. of California at Berkeley Graduate School of Public Affairs, 1978.

Break, George. *Intergovernmental Fiscal Relations in the United States.* Washington, D.C.: Brookings Institute, 1966.

Kotler, Philip. *Marketing Decision Making: A Model Building Approach.* New York: Holt, 1971.

Hirsch, Werner. *The Economics of State and Local Government.* New York: McGraw-Hill, 1970.

Lineberry, Robert. *Equality and Urban Policy.* Beverly Hills, Ca.: Sage, 1977.

McMillan, Claude Jr. *Mathematical Programming: An Introduction to the Design and Application of Optimal Decision Machines.* New York: Wiley, 1970.

Nagel, S. "Minimizing Costs and Maximizing Benefits in Providing Legal Services to the Poor." In *Improving the Legal Process: Effects of Alternatives*. Lexington, Mass.: Lexington-Heath, 1977.

Nagel, S. "Developing an Optimum-Mix Strategy for Civil Rights or Other Multipolicy Activities." In *Legal Policy Analysis: Finding an Optimum Level or Mix*. Lexington, Mass.: Lexington-Heath, 1977.

Noam, Eli. "The Optimal Distribution of Government Expenditures." Unpublished paper, Columbia Graduate School of Business, 1979.

Raskin, Ira. "A Conceptual Framework for Research on the Cost-Effective Allocation of Federal Resources." 9 *Socio-Economic Planning*, 1-10, 1975.

Savas, E.S. "On Equity in Providing Public Services." 24 *Management Science*, 800-8, 1978.

Optimum Allocation in the Crime Context

Atkinson, David, and James Dunn. "The Impact of Expenditures on the Operation of the Criminal Justice System." 12 *Washburn Law Journal*, 269-80, 1973.

Block, Peter. *Equality of Distribution of Police Services*. Washington, D.C. Urban Institute, 1972.

Yong Hyo, Cho. *Public Policy and Urban Crime*. Cambridge, Mass.: Ballinger, 1974.

Comptroller General. *Evaluation Needs of Crime Control Planners, Decision Makers, and Policymakers Are Not Being Met*. Washington, D.C.: General Accounting Office, 1978.

Haries, Keith. *The Geography of Crime and Justice*. New York: McGraw-Hill, 1974.

Kannensohn, et al. *State Subsidies to Local Corrections*. Lexington, Ky.: Council of State Governments, 1977.

Lynch, Beth, and Nancy Goldberg. *The Dollars and Sense of Justice*. Washington, D.C.: National Legal Aid and Defender Association, 1973.

Nagel, S. "Finding an Optimum Geographical Allocation for Anticrime Dollars and Other Governmental Expenditures." In *Legal Policy Analysis: Finding an Optimum Level or Mix*. Lexington, Mass.: Lexington-Heath, 1977.

Shoup, Carl. "Standards for Distributing a Free Governmental Service: Crime Prevention." 19 *Public Finance* 385, 1964.

Skogan, Wesley. "Efficiency and Effectiveness in Big-City Police Departments." 35 *Public Administration Review* 278-86, 1976.

Chapter 13
Allocation Logic

The purpose of this chapter is to show how virtually any public policy problem that involves allocating scarce resources to activities or places can be solved through simple logic if two prerequisites are met. First, one should be able to express quantitatively (1) the goal to be maximized, and (2) the constraints to be complied with. Second, the goal and the constraints should be expressed as statistical, mathematical, or other functions (i.e., equations or inequalities) of (1) the potential allocations to the alternative activities, or (2) the potential allocations to the alternative places. Solving such problems normally does not require the use of complicated and sometimes unreliable linear or nonlinear programming routines. By using a logical approach, one can also obtain better insights into what is happening which in turn can improve the policy recommendations.[1]

SITUATIONS, SYMBOLS, AND SOLUTIONS

To better understand the allocation methodology being presented, it is helpful to classify our government allocation problems. Table 13-1 provides us with a 6 by 4 classification scheme that yields 24 common allocation situations. The main dimension (on the top) is whether the relation between the goals and the allocations are linear or nonlinear. Within each of those two categories, we can talk in terms of whether we are seeking to maximize benefits subject to a maximum cost constraint, or seeking to minimize costs subject to one or more minimum benefit constraints. A third dimension (shown on the side) is whether we are allocating to interacting activities, or allocating to noninteracting places. Within each of those two categories, we can talk in terms of whether or not there are minimum (and possibly maximum) constraints on what can be given to the activities and places. Each of the 24 situations involves a somewhat different reasoning process. There are also variations on these basic 24 situations which will be discussed.

To simplify the discussion, it would be helpful to define a set of symbols that we will frequently use. They are as follows:

Y = the overall goal to be achieved.

Y_1 = the first subgoal, or the amount of Y achieved by Place 1.

TABLE 13-1. COMMON ALLOCATION SITUATIONS

	LINEAR RELATIONS			NONLINEAR RELATIONS		
	Maximize Y	Minimize TC		Maximize Y	Minimize TC	
	(One Y)		(2Y's)	(One Y)		(2Y's)
ACTIVITIES						
Unconstrained	1	5	9	13	17	21
Constrained	2	6	10	14	18	22
PLACES						
Unconstrained	3	7	11	15	19	23
Constrained	4	8	12	16	20	24

Y_2 = the second subgoal, or the amount of Y achieved by Place 2.

X_1 = the dollars allocated to Activity 1 or Place 1.

X_2 = the dollars allocated to Activity 2 or Place 2.

G = the grand total of dollars-available to be allocated to the activities or places after the minimums have been allocated or considered. G can be a given or an amount to be calculated.

M_1 = the minimum amount to be allocated to Activity 1 or Place 1.

M_2 = the minimum amount to be allocated to Activity 2 or Place 2.

$M\%_1$ = the minimum percent of G to be allocated to Activity 1 or Place 1.

$M\%_2$ = the minimum percent of G to be allocated to Activity 2 or Place 2.

X_1^* = the optimum amount to allocate to Activity 1 or Place 1.

X_2^* = the optimum amount to allocate to Activity 2 or Place 2.

Y^* = the overall goal achievement when optimum amounts are allocated to activities when optimum amounts are allocated to activities or places (and likewise with Y_1^*, Y_2^*, and G^*).

a or A = the Y-intercept in a linear function, or the scale coefficient in a nonlinear function. Lower case letters refer to Place 1 or Goal 1, and upper case to Place 2 or Goal 2.

b or B = the slope in a linear function, or the elasticity coefficient in a nonlinear function. Subscript 1 refers to Activity 1, Place 1, or Goal 1 depending on the context.

The discussion begins with the simplest situations which may be almost too simple. They are presented, however, because they are useful on which to build more complex situations that one normally would think could not be solved by simple logic, and instead would require a computerized optimizing routine. Even nonlinear relations with many activities and/or places to be allocated to and many constraints can usually be solved through simple logic and algebra. The solutions recommended below at least provide good starting points in the allocation reasoning process. One possibly may be able to devise unusual hypothetical situations where the decision rules may not apply. The author welcomes learning of such situations so as to be able to further extend this logical allocation approach.

LINEAR RELATIONS BETWEEN GOALS AND ALLOCATIONS

By linear relations between goals and allocations, we mean that it is meaningful to express the relation between the Y's and the X's by an equation of the following form for two interacting activities:

$$Y = a + b_1 X_1 + b_2 X_2 \qquad (1)$$

The analogous form for two noninteracting places is:

$$Y_1 = a + b X_1 \qquad (2a)$$

$$Y_2 = A + B X_2 \qquad (2b)$$

The numerical values for a, b_1, and b_2 in Equation 1 and for a, b, A, and B in equations 2a and 2b can be induced from statistical analysis or deduced from accepted premises. The numerical parameters for an *activities* equation often come from an analysis across agencies or places. The numerical parameters for the *places* equations often come from an analysis over time for each place. One can also carefully ask knowledgeable people what they perceive the parameters to be and average their responses. The Y-intercept generally should be fixed at zero since spending nothing should generally produce no benefits. That would be an example of arriving at one of the numerical parameters by way of an assumption rather than through induction or deduction.[2]

Maximizing Total Goal Achievement

The simplest set of situations is probably the set that involves maximizing Y subject to a maximum cost constraint. If we are allocating to the activities in the context of Equation 1, we should give all of G or the grand total of dollars available, to the activity with the highest positive slope and nothing to any of the other activities, unless there are some minimum or maximum constraints. If there are two activities tied for best in terms of their slopes, then they should divide G equally. If there are minimum constraints, we should give each activity the minimum to which it is entitled, and then allocate all of the remainder to the activity with the highest positive slope. If there is a maximum constraint, then we can only allocate up to that maximum and then switch to the activity with the next to highest positive slope, and so on. The same rules apply if we are allocating to places where linear relations are involved and the goal is to maximize benefits subject to a budget constraint.

This applies to situations 1 through 4. One variation on the basic idea that cuts across all 24 situations is dealing with an objective that is to be minimized, like crime, rather than an objective that is to be maximized, like cases resolved. When the goal is a bad rather than a good, one simply reverses the rules and concentrates on the activities or the places that have the highest negative slope with Y rather than the highest positive slope. Another variation involves more than two activities or two places, but the same rules often apply, as they do here. One could also talk in terms of allocating to both activities and places. This might simply involve allocating first to activities and then suballocating those allocations among the places, or allocating first to places and then suballocating within those places to their activities. Another variation involves expressing the minimum constraints in terms of percentages rather than dollar amounts. In this first set of situations, that would merely involve calculating the minimums for each activity or place by applying their minimum percentages to the grand total to be allocated and then allocating the remainder to the activities or places with the best slopes.

In all 24 situations, it is assumed that X_1, X_2, and other activities or places must have values of zero or more, meaning there are implicit nonnegativity constraints. If we are allocating a budget or effort to activities or places, there is no meaningful way we can give an activity or place less than nothing. We could take away something previously given, but allocation problems by definition only refer to giving, not taking. If an activity or place could be allocated a negative amount, rather than a zero amount, then one could develop nonsense solutions analogous to being able to divide zero by zero. For example, with Equation 1, if b_1 is greater than b_2, the logical solution would be to give a large negative amount to X_2 and the same large positive amount to X_1. By doing so, we would achieve a large amount of Y while spending nothing, since the sum of the expenditures on X_1 plus X_2 would be zero.

Minimizing Total Expenditures

SATISFYING ONE GOAL CONSTRAINT

In Situation 5, we are still working with Equation 1. Now, however, we do not want to give all of G to the X that has the best slope, but just enough to achieve whatever the minimum Y level is. In other words, if b_1 is greater than b_2, then give nothing to X_2, and solve for X_1 in the equation Minimum Y = $a + b_1 X_1$. It is possible that there is no value of X_1 that will achieve the minimum Y level. In any of these allocation problems, there may be no solution given the realities of the actual situations. The solution under those circumstances may be:

1. Obtain more G to allocate.
2. Set a lower minimum Y level.
3. Set lower minimum allocations to the activities or places.
4. Improve the efficiency of the activities or places, which means increasing their slopes so they produce more Y with less money.

Situation 6 involves minimum constraints on the activities. Thus with Equation 1, one would give the required minimum X_2 and then solve for X_1 in the equation, Minimum $Y = a + b_1X_1 + b_2(M_2)$. If the minimums to be given to X_1 and X_2 are expressed as percentages (like .20 per X) rather than dollar amounts, one would solve for G in an equation, for example, Minimum $Y = a + b_1(.80G) + b_2(.20G)$. A more general statement would be, Minimum $Y = a + b_1[(1 - M\%_2)(G)] + b_2[(M\%_2)(G)]$. After solving for G in this equation, X_1^* is the numerical value of what is in the first set of brackets, and X_2^* is in the second set.

Situations 7 and 8 involve the same kind of reasoning as situations 5 and 6 except the total goal achievement equals Y_1 plus Y_2. Thus in Situation 7, one would give nothing to X_2 if b_1 is greater than b_2. One would determine X_1^* by solving for X_1 in the equation, Minimum $(Y_1 + Y_2) = a + bX_1$. In Situation 8, one would determine the optimum allocation to X_1 by solving for X_1 in the equation Minimum $(Y_1 + Y_2) = a + bX_1 + A + B(M_2)$.

SATISFYING TWO OR MORE GOAL CONSTRAINTS

Allocating to Activities. The problem becomes slightly more complicated if we have two goals or two kinds of benefits on which we want minimum achievement levels. In Situation 9, for instance, the problem might be to minimize total costs while providing a minimum Y_1 level and minimum Y_2 level. Suppose, for example, the problem is one of reaching a minimum client satisfaction level (Y_1) and a minimum lawyer satisfaction level (Y_2) in the allocation of dollars to law reform work (X_1) and routine case handling (X_2) in the Office of Economic Opportunity Legal Services Agencies. That might mean a pair of constraints like the following:

$$a + b_1X_1 + b_2X_2 \geq \text{Minimum } Y_1 \tag{3a}$$

$$A + B_1X_1 + B_2X_2 \geq \text{Minimum } Y_2 \tag{3b}$$

The easiest way to determine at least an initial set of optimum values for X_1 and X_2 is to reason that if we are trying to minimize total costs, then we should not seek more than the minimum Y_1 and Y_2 levels. Doing so means converting the "greater than or equal to" signs in inequalities 3a and 3b into equals signs. If X_1 is better than X_2 in both equations (meaning it has a larger slope), then set X_2 equal to zero and solve for X_1 in both equations. The larger value for X_1 is X_1^*, since that amount is needed to achieve both minimum Y_1 and minimum Y_2 at the lowest total cost. One would do the opposite if X_2 were better than X_1. If, however, X_1 is better in one equation, but worse in the second equation, then something should be given to both X_1 and X_2. To determine what those amounts are, solve both equations simultaneously. The resulting solutions for X_1 and X_2 should be optimum values in the sense of achieving minimum Y_1 and minimum Y_2 while spending a minimum total costs.

If there are minimum constraints on X_1 and X_2 as in Situation 10, then follow the same procedures as in Situation 9, except give the worse X its minimum value rather than nothing. If one X is worse on only one of the two equations, and the equations are solved simultaneously, one may find that one or both of the solutions fall below the minimum level. If, for example, X_1^* is below M_1, then consider M_1 to be X_1^*, and solve for X_2 in both equations. The higher value for X_2 under those circumstances is X_2^*. That way one satisfies minimum Y_1, minimum Y_2, minimum X_1, and minimum X_2, while minimizing the total expenditures.

If there were three subgoals and thus three inequality constraints instead of two, an appropriate approach would be to simultaneously solve (1) equations 1 and 2, (2) equations 1 and 3, and (3) equations 2 and 3. That would give three pairs of possible optimum values. One should then sum the X_1 and X_2 for each of those three pairs to see which sum is the smallest since we are seeking to minimize total costs. The pair that yields the smallest sum is the optimum pair assuming that pair can also satisfy the third constraint. If not, then one should turn to the pair that yields the next to the smallest sum, and so on. No matter how many such constraints there are, by solving them in pairs one should be able to arrive at the optimum allocation, since that is the equivalent to finding the key corner points in a linear programming graph. By key corner points we mean solutions that involve giving something to each of the activities rather than everything to only one activity. If after giving something to each activity with three subgoals, one finds that an activity like X_1 is not getting its minimum, then substitute M_1 for X_1 and solve for X_2 in the three equations. X_2^* then equals the largest of those three solutions, and X_1^* equals M_1.

If there are three activities and only two constraints, as in 3a and 3b, we cannot solve a pair of equations simultaneously that has three unknowns. The simple thing to do under those circumstances is to think in terms of allocating only to the X that has the best slope on the first constraint and to the X that has the best slope on the second constraint. All the other Xs can be dropped out. We are then left with two equations and two unknowns which should then be capable of being solved if a solution exists. If the same X is best on both equations, then we simply give that activity all the G rather than divide it between two activities.

Allocating to Places. Situations 11 and 12 involve allocating to places rather than to activities. Under those circumstances, the constraints would be like the following, relating each goal to the place allocations:

$$(a_1 + b_1X_1) + (A_1 + B_1X_2) \leq \text{Minimum}\,Y_1 \qquad (4a)$$

$$(a_2 + b_2X_1) + (A_2 + B_2X_2) \leq \text{Minimum}\,Y_2 \qquad (4b)$$

They differ from constraints 3a and 3b in that each place has its own Y-intercept, whereas the activities share a common Y-intercept. The minimum Y_1 is arrived at by summing the Y_1 from Place 1 and the Y_1 from Place 2, and likewise with the minumum Y_2. Therefore, if we want to minimize the total costs and meet these minimum goal constraints, it makes sense to solve both equations simultaneously unless one of the two places is better on both of the subgoals. If so, we would simply give that better place enough of the G so as to achieve at least the minimum desired level on both Y_1 and Y_2. Whatever that optimum allocation might be, it might produce more than the minimum Y_1 in order to get the minimum Y_2 or vice versa.

In Situation 12 where there are minimum amounts that have to be allocated to each place, solve the equations for 4a and 4b simultaneously provided that X_1 is better on one goal and X_2 is better on the other goal. If the solution to X_1 is below M_1, then substitute M_1 for X_1, and solve for X_2. Do the same if the solution for X_2 is below M_2. If X_1 is better on both goals, then give X_2 its minimum (M_2) and determine what is the smallest allocation needed to X_1 in order to achieve at least the minimum on Y_1 and the minimum on Y_2, taking into consideration what has been allocated to X_2 and the slope of X_2. In other words, if X_1 has the better slope on both Y_1 and Y_2, then (1) substitute M_2 for X_2 in equations 4a and 4b, and (2) solve for X_1 in each of those two equations. X_2^* thus equals M_1, and X_1^* equals the larger of the two solutions for X_1.

Whatever has been said about minimum values on X_1 and X_2 should apply equally to maximum values on X_1 and X_2, although government allocation problems are more likely to specify minimums to activities or places, rather than maximums. For example, in Situation 12, if the solution to X_1^* exceeds a maximum value, then substitute that maximum value for X_1^* and solve for X_2, just as one would substitute the minimum value for X_1^* and solve for X_2 if the original X_1^* fell below M_1. Similarly, in these various situations, if the minimums are expressed as percentages of G rather than as absolute amounts, then substitute $(M\%_2)(G)$ for X_2 and $(1 - M\%_2)(G)$ for X_1 when X_1 has the better slope in both equations. If X_1 has the better slope in only one of the two equations, then solve the equations simultaneously, and make adjustments to consider $M\%_1$ and $M\%_2$ analogous to the adjustments to consider M_1 and M_2 in Situation 12.

As an additional type of constraint, a problem could conceivably provide for a maximum goal achievement or maximum Y level. Normally, goal achievement has a ceiling placed on it indirectly by a budget constraint. There may, however, be situations where the policy makers are willing to allow goal achievement to rise to a point, regardless of cost or in anticipation that the specified point can be afforded. Such a situation is like 1, 2, 3, or 4, except in those situations G is determined by the budget constraint, rather than by calculating the amount needed to achieve the maximum Y. The maximum Y situation would be resolved by giving nothing to the X or Xs with less than the best slope. One would then solve for the value of the best X in an equation of the form, Maximum Y = a + bX, since the other Xs would be set to zero or set to their minimum values. That is the same approach one would use if the policy problem specified a desired or fixed Y level, rather than a maximum Y level. It is also the same approach when the problem specifies a minimum Y level with one goal as in situations 5, 6, 7, and 8. In other words, the same optimizing analysis can often be applied to substantially different situations by seeing the underlying logical similarities.

NONLINEAR RELATIONS BETWEEN GOALS AND ALLOCATIONS

By nonlinear relations between goals and allocations, we mainly mean relations that involve diminishing returns between inputs and outputs. Such a relation may mean that increasing the inputs will cause increased beneficial outputs, but with a plateau effect like the left side of a hill. A nonallocation example might be dollars spent to provide legal services for the poor with the goal being client satisfaction (Y). An allocation example might involve allocating the budgets of legal services agencies between law reform activities (X_1) and routine case handling (X_2). A diminishing returns relation may also look like the left side of a valley if the output is a detriment like crime (Y), and the inputs are anticrime expenditures to Place 1 (X_1) and Place 2 (X_2).[3]

Maximizing Total Goal Achievement

ALLOCATING TO INTERACTING ACTIVITIES

There are a variety of ways of expressing nonlinear relations. The simplest way to show diminishing positive or negative returns where two or more activities are involved is through an equation of the form:

$$Y = a(X_1)^{b_1}(X_2)^{b_2} \tag{5}$$

One can obtain the numerical values for the three parameters from the same data used in determining the numerical values for those parameters back in linear Equation 1. The only difference is that when inputting the data into a computer as part of a regression analysis, one instructs the computer to work with the logarithms of Y, X_1, and X_2, rather than their raw scores. Numerical values can also sometimes be deduced from accepted premises.

What makes that type of relationship between goals and activities so easy to work is not only the simplicity of how those values can be used to determine an optimum allocation, as can be illustrated with Situation 13. If b_1 is greater than b_2, one would probably not want to allocate all of one's 100 dollar budget to X_1 because as the relation between Y and X_1 plateaus out, an incremental dollar given to X_1 is likely to produce a smaller return than using that same dollar as the first dollar given to X_2. The object is to allocate the 100 dollars in such a way as to spend all of the 100 dollars, but with a given amount allocated to each activity so that they are in a state of equilibrium, whereby they both have the same incremental rate of return.

To be more specific, we want to solve for X_1 and X_2 simultaneously in the following pair of equations:

$$X_1 + X_2 = G \tag{6a}$$

$$b_1 a X_2^{b_2}(X_1)^{b_1-1} = b_2 a X_1^{b_1}(X_2)^{b_2-1} \tag{6b}$$

The first equation says spend all of the grand total on X_1 and X_2. The second equation follows from the fact that if $Y = aX^b$, then the marginal rate of return of Y to X is baX^{b-1}. Thus the second equation is setting the MRR of X_1 equal to the MRR of X_2. If we simultaneously solve both those equations, we will find that $X_1^* = [b_1/(b_1 + b_2)](G)$, and that $X_2^* = [b_2/(b_2 + b_2)](G)$. Those solutions tell us we should allocate G to the activities in proportion to their exponents or elasticity coefficients, provided that each activity has a positive exponent and Y is desired. That rule of proportionality also follows from the fact that in Equation 5, the relations between each activity and Y depend solely on their respective exponents since they share a common scale coefficient or "a" value.[4]

If any activity has a negative exponent, then it gets allocated nothing (or whatever minimums are provided in Situation 14), and the remaining G is allocated among the activities with positive exponents in proportion to those exponents. Under Situation 14, (1) the minimums are allocated to all the activities; (2) the sum of the minimums is subtracted from G; and (3) the remainder of G is then allocated to the activities with positive exponents in proportion to their exponents. Activities with positive exponents would normally have exponents with values between zero and 1, which indicates diminishing returns between X and Y. If an exponent in this context equals 1 (showing a linear relation between X and Y) or a number greater than 1 (showing an increasing returns relation), then one still allocates in proportion to those exponents in order to obtain a maximum Y (or goal achievement) for a given G (or amount to be allocated).

In order to keep the allocation system simple, the X_1 and X_2 units should be dollars, hours, or other effort units rather than physical units. For example, the system becomes substantially more complicated if we are talking about allocating a budget of 100 monetary units or 100 dollars between equipment versus labor when equipment is measured in tons and labor in quantity of people. Suppose one ton of equipment costs 5 dollars and one person's labor costs 2 dollars. One could therefore express the budget constraint as $5X_1 + 2X_2 = 100$. We would then be solving for tons of equipment (X_1) and number of employees (X_2), rather than dollars to spend on X_1 and X_2. This would also change the coefficients or parameters in all the equations in this chapter. The change would be contrary to our concern for being able to solve governmental allocation problems through simple logic, albegra, and calculator-aided arithmetic. Once we solve for X_1 and X_2 in dollars, we can always translate those dollars into tons of equipment and numbers of people since we know that one ton costs 5 dollars and one person costs 2 dollars.

If the minimums for X_1 and X_2 are expressed as percentages of G, the logical allocation system has to be modified slightly. Suppose, for example, b_1 in Equation 5 is .2, and b_2 is .4. That tells us the optimum allocation to X_1 is 2/6 of G, and the optimum to X_2 is 4/6 of G. If, however, the minimum constraints specify X_1 must receive .40 G, then we would give .40 G to X_1, rather than .33 G, and X_2 should receive the remainder, or .70 G. If there were an X_3 with a b_3 of .6, then X_1 should receive 2/12 of G, X_2 should receive 4/12, and X_3 should receive 6/12. If, however, the constraints require that X_1 get at least 40 percent, then we have to give .40 to X_1, rather than .17, and allocate the remaining 60 percent between X_2 and X_3. The logical way to do this allocating is in proportion to their elasticity coefficients. Thus, X_2 would get 4/10 of the remaining .60, and X_3 would get 6/10 of the remaining .60. Through a similar reasoning process, one could solve any allocation problem involving (1) the allocation of scarce resources among interacting activities; (2) the objective of maximizing goal achievement; (3) a relation between goal achievement and the activity allocations which is expressed as a nonlinear multivariate power function like Equation 5, and (4) minimum constraints on one or more activities expressed as percentages of the grand total to be allocated. The same reasoning can apply to Situation 16 discussed later.

ALLOCATING TO NONINTERACTING PLACES

The simplest way to show diminishing positive or negative returns where two or more places are involved (as in Situation 15) is through a set of equations of the form:

$$Y_1 = a + b \log X_1 \tag{7a}$$

$$Y_2 = A + B \log X_2 \tag{7b}$$

These two equations are analogous to equations 2a and 2b, except they are nonlinear because X_1 and X_2 are logged in determining the numerical values for the parameters through statistical regression or other analysis.

This type of relation between goals and places is also easy to work with in arriving at optimum allocations. If b is greater than B, one would still want to allocate something to X_2 since it might be wasteful to allocate all of G to X_1 when the plateau effect becomes too great. More specifically in this context, we want to solve for X_1 and X_2 simultaneously in the following pair of equations:

$$X_1 + X_2 = G \tag{8a}$$

$$b/X_1 = B/X_2 \tag{8b}$$

The first equation says spend the grand total on X_1 and X_2. The second equation follows from the fact that if $Y = a + b \operatorname{Log} X$, then the marginal rate of return of Y to X is b/X. Thus the second equation is setting the MRR of X_1 equal to the MRR of X_2. If we simultaneously solve both these equations, we will find that X_1^* equals G multiplied by the ratio between b and the sum of b and B. Similarly, X_2^* equals G multiplied by the ratio between B and the sum of b and B. In other words, we can optimally allocate to noninteracting places by allocating in proportion to their semi-log regression coefficients. This rule also follows from the fact that the marginal rates of return for equation 7a and 7b depend only on the values of b and B. The values of a and A have no bearing on the MRR's, because they are constants, rather than multipliers or exponents of the allocations.[5]

One might ask, why not express the relation between goal achievement and inputs for each place using power functions of the form, $Y_1 = a(X_1)^b$ and $Y_2 = A(X_2)^B$? The answer is that doing so would greatly complicate the optimum allocations, since it would mean solving a pair of simultaneous equations in which the first equation is of the form $X_1 + X_2 = G$, and the second equation is of the form $ba(X_1)^{b-1} = BA(X_2)^{B-1}$. That pair of equations cannot be solved by simply (1) expressing X_1 in the terms of X_2 using the second equation; (2) substituting that expression for X_1 in the first equation; (3) solving the first equation, which is now one equation, in one unknown (X_2); and then (4) using the first equation to solve for X_1. Doing steps 1 and 2 yields an equation of the form, $c(X_2^d) + X_2 = G$. If d is not an integer, one has to use a reiterative guessing approach until a solution for X_2 is found. That is not too difficult with two places or two unknowns, but becomes virtually impossible to handle with 50 states, 100 cities, or any substantial number of places, where each place or X is an unknown allocation to be solved. The semi-log equations 7a and 7b enable one to allocate easily to any number of places by simply allocating in proportion to their semi-log regression coefficients (i.e., $b_i/\Sigma b$), provided that each place has a positive coefficient and Y is desired.

If any place has a negative coefficient, then it gets allocated nothing (or whatever minimums are provided in Situation 16), and the remaining G is allocated among the places with positive coefficients in proportion to those coefficients. Under Situation 16, (1) the minimums are allocated to all the places; (2) the sum of the minimums is subtracted from G; and (3) the remainder of G is then allocated to the places with positive coefficients in proportion to their coefficients. If we are spending to fight crime or a negative goal, then we allocate proportionately to the activities or places with negative exponents or coefficients.

Minimizing Total Expenditures

SATISFYING ONE GOAL CONSTRAINT

Allocating to Activities. Situation 17 involves allocating to two or more activities in such a way as to minimize total expenditures while satisfying a minimum level of Y. This simply involves solving for G in the following equation:

$$\text{Minimum Y} = a[b_1/\Sigma b)(G)]^{b_1}[(b_2/\Sigma b)(G)]^{b_2} \tag{9}$$

This equation tells us that what needs solving is the grand total to allocate to the activities. The grand total should be less than the maximum budget available if we are trying to minimize expenditures, rather than maximize goal achievement. This equation also tells us that the percentage of G to be allocated to Activity 1 should be proportionate to the elasticity coefficient of Activity 1, and similarly with Activity 2. We know what minimum Y is supposed to be. We also know values for a, b_1, and b_2 probably from a regression analysis in which all the variables have been logged. Once we solve for G as the one unknown in the above equation, we can easily solve for X_1^* and X_2^*, since they are the amounts in the first and second set of brackets, respectively. In other words, X_1^* and X_2^* are the minimum amounts possible for achieving the desired minimum Y, given the known relations between Y and both X_1 and X_2, as shown in Equation 5. Solving for G can be done by getting G to stand by itself on the left side of the equation by applying the rules of high school algebra, including the rules for simplifying expressions that contain exponents.[6]

In Situation 18, each activity is entitled to a certain minimum allocation as a matter of equity, politics, law, or other considerations while the remaining funds are allocated in accordance with the relative productivity of each activity. The best way to handle this kind of allocation problem is to solve for G in Equation 9 (as in Situation 17), and then to follow these rules:

1. If X_1^* is above M_1, and X_2^* is above M_2, then the solution of Equation 9 for Situation 17 is also the solution to Situation 18.

2. If X_1^* is below M_1, and X_2^* is below M_2, then insert M_1 into the first set of brackets as X_1^*, and insert M_2 into the second set of brackets as X_2^*.

3. If X_1^* is below M_1, and X_2^* is above M_2, then insert M_1 into the first set of brackets, insert X_2 into the second set of brackets, and solve for X_2.

4. If X_1^* is above M_1 and X_2^* is below M_2, then insert M_2 into the second set of brackets, insert X_1 into the first set of brackets, and solve for X_1.

These rules will provide the lowest possible allocations to X_1 and X_2 in order to satisfy both the minimum Y level and the minimum X_1 and X_2 levels.

If the minimums for X_1 and X_2 are expressed as percentages of G, the solutions are even easier than when they are expressed in absolute amounts. Suppose, for example, b_1 is 3 and b_2 is 5, then when we insert those amounts into Equation 9 the first set of brackets will show (3/8)(G), and the second set will show (5/8)(G). That will yield an acceptable solution if $M\%_1$ is equal to or less than .375 and if $M\%_2$ is equal to or less than .625. Suppose, however, $M\%_1$ is .40 and $M\%_2$ is zero, meaning no minimum for X_2. We would then insert into the first set of brackets (.40)(G), insert into the second set of brackets (.60)(G), and then solve for G, assuming we also have a numerical value for the "a" and minimum Y. In other words, $b_i/\Sigma b$ has to be replaced by $M\%_i$ if $M\%_i$ is greater than $b_i/\Sigma b$. By applying that kind of reasoning, we can also handle minimum X_1 and X_2 percentage constraints for places in Situation 20.

Allocating to Places. Situation 19 is like 17 in that it involves allocating to minimize expenditures while satisfying a minimum goal achievement with no minimum constraints on how much can be allocated to each place or activity. Situation 19 is also like 15 in that it involves allocating to places rather than activities, which means working with semi-log functions like 7a and 7b, rather than a power function like that of Equation 5. Thus what is basically involved is solving for G in the following equation:

$$\text{Minimum } Y = a + b \, \text{Log}\{[b/(b + B)]G\} + A + B \, \text{Log}\{[B/(b + B)]G\} \quad (10)$$

This equation tells us that all we need to do is solve for G, as in Equation 9. The expression in the first pair of braces is equal to X_1^*, or the optimum amount to allocate to Place 1 in order to achieve the minimum Y level. Similarly, the expression in the second pair of braces is equal to X_2^*. Each place receives an allocation in proportion to its semi-log regression coefficient. Minimum Y is the minimum goal achievement that we want the total allocation to have across both places. If there were more than two places we would simply add a third expression like the two which are now in Equation 10, although we would have to switch using subscripts to distinguish between the places, rather than using lower and upper case letters. Equation 10 can be solved by getting G to stand by itself on the left side of the equation by using the rules of high school algebra dealing with logarithms, especially the rule that says the logarithm of a product is equal to the sum of the log of the first factor plus the log of the second factor.[7]

Situation 20 is like 19, except each place is entitled to a minimum allocation, before allocating additional resources to satisfy the minimum Y level. That means following the same four rules described in connection with situation 18, but substitute "braces" for "brackets" in those rules.

Braces are needed in Equation 10 because the sum of the place-coefficients is symbolized (b + B), rather than Σ b which is used to show the sum of the activity coefficients in Equation 9. If the minimum Y level can be satisfied by going below the minimum place or activity allocations, then we have a conflict between the objective that says minimize expenditures, and the constraint that says provide each place with certain minimum allocations. Under those circumstances, it might be appropriate to lower the minimums, since lower allocations will still achieve a minimum Y level. Exactly what the new minimums should be is an equity matter that cannot be deductively determined the way we can logically deduce optimum allocations with various situations (like those specified in Table 1) and various empirical relations (like those specified in equations 1, 2, 5, and 7).

SATISFYING TWO OR MORE GOAL CONSTRAINTS

Allocating to Activities. In nonlinear situations 21 through 24, two or more goal constraints are involved which generally means solving pairs of equations simultaneously, as with linear situations 9 through 12. Allocating to activities under such circumstances means solving simultaneously a pair of equations like the following:

$$\text{Minimum } Y_1 = a(X_1)^{b_1}(X_2)^{b_2} \tag{11a}$$

$$\text{Minimum } Y_2 = A(X_1)^{B_1}(X_2)^{B_2} \tag{11b}$$

This means going through steps like:

1. Use Equation 11b to express X_1 in terms of X_2.
2. Substitute that expression for X_1 in Equation 11a.
3. Solve Equation 11a, which is now one equation in one unknown. This gives X_2^*.
4. After solving for X_2 in Equation 11a, then solve for X_1 in the same equation. This gives X_1^*.

The results represent the lowest possible allocations to X_1 and X_2 that can satisfy Y_1 at its minimum and simultaneously satisfy Y_2 at its minimum. If there is a minimum Y_3 equation, then solve the Y_1 and Y_2 equations, the Y_1 and Y_3 equations, and the Y_2 and Y_3 equations. The best pair of solutions is the pair in which (1) the sum of X_1 and X_2 is the lowest, and (2) all three equations are satisfied.

In situation 22, we not only have minimums on Y_1 and Y_2 to satisfy, but also on X_1 and X_2. The logical approach involves solving equations 11a and 11b simultaneously. In doing so, if X_1^* and X_2^* equal or exceed M_1 and M_2 respectively, then situation 22 has been resolved. If X_1 is below M_1, then substitute M_1 for X_1^*, and solve for X_2 in each of the two equations. The larger solution for X_2 is X_2^*. Do the opposite if X_2 is below M_2. If both Xs are below both Ms, the $X_1^* = M_1$ and $X_2^* = M_2$.

As an alternative, suppose the minimums are expressed as percentages of G and the solutions to X_1 and X_2 do not satisfy those minimums because, for example, X_1^* is less than $(M\%_1)(G)$. Under those circumstances, substitute $(M/_1)(G)$ for X_1 in Equations 11a and 11b, substitute $(1 - M/_1)(G)$ for X_2, and then solve for G in each equation. G^* is the larger of the two Gs in order to be able to achieve both minimum Y_1 and minimum Y_2. X_2^* is $(M/_1)(G^*)$ and X_2^* is $G^* - X_1^*$. The same reasoning can be applied to other variations on the idea of percentage minimums in situations 22 and 24.

Allocating to Places.   In situation 23 where noninteracting places are being allocated to, the pair of equations that needs to be solved separately or simultaneously might be like the following:

$$\text{Minimum } Y_1 = a + b \operatorname{Log} X_1 \tag{12a}$$

$$\text{Minimum } Y_2 = A + B \operatorname{Log} X_2 \tag{12b}$$

As a concrete example, one can consider the two places to be Chicago and New York. The problem is how to allocate an anticrime budget in such a way as to minimize expenditures while seeing to it that Chicago does not have more than 10 crime units and New York does not have more than 15 crime units. We would thus be talking about a maximum Y_1 and a maximum Y_2, rather than minimums on those two goals, but the logical analysis is still the same. The coefficients would also be negative rather than positive, but that also does not affect the logical analysis. The solution under these circumstances is simply to solve for X_1 in Equation 12a and solve for X_2 in Equation 12b.

To make the problem more challenging, we can move to Situation 24 where Chicago has a minimum allocation of M_1, and New York has a minimum allocation of M_2. If the X_1^* solution to Equation 12a is below M_1, then $X_1^* = M_1$, and similarly if the X_2^* is below M_2. That will mean X_1^* will produce a higher Y_1 level than if X_1^* had been above M_1. Doing better than the minimum Y_1 level, however, is consistent with the constraint which says we should do at least as well as minimum Y_1.

As an even more challenging alternative, we can change the problem to say we want certain Y_1 and Y_2 levels across both cities. That might mean solving simultaneously a pair of equations like:

$$\text{Maximum } Y_1 = b_1 \operatorname{Log} X_1 + b_2 \operatorname{Log} X_2 \tag{13a}$$

$$\text{Maximum } Y_2 = B_1 \operatorname{Log} X_1 + B_2 \operatorname{Log} X_2 \tag{13b}$$

The Y_1 in this context might be crimes against property (lower-case slopes) and Y_2 crimes against persons (upper-case slopes). For the sake of simplicity, the ''a'' and A coefficients here are considered to be zero. Equation 13b can be used to express X_1 in terms of X_2, with this expression substituted in Equation 13a for solving Equation 13a. If there are minimums for X_1 and X_2, they can be handled as previously described in situations 18, 20, and 22.

For a grand finale challenge, we could pose a problem of minimizing expenditures when allocating across places subject to constraints like 13a, 13b, 12a, 12b, and 10. The logical thing to do under those circumstances is solve for X_1^* and X_2^* under 10, 12, and 13. This will give three pairs of possible solutions. The best pair is the one in which X_1 plus X_2 is lowest and which is also capable of satisfying the constraints on total crime (Equation 10), crime in Chicago and New York (Equations 12a and 12b), and property-person crimes (Equation 13a and 13b). If we had lots of places to allocate to (not just two), then there would be more calculations and more solutions to check against those criteria. The amount of places or activities, however, should not deter one from using a logical algebraic approach like that advocated here, although a computer or good calculator would be helpful for doing the calculating and checking.

To tie the linear part of this article with the nonlinear part, we could pose an allocation problem involving two activities or places, in which the first activity has a linear relation with goal achievement and the second relation, like that shown below:

$$Y = a + bX_1 + A(X_2)^B \tag{14}$$

At first glance, one might think combining both kinds of relations might complicate things. It actually simplifies them. For example, suppose the problem is how to allocate a given budget (G) between X_1 and X_2 in light of Equation 14. The solution simply involves setting the marginal rates of return for X_1 and X_2 equal to each other which means $b = BA(X_2)^{B-1}$. This, however, is just one equation in one unknown, where we can easily solve for X_2^*. After doing so, we substitute that value in the budget constraint equation, $X_1 + X_2 = G$, and solve for X_1^*. For another example, suppose the problem is how to allocate an undetermined budget (G) between X_1 and X_2 so as to minimize expenditures while achieving at least a minimum Y level. Like the previous example, we set the MRRs equal to each other, since we want to be operating efficiently, regardless of whether we are maximizing goal achievement or minimizing expenditures. This enables us to solve for X_2^*. We can then substitute that value for X_2 in Equation 14, set the left side of the equation at minimum Y, and then solve for X_1^*.

The other 22 situations are about as easy to figure out by manipulating varations on the three basic equations of: (1) $Y = a + bX_1 + A(X_2)^B$ which shows the relations between goal achievement and the allocations to the activities or places, (2) $b = BA(X_2)^{B-1}$, which equalizes the marginal rates of return or slopes, and (3) $X_1 + X_2 = G$, which shows the relation between total costs and the allocations to the activities or places. The situations can be similarly handled if we combine a linear relation and a semi-log function in Equation 14 (rather than a linear relation and a power function), or a power function and a semi-log function.[8]

SOME CONCLUSIONS

The simple logic which this chapter proposes as a substitute or supplement for more complex linear programming and nonlinear programming methods can be reduced to five general rules as follows:

1. When allocating resources to activities or places with linear relations, allocate to the activity or place that has the best slope with goal achievement and nothing to the other activities or places, unless there are minimum or maximum constraints on the activities or places.

2. When allocating to interacting activities with nonlinear relations, allocate in proportion to the elasticity coefficients which each activity has in a power function relation between goal achievement and the activity allocations.

3. When allocating to noninteracting places with nonlinear relations, allocate in proportion to the regression coefficients which each place has in a semi-log relation between goal achievement and each place allocation.

4. When allocating to either activities or places with either linear or nonlinear relations, allocate all the resources available if one is seeking to maximize goal achievement, but allocate just enough to satisfy a minimum goal level or levels if one is seeking to minimize expenditures.

5. The above rules should be applied after minimum amounts have been allocated to the activities or places, or else the minimums or maximums should be inserted in place of the optimum allocations when the optimums are below the minimums or above the maximums, regardless whether those constraints are expressed as absolute amounts or percentages.

There are a number of benefits or advantages that come from using this type of simple logic approach as contrasted to using linear and nonlinear programming routines for allocation problems. These include:

1. By reasoning out the answer, one obtains insights into the relationships that may enable a revision of the objective function or the constraints.

2. By reasoning out the answer, one can better communicate its meaning to policy makers and policy appliers.

3. By reasoning out the answer, one is more likely to catch nonsense results.

4. Linear and nonlinear programming routines often requires stating the objective and the constraints in an awkward way that increases the likelihood that they will be misstated.

5. Linear programming routines will not work for nonlinear situations.

6. Nonlinear programming routines often get stuck in intermediate solutions especially where there are many activities or places to be allocated to.

7. A logical algebraic approach with a hand calculator saves time by avoiding the punching of cards and the processing of a computer program.

8. A logical algebraic approach is also faster and easier to apply than a graphing approach. Graphing also tends to be confined to two activities or two places, and it is quite inaccurate where nonlinear relations are involved.

In light of these advantages, it is hoped that this article will stimulate more analysis and use of a logical algebraic approach to allocation and other optimizing problems. The essence of the approach is to express relations between goals and alternative decisions in terms of simple regression equations that are linear (with none of the variables logged), log-linear (with all of the variables logged), or semi-log (with the independent variables logged). Doing so enables one to capture the reality of the relations between goals and alternative decisions, and it enables one to easily manipulate the results to arrive at optimum decisions. More complicated rules may be needed in natural science, engineering, and business problems, but this approach seems well suited to solving government allocation problems through simple logic after the appropriate statistical analysis has been done. What may be needed now is more analysis of the implications of that kind of approach to optimization, and more applications of the relatively simple logical rules which develop from that kind of analysis.

NOTES

1. On the general methodology of allocating scarce resources, see David Himmelblau, *Applied Nonlinear Programming* (Hightstown, N.J.: McGraw-Hill, 1972); Philip Kotler, *Marketing Decision Making: A Model Building Approach* (New York: Holt 1971); Sang Lee, *Linear Optimizing for Management* (Princeton, N.J.: Petrocelli/Charter, 1976); Robert Llewellyn, *Linear Programming* (New York: Holt, 1963); and Claude McMillan, Jr., *Mathematical Programming: An Introduction to the Design and Application of Optimal Decision Machines* (New York: Wiley, 1970). In addition to the authors of the above books, I would like to thank such people as Judith Liebman and Wayne Davis of the University of Illinois, Ron Dembo of Yale, Paul Zipkin of Columbia, and Leon Lasdon of the University of Texas for their helpful suggestions concerning linear and nonlinear programming.

Earlier, more abbreviate attempts than this present chapter to develop a logic of allocation include S. Nagel, "Finding an Optimum Mix or Optimum Level for Public Policies," in Frank Scioli and Thomas Cook (eds.), *Methodologies for Analyzing Public Policies* (Lexington, Mass.: Lexington-Heath, 1975), pp. 79-87; and S. Nagel and M. Neef, "A Simplified Approach to Solving Optimum Mix Problems," in *Policy Analysis: In Social Science Research* (Beverly Hills, Ca.: Sage, 1979), pp. 161-65.

2. For examples of allocation problems that emphasize linear relations, see Edward Beltrami, *Models for Public Systems Analysis* (New York: Academic Press, 1977); C. Laidlaw, *Linear Programming for Urban Development Plan Evaluation* (New York: Praeger, 1972); S. Nagel and M. Neef, *The Application of Mixed Strategies: Civil Rights and Other Multiple-Activity Policies* (Beverly Hills, Ca.: Sage, 1976); and S. Nagel, *Minimizing Costs and Maximizing Benefits in Providing Legal Services to the Poor* (Beverly Hills, Ca.: Sage, 1973).

On linear regression analysis, see Allen Edwards, *An Introduction to Linear Regression and Correlation* (San Francisco: Freeman, 1976); and Jacob Cohen and Patricia Cohen, *Applied Multiple Regression/Correlation Analysis for the Behavioral Sciences* (Hillsdale, N.J.: Erlbaum, 1975). On asking questions designed to elicit perceptions of slopes or marginal rates of return, see Kotler, op cit., and George Huber "Methods for Quantifying Subjective Probabilities and Multi-Attribute Utilities," 5 *Decision Sciences* 430-58 (1974). Meaningful questions might include, "If X is zero, what do you think the value of Y would tend to be?" or "If X increases by one unit, then by how many units do you think Y would tend to increase or decrease?" A deductive approach to determining the numerical parameters might involve knowing the relation between X and Z and the relation between Z and Y, and then deducing the relation between X and Y. See S. Nagel and M. Neef, "Deductive Modeling in Policy Analysis," in *Policy Analysis: In Social Science Research* (Beverly Hills, Ca.: Sage, 1979), pp. 177-96. On the making of assumptions to arrive at the numerical parameters, see S. Nagel and M. Neef, *Legal Policy Analysis: Finding an Optimum Level or Mix* (Lexington, Mass.: Lexington-Heath, 1977) pp. 232-34, 242-43. The numerical parameters should reflect causal relations between the goals and the alternative allocations, not just spurious correlations. On causal analysis, see Hans Zeisel, *Say It With Figures* (New York: Harper and Row, 1968); Hubert Blalock, *Causal Inferences in Non-Experimental Research* (Chapel Hill: U. of North Carolina Press, 1964); and S. Nagel and M. Neef, "Determining and Rejecting Causation," in *Policy Analysis: In Social Science Research* (Beverly Hills, Ca.: Sage, 1979), pp. 69-102.

3. For examples of allocation problems that emphasize nonlinear relations, see Donald Shoup and Stephen Mehay, *Program Budgeting for Urban Police Services* (New York: Praeger, 1971); Walter Helly, "Allocation of Public Resources," in *Urban Systems Models* (New York, Academic Press, 1975); S. Nagel and M. Neef, "Finding an Optimum Geographical Allocation for Anticrime Dollars and Other Governmental Expenditures," in *Legal Policy Analysis: Finding an Optimum Level or Mix* (Lexington, Mass.: Lexington-Heath, 1977), pp. 225-74; and S. Nagel, "Optimally Allocating Campaign Expenditures," *Public Choice* (Winter, 1980).

On nonlinear regression analysis, see Don Lewis, *Quantitative Methods in Psychology* (Iowa City: U. of Iowa Press, 1966); and Edward Tufte, *Data Analysis for Politics and Policy* (Englewood Cliffs, N.J.: Prentice-Hall, 1974). The use of subjectively perceived parameters or assumed parameters applies to nonlinear relations as well as linear ones. For example, knowledgable people can sometimes handle questions of the form, "If X is one unit, what do you think the value of Y would tend to be?" where we are trying to ascertain "a" in the nonlinear equation, $Y = aX^b$. Similarly, one can ask, "If X increases by one percent, then by how much of a percent do you think Y would tend to increase or decrease?" where we are trying to ascertain the numerical value of the exponent "b". Under some circumstances, it might also be reasonable to assume a square-root relation where $b = .5$, a rectangular hyperbola where $b = -1$, or a quadratic equation where $b = 2$.

4. The simultaneous solution to equations 6a and 6b is as follows:

1. $(X_1)^{b_1-1}/(X_1)^{b_1} = [b_2a(X_2)^{b_2-1}]/[b_1a(X_2)^{b_2}]$
   (X_1 expressed in terms of X_2 using equation 6b)

2. $(X_1)^{b_1-1-b_1} = [(b_2)(X_2)^{b_2-1-b_2}]/b_1$
   (Cancelling the "a" values and showing division with exponential expressions)

3. $(X_1)^{-1} = [(b_2)(X_2)^{-1}]/b_1$
   (Doing the subtraction within the exponents)

4. $1/X_1 = b_2/(b_1X_2)$
   (A $-$ 1 exponent is the same as a reciprocal)

5. $X_1 = (X_2b_1)/b_2$
   (Inverting both sides)

6. $[(X_2b_1)/b_2] + X_2 = G$
   (Substituting the right side of step 5 for X_1 in Equation 6a)

7. $X_2[(b_1/b_2) + 1] = G$
   (Factoring out X_2)

8. $X_2 = G/[(b_1/b_2) + 1]$
   (Dividing both sides by what is in brackets)

9. $X_2 = G/[(b_1/b_2) + (b_2/b_2)]$
   (Anything divided by itself equals 1)

10. $X_2 = G/[(b_1 + b_2)/b_2]$
    (Addition of fractions)

11. $X_2^* = G[b_2/(b_1 + b_2)]$
    (To divide by a fraction, invert and multiply)

12. $X_1 + G[b_2/(b_1 + b_2)] = G$
    (Substituting the right side of step 11 for X_2 in Equation 6a)

13. $X_1 = G - G[b_2/(b_1 + b_2)]$
    (Subtracting from both sides)

14. $X_1 = G[1 - b_2/(b_1 + b_2)]$
    (Factoring out G)

15. $X_1 = G[(b_1 + b_2)/(b_1 + b_2) - (b_2)/(b_1 + b_2)]$
    (Anything divided by itself equals 1)

16. $X_1^* = G[b_1/b_1 + b_2)]$
    (Subtraction of fractions)

5. The simultaneous solution to equations 8a and 8b is as follows:

1. $X_1/b = X_2/B$
   (Inverting both sides of Equation 8b)

2. $X_1 = X_2b/B$
   (Multiplying both sides by b)

3. $(X_2b/B) + X_2 = G$

(Substituting the right side of step 2 for X_1 in Equation 8a)

4. $X_2[(b/B) + 1] = G$
   (Factoring out X_2)
5. $X_2 = G/[(b/B) + 1]$
   (Dividing both sides by what is in brackets)
6. $X_2 = G/[(b/B) + (B/B)]$
   (Anything divided by itself is 1)
7. $X_2 = G/[(b + B)/B]$
   (Addition of fractions)
8. $X_2^* = G[B/b + B)]$
   (When dividing by a fraction, invert and multiply)
9. $X_1 + G[B/(b + B)] = G$
   (Substituting the right side of step 8 for X_2 in Equation 8a)
10. $X_1 = G - G[B/(b + B)]$
    (Subtracting from both sides)
11. $X_1 = G(1 - [B/(b + B)]$
    (Factoring out G)
12. $X_1 = G[(b + B)/(b + B) - (B)/(b + B)]$
    (Anything divided by itself is 1)
13. $X_1^* = G[b/(b + B)]$
    (Subtraction of fractions)

6. For example, if $a = .5$, $b_1 = 2$, $b_2 = 3$, and Minimum Y $= 10$, then

1. $10 = .5[(2/5)(G)]^2[(3/5)(G)]^3$
   (Inserting numerical values)
2. $10 = .5(.40G)^2(.60G)^3$
   (Doing the division)
3. $10 = .5(.16G^2)(.22G^3)$
   (Raising each factor in the parenthesis to the power outside the brackets)
4. $10 = .02G^5$
   (Doing the multiplication)
5. $G^5 = 500$
   (Dividing both sides by .02)
6. $G^* = 3.47$
   (Finding the one-fifth root)
7. $X_1^* = (.40)(3.47) = 1.39$
   (Substiting G^* in the first brackets)
8. $X_2^* = (.60)(3.47) = 2.08$
   (Substituting G^* in the second brackets)

7. For example, if $a = .50$, $b = 2$, $A = .25$, $B = 3$, and Minimum Y $= 10$, then:

1. $10 = .50 + 2 \log [(2/5)G] + .25 + 3 \log [(3/5)G]$
   (Inserting numerical values)

2. $10 = .75 + 2 \text{Log} (.40\text{G}) + 3 \text{Log} (.60\text{G})$
   (Doing the division and some addition)
3. $10 = .75 + 2(-.40 + \text{Log G}) + 3(-.22 + \text{Log G})$
   (Taking the log of each factor in the parentheses)
4. $10 = .75 - .80 + 2 \text{Log G} - .66 + 3 \text{Log G}$
   (Doing the multiplication)
5. $10 = -.71 + 5 \text{Log G}$
   (Doing the rest of the addition and subtraction)
6. $5 \text{Log G} = 10 + .71$
   (Adding $+.71$ to both sides)
7. $\text{Log G} = 10.71/5 = 2.14$
   (Dividing both sides by 5)
8. $\text{G}^* = 138.68$
   (Finding 10 raised to the 2.14 power)
9. $X_1^* = (.40)(138.68) = 55.47$
   (Substituting G^* in the first brackets)
10. $X_2^* = (.60)(138.68) = 83.21$
   (Substituting G^* in the second brackets)

8. Other combinations could be developed using exponential relations of the form $Y = ab^X$, S-shaped relations of the form, $Y = a + b_1X_1 + b_2X_1^2 + b_3X_1^3$, and quadratic relations of the form $Y = a + b_1X_1^2$. The same basic principles apply for dealing with the 24 types of situations when they consist of or include those relations. Some of these situations, however, cannot be solved through the kind of proportional allocation that this article emphasizes, or even through equation-solving where one solves for an unknown by getting it to stand by itself on the left side of an equation. Such situations may require reiterative guessing of values until an optimum is arrived at. This may necessitate or benefit from the use of nonlinear programming routines like those discussed in the books cited in note 1. For further discussion of the applicability of the logic-algebra approach of this chapter to those more complicated relations, see S. Nagel, "Solving Optimum Policy Level Problems Through Simple Logic and Algebra" (Unpublished paper available from the author upon request, 1980).

Part V
Reaching Decisions
That Optimize Time

The purpose of this section is to discuss three sets of policy evaluation methods relevant to minimizing time consumption or forecasting the future. The first set of methods emphasizes factors that are responsible for time consumption, such as (1) queueing theory which stresses the number of arrivals to be processed, the length of time to process the average case, and the number of processors; (2) sequencing theory, which stresses the order in which cases are heard; and (3) critical path theory, which stresses bottlenecks where there are multiple paths that converge from start to finish. The second set of methods emphasizes the prediction of future events from (1) probabilistic relations between events, as in Markov chain analysis; (2) trend lines, as in time series analysis; and (3) equations in which the time period is a predictor variable, as in difference/differential equations. The third set of methods emphasizes optimum level, mix, and choice analysis, as applied to delay minimization.

Chapter 14
Queueing, Sequencing, and Critical Paths

The following prescriptive or optimizing models are primarily concerned with saving time. In that sense they have a normative, prescriptive, or optimizing goal. They also have descriptive or predictive elements in the sense that they often attempt to describe or predict how much time will be saved by alternative procedures or whether time will be saved.

QUEUEING THEORY

The Basic Model

Queueing theory involves a set of mathematical models or formulas which take as their main inputs the number of cases arriving in a system per day or per time unit, and the number of days or time units needed to process each case. From those formulas and inputs, one can deduce such predictive outputs as the average amount of time spent in the system. More important, one can deduce such prescriptive outputs as how to reduce the average amount of time spent in the system.[1]

As a concrete example, suppose we are concerned with the legal process from arrest through arraignment in misdemeanor cases in middle-sized cities. By arraignment, we mean appearing before a judge who mainly determines (1) whether there is probable cause for going ahead with a trial; (2) whether a defendant wants to plead guilty or not guilty if there is probable cause; and (3) whether the defendant wants a bench or jury trial if pleading not guilty. Between arrest and arraignment there is a preliminary hearing where a judge mainly determines what the defendant's bond should be and whether the defendant is indigent enough to qualify for court-appointed counsel.

Suppose further that we have data for 10 separate working days for a given arraignment court system. On 4 of those working days, 10 cases arrived in the system as a result of people being arrested, and on the other 6 days, 20 cases arrived in the system. This means that on the average day, 16 cases arrived in the system, since $16 = [(4)(10) + (6)(20)]/10$. That figure is one of the key inputs and can be symbolized "A" for arrival rate. Suppose also that we observe that within those 10 working days, there are 7 days in which 18 arrested persons were given an arraignment hearing, and 3 days in which 12 cases were similarly serviced. This means that on the average day, 16.2 cases were serviced or departed from the arraignment system since 16.2 = [(7)(18) + (3)(12)]/10. That figure is the second of the key inputs and can be symbolized "S" for service rate. The service *rate* (S) of so many cases completed per day should be distinguished from the service *time* (T_S), which tells us in this context how long an arraignment hearing takes, usually about a half-hour. The two are related, however, in that the shorter the service time, the higher the service rate is likely to be. A sample of only 10 days is probably too small for calculating a reliable average arrival rate or service rate, but for the sake of illustration, let us assume those figures (A = 16, and S = 16.2) do capture the true averages although not necessarily the true spread of types of days around those averages.

What now does one do with those input figures? One useful output as mentioned above is to deduce or predict from those two figures an expected or likely amount of time that the average case will spend in the system. Time in that context means both waiting time (i.e., sitting in jail if the defendant has not been released on bond or awaiting the arraignment hearing while released on bond), and servicing time (i.e., the time actually consumed by the arraignment hearing). The formula for calculating the average time spent in the system is $T = 1/(S - A)$. Given our hypothetical numbers, the average time would be $T = 1/(16.2 - 16) = 1/.2 = 5$ working days, or one working week. The formula operates under assumptions that have been repeatedly validated with various kinds of case processing concerning the distribution or spread around the arrival rate and around the service rate.[2] Knowing the mathematics behind these assumptions is not necessary in order to make use of the formula and other queueing formulas. One can, however, see that the total time formula intuitively makes sense since we know that if 16.2 cases are processed on an average day, then an average case takes $1/16.2$ days to process (i.e., 6 percent of an 8-hour day or a half-hour), which is part of the right side of the formula. We further know that if the arrival rate (A) were equal to or greater than the service rate (S), then cases would arrive so fast relative to the servicing time that we would build up an infinitely long backlog and any new case would take infinitely long for its total time in the system (i.e., it would never get serviced), which is reflected in the denominator of the formula.

Variations and Implications

Other useful formulas include the formula for determining the average waiting time before service begins. That formula is $T_W = T(A/S)$. In other words, waiting time equals total time multiplied by the arrival/service ratio. Given our numbers for A and S and the previously calculated T, we would deduce that waiting time is 4.94 working days since 4.94 = (5)(16)/(16.2). Since total time also equals waiting time plus servicing time (i.e., $T = T_W + T_S$), we can easily calculate predicted servicing time by just subtracting 4.94 from 5, which tells us that the servicing time or arraignment hearing time is about .06 of an 8-hour working day, or .49 hours which is about 30 minutes at 60 minutes to an hour. T_W and T_S could also be expressed in terms of A and S, but it is simpler to calculate them in terms of the previously calculated T or total time.[3]

Queueing theorists have not only worked out formulas dealing with time consumption, but also formulas dealing with backlog.[4] For example, the formula for predicting or estimating the total number of cases backed up in the system is $N = (A/S)/(1 - A/S)$. In other words, the size of the backlog varies directly with how bad the arrival/service ratio is and inversely with the complement of that ratio. A bad arrival/service ratio is one in which the arrival rate approaches or exceeds the service rate. Given our numbers, we would expect on an average day for 80 cases to be backed up in the system, since $80 = (16/16.2)/(1 - 16/16.2)$. This means that on an average day there are 80 arrested defendants in the city who have not yet been completely arraigned. Of those 80 cases, one case is in the process of being arraigned or serviced, and the other 79 are in a sense in the waiting line. In other words, the total backlog (N) equals the backlog being serviced (N_S) and the backlog that is awaiting servicing (N_W). Just as T_W can be calculated by the formula $T_W = T(A/S)$, likewise N_W can be calculated by the formula $N_W = N(A/S)$. Calculating N_W that way also gives 79 since $79 = 80(16/16.2)$.

Other formulas have been developed in which the outputs are various kinds of probabilities rather than amounts of time or amounts of cases.[5] For example, there is a formula which uses the average arrival rate as an input (A = 16), and can give outputs showing the probability of having 14 arrivals, 19 arrivals, or any number of arrivals that one might be interested in. Another formula uses the average service rate as an input (S = 16.2) and can give outputs showing the probability of servicing 15 cases, 17 cases, or any number of cases per day that one might be interested in. Still another formula uses both A and S as inputs and can give outputs showing the probability of having a day in which there are zero cases in the backlog of the system, 5 cases, 37 cases, or any number of cases. All these probabilities can also be interpreted as percentages out of 100 random working days.

Still other queueing formulas calculate time consumed (T, T_W, or T_S), backlog (N, N_W, or N_S), and the above probabilities (P's) when one varies the number of servers, channels or courts who are processing cases. In other words, there are formulas for calculating different T's, N's, and P's when C or the number of channels is included as a variable. The formulas we have been working with have assumed there is only one arraignment court, rather than more than one operating simultaneously. Those basic T, N, and P formulas can also be modified to take into consideration unusual distributions or spreads around the average arrival rate or the average service rate.[6] The formulas can also be varied to consider (1) rules that provide for priority servicing of certain types of cases, which is called queue discipline; (2) procedures that allow lawyers to pick what courts or judges will hear their cases, which is called jockeying; (3) rules that set a maximum on the number of cases or cases of certain types that can be processed, such as divorce cases in a legal services agency in a given month, which is called truncating the arrivals; and (4) multiple stages of processing, such as waiting and being processed in a preliminary hearing, waiting and being processed in the arraignment, and waiting and being processed in the trial stage.[7]

Queueing formulas are useful for making reasonably accurate estimates of how the time and backlog would be reduced by changing the average arrival rate, the average service rate, the number of courts, the system of priorities, and other queueing variables. The formulas are also helpful in emphasizing that the only way to reduce time and backlog is through those variables. For example, we can reduce the initial arrival rate by resolving more complaints to the police without making arrests. We can also reduce the arrival rate at the processing or servicing stage by encouraging more settlements between arrest and arraignment. We can reduce the service time and thus increase the service rate by having arraignment hearings follow a more standardized script and thus avoid unnecessary matters.[8] In that regard, if an average two-day trial can be reduced to one day and there are 500 cases waiting in line, then the 500th case will be heard 500 working days sooner as the result of one day saved per case. In other words, total time (T) saved equals not just one day (i.e., the reduction in T_S), but rather the reduction in T_S multiplied by the number of cases in the waiting line (N_W). The queueing model also points up the need for more courts, more judges, and more judge time per year since T and N are influenced by the availability of processing channels which those matters relate to. Time and backlog can also be reduced through systems of priorities for types of cases, which is partly the subject of dynamic programming in the next section of this chapter. Similarly, time and backlog can be reduced by reducing the number of stages in the total process, and by a central administration which directs what paths cases should follow, both of which are partly the subject of critical path modeling in the subsequent section.[9]

DYNAMIC PROGRAMMING OR OPTIMUM SEQUENCING

Sequencing of Cases

The essence of dynamic or sequential programming involves finding an optimum sequencing of events so as to minimize the total time consumed or some other benefit-cost considerations. At first glance, one might not think that the sequence in which cases are processed would influence the total time. For example, suppose we have a set of three cases in which one case takes 20 days in trial, a second case 10 days, and a third case 5 days. One might think processing those cases would take 35 days no matter what order they are processed in. That thinking, however, does not take into consideration that total time (T) equals waiting time (T_W) and processing or servicing time (T_S), not just processing time.[10]

Bearing this in mind, if we process the 3 cases starting with the longest first, then the first case will take 20 days (T = 0 + 20); the second case will take 30 days, since it has to wait 20 days for the first case to be processed (T = 20 + 10); and the third case will take 35 days to be processed, since it has to wait 30 days for the first two cases (T = 30 + 5). The total amount of time for all three cases is thus 85 days, meaning an average of 28 days per case. The object of dynamic programming in this simple situation is to develop an optimum order for those three cases that will minimize the average time per case, and then generalize some rules applicable to larger samples of cases and to more complicated variations on this basic example.

With three cases, there are six possible ways to order them, since the number of permutations for N items is N factorial, which means (N)(N − 1)(N − 2) . . . (N − N + 1). Thus if there are three cases, there are (3)(3 − 1)(3 − 3 + 1) or 3 × 2 × 1 permutations or orderings. More specifically, these six orderings are shown in Table 14-1. Notice that each order generates a different average amount of time consumed per case.

TABLE 14-1. WAYS OF ORDERING THREE CASES

Order #1				Order #2				Order #3			
Case	$T_W + T_S$		= T	Case	$T_W + T_S$		= T	Case	$T_W + T_S$		= T
20	0	20	20	10	0	10	10	5	0	5	5
10	20	10	30	20	10	20	30	20	5	20	25
5	30	5	35	5	30	5	35	10	25	10	35
		Sum =	85			Sum =	75			Sum =	65
		Avg =	28			Avg =	25			Avg =	22

Order #4				Order #5				Order #6			
Case	$T_W + T_S$		= T	Case	$T_W + T_S$		= T	Case	$T_W + T_S$		= T
20	0	20	20	10	0	10	10	5	0	5	5
5	20	5	25	5	10	5	15	10	5	10	15
10	25	10	35	20	15	20	35	20	15	20	35
		Sum =	80			Sum =	60			Sum =	55
		Avg =	27			Avg =	20			Avg =	18
											(optimum)

T_W = Waiting time, T_S = Servicing time, T = Total time.

The optimal order is #6, which involves sequencing the cases from the shortest to the longest. This produces an average time consumed per case of only 18 days as contrasted to the 28 days when the longer cases are handled first. We could generalize that finding to say that the cases always should be sequenced so the shorter cases are handled first, provided the only goal is to minimize the average time spent per case and there are no maximum time constraints on the cases.

If, however, we more realistically provide that no case can be allowed to take more than a certain amount of time, then the optimum sequencing would not be simply to take the shorter cases first, since the longer cases would then either never get processed or their processing plus waiting time would probably exceed the maximum constraint. For example, if we specify that no case should be allowed to take more than 30 days, then order #6 is no longer feasible, since it does not satisfy that maximum constraint by virtue of the fact that the third case takes 35 days.[11] No matter how the cases are ordered, the total waiting time and servicing time for the last case will equal the sum of the servicing time for all the cases. This sum is 35 days and thus the last case for all six orders would violate a 30-day maximum constraint.[12]

To comply with the 30-day maximum constraint in light of queueing theory, we would then have to reduce the number of arrivals (i.e., the number of cases), reduce the service time (i.e., lower T_S for some or all of the cases), or else add additional channels or courts.[13] Table 14-2 shows all the possible ways we could order the cases if we had two courts for them to be processed in. There are still six possible ways of ordering the cases because we are still working with three cases although in two courts. The average time per case for these six orders, however, is less than the six orders where there was only one court, since with two courts there are two cases at the processing stage rather than one, and there is only one case at the waiting stage rather than two. The optimum order now is not order #6, which was optimum without constraints, or order #3, which was optimum with a 35-day constraint. Rather, the optimum order is either #4 or #5, both of which satisfy the new 30-day constraint and have the relatively low average time per case of 13. The most meaningful way to resolve the tie is to add a third criterion, namely that when two orders satisfy the maximum constraints and both have equally minimum average times per case, then pick the order that has the smallest maximum. This criterion involves noticing that the maximum time for order #5 is 25 days. Thus, order #4 has the smallest maximum, is thus better than order #5, and is thus the optimum of the six orders of Table 14-2. From this analysis one can generalize that within each court the shorter cases should be taken first, and the shorter cases should be given to the court with the greater quantity of cases.

The above principles for optimum ordering or sequencing of cases can be applied by computer programs to large quantities of cases where the

TABLE 14-2. WAYS OF ORDERING THREE CASES WITH TWO COURTS

Order #6		#3		#5		#2		#4		#1	
Case	Time	Case	Time	Case	Time	Case	Time	Case	Time	Case	Time
Court 1											
5	5	5	5	10	10	10	10	20	20	20	20
Court 2											
10	10	20	20	5	5	20	20	5	5	10	10
20	30	10	30	20	25	5	25	10	15	5	15
SUM=45		SUM=55		SUM=40		SUM=55		SUM=40		SUM=45	
AVG=15		AVG=18		AVG=13		AVG=18		AVG=13 (Optimum)		AVG=15	

quantities are too large to otherwise work out all the possible permutations. Each new case entering into the system can be analyzed to estimate how much trial time the case will need. These estimates or predictions can be based on a statistical analysis that considers such variables in criminal cases as severity of the crime type, whether the defendant has asked for a jury or bench trial, and whether the defendant has private counsel or a public defender. In personal injury cases, time predictions can be made from such variables as the plaintiff's latest settlement demand, the defendant's latest settlement offer, and the type of personal injury is involved. Regression equations of the form $T = a + b_1X_1 + b_2X_2 \ldots + b_nX_n$, or $T = aX_1^{b_1}X_2^{b_2} \ldots X_n^{b_n}$ can be developed by computerized regression analysis programs after inputting data for many prior cases where each X corresponds to the score of the case on one of the above-mentioned or other variables.[14]

Sequencing of Stages

An additional type of dynamic programming is the optimum sequencing of *stages* of cases. For the sake of simplicity, let's assume that all cases have only two stages, namely pretrial pleadings and the trial stage. By optimum sequencing of stages we do not mean in this context whether it is better to have the pleadings precede or follow the trial. This kind of sequencing is not an available option since the pleadings or preliminary filing of papers must always legally and logically precede the trial. Optimum sequencing of stages, however, could include the question of whether the verdict and damages decision should be decided simultaneously at the trial stage or sequentially in what would amount to two trials for some cases, with one trial deciding whether the defendant is liable to the plaintiff and the second trial deciding how much the damages should be. Sequential trials of this kind do save time. First, if we have 100 typical personal injury cases, only about 64 are likely to result in a judgement for the plaintiff, and thus 36 of the cases only need half a trial since they never get to the damages question. Second, about 32 cases or half of the 64 cases in which the defendant is found liable are likely to be settled before the damages trial, since damages is a matter easier to agree upon than is liability. If we assume that the combined trial takes 10 days, the separate liability trial 7 days, and the separate damages trial 6 days, then under the combined system, 100 cases would consume 1,000 trial days. Under the split trial system, 100 cases would consume 448 days (i.e., 64 times 7) plus 192 days (i.e. 32 times 6) for a total of 640 trial days. This is a substantial saving from 1,000 days, especially when at first glance one would think a split trial system might double the trial time rather than reduce it.[15]

However, under a split trial system, the 64 percent liability rate may drop to 40 percent since the jury cannot deduct from the plaintiff's damages for the plaintiff's contributory negligence, and therefore must decide against the plaintiff if he has contributed to his own injury. This result provides an unforeseen time benefit since only 40 percent of the cases are eligible for the second trial, and thus only 20 percent are likely to take advantage of that eligibility if half of those 40 percent are settled between the liability trial and the damages trial. This result, however, provides a substantial unforeseen detriment since this sequencing reform is only supposed to reduce delay in the processing of cases, not change their outcomes. Often time-saving reforms do have effects on outcomes that should be taken into consideration in analyzing whether the reform is worth adopting.[16]

Optimum sequencing of stages, however, normally does not refer to the splitting of a stage in the process into two sequential stages, but rather the extent to which the early stages in one case should be handled before the later stages in other cases. Let's assume we have two cases, each of which has a pleading stage and a trial stage. Let's further assume that pleading for case 1 is estimated to take one hour (P_1), pleading for case 2 two hours (P_2), trial for case 1 three hours (T_1), and trial for case 2 four hours (T_2). Table 14-3 shows all the possible ways we could sequence the stages of those cases without violating the rule that pleadings have to precede trial. Each order shows the servicing time for each stage, the waiting time, and the total time. The servicing time is the same for each stage regardless of the order. The waiting time refers to the number of hours that a stage of case 1 has to wait for a stage of case 2 to be processed, or vice versa. In other words, waiting time only refers to waiting for the other case, not waiting for an earlier stage of one's own case.

Table 14-3 shows that the optimum sequencing does all the stages for case 1 before starting any of the stages for case 2. Case 1 is preferred over

TABLE 14-3. WAYS OF ORDERING TWO STAGES OF TWO CASES

Order #1

Stage	Ts	Tw	T
P1	1	0	1
T1	3	0	3
P2	2	4	6
T2	4	0	4

SUM = 14
AVG = 7 (Optimum)

Order #2

Stage	Ts	Tw	T
P2	2	0	2
T2	4	0	4
P1	1	6	7
T1	3	0	3

SUM = 16
AVG = 8

Order #3

Stage	Ts	Tw	T
P1	1	0	1
P2	2	1	3
T1	3	2	5
T2	4	3	7

SUM = 16
AVG = 8

Order #4

Stage	Ts	Tw	T
P2	2	0	2
P1	1	2	3
T1	3	3	6
T2	4	4	8

SUM = 19
AVG = 9.5

Order #5

Stage	Ts	Tw	T
P1	1	0	1
P2	2	1	3
T2	4	0	4
T1	3	6	9

SUM = 17
AVG = 8.5

Order #6

Stage	Ts	Tw	T
P2	2	0	2
P1	1	2	3
T2	4	0	4
T1	3	4	7

SUM = 16
AVG = 8

T_S = service time
T_W = waiting time
T = total time

P_1 = pleading time for case 1
T_1 = trial time for case 1

263

case 2 because it is a shorter case. Doing all the stages of one case without interruption by the other case is preferred because waiting time only occurs while waiting for the other case. This assumes as we mentioned, that the only stages in our simplified illustrations are pleadings and trial, which means there is no stage between pleadings and trial called preparation for trial. When there is such a stage because the parties are not ready to go to trial immediately after pleadings, then it would make sense to move the pleadings for case 2 in between the pleadings and trial for case 1 while the parties in case 1 are preparing for trial.

At first glance it might seem that even if we assume only the two stages of pleading and trial, then it might still be meaningful to interrupt P_1 and T_1 with P_2 if case 1 were not shorter for both pleadings and trial, but only for pleadings. As a matter of fact, cases that are short on pleadings do tend to be short on trial length too. As a matter of logic though, even if case 1 were only shorter on pleadings and longer on trial (e.g., $T_1 = 4$ and $T_2 = 3$, rather than $T_1 = 3$ and $T_2 = 4$), then one could prepare a table like Table 14-3, which would show the rule of processing the stages of a given case in uninterrupted succession still makes sense in order to minimize the average time per case. However, if we shorten the trial time for case 2 enough to make its total time less than case 1, then all of case 2 should be done before all of case 1.

The rule of processing the stages of a given case in uninterrupted succession applies whether there is one court or two courts so long as each court or channel is capable of processing cases at both the pleading stage and the trial stage. If one court specializes in nothing but pleadings and the other court specializes in nothing but trials, then the optimum sequencing involves first finding the shortest time unit among all the stages and cases. If, for example, the shortest time unit among all the stages is the *pleading* stage for case 9, then that case is scheduled *first*. If the shortest time unit is the *trial* stage for case 7, then that case is scheduled *last*. After finding the shortest time unit, then one looks for the next to the shortest time unit and continues to follow the rule that if the unit is a pleading unit, then the case with which it is associated is heard next to the top. If, on the other hand, the unit is a trial unit, then the case with which it is associated is heard next to the bottom. By following these rules, we will minimize the average length of time per case. Few court systems involve this kind of specialization, but doing so could save time unless trials become substantially longer as the result of trial judges having to learn about cases anew by virtue of not having participated in the pleadings stage.

Like case sequencing, stage sequencing can be computerized so that one does not have to enumerate all the possible orders, which can become quite cumbersome if there are many cases, stages and specialized channels for processing the stages. The input to such computerized scheduling or sequencing programs, like the case scheduling, involves time consumption figures for the stages based on characteristics of the cases that have been found to correlate substantially with how much time cases tend to take at each stage. Dynamic programming routines also exist which can take into consideration that the amount of trial time at trial court 3, 4, or 5 may depend in part on whether the pleading work was done in pleading court 1, 2, or 3.[17]

CRITICAL PATH METHOD
AND FLOW CHART MODELS

Critical Path

Critical path method (CPM), or Program Evaluation and Review Technique (PERT) emphasizes that if total time is going to be reduced in cases, one should not concentrate on reducing all the stages, but only on those stages that are especially influential on the total time. By influential in this context we mean two things. First, the stage is essential to some subsequent stage which cannot be started until the earlier stage is completed. Second, the stage takes longer than other stages that are also essential to the subsequent stage. For example, preparation by the public defender and preparation by the prosecutor are both normally essential for going to trial, as is indicated in Figure 14-1. If, however, the public defender, on the average, takes three weeks to prepare for trial and the prosecutor only takes two weeks, then the critical path from pleading to trial is through the lower arrow of preparation by the public defender. This is so because reducing the prosecutor's preparation time would not make trials occur any sooner. Reducing the public defender's preparation time by, for example, providing additional resources would, however, enable trials to occur sooner. If the public defender's preparation time is reduced to less than two weeks, then preparation by the prosecutor becomes a critical path.[18]

FIGURE 14-1. A SIMPLE CRITICAL PATH MODEL

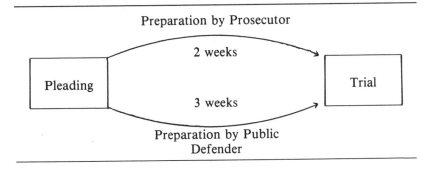

Preparation by Prosecutor

2 weeks

Pleading

Trial

3 weeks

Preparation by Public
Defender

This kind of analysis could be expanded to include the total criminal justice process from arrest to parole or the civil justice process from complaint to collecting on the judgment. Many of the stages in either kind of legal process, however, do not involve two or more procedures coming together as prerequisites to a subsequent stage. Rather, the legal process tends to be more like the kind of assembly line in which each stage follows the preceding stage in boxcar fashion. Other jointly converging stages, however, include bringing together information by the defense and prosecutor on the matter of pretrial release, and bringing together information by the defense, prosecutor, and probation department on postconviction sentencing.[19] Normally, the probation department's presentence report follows the conviction of the defendant, but substantial time might be saved by having the probation department prepare presentence reports on all defendants before they are convicted, rather than only for the approximately 70 percent who are convicted.[20] The extra cost of preparing unnecessary reports for the 30 percent of defendants who are not convicted may be more than offset by the time wasted waiting for reports whose preparation does not begin until conviction. More specifically, the extra cost of reporting on all defendants would be .30 times the number of defendants times the average cost per report, whereas the extra cost of not reporting on all the defendants equals (1) the extra cost of storing defendants in the county jail when they could be free if their release on probation is recommended, and (2) the extra cost to the county if the defendant could be shipped sooner to the state prison where imprisonment is recommended.

In Figure 14-1, we indicated that preparation by the prosecutor would be two weeks by implicitly averaging the prosecutor's preparation time over a set of cases and then doing the same for the public defender. Often this kind of data is not available. A commonly used substitute is to ask the prosecutor for a subjective estimate, or better yet, three subjective estimates. One estimate would be the most likely or most common time (comparable to the mode in statistical analysis), the second estimate would be an optimistic time (which occurs about once in 100 cases), and the third estimate would be a pessimistic time (which also occurs about once in 100 cases). From these three estimates an average or mean time is computed by the formula: T_E (for expected time) equals the optimistic time plus four times the most likely time plus the pessimistic time, with the sum divided by six. This formula is based on (1) the idea that people cannot directly estimate averages, but they can more easily estimate optimistic, modal, and pessimistic figures as above defined; (2) assumptions concerning how averages tend to relate to those figures; and (3) the usefulness of those input figures in PERT-CPM outputs.

By inputting into a PERT or CPM computer program information concerning the ordering of the stages and the optimistic, modal, and pessimistic estimates for each stage, one can obtain a variety of useful outputs. These outputs include (1) estimates of the date by which each stage is likely to be completed; (2) estimates of the time accumulated as of each stage; (3) the stages that constitute the critical path from start to finish, (4) the amount of slack or dead time at the end of each stage that has to wait for an adjacent stage to be completed in order to bring the results from the two together at the next stage; and (5) the probability that a subsequent stage will have to wait for a previous stage not on the critical path. These informational outputs can be helpful to better plan big cases and also routine cases.[21] Such planning should not equally emphasize all stages that are on the critical path, but rather those stages on the critical path from start to finish that consume the most time and that are most subject to time reduction as indicated by the amount of spread between the optimistic, modal, and pessimistic estimates. The more spread or diversity there is regarding the time consumed at a given stage, the more that stage may be subject to time reduction if one can determine what correlates with that variance or spread across cases, over time, or across courts.[22]

An interesting problem, closely related to critical path method, is to which court one should take one's case to minimize time consumption and other costs, when one has a choice of courts. For example, suppose a personal injury plaintiff could follow the path going to a federal court (on the jurisdictional grounds that the plaintiff and defendant are from different states), or go to the state court in which the defendant can be sued. Suppose further if the plaintiff goes to the federal court, the case will be heard within one year, and the plaintiff will collect about 15,000 dollars if victorious, but with only a 20 percent chance of winning. If, on the other hand, the plaintiff goes to the state court, the case will be heard within two years, and the plaintiff will collect 10,000 dollars if victorious, with a 40 percent chance of winning. Which path should be followed?[23]

The expected value of the federal path is 3,000 dollars (i.e., 15,000 dollars discounted by the .20 probability of winning it) without considering the time element, and the expected value of the state path is 4,000 dollars (i.e., 10,000 dollars discounted by the .40 probability of winning it). If, however, we take into consideration that one has to wait two years for the 10,000 dollars from the state court, its value substantially decreases. More specifically, the present value of a future amount is calculated by formula $P = A/(1 + r)^t$ where r is the interest rate that could be obtained by putting money in a savings account for t years. If we assume the interest rate is 6 percent, then the present value of the state's 10,000 dollars two years from now is 8,900 dollars. If we now discount that present value by the .40 probability of achieving it, the expected value of the state case becomes 3,560 dollars. Applying the same formlula to the federal case, the present value of its 15,000 dollars award would be 14,151 dollars since $\$14,151 = \$15,000/(1 + .06)^1$. If we now discount that present value by the .20 probability of achieving it, the expected value of the federal path becomes 2,830 dollars which is still less than the state path, but not as much less as taking the difference in time consumption into consideration. We, of course, could have offered a hypothetical example where taking the time consumption into consideration reverses the rank order of which is the better path.

Flow Chart Models

Flow chart models are related to critical path method in that they consist of a series of rectangles or other geometric shapes which represent the beginnings or endings of stages in the legal process, and a series of arrows connecting the rectangles. On the arrows are generally written the quantity of time needed to go from the beginning to the end of each stage. The arrows also show how the stages flow into each other or how the stages represent either-or possibilities, including the possibility or probability of dropping out rather than going ahead. Flow chart models are useful as a visual aid for seeing the general case processing more clearly, which can be quite suggestive of ideas for how time can be reduced. They can also be computerized to show the output effects of changes in the times, case quantities, stages, or other inputs.

One overly simple hypothetical illustration would be to observe that on a flow chart the total time consumed by the average felony case is 100 days and 20 of these days involve waiting after the preliminary hearing for a grand jury proceeding, which then averages one day. Thus the flow chart implies that if the grand jury proceeding could be eliminated, then 21 days would be saved or 21 percent of the total time. This assumes, however, that what replaces grand jury indictment, namely a formal complaint by the prosecutor alone, takes no time, which is unlikely to be true. Another flow chart for cases involving formal complaint by the prosecutor alone might show 10 days waiting for the prosecutor's indictment, meaning the net saving from replacing the grand jury with the prosecutor would be 11 days. This assumes that grand jury cases, if shifted to prosecutor indictment, would only take the 10 days that previous cases handled by the prosecutor had been taking, which may not be so, given differences in the types of cases involved and his new extra load, meaning a saving of less than 11 days per shifted case. As an aside, one might note that grand jury indictment can only be eliminated at the state level, not the federal level, in light of the national constitution. Such legal constraints are important to consider in any prescriptive modeling designed to minimize time consumption.

Table 14-4 constructs a flow chart from previously unpublished data (shown in Figure 14-2), for a sample of state criminal cases from across the United States compiled in 1961 by the American Bar Foundation. This data has the advantage of being based on a nationwide sample of 11,000 cases rather than cases from a single court jurisdiction, as is usually the case with flow chart models. Table 14-4 shows the average time consumed in days from one event to another for a subset of the 11,000 cases in which those two events occurred and for which information was available. Table

TABLE 14-4. TIME CONSUMPTION AT VARIOUS STAGES IN STATE CRIMINAL CASES ACROSS THE UNITED STATES

Time Number	Start Node	End Node	Time Description	# of Cases with Info.	Mean Days	Standard Deviation	Coefficient of Variation
1	1	3	Arrest to counsel	2114	29	31	1.07
2	2	3	Preliminary to counsel	1147	25	33	1.32
3	3	4	Counsel to bail release	1145	24	34	1.42
4	1	8	Arrest to nontrial disposition	2907	95	96	1.01
5	1	9	Arrest to trial begins	409	160	128	.80
6	3	8	Counsel to nontrial disposition	2355	61	61	1.00
7	3	9	Counsel to trial begins	338	93	69	1.03
8	7	8	Arraignment to non-trial disp.	3491	48	57	1.19
9	7	9	Arraignment to trial beginning	507	81	70	.86
10	1	4	Arrest to bail release	1313	22	40	1.82
11	1	2	Arrest to preliminary hearing	1516	12	13	1.08
12	1	7	Arrest to arraignment	3003	46	60	1.30
13	6	8	Indictment to nontrial disposition	3815	71	88	1.24
14	6	9	Indictment to trial begins	544	114	101	.89

14-4 also shows the standard deviation for each of those time consumption figures. If the actual time consumption figures for the cases at any given time passage have a bell-shaped distribution around the average, then approximately two-thirds of the cases should be within one standard deviation as a measure of spread is mainly useful for indicating which time passages have the greatest variation and are thus most subject to having their excessive cases pushed more toward the mean.[24] The coefficient of variation, which is the ratio between the standard deviation and the mean, is a preferred better measure since one would expect a bigger spread where there is a bigger mean.[25] This kind of measure shows that on percentage of days saved, improvement can be especially made from arrest to bail release where the coefficient of variation is almost 2 to 1. Many days can be saved from arrest to the beginning of trial, since there are so many days in that time passage, since that time passage is the sum of all the component time passages. There are other measures of spread and distribution but they are either less useful or less easy to calculate.

In the flow chart, the modes or events in regular rectangles are generally required events in the sense that each of these felony cases require an arrest, indictment, and arraignment and either a nontrial disposition or a trial. The modes or events in the dashed rectangles are optional events in the sense that a large proportion of the cases do not involve bail release, preliminary hearing, or counsel. The numbers on the arrows indicate the average time consumed between events. The numbers in the rec-

FIGURE 14-2. FLOW CHART OF TIME CONSUMPTION AT VARIOUS STAGES IN CRIMINAL CASES ACROSS THE UNITED STATES

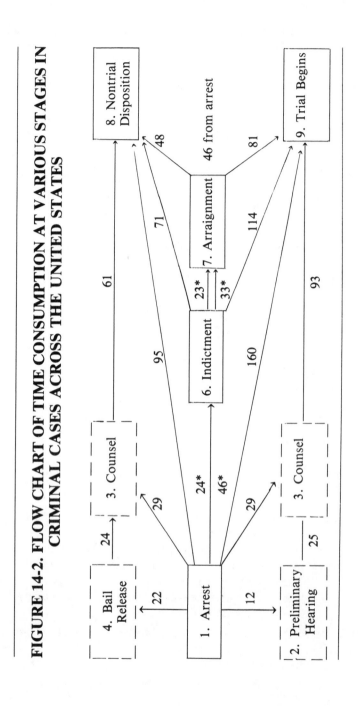

tangles indicate the event number arranged in the usual chronological order. Time consumption figures without asterisks are calculated from the raw data supplied by the American Bar Foundation now available from the Inter-University Consortium for Political and Social Research at Ann Arbor, Michigan.[26] This data provides information for the 14 time passages or variables shown in Table 14-4 and Figure 14-2. Time consumption figures with asterisks (X times) are determined by subtracting the shorter time (S time) from the longer time (L time) where X + S should equal L if there were perfect consistency in the data. For example, arrest to indictment is calculated at 24 days in nontrial disposition cases, since arrest to nontrial disposition is 95 days and indictment to nontrial disposition is 71 days. The numbers are consistent if one recognizes that certain events are optional, and that there is missing information for some of the cases. Thus it takes an average of 29 days from arrest to counsel with or without a preliminary hearing, but 37 days (12 + 25) from arrest to counsel in those cases that had a preliminary hearing.

Observing the flow chart shows that trial disposition is more time consuming than nontrial disposition to the extent of 160 days versus 95 days. This indicates that if a trial could be eliminated, a saving of about 65 days or two months might be saved for each such case. The flow chart also shows a rather large period of three weeks from arrest to bail release in those cases where the defendant is released on bail. It also indicates a rather large delay of about a month from arrest until the time defense counsel enters, when there is defense counsel. One might also note that almost a month is consumed from the time of indictment until the defendant is arraigned (indicating a guilty plea or not, and a jury or bench trial if pleading not guilty), although during that time important plea bargaining may occur. Arrest to indictment tends to take a month in nontrial cases, followed by more than two months for nontrial disposition, and arrest to indictment tends to take 1.5 months in trial cases followed by 3 months for the trial to begin.[27]

Processed data like that shown in Table 14-4 and Figure 14-2 has been generated from the raw data in the American Bar Foundation files for six different types of crime, namely, armed robbery, aggravated assault, grand larceny, rape, burglary, and auto theft. A table and a figure have also been generated for cases from metropolitan counties having more than a 400,000 population, urban counties having populations between 100,000 and 400,000, and for rural counties having populations under 100,000. Similarly, we have a separate table and figure for each of the 50 states. This kind of data can be especially useful for determining what kinds of procedures, demographic characteristics, and governmental characteristics correlate with high or low time consumption at various stages in the criminal justice process although the data is still being analyzed for that purpose.[28]

Much more complicated flow charts than Figure 14-2 could be developed with detailed data. More complicated variations include showing, in one or more flow charts, average time consumption for each passage, measures of spread or distribution, optimistic or desired time consumption as determined by asking experts, the proportion of cases that move from one event to another where there is provision for branching or dropping out, and the dollar-cost of each event or time passage to the legal system or the parties. In addition to rectangles and arrows, one can also develop a great variety of geometric forms to show events or nodes that begin the process, end the process, or are both beginning and ending points within the process, time passages that always occur or that occur with given probabilities, as well as to provide queueing, critical path, and other information. This mass of information can then be used as input into a computerized simulation program. This program would provide a variety of outputs showing how all the numbers change, if there is a change, in such things as the number of cases entering the system, or the proportion of cases that take one turn rather than another at a branching point.[29]

APPENDIX 14-1. GLOSSARY OF TERMS IN QUEUEING, SEQUENCING, AND CRITICAL PATHS

See the list of formulas in Appendix 14-2 for how various concepts are calculated.

Symbol	Represents

QUEUEING THEORY

1. Basic Rates

A	Arrival rate of cases per unit of time into the processing system
S	Service rate of cases completed per unit of time by the processing system
A/S	Ratio of cases arrived to cases serviced per unit of time

2. Time Spent

T	Total time spent in the system by an average case
T_W	Time spent waiting before service begins by an average case
T_S	Time spent servicing an average case

3. Number in Backlog

N	Total number of cases backed up in the system
N_W	Number of cases in backlog that is awaiting servicing
N_S	Number of cases in backlog being serviced

4. Other Symbols

P	Probability of a certain amount of time spent by a case (total, waiting, or being serviced) or a certain number of cases being in the backlog (total, waiting, or being serviced)
C	Number of processing channels

OPTIMUM SEQUENCING

P_1, P_2	Pleading time for case 1 and 2
T_1, T_2	Trial time for case 1 and 2
X	A characteristic of a case used to predict the amount of time cases will consume including such characteristics as the plaintiff or defendant's settlement offer and the type of personal injury or crime involved

CRITICAL PATH METHOD
1. Estimated Time for Each Processing Stage

T_O — Optimistic time, i.e. estimated time if things go well.

T_P — Pessimistic time, i.e. estimated time if things go poorly.

T_L — Likely time, i.e. estimated time in light of what usually happens.

T_E — Expected time calculated from T_O, T_P, and T_L.

2. Present Value of Future Payoff

t — A given time period, or the quantity of time periods

r — The interest rate that could be obtained by putting money in a savings account or other investment for t years.

APPENDIX 14-2. BASIC FORMULAS USED IN QUEUEING, SEQUENCING, AND CRITICAL PATHS

See the glossary in Appendix 14-1 for definitions of the symbols.

Formula	Represents

QUEUEING THEORY
1. Time Spent

$T = 1/(S\text{-}A)$ — Waiting time

$T_W = T(A/S)$ — Total time

$T_S = T\text{-}T_W$ — Servicing time

2. Number of Cases in Backlog

$N = (A/S)(1\text{-}A/S)$ — Total number of cases in backlog

$N_W = N(A/S)$ — Number which are in waiting line

$N_S = N\text{-}N_W$ — Number being serviced

OPTIMUM SEQUENCING
1. Average Time

Avg. $T = (T_1 + \ldots + T_n)/N$ — Where $T = T_W + T_S$

2. Equation for Predicting Time Consumed for Case Characteristics

$T = a + b_1X_1 + \ldots + b_nX_n$ — Assuming linear or constant relations

$T = aX_1^{b_1} \ldots X_n^{b_n}$ — Assuming nonlinear relations, diminishing effects, or increasing effects

CRITICAL PATH METHOD

$T_E = (T_0 + 4T_L + T_P)/6$	Relating expected time to optimistic, likely, and pessimistic time
$P = A/(1 + r)^t$	The present value of a future amount considering the interest rate and the number of time periods

NOTES

1. On queueing theory, see Jack Byrd, *Operations Research Models for Public Administration* (Lexington, Mass.: Lexington-Heath, 1975) pp. 198-208; Donald Gross and Carl Harris, *Fundamentals of Queueing Theory* (New York; Wiley, 1974); Alec Lee, *Applied Queueing Theory* (New York: Macmillan, 1966); Samuel Richmond, *Operations Research for Management Decisions* (New York: Ronald Press, 1968) pp. 405-38; and Thomas Saaty, *Elements of Queueing Theory: With Applications* (Hightstown, N.J.: McGraw-Hill, 1961).

2. See note 1.

3. Queueing theory considers time consumed to be a function or effect of the arrival rate and the service rate, and not the other way around. In reality, however, there may be dynamic reciprocal causation whereby if the arrival rate goes down, time consumed will go down, but if time consumed goes down, this may cause more people to be willing to enter the line, thereby causing the arrival rate to go back up at least partly. If, however, the arrival rate then goes back up, that will cause time consumed to increase, which in turn is likely to decrease the willingness of people to enter the line (i.e., decrease the arrival rate) and thereby decrease the time consumed, and so on. If the arrival rate has a positive effect on time consumed (i.e., when the arrival rate increases, time consumed increases) which is exactly equal to the negative effect that time consumed has on the arrival rate (i.e., when time consumed increases, the arrival rate decreases), then these two relations would exactly offset each other and the arrival rate and time consumed would tend to remain in a stable equilibrium in the long run. It is, however, an empirical question the extent to which those two relations are equal in strength.

Similarly, there may be a dynamic reciprocal causation between the service rate and time consumed such that when the service rate increases (i.e., faster servicing), time consumed goes down; but that may cause the processors to relax their efforts which means the service rate will go back down, wiping out part of, all of, or more than the previous reduction in time consumed. If time consumption thereby increases as a result of the service rate going back up, this may cause the processors to feel the need to accelerate their efforts, which means the service rate increases, the time consumed thus increases, and the cycle goes on again. Also an empirical question is the extent to which the inverse effect of the service rate on time consumed is as strong as the positive effect of time consumed on the service rate.

4. See note 1.

5. Ibid.

6. The usual distribution for arrival rates is called a Poisson distribution. This distribution involves a few days that have extremely low arrivals, many days that have low to moderate arrivals, and a few days that have high arrivals. It is a distribution that when plotted is peaked to the left such that it quickly goes up and

then gradually goes down. The usual distribution for service rates is called an exponential distribution. This distribution involves many days that have relatively low service rates, and a few days that have moderate or high service rates. It is a distribution that when plotted looks like a children's slide that goes continuously although gradually down.

7. Standard queueing theory formulas assume that the arrival rate and service rate are independent of each other. In reality, this may not be the case. For example, if the service rate is increased, meaning more cases are being serviced in a given unit of time, this may encourage more people to bring cases to court that otherwise they might settle out of court. Thus by speeding the servicing, the arrival rate may be increased, thereby offsetting some of the time saving benefits of the improved service rate. Similarly, if the arrival rate is reduced, meaning fewer cases are entering the system in a given unit of time, this may encourage people who are involved in processing the cases to slow down a bit in their processing. Thus by decreasing the arrivals the service rate may be worsened, thereby offsetting some of the time saving benefits of the improved arrival rate. It also follows that worsening the service rate may favorably decrease the arrivals, and also worsening the arrival rate (i.e., encouraging more arrivals) may stimulate faster service. The extent to which A and S correlate with each other is an empirical question on which data needs to be gathered, as contrasted to the more deductive approach that is used in determining the standard queueing theory formulas.

8. A recent study of delay in the courts indicates that it might be wasteful to try to shorten case processing time because the study finds that cases with a short processing time involve almost the same total time as cases with a long processing time. Kent Portney, "Per Curiam Opinions and Appellate Court Delay: A Research Note" (unpublished paper available from the author at Florida State University Political Science Department, 1978). One, however, would expect both short and long cases to take about the same total time because total time equals waiting time plus processing time, and in some court systems waiting time may be almost 100 percent of the total time. Thus a relatively long processing time has little incremental detriment. The amount of waiting time, however, is a function of the amount of processing time. Thus by reducing an average processing time of two days in half, the waiting time for cases waiting in line can also be reduced in half, thereby reducing total time in half.

9. For additional examples of queueing theory applied to the legal process, see Haig Bohigian, *The Foundations and Mathematical Models of Operations Research with Extensions to the Criminal Justice System* (Tarrytown, N.Y.: Gazette Press, 1971) pp. 191-209; Jan Chaiken and P. Dormont, *Patrol Car Allocation Model* (Chicago: Rand, 1975); Jan Chaiken, et al. *Criminal Justice Models: An Overview* (Chicago: Rand, 1975); and John Reed, *The Application of Operations Research to Court Delay* (New York: Praeger, 1973). Also see Hans Zeisel, Harry Kalven, Jr., and Bernard Buchholz, *Delay in the Court* (Boston: Little Brown, 1959), since that book is organized in accordance with queueing concepts by being divided into parts on "Reducing the Trial Time" (i.e., increasing service rates), "Increasing Settlements" (i.e., decreasing arrival rates), and "More Judge Time" (i.e., increasing the channels or processors).

10. On dynamic and sequential programming, see Jack Byrd, op. cit. pp. 139-56; Richard Conway, William Maxwell, and Louis Miller, *Theory of Scheduling* (Reading, Mass.: Addison-Wesley, 1967); A. Kaufman, *Graphs, Dynamic Programming, and Finite Games* (New York: Academic Press, 1967); Kenneth Baker, *Introduction to Sequencing and Scheduling* (New York: Wiley, 1974); Samuel Richmond, op. cit. pp. 461-80; George Nemhauser, *Introduction to Dynamic Programming* (New York: Wiley, 1966); and Brian Gliess, *An Elementary Introduction to Dynamic Programming* (Rockleigh, N.J.: Allyn and Bacon, 1972).

11. Saying that the shortest-case-first rule will not work meaningfully unless maximum constraints are provided for, is not to deprecate the rule, or to say it is a fallacious rule. Rather, providing for maximum constraints is simply a recognition that one cannot apply management science or operations research principles to the legal process without taking into consideration the constitutional, statutory, and precedent constraints under which the legal process operates, and that these constraints, in this context, do sometimes include speedy trial rules. We could have changed our hypothetical constraint to be a 40-day constraint rather than a 30-day one. But we thereby would forego the opportunity to ask, what alternative options does queueing theory provide for satisfying a maximum constraint, which in the absence of alternative options would otherwise be violated, given the data of Table 14-1.

12. In other subject matters, an appropriate goal might be something other than minimizing the average time spent per case with or without a maximum constraint. For example, in handling jobs in a business firm, the goal might be to minimize the number of late jobs, the average lateness of the jobs, the average cost of lateness, the maximum lateness, or the maximum lateness cost. These alternative goals are discussed in J. Byrd, op. cit., pp. 139-56. Alternative procedures for achieving one's goals might include (1) a rule of a first-come-first-serve that is generally applied; (2) a rule of shortest-cases-first where a set of cases come in within about the same week as advocated here; (3) a rule that gives top priority to the job that has the earliest due date, which is a concept that may be applicable in business jobs, but not so applicable in court cases; or (4) a more complicated business rule that schedules jobs first that have the smallest ratio between the time required for the job and the adverse consequences of the job being later per unit of time, or stated differently that schedules jobs last that have the largest ratio between the time required and the lateness consequences.

13. If there is only one court, judge, or channel, then any maximum constraint will either be violated by all the orders or by none of them. This is so because when there is one processor, the last case will consume a quantity of time equal to the sum of the servicing times for all the cases being considered. This can be seen in Table 14-1 where the last case always took 35 days total time. The notion of a maximum constraint, however, is quite meaningful in the legal process because in any court system there is almost always more than one judge or the possibility of having more than one judge. The notion is also meaningful even if there was no possibility of having more than one judge, since the constraint can still possibly be satisfied by reducing the arrival rate or improving the servicing rate, even though the maximum time cannot be improved by manipulating the order of the cases or the number of judges.

14. On the subject of how much time is consumed by cases of various types and by various case stages, see Steven Flanders, *District Court Studies Project* (Federal Judicial Center, 1976); USDA Statistical Reporting Service, *The 1969-1970 Federal District Court Time Study* (Washington, D.C.: Federal Judicial Center, 1971); and Robert Gillespie, "Economic Modeling of Court Services, Work Loads, and Productivity," in Stuart Nagel (ed.), *Modeling the Criminal Justice System 175*(Beverly Hills, Ca.: Sage, 1977). The first two items are reports of the Federal Judicial Center.

15. The 64 percent victory rate for plaintiffs in personal injury cases reflects the approximate findings of the Jury Verdict Research Corporation as indicated in its loose leaf Jury Verdict Expectancies Service. The sample of cases used for the University of Chicago jury project showed a 56 percent victory rate. The exact victory rate within that range influences how much time can be saved by splitting the trial work into a liability decision and a damages decision, but pinpointing the rate cannot eliminate the substantial saving, since much of the saving comes from the

fact that (1) many of the cases in which liability is established are then settled out of court without a trial on the damages matter; and (2) the plaintiff's victory rate tends to drop substantially when (a) the jurors are instructed that they cannot find the defendant liable if the plaintiff is partly negligent and (b) they cannot offset the plaintiff's negligence by reducing the damages over which they have no control. Similarly, the figures in this example for the post-liability out-of-court settlement rate and the reduction in the plaintiff's victory rate can range somewhat widely and still allow for a substantial saving of time. The key point, however, is whether the legal system is willing to achieve time-saving at the cost of changing the outcomes of cases, as contrasted to preserving accepted outcomes while having cases take less time.

16. For a statistical study of a sample of cases in which the split trial method was compared with integrated trials (producing findings like those described above), see Hans Zeisel and Thomas Callahan, "Split Trials and Time saving: A Statistical Analysis," 76 *Harvard Law Review* 1606 (1963).

17. For additional examples of dynamic and sequential programming applied to the legal process, see Haig Bohigian, op. cit, pp. 171-90; John Jennings, *Evaluation of the Manhattan Criminal Courts Master Calendar Project* (Santa Monica, Ca.: Rand, 1971); Raymond Nimmer, *The System Impact of Criminal Justice Reforms: Judicial Delay as a Case Study* (Chicago: American Bar Foundation, 1974) pp. 62-68; *Programming Methods Incorporated, Justice: Judicial System to Increase Court Effectiveness* (New York: Programming Methods Incorporated, 1971); Hans Zeisel, op. cit., pp. 201-5; and Jack Hausner, Thomas Cane, and Gary Oleson, "Automated Scheduling in the Courts," in Sidney Brownstein and Murray Kamrass (eds.), *Operations Research in Law Enforcement, Justice, and Societal Security* (Lexington, Mass.: Lexington-Heath, 1976) p. 217. See also the final report on the operation and capabilities of the use of computers to aid in case calendaring and judge assignment as reported in 10 *The Third Branch* 4 (August, 1978).

18. On critical path method and flow chart modeling, see Russell Archibald and Richard Villoria, *Network-Based Management Systems* (PERT1CPM) (New York: Wiley, 1967); Jack Byrd, op.cit., pp. 115-38; H.F. Evarts, *Introduction to PERT* (Rockleigh, N.J.: Allyn and Bacon, 1964); B.J. Hansen, *Practical PERT* (Washington, D.C.: America House, 1964); Samuel Richmond, op. cit., pp. 481-500; and Gary Whitehouse, *Systems Analysis and Systems Design* (Englewood Cliffs, N.J.: Prentice-Hall, 1973).

19. If one prepares a flow chart from arrest to sentencing showing all the connecting and converging paths, then the overall critical path would be the combination of all the longest paths starting from sentencing and working back to arrest. A more sophisticated approach would also recognize that if one comes to a fork when determining a critical path, one should not automatically choose path A over path B, merely because path A takes 10 days and path B takes 5 days if path A is connected to path C, which takes 2 days, and path B is connected to path D, which takes 15 days. In other words, we should look to the sums of all the connecting paths that converge on a stage in determining the alternative path that is critical for reducing the total time consumed from arrest to sentencing. We could extend the hypothetical data of Figure 14-1 to show this kind of flow chart. Unfortunately, the real data that is available on time consumption at various stages in the criminal justice process does not deal with such converging matters as the time needed by various participants to prepare for various stages. This is illustrated later by Figure 14-2, which does contain real data, but only for connecting paths, not for converging paths like Figure 14-1. One could, however, obtain information from the participants concerning their preparation times by examining files and other records, or by questionnaires and interviews.

20. On the presentence reporting process, see John Kaplan, *Criminal Justice:*

Introductory Cases and Materials (St. Paul: Foundation Press, 1973) pp. 454-62, and Donald Newman, *Introduction to Criminal Justice* (Philadelphia: Lippincott, 1975) pp. 246-60.

21. A form of PERT analysis is to determine for each activity stage how much it costs in dollars and time to conduct the activity in the normal way and how much it costs in dollars and time to conduct the activity in as fast a way as possible (i.e., in a manner that is referred to as "crashing"). One can then determine for each activity the cost of crashing in dollars per day or other time unit. With that information, one can then determine which activities are worth crashing or accelerating and to what extent. Some activities are not worth accelerating because the total job would still have to await the completion of other activities. The activities most worth accelerating are the ones that can be accelerated at relatively little cost and that when completed move the whole job forward. On the matter of developing an optimum crash program, see William Greenwood, *Decision Theory and Information Systems* (Cincinnati, Ohio: South-Western, 1969).

22. S. Nagel, "Measuring Unnecessary Delay in Administrative Proceedings: The Actual versus the Predicted," 3 *Policy Sciences* 81 (1972).

23. Technically speaking, this problem is not a critical path method problem since it does not involve two or more processes converging to generate another process. It is, however, closely related to the critical path idea since the decision maker is faced with a choice of following one path that leads to a federal courthouse, or an alternative path that leads to a state courthouse. More important to our concern for time-oriented models is the fact that time consumed is an important benefit-cost determinant on each of the alternative paths. In that sense, the path that has the highest expected value is the critical path. By "expected value" we mean the perceived benefits minus costs discounted by the probability of their occurring and discounted by how far from the present they will occur. The problem of choosing between two time-related alternatives like these can also be labeled a decision theory problem for an optimum choice problem with the paths being the branches of a decision tree. As such, the problem is related to optimum choice analysis discussed earlier. The problem is also related to the use of differential equations where the emphasis is on the defendant's rather than the plaintiff's perspective in planning personal injury case strategies.

24. The standard deviation is calculated by (1) summing the time consumption at a given passage for the cases and dividing by the number of cases; (2) subtracting this mean from actual time consumed for each case; (3) squaring these differences; (4) dividing the sum of these squares by the number of cases; and (5) taking the square root of this quotient.

25. For example, one would expect the standard deviation of the length of mosquitoes to be measured in millimeters since the average mosquito is measured in millimeters, but one would expect the standard deviation or spread to be smaller on the stage from arrest to indictment than on the stage from arrest to trial, not because the first stage is being processed more efficiently or uniformly, but simply because its average is smaller. For further details on the interpretation of such statistical measures as the mean, standard deviation, coefficient of variation, and other measurements of central tendency and spread, see Hubert Blalock, *Social Statistics* (New York: McGraw Hill, 1972); and John Mueller, Karl Schuessler, and Herbert Costner, *Statistical Reasoning in Sociology* (Boston: Houghton Mifflin, 1970).

26. See Lee Silverstein and S. Nagel, "American Bar Foundation: State Criminal Court Cases" (ICPR, 1974) for a description of the dataset. The same IBM card data has been used to generate such articles as S. Nagel, "Disparities in Criminal Procedure," 14 *University of California at Los Angeles Law Review* 1272 (1967).

27. The figures given above come from Table 14-4 and Figure 14-2, which in turn come from the IBM card dataset, dealing with state criminal court cases referred to in note 26.

28. Those more detailed versions of Table 14-4 and Figure 14-2 are available from the author upon request.

29. Additional examples of flow chart modeling applied to the legal process include Jan Chaiken, et al. op cit.; Albert Blumstein, "A Model to Aid in Planning for Total Criminal Justice System," in *Quantitative Tools for Criminal Justice Planning* ed. Leonard Oberlander (Washington, D.C.: LEAA, 1975) p. 129; Joseph Navarro and Jean Taylor, "Data Analyses and Simulation of a Court System for the Processing of Criminal Cases," in The President's Commission on Law Enforcement and Administration of Justice, *Task Force Report: Science and Technology* (Washington, D.C.: GPO, 1967); R. Gordon Cassidy, "A Systems Approach to Planning and Evaluation in Criminal Justice Systems," 9 *Socio-Economics Planning Sciences* 301 (1975); William Biles, "A Simulation Study of Delay Mechanisms in Criminal Courts" (Unpublished paper presented at the 1972 meeting of the Operations Research Society of America at New Orleans, Louisiana); and Gary Hogg, Richard DeVor and Michael Handwerker, "Analysis of Criminal Justice Systems via Stochastic Network Simulation" (unpublished paper presented at the Workshop on Operations Research in the Criminal Justice System at San Diego, California, 1973).

Chapter 15
Time-Oriented
Predictive Models

The purpose of this chapter is to discuss three commonly used predictive models that are time oriented. Most predictive models in the social sciences are not time oriented. They involve making predictions from independent variables in which the units of analysis are persons, places, or things other than time periods. For example, it is common in legal process research to attempt to predict decisional propensities from the background characteristics of the decision makers, using a set of decision makers or cases as of one-point-in-time, or as of many-points-in-time but ignoring or downplaying the time element. Time oriented predictive models include (1) Markov chain analysis which predicts subsequent events by determining the probability that one event will follow another; (2) time series analysis which involves measuring variables or establishing relations with time periods as the units of analysis; and (3) difference/differential equations in which one right side of the equations involve time as a variable and the equations are generally deductively rather than inductively derived.

Predictive time-oriented models are common in optimizing textbooks.[1] Differential equations are particularly relevant to handling the problems of time-discounting, whereby future benefits and costs need to be discounted since they tend to provide less satisfaction or dissatisfaction than present ones. Many optimizing models are also predictive in the sense that one can often predict behavior by assuming the decision makers are seeking to maximize benefits minus costs. Time-oriented optimizing models are often both predictive of delay and useful in seeking to minimize delay. Similarly time-oriented predictive models can be useful in reducing delay, decreasing other costs, or increasing benefits by helping to predict the effects of alternative delay-reduction policies or other policies, and by aiding the preparation for forthcoming events.

MARKOV CHAIN ANALYSIS

The essence of Markov chain analysis involves the prediction of subsequent events by knowing the probability of one event leading to another. As an oversimplified example, if we know that 60 percent of the convicted defendants in a given court system go to prison and 40 percent receive probation, then from those percentages or probabilities, we know something about what would happen if the number of convictions increased from 200 to 300 per year. More specifically, they tell us that before the increase, the prison caseload was 120 cases per year (.60 times 200) and the probation caseload was 80 cases, and after the increase, the prison caseload will probably be 180 cases per year (.60 times 300) and the probation caseload 120 cases. This simple example could be made substantially more interesting if it were part of a chain of branching events, such that a change in one of the early events has a kind of domino effect moving out across the branches, where the ultimate effects are not so readily predictable in the absence of a Markov chain analysis.[2]

Figure 15-1 provides an example of Markov chain analysis used to predict the effect on the public defender's caseload of a change in the probability of being held in jail pending trial. More specifically, if 100 cases enter the system and previously 10 percent were released on their own recognizance, 30 percent were released on bond, and 60 percent were held in jail pending trial, then how much of an increase or a decrease would there be in the public defender's caseload if those probabilities were to change to .40, .20, and .40 respectively as the result of a bail reform movement? To answer that question we need to know the probability of pleading not guilty rather than guilty for each of these categories of pretrial release and of those who plead not guilty, what is the probability of having a public defender appointed to represent them.

This data tends to indicate that those in jail pending trial are more likely to plead guilty than those released. The data also indicates that of those defendants who plead not guilty, the ones most likely to be indigent and thus eligible for the public defender are the defendants who have been kept in jail pending trial unable to make bond. Of those released, the defendants who put up bond money are possibly less likely to be indigent enough to have a public defender appointed than those who are released on their own recognizance (ROR). The hypothetical data implicitly assumes that about one-half of the ROR cases are middle-class defendants who are considered good risks for ROR but are not eligible for a public defender, and the other half are poor defendants who are also considered good risks for ROR but who are eligible for a public defender.

The analysis simply involves allocating the entering 100 cases in accordance with the first tier of probabilities to the second column of events, then allocating these allocations in accordance with the second tier of probabilities to the third column of events, and then allocating these allocations in accordance with the third tier of probabilities to the fourth column of events. The last step in the analysis involves summing the number of cases probabilistically allocated to the public defender in various rows of the fourth column of events to determine the total public defender caseload. The same thing is done both with the "before" probabilities and the "after" probabilities. Doing so indicates that the predicted "before" caseload for 100 cases is 25.5 cases to the public defender and the predicted

FIGURE 15-1. APPLYING MARKOV CHAIN ANALYSIS TO PREDICTING THE EFFECTS ON PUBLIC DEFENDER CASELOADS OF CHANGES IN PRETRIAL RELEASE

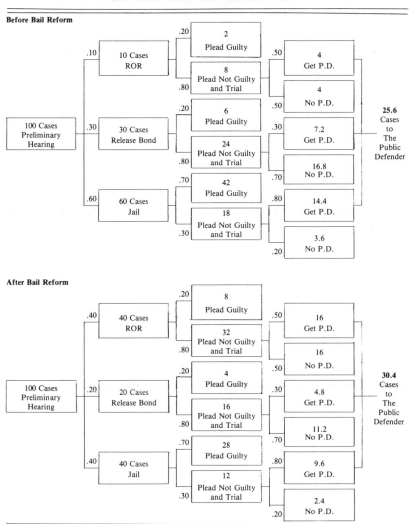

"after" caseload for 100 cases is 30.5 cases. This means an increase of 19 percent in the public defender's caseload since (30.4 − 25.6/25.6 is 19 percent.) This means that if the public defender's office is going to continue to operate at the same caseload per assistant public defender, there possibly should be hiring of 19 percent more assistants without waiting for the backlog to build up.[3]

The falling-dominoes thinking associated with Markov chain analysis can be helpful even when one does not have probabilities but merely a knowledge of how a change in a previous event affects a subsequent event. A good example of how thinking in terms of a chain of events can provide insights that otherwise might be missed involves the relation between increasing pretrial release rates and the size of the jail population. By only thinking in terms of these two events or variables without thinking through the intervening chain, one might logically jump to the conclusion that if pretrial release rates are increased, then of course the pretrial detention population will be decreased. But is this necessarily so?

Figure 15-2 shows what relevant things may happen as the result of increasing pretrial release. An increase in pretrial release is likely to result in a decrease in guilty pleas, since many defendants who plead guilty do so in return for a promise from the prosecutor to recommend a sentence equal to the time they have already served waiting in jail, or to recommend probation which will also mean they can immediately get out of jail.[4] Defendants waiting in jail who demand a trial to prove their innocence may have to wait additional months in jail, and may still lose their case and have to serve additional jail time. If many defendants who were formerly held in jail are now released, they will be less vulnerable to that kind of prosecutor offer and more likely to plead not guilty. If there is a decrease in guilty pleas, there is likely to be an increase in trials, since a defendant pleading not guilty is in effect asking for a trial. If there is an increase in trials, there is likely to be increased delay in the system, since queueing models and common sense indicate that more trials mean more delay for those awaiting trial in jail or out. If those awaiting trial in jail now have to wait longer, then the jail population will increase since it is a function of the number of people going to jail, which has gone down as a result of increased pretrial release, but also a function of how long they stay there, which has gone up because of the increased pretrial release and its intervening effects. This increase in jail length may more than offset the decrease in jail entries, thereby increasing rather than decreasing the pretrial jail population, all because of an increase in pretrial release.

It is interesting to note how each of the four relations or causal arrows in Figure 15-2 is explained by a deductive model. The first relation is explained by bargaining models which say that successful plea bargains are a function of the litigation costs, the probability of conviction, and the sentence if a conviction occurs, all as perceived by the defendant and the prosecutor. One of the defendant's most important litigation costs is the cost of possibly having to sit in jail awaiting trial if the defendant demands a trial.[5] By lowering that litigation cost, the defendant's upper limit to the extended offers is likely to be lowered, reducing the possibility that the defendant's upper limit will be above the prosecutor's lower limit, and thereby reducing the possibility of a settlement. The second relation is explained by the queueing model for determining backlog sizes, and the third

FIGURE 15-2. IMPACT OF PRETRIAL RELEASE ON THE PRETRIAL JAIL POPULATION

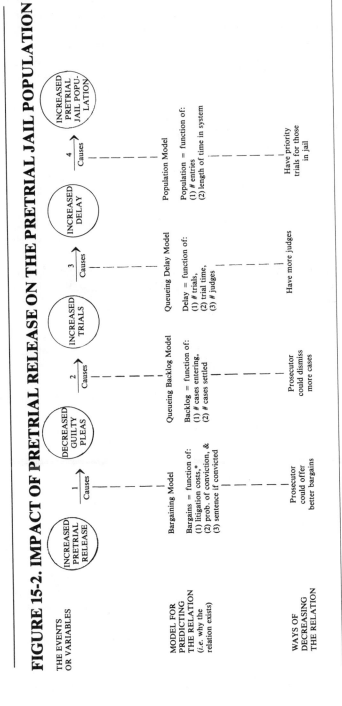

*including the cost of sitting in jail awaiting trial

285

relation is explained by the queueing model for determining the amount of delay or time consumption per case. The fourth relation involves a population model which says the world's population is a function of the number of births and how long people live. Similarly, the jail population is a function of (1) the number of people entering the jail by not being released prior to trial, which has gone down; and (2) the length of time the average detained defendant lives in the jail, which has gone up.

It is especially interesting that each of these models not only predicts and explains the chain of relations from pretrial release to the size of the jail population, but they also suggest meaningful ways of lessening the extent to which those undesired relations occur. The bargaining model suggests that the prosecutor could hold constant the percentage of guilty pleas even in the face of an increasing pretrial release rate by making better offers to those who are released. The better offers might consist of shorter sentences and more probation than the expected value of the sentence if convicted, discounted by the probability of being convicted. Even if the guilty plea goes down, the prosecutor can still hold constant the quantity of trials by dismissing more cases, since he is under no obligation to prosecute simply because the defendant pleads not guilty. Even if the quantity of cases increases, the amount of delay can be held constant by providing more judges and other court personnel. If delay does increase, there need not be an increase in the length of time spent in jail awaiting trial if the prosecutor provides for priority trials to those who are in jail whereby their cases are tried ahead of defendants who are out of jail. If we had numbers to insert in Figure 15-2 somewhat like those we had in Figure 15-1, we could be more precise about (1) the effects of prior events on subsequent events, and (2) how much these suggestions could lessen those effects. Even without that quantitative information, however, the chain analysis reasoning process can produce useful descriptive and prescriptive insights.

In the legal process literature there have now appeared a number of examples of Markov chain reasoning as applied to trying to predict the probability that a given convicted defendant will re-engage in criminal behavior within a certain number of time periods after being released from prison.[6] A paper by David White, for example, finds that a released juvenile who was not referred back to the court during the first three months after being released has a .978 probability of not being referred back in the fourth month, a .019 probability of committing a minor crime in the fourth month, and a .003 probability of committing a major crime. Other probabilities can be calculated for subsequent months (either empirically from direct data or deductively from probability formulas) for other combinations of nonreferrals, minor crimes, and major crimes in the preceding months. This kind of an analysis can be useful in predicting behavior, comparing different types of convicts or treatments, and developing recommendations for special supervision of certain types of convicts.

TIME SERIES ANALYSIS

An especially common way of predicting the future from the past in social science is through the use of time series analysis. Such an analysis involves obtaining and processing data on one or more variables for many points in time. This type of analysis is sometimes referred to as longitudinal or over-time analysis.[7] It is generally contrasted with cross-sectional or over-space analysis where data is obtained and processed over one or more variables for many places at a single point-in-time. The processing of the data in either kind of analysis tends to emphasize the development of linear regression equations of the form $Y = a + bX$ or nonlinear regression equations of the form $Y = ax^b$, where Y is the variable being predicted to, and X is the variable being predicted from. The "a" and "b" coefficients are determined by the computer when one inputs the Y and X scores or their logarithms for each time point or for each place point along with a regression analysis program.[8]

There are many ways of classifying time series analyses. One useful way is in terms of whether the analysis is univariate, bivariate, or multivariate. By univariate we mean where information is used only on the Y variable, and the X variable simply consists of consecutive numbers corresponding to the time periods. For example, if we input into the computer (1) nationwide crime scores for each of the last ten years as variable Y; (2) the numbers 1 through 10 as variable T; and (3) a regression analysis program, then the computer will provide us with numerical values for the "a" and "b" parameters of the equation: Crime = a + b(Time Period). To use that equation to predict how much crime there will be in the 11th or 20th time period, we simply insert an 11 or 20 into the parentheses, multiply by the value of "b", and add on the value of "a". We will in effect be extending a trend line to the dots corresponding to the 10 time data points. If we suspect that crime is not increasing at a constant rate, but rather at an increasing rate or a decreasing rate, then we can input into the computer (1) the logarithms of the crime scores for the last 10 years; (2) the logarithms of the numbers 1 through 10; and (3) the same regression analysis program. The computer will then provide us with numerical values for the "a" and "b" parameters of the equation: Crime = a(Time Period)^b. If the numerical value of "b" is greater than zero but less than 1, then crime is increasing at a diminishing rate. If the numerical value of "b" is greater than 1, then crime is increasing at an increasing rate. The computer will also inform us what percent of the variation on Y is explained by the variation on T using both the linear and nonlinear approach so that we can see which approach has the greater explanatory power.[9]

In bivariate time series, information is obtained on the Y variable and for an X variable that is other than a time period counter. For example, the Y variable might be murders for each year since 1900, and the X variable might be capital punishment executions for each of the same years in order to determine how these variables relate to each other. The computer analysis would then yield an equation of the form: Murders = $a_1 + b_1$ (Executions) if we are predicting murders from executions, or Executions = $a_2 + b_2$ (Murders) if we are predicting executions from murders. We might be able to predict better (i.e., account for more of the variance on the dependent variable) by using a lagged independent variable. Doing so in predicting murders from executions might mean for each Y and X data pair, the Y score is at time t and the X score is at time t − 1. This kind of analysis would yield numerical values for the parameters of the equation: $\text{Murders}_t = a + b\,(\text{Executions}_{t-1})$, on the assumption that it takes about one year for executions to influence the subsequent murder rate. One can experiment with a two-year lag or longer to see which bivariate lagging accounts for the most variation on the murder variable.

If one suspects the unemployment rate influences the relation between executions and murders, possibly by causing would-be murderers to have more or less of a stake in not risking an execution, then one can split the 77 data pairs into two subsets. One subset can consist of murder years in which unemployment was relatively low and the other subset in which unemployment was relatively high. One would then obtain two separate regression equations of the form Murders = a + b (Executions) for each subset of data. The multivariate alternative approach is to input into the computer scores for each year on murder, execution, and unemployment. The computer would then give numerical values to the parameters in an equation of the form: Murders = a + b_1(Executions) + b_2(Unemployment Rate). With this equation, one could insert a future value for executions (such as zero if executions are abolished) and a future unemployment rate. By doing the multiplication and addition one obtains a future predicted quantity of murders. Additional variables can be similarly added to such a multivariate analysis. The analysis can also work with some variables that are lagged to show delayed relations, or that are logged to show nonlinear relations.

Another important way of classifying time series analysis, which is quite relevant to legal process research, is in terms of whether the independent variable (often a policy variable) undergoes continuous change or undergoes a single interruption. An example of a policy variable undergoing continuous change would be the number of executions over the last 77 years. An example of a policy variable with more of an off and on status is the Connecticut speed crackdown in the 1960s or the British Adoption of compulsory breathalyzer testing, both of which used highway accidents as the dependent variable in the time series analysis.[10] Interrupted time series may show a strong relation between the X policy and the Y alleged effect that is noncausal in nature. The relation may exist without the change in X being the cause of changes in Y because (1) Y has changed due to a third variable; (2) Y recently increased or decreased before the policy changed and was merely regressing back to its average position; (3) Y was already moving upward or downward and did not change its direction or rate when X changed; and (4) Y fluctuates over time and its fluctuation when X changed was part of that normal pattern. These alternative explanations need to be eliminated before one can conclude that the change in X was responsible for the change in Y. These alternative explanations are less likely to be important if X changes frequently and Y almost consistently changes in a corresponding manner.[11]

Another way of classifying time series analysis is in terms of whether its purpose is (1) to describe graphically how a variable changes over time; (2) to predict future scores on a variable from knowing the time period T, its prior Y score, or from a score on another X variable; or (3) to determine what causes change over time on the Y variable. The causal analysis may involve a variety of methods and alternative explanations. For example, one might try to determine which relation is valid or stronger: (1) the extent to which making divorce laws more lenient causes increases in divorce rates, or (2) the extent to which increases in divorce rates causes divorce laws to become more lenient. Making that determination with time series data may require holding a third variable like urbanism statistically constant in a multivariate relation since increased urbanism may be causing both an increase in divorce law leniency and an increase in divorce rates rather than these two variables causing each other. This determination may also require looking for joint causation relations, since divorce rates may not be affected by more lenient divorce laws unless the laws are accompanied by educational or other demographic changes in the population. Special forms of bivariate regression analysis (called cross-lagged panel analysis), multivariate regression analysis (called two-stage least squares analysis), and interrupted time series may be used to try to separate out (1) the effects on divorce rates by divorce laws from (2) the effects on divorce laws by divorce rates.[12]

A computerized time series analysis not only gives "a" and "b" coefficients and percentages of variance accounted for (R^2), but also numbers that can be taken to probability tables to determine what is the probability that the a's, b's, and R^2 can be as large as they are given the number of time points when they might really be zero due to the chance occurrence of having drawn a distorted sample of time points. This kind of testing for statistical significance is virtually the same whether one is doing a regression analysis over time points or an analysis over places at one point in time. One difference, however, is that time series is more likely to involve what is known as autocorrelation which can disrupt those probability calculations.[13] To determine the extent to which autocorrelation is present, each time point needs to be given a residual score (Y'_t) which equals its actual score (Y_t) minus its predicted score ($\hat{Y}_t$), predicted from the equation $Y_t = a + bX_t$. Each time point also needs to be given a lagged residual score (Y'_{t-1}) which equals $Y_{t-1} - \hat{Y}_{t-1}$. One then inputs those Y'_t and Y'_{t-1} scores into the computerized regression analysis for each time point to see how well one can predict one from the other. If these residual scores correlate highly, then adjustments have to be made in the original regression equation ($Y_t = a + bX_{t-1}$) by lagging it, logging it, using other transformations, or adding additional variables if one wants to reduce the autocorrelation so that the chance probability calculations will be more meaningful. One can, however, ignore the chance probability calculations if one is willing to assume that the sample of time points with which one is working constitutes or is representative of the universe that one is seeking to generalize.

Various research examples could be given from the legal process field to illustrate how time series analysis is able to clarify predictive relations that are muddied when one only does an analysis of many places at one point-in-time. It would, for instance, be more meaningful to compare judicial behavior in the state of Missouri before and after the 1940 switch from an elected judiciary to an appointed judiciary than it would be to compare the appointed judiciary of Missouri with the elected judiciary of Illinois at the same 1960 point-in-time. This is so because we suspect that other variables in Missouri are roughly held constant before and after 1940 that might affect judicial behavior besides the change in judicial selection, whereas we suspect that those other influential variables might be substantially different between Illinois and Missouri in addition to differences in their judicial selection system.[14] Similarly, it might not be so meaningful to compare Michigan, which has abolished capital punishment, with Mississippi, which has not, to see how their murder rates differ. However, it might be more meaningful to compare Michigan before and after it abolished capital punishment, or even more meaningful to do that type of analysis on all the states that have abolished capital punishment. Instead of that kind of interrupted time series, one could also do a continuous time series relating homicides to executions for many states and/or for the nation as a whole.[15]

A particularly good example to illustrate the value of time series in clarifying legal process relations involves the relation between crime occurrence and anticrime expenditures. If one inputs into a regression analysis crime figures and expenditure figures for many cities at one point in time, the resulting regression equation of the form: Crime = a + b(Expenditures) will have a positive "b" coefficient. This implies that the more money spent to fight crime, the more crime occurs, contrary to our common sense notion of the possible relation. No matter how much we lag or log the expenditure variable and no matter how many other variables we hold constant, that spurious positive relation tends to remain. However, if we input into a computer the crime and expenditure scores for many points in time for each city in which we are interested, then we are somewhat more likely to get a negative "b" coefficient which implies that the more money spent to fight crime, the less crime occurs.

This coefficient or slope, however, is more likely to be negative if we also hold constant these variables over-time, which may simultaneously influence both crime and expenditures. One meaningful way to do that (called cross-lagged panel analysis) is to input into a computer for each city in which we are interested a crime score for each year (Y_t), an expenditure score for each prior year (X_{t-1}), and a crime score for each prior year (Y_{t-1}). We then obtain numerical values for the coefficients in the equation: $Y_t = a + b_1(X_{t-1}) + b_2(Y_{t-1})$. Crime at time t is related to expenditures at time $t - 1$ in order to take into consideration that crime tends to reflect anticrime expenditures in the previous year more than the present year. Crime for the previous year is in effect held constant in this equation because doing so tends indirectly to hold constant the variables other than anticrime dollars that influence previous crime and thus probably present crime.[16] One can also work with the logarithms of these three variables in the regression analysis in order to take into consideration that anticrime expenditures, and the other variables, probably have a diminishing returns relation with crime occurrence, rather than a constant returns relation. This produces the numerical values for the coefficients or parameters in the equation: $Y_t = a(X_{t-1})^{b_1}(Y_{t-1})^{b_2}$. [17]

In that nonlinear multivariate time series equation the marginal rate of return in crime reduction for an extra monetary unit spent is $b_1 A(X)^{b_1-1}$, where A is the product of a $(Y_{t-1})^{b_2}$ with Y_{t-1} being last year's crime score and the coefficients being provided by the computerized regression analysis. This marginal rate of return follows from the rule that says if $Y = aX^b$, then the slope of Y to X is baX^{b-1}, as mentioned in discussing optimum level and optimum mix analysis. With that information, one can then allocate funds to the cities in at least three ways, namely, (1) in proportion to the multipliers and the exponents in each city's marginal rate of return; (2) by simultaneously solving a series of equations where the marginal rates of return are set equal to each other as in optimum mix analysis; or (3) by working with one of the newly developed nonlinear programming routines available at many computer centers. This time series analysis is thus capable of both describing the relation between crime occurrence and anticrime expenditures within each city, and of being used in a prescriptive way for better allocating scarce resources in the legal system.[18]

DIFFERENCE EQUATIONS AND DIFFERENTIAL EQUATIONS

A difference equation involves a dependent variable or variable to be predicted as of a given point-in-time (Y_t) which is expressed as a function of itself at an earlier point-in-time (Y_{t-n}). Each point-in-time is an integer, and at each point-in-time the value of Y jumps upward or downward. A difference equation can be contrasted with a differential equation where it is meaningful to talk in terms of decimal points-in-time and especially where changes in Y are smooth and continuous, not in staircase jumps. Both difference and differential equations differ from time series regression equations in that the former are deduced from the nature of the subject matter, whereas the latter are inductively arrived at by in effect fitting a curve to many time data points. Difference and differential equations do not necessarily refer to time, but in this context we are only discussing time-oriented difference and differential equations.[19]

A good example of difference equations in the legal process is the equations for describing the relations in plea bargaining between (1) the first counter offer and the initial offer; (2) any counter offer and the immediate prior counter offer; and (3) any counter offer and the initial offer. From the nature of the subject matter it seems logical that the first counter offer for the defendant (D_1) would be equal to the defendant's initial (D_0) plus an increment. It also seems logical that that increment would represent a portion or percent (%) of the distance from the defendant's upper limit (L) down to the defendant's initial offer (i.e., the distance $L - D_0$). Put another way, the relation between the first counter offer and the initial offer of the defendant can be symbolized $D_1 = D_0 + \% (L - D_0)$. Similarly the first counter offer for the prosecutor (P_1) is equal to the prosecutor's initial offer (P_0) minus a decrement. This decrement represents a percent (%) of the distance from the prosecutor's lower limit (L) up to his initial offer (i.e., the distance $P_0 - L$). Thus, the relation between the first counter offer and the initial offer of the prosecutor can be symbolized $P_1 = P_0 - \%(P_0 - L)$ where % and L for the prosecutor are unlikely to be the same as % and L for the defendant.

From the above reasoning, we can generalize that the relation between any counter offer and the immediately prior counter offer for either the defendant or the prosecutor can be symbolized $F_t = F_{t-1} + \%(L - F_{t-1})$. In that equation, F represents an offer from either the defendant or the prosecutor of years in jail for which they are willing to settle the case without a trial. The t represents the time period or the round in the series of paired offers and counter offers. The equation makes sense for the defendant whose limit is always higher than or equal to the corresponding previous offer, and thus $\%(L - F_{t-1})$ represents a positive number of years to be added to those previous offers. The equation also makes sense for the prosecutor whose limit is always lower than or equal to the corresponding previous offer, and thus $\%(L - F_{t-1})$ represents a negative number of years to be subtracted from the prosecutor's previous offer.

Solving a difference equation generally means expressing Y_t in terms of Y_0 rather than in terms of Y_{t-1}. If Y can only be expressed in terms of Y_{t-1}, then to determine the value of Y_6 would mean first determining the value of Y_0, Y_1, Y_2, and so on through Y_5. In our plea bargaining example, expressing F_t in terms of F_0 involves experimenting with the above equations by expressing F_1 in terms of F_0, expressing F_2 in terms of F_1, which is expressed in terms of F_0, and so on until one observes a pattern of how F_t relates to F_0. This kind of experimentation reveals that the relation is $F_t = L + [(1 - \%)^t(F_0 - L)]$. This equation tells us that to find F_t, we should subtract from the defendant's upper limit the decrement which is in brackets, and we should add to the prosecutor's lower limit the increment which is in brackets. The bracketed material will be a decrement for the defendant whose initial offer (F_0) will be lower than the corresponding limit (L), and it will be an increment for the prosecutor whose initial offer (F_0) will be higher than the corresponding limit (L). The $(1 - \%)^t$ indicates that a smaller portion of what $F_0 - L$ distance is added to or subtracted from L at each successive t stage. In other words, $(1 - \%)^3$ is a smaller portion than $(1 - \%)^2$, assuming the splitting rate (or $\%$) remains roughly constant from stage to stage.

This kind of analysis can be useful in a variety of ways. It can enable one to predict whether the prosecutor and defendant are likely to converge or settle. They are likely to settle if the defendant's upper L limit is higher than the prosecutor's lower L limit. It can enable one to predict in how many stages or time periods they are likely to converge if one knows their respective L, $\%$, and F_0 figures. This in turn tells us that if we want faster and surer convergence we should seek to (1) increase the defendant's upper L limit and initial F_0 offer; (2) decrease the prosecutor's lower L limit and initial F_0 offer; and (3) increase the splitting rate or percent for both the defendant and the prosecutor. The analysis also leads one into thinking about what goes into determining L, $\%$, and F_0, especially L since F_0 and $\%$ seem to be partly to be a function of L and since the components of L seem more subject to manipulation by the legal system. These components include such things as the predictability of conviction and sentence, and the litigation costs of the defendant and prosecutor. In addition, the analysis leads one into thinking about how plea bargaining could come closer to arriving at sentences equal to trial sentences without the time and expense of trials, namely by increasing the above predictability to avoid misperceptions and decreasing the above litigation costs to avoid coerced settlements. The same kind of analysis can also be usefully applied to analyzing and improving civil out-of-court settlements.[20]

A good example of a differential equation that can be applied to the legal process is the equation $Y_t = Y_0(1 + r)^t$ where Y_t is the future value of an amount of money, Y_0 is the initial value, r is the interest rate per year, and t is the number of years. Its practical application occurs when, for example, the defendant in a civil case is told by the plaintiff that the plaintiff will withdraw the lawsuit if the defendant will pay 3,000 dollars. The defendant thinks that if the case goes to trial five years from now and the defendant loses, of which there is a ⅔ chance, the plaintiff will be awarded 6,000 dollars. The defendant thus perceives the case as having an expected value of 4,000 dollars. The question then becomes, is the defendant better off paying the plaintiff 3,000 dollars now or 4,000 dollars five years from now? Answering this question involves working with the above differential equation and the current interest rate, which we might assume is .06. The equation thus becomes $Y_t = 3000(1.06)^5$, and Y_t thus equals 4,015 dollars. The defendant, therefore, would be better off putting the 3,000 dollars into a savings account at 6 percent, waiting 5 years, and then paying 4,000 dollars to the defendant and having 15 dollars left over, than simply paying the 3,000 dollars to the plaintiff.

This conclusion assumes that the litigation costs are less than 15 dollars, which they are not likely to be. The conclusion also makes more sense if the defendant is, for example, an insurance company that has many similar cases such that it loses two-thirds of them and wins one-third, whereas the single defendant, by not accepting the plaintiff's willingness to settle for 3,000 dollars, stands to be out 3,000 dollars (i.e., 6,000 dollars damages minus the 3,000 dollars rejected offer if the case is lost) or to save 3,000 dollars (if the case is won). Inflation is partly taken into consideration in saying that five years from now, if the case is won by the plaintiff, the plaintiff will get 6,000 dollars. With greater inflation, the figure would be more than 6,000 dollars; and with less inflation, less than 6,000 dollars. This differential equation example is the opposite of the example previously given in discussing whether the plaintiff should follow the federal path or the state path in the section on "Critical Path Analysis." There, the plaintiff wanted to know what is the present value of future money, which can be determined by the formula $Y_0 = Y_t/(1 + r)^t$, rather than the defendant's question of what is the future value of present money.[21] Both are differential equations because (1) they express Y at one point-in-time in terms of Y at another point-in-time; (2) they are deductively arrived at from the nature of the subject matter rather than inductively arrived at from time data points, unlike a time series regression equation; and because (3) it is meaningful for t to be any decimal part of a year, unlike a difference equation which involves integer jumps.[22]

APPENDIX 15-1. GLOSSARY OF TERMS IN TIME SERIES AND DIFFERENCE/ DIFFERENTIAL EQUATIONS

See the list of formulas in Appendix 15-2 for how various concepts are calculated.

Symbol	Represents

TIME SERIES ANALYSIS

Y_t	Actual score at time t
Y_{t-1}	Actual score at time t-1 or the immediate prior time point
$\hat{Y}_t$	Predicted score at time t
$Y't$	Residual score at time t, or difference between actual and predicted
R^2	Percentage of variance accounted for
Log	Logarithm to the base 10, that is, an exponent such that $10^N = Y$

DIFFERENCE EQUATIONS (E.g. Plea Bargaining)

D_0, P_0	Initial offer of defendant or prosecutor
D_1, D_2	Counter offers of defendant at time 1 and 2
P_1, P_2	Counter offers of prosecutor at time 1 and 2
L	Defendant's upper limit or prosecutor's lower limit
F	Offer of either defendant or prosecutor of the years in jail he is willing to offer to settle the case without a trial
%	Portion or percent of the distance from the defendant's upper limit down to his initial offer, or from the prosecutor's lower limit up to his initial offer

DIFFERENTIAL EQUATIONS (E.g. Future Value of Present Investment)

r	The interest rate that could be obtained by putting money in a savings account or other investment for t years
t	A given time period, or the quantity of time periods
Y_0	The initial or present value of an investment or a damage award

APPENDIX 15-2. BASIC FORMULAS IN TIME SERIES AND DIFFERENCE/DIFFERENTIAL EQUATIONS

Symbol	Represents

TIME SERIES ANALYSIS

1. Univariate and Bivariate Relations

Crime = a + b(Time Period)	Predicting crime for various time periods
Murders = a_1 + b_1(Executions)	Predicting murders from executions
Executions = a_2 + b_2 (Murders)	Predicting executions from murders

2. Cross-Lagged Panel Analysis to Relate Crime to Expenditures

$Y_t = a + b_1(X_{t-1}) + b_2(Y_{t-1})$	Linear relation with b_1 as the marginal rate of return
$Y_t = a(X_{t-1})^{b_1}(Y_{t-1})^{b_2}$	Nonlinear relation with $b_1 a (Y_{t-1})^{b_2}{}_{(X)}^{b_1-1}$ as the marginal rate of return

3. Deserializing to Relate Crime to Expenditures

$\hat{Y}_t = a + bY_{t-1}$	Predicting crime at time t from crime at time t-1
$Y' = Y_t - \hat{Y}_t$	Defining residual or unexplained crime as the difference between actual crime and predicted crime
$Y' = a + bX$	Predicting residual crime fron anti-crime dollars, with b as the marginal rate of return

DIFFERENCE EQUATIONS

$D_1 = D_0 + \%(L-D_0)$	Relation between first counter offer and initial offer of defendant considering the defendant's upper limit
$P_1 = P_0 - \%(P_0-L)$	Relation between first counter offer and initial offer of prosecutor considering the prosecutor's lower limit
$F_t = F_{t-1} + \%(L-F_{t-1})$	Relation between any counter offer at time t and the immediate prior counter offer
$F_t = L + [(1-\%)^t(F_0-L)]$	Relation between any counter offer and the initial offer considering the percentage rate at which the defendant or prosecutor splits

DIFFERENTIAL EQUATIONS	the difference between his last offer and his outer limit
$Y_t = Y_0(1 + r)^t$	The future value at time t of an amount of money offered to settle a case now, given the interest rate per time period and the number of time periods until time t is reached

NOTES

1. Edith and Richard Zeckhauser, *A Primer for Policy Analysis* (New York: Norton, 1978) and Michael White, et al., *Managing Public Systems: Analytic Techniques for Public Administration* (Scituate, Mass.: Duxbury, 1980).

2. On Markov chain analysis, see Dean Isaacson and Richard Madsen, *Markov Chains Theory and Applications* (New York: Wiley, 1975); Jan Kemeny and J. Laurie Snell, *Finite Markov Chains* (Englewood Cliffs, N.J.: Prentice Hall, 1960); Samuel Richmond, *Operations Research for Management Decisions* (New York: Ronald, 1968) pp. 439-60; and Sidney Ulmer, "Stochastic Process Models in Political Analysis," in James Herndon and Joseph Bernd (eds.), *Math Applications in Political Science* (Blacksburg: Virginia Polytechnic Institute, 1967).

3. The above analysis assumed that the only percentages or probabilities undergoing change are the percentage of cases involving release on recognizance, release on bond, and jail detention. In some situations a change in the percentages on one tier can affect the percentages on another tier as well as the quantity of cases. For example, after bail reform, only the relatively bad-worse risk prisoners are now in jail. They may be less likely to plead guilty at a .70 rate because they may be more street-wise and jail-hardened, and thus be *less* vulnerable to the prosecutor's offers. On the other hand, they may be more likely to be convicted if their cases go to trial and also suffer less stigma from pleading guilty, and thus be *more* vulnerable to the prosecutor's offers. Those two considerations may balance each other such that it is reasonable to assume the .70 guilty pleading rate for defendants in jail will remain after bail reform.

4. Kenneth Lenihan, "Telephones and Raising Bail: Some Lessons in Evaluation Research, 1 *Evaluation Quarterly* 579 (1977); Patricia Wald, "Pretrial Detention and Ultimate Freedom," 39 *New York University Law Review* 633 (1964).

5. For data on the costs suffered by defendants having to sit in jail awaiting trial see Caleb Foote, *Studies on Bail* (Philadelphia: University of Pennsylvania Law School, 1966) pp. 722-30; Daniel Freed and Patricia Wald, *Bail in the United States* (Washington, D.C.: Government Printing Office, 1964) pp. 39-48; and Wayne Thomas, *Bail Reform in America* (Los Angeles: University of California Press, 1976) pp. 110-18.

6. Ronald Rardin and Paul Gray, "Analysis of Crime Control Strategies," 1 *Journal of Criminal Justice* 339-46 (1973); Ronald Slivka and Frank Cannavale, Jr., "An Analytical Model of the Passage of Defendants Through a Court System," 10 *Journal of Research in Crime and Delinquency* 132-40 (1973); S.J. Deutsch, J.J. Jarvis, and R.G. Parker, "A Network Flow Model for Predicting Criminal Displacement and Deterrence" (unpublished paper, 1977); David

Greenberg, "Recidivism as Radioactive Decay" (unpublished paper, 1975); Thomas Schelling and Richard Zeckhauser, "Law and Public Policy: Policy Analysis" (unpublished course materials, 1975); David White, Soo Uh, and Kim Andriano, "Juvenile Court Records and Markov Chains: Their Use as Aids in Identification and Treatment of Delinquent Youth," 1 *Law and Human Behavior* 217-37 (1977); and Belkin, Blumstein, and Glass, "Recidivism as Feedback Process: An Analytical Model and Empirical Validation," 1 *Journal of Criminal Justice* 7 (1973).

7. On time series analysis, see Samuel Kirkpatrick, *Quantitative Analysis of Political Data* (Columbus, Ohio: Charles Merrill, 1974) pp. 385-509; David Leege and Wayne Francis, *Political Research: Design, Measurement, and Analysis* (New York: Basic Books, 1974) pp. 383-96; Robert Pindyck and Daniel Rubinfeld, *Econometric Models and Economic Forecasting* (New York: McGraw Hill, 1976); Steven Wheelwright and Spyros Makridakis, *Forecasting Methods for Management* (New York: Wiley, 1973); and Bruce Russett, "Some Decisions in the Regression Analysis of Time-Series Data," in Herndon and Bernd, op. cit.

8. In cross-sectional analysis, the units being analyzed are places which have a variety of characteristics or variables. In time series analysis, the units being analyzed are time points which also have a variety of characteristics or variables. A kind of cross-sectional analysis that has a time element in it involves places as the units of analysis, but some of the variables are expressed in terms of change-over-time. For example, the places may be cities that have NAACP chapters and variables like change in housing discrimination which is scored on a 5-point scale of big increase, little increase, no change, little decrease, or big decrease. See S. Nagel and M. Neef, *The Application of Mixed Strategies: Civil Rights and Other Multi-Policy Activities* (Beverly Hills, Ca.: Sage, 1976); and George Bohrnstedt, "Observations on the Measurment of Change," in Edgar Borgatta (ed.) *Sociological Methodology* (San Francisco: Jossey Bass, 1970) pp. 113-33.

Another type of cross-sectional analysis that includes an element of change involves working with persons as the unit of analysis and from which the variable of age is predicted. For example, if one divides a set of judges into younger judges and older judges, one may find the older judges are more conservative in their decisional propensities, and therefore conclude that aging makes for conservatism due partly to the fact that older judges were socialized in an earlier era. That kind of reasoning, however, might be fallacious as compared to analyzing the decisional propensities of judges over time. For example, as of about 1976, the older judges on the federal bench may score higher on a liberalism scale than the younger ones because the older judges might be more likely to be Democrats appointed by a Democratic president prior to 1968, although those same Democratic judges may have been more liberal in their youth. On the relation between the age of judges and some aspects of their decisional propensities, see John Schmidhauser, "Age and Judicial Behavior" in Wilma Donahue and Clark Tibbetts (eds.), *The Politics of Age* (Ann Arbor, U. of Michigan Press, 1962); J. Hogarth, *Sentencing as a Human Process* (Toronto: Toronto University Press, 1971), pp. 211-28; S. Nagel, "Multiple Correlation of Judicial Backgrounds and Decisions," 2 *Florida State University Law Review* 258 (1974); and Anthony Champagne, "Aging and Judicial Behavior," (unpublished paper presented at the annual meeting of the Southwestern Political Science Association, 1978).

9. Another type of univariate time series analysis involves crime at a time-predicted from crime at a prior point-in-time. That type of univariate time series is discussed in the example given later which deals with relating crime to anticrime expenditures.

10. Donald Campbell and Laurence Ross, "The Connecticut Crackdown on Speeding: Time-Series Data in Quasi-Experimental Analysis," 3 *Law and Society Review* 33 (1968); and Laurence Ross, Donald Campbell, and Gene Glass, "Deter-

mining the Social Effects of a Legal Reform: The British Breathalyser Crackdown of 1967," in S. Nagel (ed.) *Law and Social Change* (Beverly Hills, Ca.: Sage, 1970).

11. For materials specifically dealing with interrupted time series, see Gene Glass, Victor Willson and John Gottman, *Design and Analysis of Time-Series Experiments* (Colorado U. Press, 1975); James Caporaso and Leslie Roos (eds.), *Quasi-Experimental Approaches* (Greenwich, Conn.: JAI Press, 1973); and Donald Campbell, "Reforms as Experiments," 24 *American Psychologist* 409 (1969). Some legal policies undergo neither continuous change nor off-on status. An example would be the effect on oil productivity of the oil depletion allowance which has gone from 5 percent in 1913, to a "reasonable allowance" in 1916, to itemized deductions in 1917, to 27.5 percent in 1926, to 22 percent in 1969, to zero percent in 1976. Jon Bond, "A Longitudinal Analysis of the Effects of the Oil Depletion Allowance: Empirical Evidence to Resolve Conflicting Evaluations" (unpublished paper presented at the 1976 meeting of the Midwest Political Science Assocation at Chicago, Illinois).

12. On causal analysis with time series or cross-sectional data, see David Heise, *Causal Analysis* (New York: Wiley, 1975); and S. Nagel and M. Neef, "Causal Analysis and the Legal Process" in Rita Simon (ed.) *Research in Law and Sociology* (Greenwich, Conn.: JAI Press, 1977).

13. Autocorrelation can be defined as the extent to which the lagged residual scores of the persons, places or other units of analysis correlate with each other. A residual score is the difference between one's actual score and one's predicted score. For example, the actual crime score for a given city in 1970 may be 60 on a scale from zero to 100. The predicted crime score predicting from city size may be 80. Thus that city has a residual score of -20, meaning the actual is 20 below the predicted. A lagged residual score is a residual score for the city at an earlier point-in-time. If we are talking about a two-year lag, then the lagged residual score for 1970 would be the residual score for 1968, which might be a -15 rather than a -20. If each residual score for the city and its two-year lagged residual score is off by a difference of 5 as with the hypothetical 1970 and 1968 data, then perfect autocorrelation would be present. If, however, those relations are highly random and thus do not follow a consistent pattern, then no autocorrelation is present. The presence of autocorrelation interferes with the extent to which one can feel safe in saying that the slope of the relation between crime and city size (or other relations) is not due to chance sampling probability. On autocorrelation and other aspects of time series analysis, see the references cited in note 7. Also see Michael Brennan, *Preface to Econometrics: An Introduction to Quantitative Methods in Economics* (Cincinnati: South-western, 1973), pp. 259-364, especially pp. 353-62.

14. See S. Nagel, *Comparing Elected and Appointed Judicial Systems* (Beverly Hills, Ca.: Sage, 1973); and Richard Watson and Randall Downing, *The Politics of the Bench and Bar: Judicial Selection Under the Missouri Non-Partisan Court Plan* (New York: Wiley, 1969).

15. See Hans Mattick, *The Unexamined Death: An Analysis of Capital Punishment* (Chicago: John Howard Assoc., 1965); Adam Bedau (ed.), *The Death Penalty in America* (New York, Harper, 1967); and Isaac Ehrlich, "The Deterrent Effect of Capital Punishment: A Question of Life and Death" 65 *American Economics Review* 314 (1975). In determining the effects of reapportionment, an analysis before and after reapportioning is more meaningful than an analysis between states that are relatively malapportioned and those that are relatively well-apportioned. The across states or cross-sectional approach finds apportionment makes no difference on the nature of the legislative output, probably because there are so many other causal variables determining legislative output that cannot be meaningfully held constant when comparing two sets of states at the same point-in-time. The over-time approach, however, reveals changes in legislative output from before to after reapportionment when reapportioning states are compared with

relatively nonreapportioning states over the same time period. See William Bicker, "The Effects of Malapportionment in the States: A Mistrial," in Nelson Polsby (ed.) *Reapportionment in the 1970's* (Los Angeles: University of California Press, 1971); and William Cantrall and Stuart Nagel, "The Effects of Reapportionment on the Passage of Nonexpenditure Legislature Legislation" in Stuart Nagel, *Improving the Legal Process: Effects of Alternatives* (Lexington, Mass.: Lexington-Heath, 1975).

16. For a discussion of the relative predictive power of equations of the form $Y_t = f(Y_{t-1})$ as compared to $Y = f(X_1, X_2, \ldots X_n)$, see Jerry Goldman, Richard Hooper, and Judy Mahaffey, "Caseload Forecasting Models for Federal District Courts," 5 *Journal of Legal Studies* 201 (1976). Normally one can predict a variable better from the same variable at a prior point-in-time than from other variables. Predicting from other variables, however, may give one a much better understanding of what causes fluctuations in the variable being predicted, and more important, an understanding of how to favorably influence those fluctuations. By developing a regression equation to predict Y_t from Y_{t-1}, Y_{t-2}, and so on down to Y_1 (or from X_{t-1} down to X_1), one is in effect doing the kind of prediction done in Markov chain analysis, especially if the Y variable that one is seeking to predict is scored zero or 1 for absent or present and can be treated like a probability. A form of regression analysis called probit analysis explicity works with Y variables that are probabilities.

The above procedure is called cross-logged panel analysis because it involves crime related to both dollars and itself at an earlier point-in-time (lagged analysis) with over-time data (panel analysis) and across two variables. If one compares (1) the relationship between crime and both prior dollars and prior crime with (2) the relationship between dollars and both prior crime and prior dollars, one can thereby get at the degree of reciprocal causation between crime and anticrime dollars. The first relationship indicates the extent to which crime is influenced by anticrime expenditures, holding prior crime constant, and the second relationship indicates the extent to which anticrime expenditures are influenced by crime, holding prior expenditures constant. On the use of time series to analyze reciprocal causation see David Heise, "Causal Inference From Panel Data" in G. Bohrnstedt (ed.), *Sociological Methodology* (San Francisco: Jossey Bass, 1970); and S. Nagel and M. Neef, "Causal Analysis and the Legal Process" in Simon, op. cit.

17. An alternative procedure (called deserializing) would be to obtain numerical values for the coefficients in the equation: $Crime_t = a + b(Crime_{t-1})$. With that equation, we can obtain a predicted crime score ($\hat{Y}$) for each time point and then a residual or difference score (Y'), where $Y' = Y - \hat{Y}$. This score represents the amount of crime which occurred in the city in a given year that could not be explained from the previous year's crime and thus not from whatever social variables determine the previous year's crime. We can now input into the computer a Y' score and an expenditure score (X) for each year in order to obtain the numerical values for the equation $Y' = a + bX$. The value of "b" in that equation is the slope or marginal rate of return of an extra dollar spent on reducing the unexplained crime occurrence. The deserializing approach may in some ways sound simpler than the cross-lagged panel analysis. It, however, has the defect that so much of the variance in crime (Y_t) is explained by prior crime (Y_{t-1}) that there is virtually nothing left to be explained by the anticrime expenditures (X). This does not mean expenditures have no influence, but simply that the influence of expenditures on crime is covered by the relation of crime to prior crime, since prior crime includes the influence of prior expenditures as well as demographic and other variables.

18. S. Nagel and M. Neef, "Allocating Resources Geographically for Optimum Results," 3 *Political Methodology* 383 (1976) and S. Nagel and M. Neef, "Optimally Allocating Anticrime Dollars Across U.S. Cities and Anticrime Ac-

tivities" (Paper presented at the annual meeting of the Midwest Political Science Assocation, 1978). For additional examples of time series analysis applied to the legal process, see Hans Zeisel, Harry Kalven, Jr., and Bernard Buchholz, *Delay in the Court* 251-62 (Boston: Little Brown, 1959); Austin Sarat, "Litigation in the Federal Courts: A Comparative Perspective," 9 *Law and Society Review* 321 (1975); Christine Rossell, "School Desegregation and White Flight," 90 *Political Science Quarterly* 675 (1975-1976); Robert Kagan, "The Business of State Supreme Courts" (Unpublished paper presented at the annual meeting of the Midwest Political Science Association, 1977); and Harvey Sepler, "The Next 25 Years Facing the Criminal Justice System: Using Standard Celeration Charting for Systems Analysis" (Unpublished paper available from the author at the University of Kansas School of Education). The Rossell study tends to show that the white flight phenomenon from central cities to suburbs has been occurring over time without substantial change as a result of court desegregation orders. An analysis merely comparing desegregation-ordered cities with cities that have not been ordered to desegregate gives the appearance that white flight is greater in the desegregation-ordered cities because of the desegregation orders.

19. On difference equations and differential equations, see Michael Brennan, *Preface to Econometrics* (Cincinnati: South-Western, 1973), pp. 226-45; Ferdinand Cortes, Adam Przeworski, and John Sprague, *Systems Analysis for Social Scientists* (New York: Wiley, 1974); and Caroline Dinwiddy, *Elementary Mathematics for Economists* (Fair Lawn, N.J.: Oxford University Press, 1966), pp. 116-26, 133-49, and 199-216.

20. On difference equations applied to plea bargaining, see S. Nagel and M. Neef "Plea Bargaining, Decision Theory, and Equilibrium Models," 51 *Indiana Law Journal* 987 (1976); 52 *Indiana Law Journal* 1 (1976). This article also discusses the time discounting differential equation as applied to personal injury out-of-court settlements.

21. After one develops a difference equation or a differential equation, one can then calculate Y_t scores at various time points using the equation. One could then fit a regression equation to that data of the form $Y = a + bT$, or $Y = aT^b$. Doing so, however, would be wasteful of information since the original difference or differential equation is more capable of predicting Y values than the imperfectly-fitted regression equation.

22. There are other ways of forecasting the future besides Markov chain analysis, time series, and difference-differential equations. Other methods, however, tend to emphasize verbal qualitative analysis rather than quantitative models. See Daniel Harrison, *Social Forecasting Methodology: Suggestions for Research* (New York: Russell Sage, 1976); and S. Wheelwright and S. Makridakis, op. cit.; Wayne Boucher (ed.) *The Study of the Future: An Agenda for Research* (Washington, D.C.: National Science Foundation, 1977).

Chapter 16
Optimum Level, Mix, and Choice Applied to Delay Minimization

This chapter brings us full circle to the general analysis of finding an optimum choice, level, or mix in policy evaluation, as was discussed in Chapter 1. The difference, though, is that in this chapter, these three basic methodologies are all discussed in the context of minimizing delay. Optimum level analysis is especially helpful in determining optimum time-consumption, so that one can then subtract the optimum from the actual, in order to tell how much time consumption constitutes undesirable delay. Optimum mix analysis is helpful in allocating resources for delay minimization. Optimum choice analysis is helpful in seeking to influence the decisions of key personnel so as to encourage them to make more time-saving, rather than time-lengthening decisions.

OPTIMUM LEVEL ANALYSIS

Queueing theory tells us cases can be processed faster if we decrease arrivals, increase the servicing rate, and increase the number of processors. This is not meant to imply that we should strive to reduce arrivals to zero, or increase the servicing rate or number of processors to the point where time consumption becomes virtually zero. On the contrary, the speed-up costs may be greater than the delay costs such that we are better off keeping the delay. Optimum level analysis in the context of optimum time consumption is designed to tell us what is the optimum level of delay in the sense of minimizing the sum of the delay costs (Y_1) and the speed-up costs (Y_2).[1]

Figure 16-1 in pictorial form shows what is involved in optimum level analysis for a hypothetical metropolitan court system. To fully apply the analysis, we need to develop an equation showing the relation between delay costs and time consumed. For the sake of simplicity, we might say every extra day of time consumed in completing a criminal case is worth about 7 dollars per jailed defendant to the system. The 7 dollars represents waste in holding those defendants in jail who will receive an acquittal, dismissal, or probation when their case is tried. Of that 7 dollars, about 2 dollars are wasted in jail maintenance costs, and 5 dollars represents lost

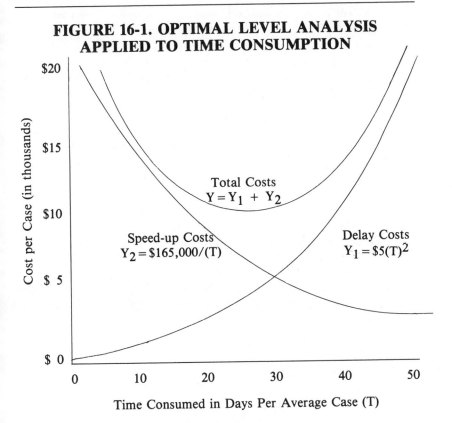

FIGURE 16-1. OPTIMAL LEVEL ANALYSIS
APPLIED TO TIME CONSUMPTION

Cost per Case (in thousands)

Total Costs
$Y = Y_1 + Y_2$

Speed-up Costs
$Y_2 = \$165,000/(T)$

Delay Costs
$Y_1 = \$5(T)^2$

Time Consumed in Days Per Average Case (T)

gross national product that could have been earned. The 2 dollars is calculated by noting that it costs 6 dollars per day to maintain a defendant in jail, and one-third of them receive nonjail dispositions upon trial, meaning 2 dollars per day is wasted by delaying the nonjail disposition. The 5 dollars is calculated by noting that a defendant can earn about 15 dollars a day if not in jail, and that about one-third of them would not be in jail if their acquitted or dismissed cases came up sooner, meaning an additional 5 dollars per day is wasted by delay. There might also be about 3 dollars per day wasted per released defendant. The 3 dollars represents waste in releasing those defendants who will be jailed when they are eventually tried and convicted, but who during the delay commit a crime or have to be rearrested for failure to appear in court. That 3 dollars is determined by calculating (1) the crime-committing cost or the rearresting cost for the average released defendant; (2) multiplied by the low probability of the occurrence of crime committing or rearresting; (3) multiplied by the middling probability of being convicted and jailed if the case were to come to disposition; and (4) divided by the number of days released. If we assume half the arrested defendants are jailed and half are released, then the 7 dollars delay cost per day per *jailed* defendant is 3.50 dollars per day per arrested defendant or per *case*, and the 3 dollars delay cost per day per *released* defendant is 1.50 dollars per day per arrested defendant or per *case*. Thus the total delay cost per day per case would be 5 dollars (or 3.50 dollars plus 1.50 dollars). If the 5 dollars per day were a constant figure, we could say delay costs (Y_1) equal 5 dollars times T days, or $Y_1 = \$5(T)$.

Since the likelihood of crime committing and the need for rearresting increase as delay increases, the relation between Y_1 and T might be better expressed by an equation of the form $Y_1 = \$5(T)^2$. This equation tells us that when T is 1 day, Y_1 is 5 dollars; but when T is X days, Y_1 is not 5 dollars times X, but rather Y_1 increases at an increasing rate. More specifically, as T goes up 1 percent, Y_1 goes up 2 percent. The values of the multiplier of T and the exponent of T can be determined by performing what is known as a log-linear regression analysis if one has data showing for a set of cases (1) the time consumed by each case; (2) the amount each case roughly costs in terms of jail maintenance and lost GNP for those held, and crime-committing and rearresting costs for those released; and (3) the proportion or probability of cases in which nonjail sentences were handed down and the proportion of crime committing and rearresting of released defendants.

The more time that is consumed, the higher the delay costs become at a possibly increasing rate. However, the more we rush cases to a disposition, the greater the speed-up costs might be. These costs mainly include the monetary cost of hiring additional personnel or introducing new facilities or procedures. Suppose either through deductive queueing theory or through the compilation of empirical data, we find that with only 20 judges, cases average 75 days per case; with 40 judges, 38 days; with 60 judges, 25 days; with 80 judges, 19 days. We can meaningfully assume that with zero judges, the number of days would rise to infinity, and in order to get the number of days down to zero, we would have to have an infinite number of judges.

The speed-up costs curve shown in Figure 16-1 incorporates this data and these assumptions. A curve of this kind can be expressed by the equation of $J = a/T$, where J stands for the number of judges, and T stands for time in days per average case. If $J = a/T$, then $T = a/J$. The "a" in the $J = a/T$ equation is the number of judges needed to get time down to one day per case (i.e., $T = 1$), and the "a" in the $T = a/J$ equation is the number of days consumed when there is only one judge (i.e., $J = 1$) if the relationships are carried out to their logical extremes even though at the extremes the empirical data does not apply. From the above data and a computerized regression analysis, we can determine that $a = 1,500$. This means, according to our data, that $J = 1500/T$ and $T = 1500/J$.

Instead of talking in terms of the relation between the number of judges and the number of days consumed, we should be talking in terms of the cost of judges and the number of days consumed. If one judge costs 40,000 dollars a year, that means 110 dollars per day at a 365-day year. Thus the equation $J = 1500/T$ should be changed to $Y_2 = \$165,000/T$. The Y_2 is the speed-up costs or the additional judge costs, and the 165,000 dollars is simply 110 dollars times the previous "a" (also called the scale coefficient) of 1500 to show we have increased the scale by 110 dollars per judge per day. Our equation of $Y_2 = 165,000/T$ is algebraically the equivalent of the equation shown in Figure 16-1 of $Y_2 = 165,000(T)^{-1}$. This equation perfectly fits the above data, although in real life the equation might provide a good fit, but not a perfect fit.

Given the relationship between delay costs and time consumed of $Y_2 = \$5(T)^2$ and the relation between speed-up costs and time consumed of $Y_1 = \$165,000(T)^{-1}$, the relation between total costs (Y) and time consumed is logically $Y = \$5(T)^2 + \$165,000(T)^{-1}$. We are now ready to calculate the optimum level of time consumed which is graphically the value of T where the total costs curve hits bottom. Doing so involves recognizing that the total cost curve has a negative slope before it hits bottom, a positive slope after it hits bottom, and a zero slope when it bottoms out. Therefore we need to know the slope of Y to T. We can then set that slope equal to zero and solve for T. In elementary calculus, one learns that in an equation of the form $Y = aX^b$, the slope of Y to X is baX^{b-1}. Therefore, in our total cost equation, the slope of Y to T is $(2)(\$5)(T)^{2-1} + (-1)(\$165,000)(T)^{-1-1}$. If we set that expression equal to zero and solve for T, we get $10(T) - 165,000/(T)^2 = 0$, or $T = (16,500)^{.33}$, which means $T = 25$ days where the total costs hit bottom.[2]

This means that 25 days or about one month is the optimum level of time consumption in order to minimize the sum of the delay costs and the speed-up costs as we have calculated them. We could also say that the optimum level of judges is 60 judges, since $J = 1500/T$, or $60 = 1500/25$. This means that our court system would be minimizing its total costs if we have about 60 full-time judges. We could make this optimum level analysis more complicated by taking into consideration that speed-up costs (Y_2) may only be accurately indicated as a combination of the cost of judges, prosecutors, public defenders, other personnel, courtrooms, and other costs rather than only judges. The methodology, however, is basically the same, namely, (1) obtaining an empirical equation relating speed-up costs to time and delay costs to time; (2) finding the slope of the sum of those two equations; (3) setting that slope equal to zero and solving for T to determine the optimum number of days per average case for minimizing total costs; and (4) thereby indirectly determining the optimum number of judges, prosecutors, public defenders, other personnel, courtrooms, and other costs.[3]

OPTIMUM MIX ANALYSIS

Queueing theory tells us cases can be processed faster if we decrease arrivals, increase the servicing rate, and increase the number of pro cessors. If we concentrate on the number of processors, we might conclude that we can solve the time consumption problem by simply adding more judges, prosecutors, and public defense attorneys. We saw, however, in the previous section that to reduce time consumption to close to zero might require so many judges as to make the cure more expensive than the problem. We therefore calculated an optimum level of judges that would minimize the sum of the delay costs and judge costs. We could do a similar analysis to determine the optimum level of lawyers in the prosecutor's office and the optimum level of lawyers in the public defender's office. Doing three separate optimum level analyses, however, would not make sense because deciding on an optimum level for each of those activities requires taking the other activities into consideration.[4]

What basically is involved in an optimum mix analysis? By that kind of analysis in this context, we generally mean allocating a given budget to judges, prosecutors, and defense counsel so as to minimize time consumption. Suppose through an optimum level analysis, we find the optimum level of expenditure on judges is 700,000 dollars, on prosecutors is 400,000 dollars and 200,000 dollars on defense counsel for a total of 1.3 million dollars. If our total budget is only 1 million dollars, it would be quite inefficient to reduce each activity by 100,000 dollars.[5] It would also be inefficient to say that since judges constitute 54 percent of the 1.3 million dollar budget, they should get 54 percent of the 1 million dollar budget; prosecutors should get 31 percent; and defense counsel 15 percent. Either of these ways of bringing the separate expenditures within the total budget fails to consider the marginal rates of return of an extra dollar spent on each activity. By taking this perspective, we can arrive at a meaningful optimum mix analysis.

We previously determined for our hypothetical court system that the relation between time consumed and quantity of judges is $T = 1500/J$. Given the cost of a judge as being 40,000 dollars, the relation between time consumed and the cost of judges is $T = 165,000/\$J$, where $\$J$ refers to the number of dollars spent on judiciary per day. Thus if we have 10 judges and thereby spend $400,000/365$, or 1,096 dollars on the judiciary per day, then we expect the average case to consume 150 days since $150 = 165,000/1096$. By a similar analysis we could possibly determine that the relation between time consumed and the number of assistant states attorneys or prosecutors is $T = 1200/P$. This means, at the extremes, that if we only have one prosecutor in our metropolitan court system, cases would average 1200 days, ignoring for the moment the number of judges and defense counsel. If prosecutors are paid 30,000 dollars a year, the cost equation becomes $T = 98,400/\$P$, where $\$P$ refers to the number of dollars spent on prosecution, since $(1200)(30,000)/365 = 98,400$. A similar analysis for public defenders might reveal an equation of $T = 1000/D$. If assistant public defenders are paid 20,000 dollars apiece, then the third equation becomes $T = 55,000/\$D$, since $(1000)(20,000)/365 = 55,000$.

The above judicial equation of $T = 165,000/\$J$ can also be written $T = 165,000(\$J)^{-1}$. This equation informs us that the slope or marginal rate of return of T to $J is $-165,000(\$J)^{-2}$, since in the related equation of $Y = aX^b$, the slope of Y to X is baX^{b-1}. Similarly, the slope of T to $P is $-98,400(\$P)^{-2}$, and the slope of T to $D is $-55,000(\$D)^{-2}$. Given this information, we should solve for $J, $P, and $D in a set of three simultaneous equations in order to optimally allocate our 1 million dollar budget. The three equations are as follows:

$$-165,000(\$J)^{-2} = -98,400(\$P)^{-2}$$

$$-98,400(\$P)^{-2} = -55,000(\$D)^{-2}$$

$$\$J + \$P + \$D = \$1,000,000$$

By solving for the three unknowns in these three equations, we are equalizing the marginal rates of return across the three activities so that nothing can be gained by shifting dollars from one activity to another, and we are simultaneously spending no more than the total budget.

A defect in the above analysis is that it does not take into consideration the overlapping effect on time consumed of judges, prosecutors, and defense attorneys. What we need is an equation that provides a good fit to our data showing the average time consumed for various combinations of judges, prosecutors, and defense attorneys. What we need is an equation that provides a good fit to our data showing the average time consumed for various combinations of judges, prosecutors and defense counsel. One such data point might show the time consumed when we had seven judges, three prosecutors, and two public defenders. Other data points might show the time consumed when we had other combinations of judges, prosecutors and public defenders. Putting that data into a log-linear regression analysis would generate an equation of the form $T = a(\$J)^{b_1}(\$P)^{b_2}(\$D)^{b_3}$ with numbers substituted for the as and bs. Applying the same rule about finding the slope of Y to X, this equation tells us the slope of T to $J is (b_1) $(a)(\$P)^{b_2}(\$D)^{b_3}[\$J]^{b_1-1}$. Similarly the slope of T to $P is $(b_2)(a)(\$J)^{b_1}(\$D)^{b_3}$ $[\$P]^{b_2-1}$, and the slope of T to $D is $(b_3)(a)(\$J)^{b_1}(\$P)^{b_2}[\$D]^{b_3-1}$. With that new information, we can now more meaningfully find an optimum mix among $J, $P, and $D by setting those three slopes equal to each other in two equations, setting the sum of the three unknowns equal to 1 million dollars in the third equation, and then solving for the three unknowns. Using the multivariate approach is actually simpler because it can be shown algebraically. The optimum mix procedure then reduces to allocating to each "i" activity in accordance with the equation $b_iG/(b_1 + b_2 + b_3)$, where b_i is the elasticity coefficient (which is the exponent of activity i) and G is the grand total available to be allocated.[6]

Optimum mix analysis can also include deciding on a maximum

average time consumption that we are willing to tolerate and then determining what are minimum total expenditures for our three activities in
order to achieve that time consumption. In other words, optimum mix
analysis can include finding an optimum mix that will minimize expenditures subject to a maximum time constraint or that will minimize time
subject to a maximum expenditures constraint. The expenditures minimization approach involves solving for \$J, \$P, and \$D in the following three
equations if we use the slopes that do not consider the overlapping interaction among the activities:

$$-165{,}000(\$J)^{-2} = -98{,}400(\$P)^{-2}$$

$$-98{,}000(\$P)^{-2} = -55{,}000(\$D)^{-2}$$

$$165{,}000/\$J + 98{,}400/\$P + 55{,}000/\$D = 120$$

The first two equations result in an optimum mix in which each activity is
given a quantity of money such that at those three points their three marginal rates of return are equal. The third equation indicates that the sum of
the three separate time consumptions should be less than 120 days or three
months, if that is the maximum we are willing to tolerate for the average
case. A more meaningful third equation would have the form $a(\$J)^{b_1}(\$P)^{b_2}$
$(\$D)^{b_3} = 120$. If we use this more meaningful multivariate type of equa-
tion to express the maximum time constraint, then we should also use the
more meaningful slopes that are based on that equation for the first two
equations. Wherever a \$J, \$P, or \$D appears, we could also substitute
$\$J + M_1$, $\$P + M_2$, and $\$D + M_3$, where M indicates the minimum
number of dollars to be allocated to that activity before the remaining
dollars are allocated in accordance with the marginal rates of return.[7] One
could also talk in terms of an optimum allocation of a given budget to
judges, prosecutors, and public defenders in terms of a composite goal in
which delay reduction is just one of a number of criteria that one is seeking
to maximize.[8]

OPTIMUM CHOICE ANALYSIS

Both optimum level and optimum mix analysis involve working with
a variable to be optimized that has a continuum of categories, as dollars
does. Optimum choice analysis, on the other hand, involves a variable that
has discrete categories like yes/no, or do it/don't do it. This type of
analysis might be especially valuable in analyzing how to get judicial personnel like judges, prosecutors, and defense counsel to do the things that
are most likely to lead to settlements, a reduction in servicing time, or
other activities that will reduce the average time consumed per case.[9]

Optimum choice analysis operates on the assumption that when individuals choose one activity over another, they are implicitly indicating

that the expected benefits minus costs of the chosen activity are greater than the expected benefits minus costs of the rejected activity. The expected benefits equal the benefits to be received from an action discounted or multiplied by the probability of the occurrence of whatever events those benefits are contingent upon. Similarly, the expected costs equal the costs to be incurred by an action discounted by the probability of whatever events these costs are contingent upon. The general decision theory involved in optimum choice analysis is shown in Figure 5-5 in Chapter 5.

Figure 5-5 specifically applies optimum choice analysis to the problem of how to get prosecutors and assistant states attorneys to make decisions to accelerate the slow and difficult cases so that they do not exceed a maximum time threshold. Doing that could involve (1) increasing the benefits and decreasing the costs from making time-saving decisions; (2) decreasing the benefits and increasing the costs from time-lengthening decisions; and (3) increasing or decreasing the probabilies of relevant contingent events. To encourage favorable time consumption decisions, assistant states attorneys can be given monetary rewards (to increase the benefits) and be given work-saving resources (to decrease the costs). Similarly, to discourage unfavorable time consumption decisions, states attorneys can in effect be punished by providing an absolute discharge not subject to reprosecution of excessively delayed defendants, and they can be deprived of the plea bargaining benefits of lengthy pretrial incarceration by providing more release on recognizance. These devices may incur substantial monetary and nonmonetary speed-up costs to the system that may outweigh the delay costs, as discussed under optimum level analysis. Optimum choice analysis, however, does stimulate one's thinking with regard to how decision makers can be influenced to make time-saving decisions if one, at least for the moment, is primarily concerned with time-saving.

A similar optimum choice analysis could be applied to the decisions made in the public defenders office or the offices of private defense attorneys. The suggestions there for encouraging time-saving decisions, however, may conflict with the decisions applicable to the states' attorney. For example, one might recommend more pretrial release to decrease the benefit the prosecutor receives from the increased willingness to plead guilty by defendants held in jail. On the other hand, one might recommend less pretrial release in order to make the defendant, and indirectly, the defendant's attorney, suffer more from delaying the case. In such conflicting situations, one has to decide which side is more responsible for the delay, or decide on the basis of criteria other than saving time. There are also benefit-cost suggestions stimulated by this analysis applicable to the defense side that do not conflict with the previous suggestions applicable to the prosecution. For example, providing monetary rewards to assistant public defenders and more resources does not conflict with the prosecutor's suggestions, unless one assumes there is a fixed quantity of resources available to the criminal justice system, and whatever the prosecutor gets must be taken away from the public defender or other parts of the system.

A similar optimum choice analysis could also be applied to judicial decisions that affect delay. For example, as of now, judges incur virtually no personal costs from granting repeated continuances or making other delaying decisions. If, however, records were publicized showing for each judge in a given court system the average length of time taken to process cases of various types, this visibility might cause the especially slow judges to change their ways so as to come closer to the averages of the other judges. Such a publicizing system (even among only the judges rather than the general public) would have the effect of increasing the costs of making time-lengthening decisions. This kind of record keeping can also be done for making comparisons across assistant states attorneys and assistant public defenders in a given court system, or across court systems if one calculates separate averages for cases of different types of severity and different expected time consumptions.[10]

APPENDIX 16-1. GLOSSARY OF TERMS IN CHOICE, LEVEL, AND MIX

See the list of formulas in Appendix 15-2 for how various concepts are calculated

Symbol	Represents

OPTIMUM LEVEL ANALYSIS
1. Relating Time and Judges

T	Time in days per average case
J	Judges, number of
a	Either (1) time in days consumed by the average case when there is only one judge available to process cases as in $T = a/J$, or (2) number of judges needed in order to get the average time consumed down to one day as in $J = a/T$.

2. Costs

Y_1	Actual or predicted number of dollars wasted over a given number of days prior to trial for a case or an average case (delay costs).
Y_2	Actual or predicted number of dollars expended on judges in order to achieve a given number of days awaiting trial by an average case (speed-up costs)
Y	Total costs, i.e., delay costs plus speed-up costs for a given number of days

3. The Parameters or Constants for Predicting the Costs from Time Consumed

A_1	The predicted number of dollars in delay costs if only one day is consumed, as in $Y_1 = A_1(T)^{b1}$
A_2	The predicted number of dollars in speed-up costs if only one day is consumed, as in $Y_2 = A_2(T)^{b2}$
b_1	Ratio between a percentage change in delay costs and a one percent change in the number of days consumed per average case.
b_2	Ratio between a percentage change in speed-up costs and a one percent change in the number of days consumed per average case.

OPTIMUM MIX ANALYSIS

P	Prosecutors, number of
D	Defenders, number of
$J	Judges, number of dollars spent on
$P	Prosecution, number of dollars spent on
$D	Defenders, number of dollars spent on
G	Grand total of dollars available to be allocated
M_1, M_2	Minimum number of dollars to be allocated to activity 1 and 2

OPTIMUM CHOICE ANALYSIS

+ a	Benefits from making time-saving decisions
-b	Costs of making time-saving decisions
-c	Costs incurred from making time-lengthening decisions
+ d	Benefits from making time-lengthening decisions

APPENDIX 16-2. BASIC FORMULAS USED IN CHOICE, LEVEL, AND MIX

See the glossary in Appendix 16-1 for definition of the symbols

OPTIMUM LEVEL ANALYSIS

1. Basic Relations

$T = a/J$	Relation between time in days per average case and number of judges. E.g., $T = 1500/J$
$J = a/T$	Relation between number of judges and time in days per average case. E.g., $J = 1500/T$

2. Costs

$Y_1 = A_1(T)^{b1}$	Delay costs. E.g., $Y_1 = \$5(T)^2$
$Y_2 = A_2(T)^{b2}$	Speed-up costs. E.g., $Y_2 = \$165,000(T)^{-1}$
$Y = A_1(T)^{b1} + A_2(T)^{b2}$	Total costs. E.g., $\$5(T)^2 + \$165,000(T)^{-1}$

$A_1 =$ (Wasted cost per day per jailed defendant) x (Percent of defendants who are jailed) + (Wasted cost per day per released defendant) x (Percent of defendants released).
E.g., $A_1 = (\$7)(.50) + (\$3)(.50) = \$5$.

$A_2 =$ (a) x (Salary per year) / (Number of days per year)
E.g., $A_2 = (1500)(\$40,000) / (365) = \$165,000$

3. Relation Between a Change in Total Costs and a Change in Time per Case

$$\Delta Y / \Delta T = (b_1)(A_1)(T)^{b_1-1} + (b_2)(A_2)(T)^{b_2-1}$$

E.g., $\Delta Y / \Delta T = (2)(\$5)(tT)^{2-1} + (-1)(\$165,000)(T)^{-1-1} = 10(T) - 165,000/(T)^2$

OPTIMUM MIX ANALYSIS

Numerical values are generally used in the formulas below based on the hypothetical data from the text instead of using symbols for the parameters or constants. The numerical values for prosecutors and public defenders are calculated analogous to the way they were above for judges.

1. Relation between Time and Number of Judges, Prosecutors, and Defenders

   $T = 1500/J$ $T = 1200/P$ $T = 1000/D$

2. Salary per day (annual salary / 365)

   $40,000/365 = 110$ $30,000/365 = 82$ $20,000/365 = 55$

3. Relation between Time and Dollars for Judges, Prosecutors, and Defenders

   $T = 165,000/\$J$ $T = 98,400/\$P$ $T = 55,000/\$D$

4. Relation Between a Change in Time and a Change in Dollars for Judges, Prosecutors, and Defenders

   $\Delta T / \Delta \$J = -165,000(\$J)^{-2}$ $\Delta T / \Delta \$P = -98,400(\$P)^{-2}$

   $\Delta T / \Delta \$D = .-55,000(\$D)^{-2}$

5. Equation for Relating T to $J, $P, and $D to Consider Overlapping Effects

   $$T = a(\$J)^{b_1}(\$P)^{b_2}(\$D)^{b_3}$$

OPTIMUM CHOICE ANALYSIS

$EV_S = (+a) + (-b)$ Expected net value (benefits minus costs) from making a time-saving decision

$EV_l = (P)(-c) +$ Expected net value from making a time-
$(1-P)(+d)$ lengthening decision

NOTES

1. On optimum level analysis, see Michael Brennan, *Preface to Econometrics* (Cincinnati: South-Western, 1973) pp. 111-192; Jack Byrd, *Operations Research Models for Public Administration* (Lexington, Mass.: Lexington-Heath, 1975) pp. 183-98; Samuel Richmond, *Operations Research for Management Decisions* (New York: Ronald Press, 1968) pp. 87-126; and James Shockley, *The Brief Calculus: With Applications in the Social Sciences* (New York: Holt, 1971).

2. Although the above hypothetical data is realistic, the results could have been made even more meaningful by making various changes in the input data. The idea of a 25-day optimum level of time consumption is meaningful, but having an

average cost per case of approximately 10,000 dollars seems a bit high. To determine the average cost per case for a given court system (as contrasted to the optimum cost) find the total annual budget for the court system and divide the number of cases processed. Perhaps 10,000 dollars per case would not be too high if only major criminal cases were included. The exact cost per case in the above hypothetical example is 9,725 dollars as calculated by the formula $Y = \$165,000/25 + \$5(25)^2$.

3. For additional examples of optimum level analysis applied to reducing delay and other aspects of the legal process, see S. Nagel and M. Neef, *Legal Policy Analysis: Finding an Optimum Level or Mix* (Lexington, Mass.: Lexington-Heath, 1977); S. Nagel, M. Neef, and P. Wice, *Too Much or Too Little Policy: The Example of Pretrial Release* (Beverly Hills, Ca.: Sage, 1977); Hans Zeisel, Harry Kalven, Jr., and Bernard Buchholz, *Delay in the Court* (Boston: Little Brown, 1959) pp. 169-220; Llad Phillips and Harold Votey, "An Economic Basis for the Definition and Control of Crime," in *Modeling the Criminal Justice System*, ed. S. Nagel, (Beverly Hills, Ca.: Sage, 1977) p. 89; Frederic Merrill and Linus Schrage, "Efficient Use of Jurors: A Field Study and Simulation Model of a Court System," 2 *Washington University Law Quarterly* 151 (1969); and G. Thomas Munsterman and William Pabst, "Operating an Efficient Jury System" (Unpublished paper presented at the International Meeting of the Institute of Management Sciences, 1975). A recent paper that is especially relevant to this section is Eli Noam, "The Optimal Size of the Court" (Unpublished paper available from the author at the Columbia University Center for Law and Economic Studies). The above hypothetical problem arrives at an optimum level of 60 judges. Noam's related analysis of the District of Columbia's court system arrives coincidentally at an optimum level of 62 judges for processing criminal cases, although the existing level for 1976 was only 16 judges.

4. On optimum mix analysis, see Jack Byrd, op. cit., pp. 85-114; Philip Kotler, *Marketing Decision Making: A Model Building Approach* (New York: Holt, 1971); Robert Llewellyn, *Linear Programming* (New York: Holt, 1963); Claude McMillan, *Mathematical Programming* (New York: Wiley, 1970); and S. Richmond, op. cit., pp. 314-404.

5. It would be inefficient to reduce each of the three activities by 100,000 dollars in order to bring the 1.3 million dollars down to the available 1 million dollars because the marginal rate of return may differ substantially for each activity. For example, if an extra dollar given to judges produces a greater saving of time than an extra dollar given to prosecutors or defense counsel, then we would not want to take equally from each of the three activities, but rather take more from the allocation to prosecutors and defense counsel. Similarly, it would be inefficient to reduce each activity in proportion to the size of its separate optimum budget without taking into consideration the marginal rates of return for an extra dollar spent or taken away for each activity relative to each other activity.

6. Instead of inductively processing data at various points in time showing how many days were consumed for various combinations of judges, prosecutors, and public defenders in order to obtain the parameters for a multivariate regression equation, one could in part deductively reason about the interrelations between changes in the budget of judges, prosecutors, and defense attorneys. This partly deductive approach is used by Eli Noam, "The Criminal Justice System: An Economic Model," in *Modeling the Criminal Justice System*, ed. S. Nagel (Beverly Hills, Ca.: Sage, 1977) p. 41. For example, through a chain of deductions combined with some empirical data from the District of Columbia, Noam finds that if an extra 100 dollars is allocated to the judge's budget, then 110 dollars will have to be allocated to the prosecutor's budget in order to maintain the existing amount of trials per judge per time period. In other words, 10 percent more prosecutors would

be needed in order to keep the increased judges as busy as the previous set of judges. On the other hand, he finds that if an extra 100 dollars is allocated to the prosecutor's budget, then only an extra 68 dollars should be allocated to the judge's budget or else the increase in judges will offset the increase in prosecutors and thereby change the existing service levels. He also makes adjustments in those ratios to take into consideration that an increase in prosecutors may result in a decrease in crime. On the other hand, using the multivariate regression equation approach, one would answer the question of how much of an increase or decrease in $P is needed if there is a 100 dollar increase in $J by simply solving for $P in the equation when (1) T and $D are set at whatever previous T and $D were, (2) the a's and b's are those from the previous computerized regression analysis, and (3) $J is increased by 100 dollars from whatever it was.

7. The minimum figure for each activity could be arrived at by analyzing data for many court systems and seeing what is the minimum number of dollars spent on judging, prosecuting, and defending per case quantity. One could then multiply these three figures by the estimated case quantity for next year's court system to arrive at the three minimums. An alternative approach would be to give each activity, as a minimum, the lowest amount of money that it received during any recent year. Another alternative might involve asking knowledgeable people inside and outside those divisions of the court system and then averaging their responses. Whatever the minimums might be, each division is likely to receive more than its minimum provided that (1) the total budget for the court system is to be spent; (2) the minimums add to less than the total budget; (3) each activity has a favorable marginal rate of return in the sense that extra dollars spent on the activity do result in a reduction in time consumed; and (4) the reductions are nonlinear so that increased dollars mean reduced delay, but the reduction benefits tend to taper off, so it becomes efficient to switch expenditures from the generally most efficient activity to a less efficient activity when that tapering becomes substantial. In other words, if assumptions 1, 2, and 3 are met, then the most efficient allocation after satisfying the minimums is to allocate the remainder to the activities in proportion to their exponents in an equation of the form $(\$J)^{b_1}(\$P)^{b_2}(\$D)^{b_3} = 120$.

8. For additional examples of optimum mix analysis applied to the legal process, see Werner Hirsch, *The Economics of State and Local Government* (Hightstown, N.J.: McGraw-Hill, 1970) pp. 217-54; Law Enforcement Assistance Administration, *Allocation of Resources in the Chicago Police Department* (Washington, D.C.: LEAA, 1972); S. Nagel, *Minimizing Costs and Maximizing Benefits in Providing Legal Services to the Poor* (Beverly Hills, Ca.: Sage, 1973); Donald Shoup and Stephen Mehay, *Program Budgeting for Urban Police Services* (New York: Praeger, 1971); and S. Nagel and M. Neef, "Allocating Resources Geographically for Optimum Results," 3 *Political Methodology* 383 (1976).

9. On optimum choice analysis, see Robert Behn and James Vaupel, *Analytical Thinking for Busy Decision Makers* (New York: Basic Books, 1981); Ruth Mack, *Planning on Uncertainty: Decision Making in Business and Government Administration* (New York: Wiley, 1971); Howard Raiffa, *Decision Analysis: Introductory Lectures on Choices Under Uncertainty* (Reading, Mass.: Addison-Wesley, 1968); and Samuel Richmond, op. cit., pp. 301-60.

10. For additional examples of choice theory applied to the legal process, see S. Nagel and M. Neef, *Decision Theory and the Legal Process* (Lexington, Mass.: Lexington-Heath, 1978); S. Nagel and M. Neef, "Decision Theory and the Pretrial Release Decision in Criminal Cases," 31 *University of Miami Law Review* 1433 (1977); and Robert Stover and Don Brown, "Reducing Rule Violations by Police, Judges, and Corrections Officials", in S. Nagel and M. Neef, "Decision Theory Judgers, and Corrections Officials," in *Modeling The Criminal Justice System*, ed. S. Nagel (Beverly Hills, Ca.: Sage, 1977) p. 297.

Epilogue

This book, *Policy Evaluation: Making Optimum Decisions*, has emphasized what might be called the nuts and bolts aspects of policy evaluation, rather than the more philosophical aspects. Nevertheless, there is a high level of generality emphasized, particularly from the perspective of evaluating policies or programs across places and times. In fact, policy evaluation can be distinguished from program evaluation in terms of that characteristic. For example, a policy evaluation of halfway houses for released convicts might involve making systematic comparisons of the crime-committing behavior of (1) convicts who are unconditionally released after serving their full terms; and (2) convicts who are released to live in halfway houses before returning fully to the community; and (3) convicts who are released on supervised parole. A typical program evaluation, on the other hand, might involve attempting to determine how well a halfway house in Champaign, Illinois in 1980 is working, partly by asking the staff, former and present inmates, and other knowledgeable people in the community. In other words, policy evaluation as presented in this book tends to involve evaluating the effects of alternative policies or programs across places and times, whereas program evaluation tends to involve evaluating the effects of a specific policy or program in a specific place and time.

It seems fitting to end this book by attempting to pull together many of the ideas presented in such a way as to bring out various trends in policy evaluation methods. These trends cut across the more specific techniques that relate to finding an optimum choice, level, or mix in public policy analysis. Different people in the policy evaluation field would be likely to see the trends differently, but some trends that do seem fairly clear are the following:

1. Policy analysis is building on business analysis, but it is developing its own methodology. Policy analysis builds on the basic business principle of maximizing income minus expenses, although in *public sector analysis*, the words get converted to benefits minus costs. Since benefits are usually nonmonetary in policy analysis, this means developing methods for summing benefits and costs in such a way that the benefits are weighted to take into consideration (1) their normative importance relative to the costs, and (2) the differences in the measurement units used. Policy analysis also relies more on statistical inputs and less on accounting inputs. Policy analysis is more sensitive to the reactions of the people affected by the policies which may require considering special psy-

316

chological and political constraints, as well as the more traditional economic ones.

2. Policy analysts have traditionally taken policies as givens in attempting to determine their effects, especially their effects on the intended goals. There is, however, a trend more toward more taking of goals as givens, and then attempting to determine what policies will maximize or *optimize* them. The former approach is more associated with program evaluation in psychology and sociology. The latter approach is more associated with optimizing analysis from economics and operations research.

3. Policy analysts are becoming more sensitive to social values, with more *questioning of goals* when evaluating alternative policies. There are now a number of policy studies programs across the country that emphasize the analysis of goals, rather than, or in addition to, the achievement of goals, such as the programs at Notre Dame, University of Maryland, Georgetown University, Duke University, and the Hastings Institute. Goals can be analyzed through survey research to see to what extent they are supported, through relational analysis to determine how achieving them would affect higher values, or through philosophical analysis to determine how they fit into more general philosophical systems.

4. Policy evaluation is becoming increasingly proactive or *preadoption*, rather than reactive or postadoption. Too often the effects of an adopted policy cannot be meaningfully determined because of (1) the lack of availability of a meaningful control group or experimental group, or (2) the lack of availability of before-data or after-data. Waiting for policies to be adopted before they are evaluated may also lead to harm being done before the unsatisfactory policies can be changed, and it can lead to inertia and vested interests that resist needed changes. As a result, there is an increasing trend toward using preadoption projections or deductive modeling, rather than just postadoption before-and-after analysis.

5. Policy evaluation is becoming increasingly *interdisciplinary* in its methods. All the social sciences now offer courses, textbooks, journals, and other disciplinary communication media which emphasize policy evaluation methods from both a disciplinary and interdisciplinary perspective. There is particularly an increasing synthesis of statistical methodology and deductive mathematical models.

6. Policy evaluation is showing increasing sophistication with regard to considering *political and administrative feasibility*. In the past, policy evaluation has often resulted in recommendations being adopted by the political decision makers or what might happen when it came to implementing or administering the policy recom-

mendations. The concern for political and administrative feasibility reflects the increasing role of political science and public administration in policy evaluation.

7. Policy evaluation is developing increased precision in its methods, but at the same time is increasingly recognizing that *simple methods* may be all that is necessary for many policy problems. This is especially so since the typical policy problem asks which policy is best, not how much better is it than the second best policy, and not how do all the policies compare with each other on an interval scale or even a rank-order scale.

8. Systematic policy evaluation is becoming *increasingly used* in government at the federal, state, and local levels and in the executive, legislative, and judicial branches. This utilization reflects an increased sensitivity among policy analysts to dealing with actual data, not just abstractions. At the same time, policy analysis is developing broad principles that cut across specific subject matters.

9. There is substantial *growth* occurring in policy evaluation training programs, research centers, funding sources, publishing outlets, scholarly associations, and other policy evaluation institutions.

These trends all add up to making the field of policy evaluation an exciting one to be in, especially in these formative times. The benefits from developing policy evaluation skills include access to new government and academic positions, research funds, publishing outlets, conference invitations, consultantships, and other such tangible rewards. They also include psychological benefits that relate to the intellectually stimulating nature of trying to deal with policy evaluation problems, and the good feelings that come from doing things relevant to important policy matters. It is hoped that this book will help to summarize and stimulate many ideas with regard to finding optimum choices, levels, and mixes in public policy evaluations.

Name Index

Abramowitz, Alan, 201
Achen, Christopher, 201
Adamany, David, 195
Agranoff, Robert, 193
Alexander, Herbert, 193, 194
Alfini, James, 46
Andriano, Kim, 298
Aranson, Peter, 18
Archibald, Russell, 278
Atkinson, David, 229

Baker, Kenneth, 276
Baird, Bruce, 76
Baldus, David, 146
Bardach, Eugene, 228
Barkan, Joel, 201
Barron, C., 146
Baumol, William, 18, 31, 108, 174, 193, 195
Becker, Gary, 31, 146
Bedau, Adam, 299
Behn, Robert, 36, 315
Belkin, 298
Beltrami, Edward, 248
Bental, Benjamin, 201
Ben-Zion, Uri, 201
Berelson, Bernard, 195
Berk, Richard, 151
Bernd, Joseph, 297, 298
Berney, Arthur, 109
Bicker, William, 300
Biles, William, 280
Black, Guy, 17, 76, 193, 196
Blackstone, William, 88

Blalock, Hubert, 148, 175, 193, 194, 195, 248, 279
Block, Peter, 229
Bloom, Murry, 109
Blumstein, Albert, 149, 280, 298
Blydenburgh, John, 201
Bohigian, Haig, 19, 276, 278
Bohrnstedt, George, 298, 300
Bond, Jon, 299
Borgatta, Edgar, 298
Boucher, Wayne, 301
Brams, Steven, 108, 193
Break, George, 196, 228
Brennan, Michael, 146, 299, 313
Brosi, Kathleen, 105
Brown, Don, 315
Brown, Peter, 19
Brownstein, Sidney, 278
Bruno, James, 201
Buchholz, Bernard, 276, 301, 313
Bullock, Charles, 31
Burkart, Michael, 201
Burnham, Walter, 194
Byrd, Jack, Jr., 18, 107, 276, 278, 313, 314

Callahan, Thomas, 278
Campbell, Donald, 298, 299
Cane, Thomas, 278
Cannavale, Frank, Jr., 297
Cantrall, William, 300
Caporoso, James, 299
Carter, Jimmy, xviii
Cassidy, R. Gordon, 280

Subject Index

ABOUT THE AUTHOR

Stuart S. Nagel is a professor of political science at the University of Illinois and a member of the Illinois bar. He is the author or co-author of such relevant books as *The Policy-Studies Handbook* (1980), *Decision Theory and the Legal Process* (1979), *Policy Analysis: In Social Science Research* (1979), *Legal Policy Analysis: Finding an Optimum Level or Mix* (1977), *The Legal Process: Modeling the System* (1977), *Improving the Legal Process: Effects of Alternatives* (1975), and *The Legal Process from a Behavioral Perspective* (1969). He is the editor of *Improving Policy Analysis* (1980), *Policy Studies Review Annual* (1977), *Modeling the Criminal Justice System* (1977), *Policy Studies and the Social Sciences* (1975), *Policy Studies in America and Elsewhere* (1975), *Environmental Politics* (1974), and *The Rights of the Accused: In Law and Action* (1972). He has been an attorney to the Office of Economic Opportunity in Champaign, Illinois; the Lawyers Constitutional Defense Committee in Jackson, Mississippi; the National Labor Relations Board in Chicago, and the U.S. Senate Judiciary Committee in Washington. He has also been a fellow of the Ford Foundation, Russell Sage, National Science Foundation, American Council of Learned Societies, Social Science Research Council, East-West Center, Illinois Law Enforcement Commission, and the Center for the Advanced Study in the Behavioral Sciences. He has also been a grant recipient through the Policy Studies Organization from the Departments of Justice, Labor, Housing and Urban Development, Energy, Agriculture, Transportation, Education and Health and Human Services, and from the Rockefeller, Guggenheim, and Ford Foundations.

DATE DUE
